BLOOD - DRENCHED ALTARS

MEXICO

VICARIATE APOSTOLIC - ♦ ARCHBISHOPRIC - ♦ BISHOPRIC - ♀ BISHOPRIC VACATED OR TRANSFERRED

GULF

of

MEXICO

BAY OF CAMPECHE

LOUISIANA
MISSISSIPPI
ALABAMA
MOBILE
NEW ORLEANS

T E X A S
AUSTIN
HOUSTON
GALVESTON
SAN ANTONIO
LAREDO

NUEVO LEON
MONTERREY
LINARES
TAMAULIPAS
VICTORIA
TAMPICO

LUIS POTOSI
POTOSI
QUERETARO
QUERETARO
TULANCINGO
COLORES
MEXICO CITY
TEZCOCO
TLAXCALA
JALAPA
VERA CRUZ
TOLUCA
TLALPAM
PUEBLA
CUERNAVACA
MORELOS
TELOLOAPAM
IGUALA
HUAJUAPAM
GUERRERO
CHILAPA
SIERRA MADRE DEL SUR
TLAXCALA
ACAPULCO
OAXACA
OAXACA
TEHUANTEPEC
SALINA CRUZ
ISTHMUS OF TEHUANTEPEC
CORDOBA
TABASCO
S. JUAN BAUTISTA
PALENQUE
S. CRISTOBAL
CHIAPAS
SIERRA MADRE

PROGRESSO
MERIDA
YUCATAN
VALLADOLID
CAMPECHE
QUINTANA ROO
CAMPECHE

CENTRAL AMERICA
GUATEMALA
BRITISH HONDURAS
BELIZE
GULF OF HONDURAS
HONDURAS
COMAYAGUA
GUATEMALA
SALVADOR
SALVADOR

BLOOD-DRENCHED ALTARS

A Catholic Commentary on the
History of Mexico

By

MOST REV. FRANCIS CLEMENT KELLEY
Bishop of Oklahoma City and Tulsa

With Documentation and Notes by
EBER COLE BYAM

TAN BOOKS AND PUBLISHERS, INC.
Rockford, Illinois 61105

#29384959

Copyright © 1935 by The Bruce Publishing Company, Milwaukee, Wisconsin.

The typography in this book is the property of TAN Books and Publishers, Inc. and may not be reproduced, in whole or in part, without written permission from the Publisher.

Library of Congress Catalog Card No.: 87-71867

ISBN: 0-89555-319-8

Printed and bound in the United States of America.

TAN BOOKS AND PUBLISHERS, INC.
P.O. Box 424
Rockford, Illinois 61105
1987

DEDICATION

This book is dedicated to Eber Cole Byam, a devoted student of Mexican history who, weak in body but strong in mind and soul, gave generously of his few daily hours of half-comfort to the work of its documentation as each chapter was finished, thus making it possible to produce it within the short space of eight weeks.

CONTENTS

PART ONE

STUDY AND NARRATIVE

CHAPTER

CONTENTS

PART TWO

CHRONOLOGY, NOTES, AND DOCUMENTATION

ILLUSTRATIONS

PART ONE

STUDY AND NARRATIVE

I

INTRODUCTION

THE UNITED STATES of America is situated geographically between two potentially great and wealthy neighbors, Canada and Mexico. The first is still loosely bound to Europe through its membership in the British Family of Nations; the second is nominally a free Republic. Both have agricultural and mining resources of great value. Both potentially are competitors with the United States for world markets. Both, but especially Canada, are excellent customers for American industrial products. With both, nevertheless, we are on official terms of friendship. Our friendship for Canada is more than official. As to Mexico there is reason for doubt. We know that many, if not the great majority of Mexicans, dislike, to put it mildly, their Northern neighbor. Americans themselves do not dislike Mexicans. The feeling is as yet only half-formed but it is a mixture of suspicion, pity, and in many cases even half-veiled contempt. Mexico is looked upon popularly as a country of ignorant people who have never found themselves; quarrelsome, petulant, unreliable, and unstable; a people with whom it is impossible to maintain ordinary decent relations; a people with a history of violence scarcely relieved by a few favorable contrasts; a nation of robbers on the one hand and beggars on the other, unenlightened and, for the most part, miserable.

The difference of language scarcely enters into the question. Canada is a bilingual country. English and French are spoken in its Parliament and Senate. A very large part of its people speak French as their maternal tongue and it is this part which is of greater interest to us because it is so "romantically different." The question of religion might play a more important role, for more than one third of Canada's people are Catholics. Its greatest province is predominantly Catholic, but with a Protestant minority justly content, having their own institutions of worship, education, and charity. That province, Quebec, is, perhaps, the outstanding example of mutual religious understanding and peace in the whole world. Americans admire and praise it. But they have failed to note the contrast with Mexico. Mexico has a very small Protestant population, for the most part made up of its American and British residents. They are not permitted to possess a place of worship of their own, nor to teach in a school. They may not employ a Protestant clergyman of their own nationality to preach to or pray for and with them. Religious toleration joined to good-will in one part of Canada is from Protestants to Catholics. In the other it is from Catholics to Protestants. In general both are quite satisfied with the situation, especially the Protestants of Quebec. In Mexico, predominantly Catholic, the intolerance is for Catholics as well as Protestants, but for it Catholics are in no way responsible. They hate and abhor it. They would gladly accept the Canadian situation for all. The persecutor in

Mexico is the Radical, who hates the Protestant less than the Catholic only because there are fewer of him.

Since the War of 1812 with Great Britain, the thought of bringing Canada into the United States has never been even considered seriously. To the overwhelming majority of Americans and Canadians the idea is one of the unthinkable things. Nor has either country ever had a dispute that peaceful arbitration could not, and did not, settle. The two countries have traded and bartered, visited and chatted together, for far more than a century, all in good will and with even no little jollity. It never occurs to Americans to call Canadians, English or French, an ignorant, suspicious, pitiful, petulant, unreliable, or unstable people. A thought abhorrent to even the most warlike of Americans would be to quarrel with Canada and Canadians.

With Mexico it is different. Americans have been at war with Mexicans. The United States has invaded Mexico. Mexican soldiers have raided and killed American soldiers on American soil.[1] American armies have camped on and crossed the Mexican border. The American Navy has bombarded Mexican cities. Worse than all, Americans have never, during all the years of their existence as a nation, ceased to fear the possibility of a bloody encounter with their Mexican neighbors.

Who are these neighbors? By far the greater part are a very kind, a very peaceful, even a very lovable people. Americans who live or have lived among them have nothing but praise for their hospitality, their politeness, their hon-

---

[1]The "superior" figures refer to the annotations in Part Two, beginning on page 372.

esty, and their good-will; that is, for all those quite admirable traits and virtues as they are found in the poor—and in Mexico the poor are the major part of the population. These traits and virtues are found also among many, even the majority, of the upper classes. What Americans hate in Mexicans, is, strangely enough, found only in that class which, politically and socially, we take for the only Mexicans worth dealing with, the only ones as a matter of fact we have dealt with and listened to. The grace of God made the Mexican people, as a people, much to be admired. But we do not deal with them. Officially, and often unofficially, we do not know them. We accept what the others say against them. We have been doing that for well over a century.

Is it that we fear a prosperous Mexico as a neighbor? I do not think so. Certainly we are always glad to hear of the prosperity of Canada. Do we really want Mexico to have peace? I think we do. We certainly want Canada to have and keep it. We are a business people and know that the prosperity of our neighbors can bring only good to us by an interchange of the things we have or want for the things they have or want. There is nothing for us to fight about, and everything to keep us all in peaceful relations with one another. Poverty and strife in one, mean short markets and bitter words in the other.

What fate has doomed the people of the United States and the people of Mexico to be as they are to each other? It is not fate but plain ignorance, and alas! very much on our own side. We do not know the truth about Mexico, the story of her triumphs, her defeats, her beating onward against the winds of adversity. We have listened to slanders against her. We have believed the lies of the riffraff from within who robbed her. We have helped them in their robberies. In a word, we have treated Mexico not at all as we have treated Canada, for we have hurt her. The worst ill feeling always comes from the one who has done an injustice to the other.

It goes without saying that no one can read history to his or her own profit with a mind full of unconquerable prejudices. In other days, that was how history was written, and it is the reason why it could and was truthfully said that history is nothing but a recorded lie. Modern research is rapidly changing all that. Prejudice is being taken out of historical writing. It will be a more difficult task to take it out of reading. Nevertheless that too must be done. For what civilization is going to be will, to a greater extent than we now realize, perhaps, depend on what we learn of its mistakes as well as its triumphs. No history written in the English language has more need to be approached without prejudice than that of Mexico. Too much of the English record called Mexican history is the work of conscious or unconscious special pleaders.[2] We shall notice these as we go along. The present urgent necessity is to make sure of our warning against prejudice. Strange to say the necessity of this warning may not be understood, and there are good reasons for expressing the fear. Prejudice against anything Spanish is part of the inheritance of English-speaking peoples. It is in their blood. Its sources are both political and religious. To remove them it is first necessary to uncover them. That may take a little time, but it will be time well spent for those who do really wish to get at the truth.

It is not difficult to find the reasons for our dislike of Mexico and Mexico's dislike for us. For the latter the story is spread over the record of our dealings with Mexican problems; for the former, it may be had by an honest confession of what is in the minds and hearts of the majority of English-speaking people. It will profit us to take a look at both.

Bruce, in his *Romance of American Expansion,*[3] quotes from a letter of Thomas Jefferson, written from Paris, which gives us a lead in trying to learn what Mexico has against us. Speaking of the Spanish-American countries Jefferson wrote: "These countries cannot be in better hands. My fear is that they are too feeble to hold them till our population can be sufficiently advanced to gain it from them piece by piece." No statesman, and Jefferson was a statesman, ever wrote two more undiplomatic sentences. But they did represent, not only the ambition of Jefferson, but of the American statesmen of his day, and of many days and years to follow. They actually represented the ambitions of American statesmen well into our own day. One credit at least may be given to Woodrow Wilson's handling of Mexican troubles: he "sold" to the American people the conviction that they did not want Mexican territory or any other territory than that which they possessed. But the sale came too late to save us from well-grounded suspicion of our purposes in their regard, on the part of Mexicans.

Mexico to us would be no asset. It would tax our assimilative digestion into ulcers, as overeating taxes the stomachs of the strongest men, not because of the richness of the food but simply because there is too much of it. Absorption of Mexico would hurt our fruit-growing states, multiply our agricultural and labor problems, and end in movements for secession. Every advantage we could gain would be offset by greater disadvantages.

The Mexicans knew what our statesmen had in mind, for there were others besides Jefferson who let their pens and tongues betray them. Many in Mexico were not slow to take advantage and preach hatred of "The Colossus of the North," cleverly suggesting, usually for personal or political advantage, the thought that Mexico needed patriotic defenders against aggression by her neighbors, and that they could be trusted to be all of that. The United States was pictured, not only as the Colossus, but as an ugly one with an insatiable maw for territory. Religious fears likewise were played upon. That particular thought of fear especially was planted deep in the Mexican mind. It will take a stronger arm than was Wilson's to pull it out.

The revolutionary Mexican element, the self-styled liberals, saw a perfectly marvelous opportunity for themselves in all this. Within Mexico they could appeal for support to the popular fear of the Great Colossus. Outside Mexico, that is, in the United States, they could play their Gringo fish with the bait they knew would please his taste. Enemy within, friend without! That was the idea. And the American statesmen of the pre-Wilsonian age took the bait, "hook, line, and sinker." They initiated the only American policy toward Mexico that always has been consistently followed, viz., help revolution; what was in must be bad; put it out. Perhaps Polk and Buchanan, of all our Presidents, did actually distinguish themselves most in carrying out this policy. More than once Mexico came to the very brink of ruin because of it.

Now, if this policy of sympathizing and aiding every bad revolution in Mexico had been formulated officially, and handed down from administration to administration as a well-thought-out plan to achieve Jefferson's dream of Empire, it would deserve praise at least for the sagacity of it. No policy toward Mexico could be more certain to produce the result that Jefferson hoped for. From the revolt of Hidalgo in 1810 to the present time, revolutions have been sucking the very heart's blood out of the country. Once Mexico was ahead of us in practically all the things that mark an advancing civilization.[4] We passed her while revolutions halted and then sent her into a decline that Díaz stayed temporarily. The steady deterioration of the nation is an undeniable fact. Many who live today have seen much of the decline pass before their very eyes. How long can Mexico stand blood-letting and destruction before she calls from the depth of her misery for the pity and guardianship of the much-hated Colossus? And what will the Colossus do with her when that time comes? Whatever he does, if he continues to be deaf, dumb, and blind to her best interests, will only make her fate worse and his with it. But the Great Colossus will not be Mexico's worst betrayer. He may be a Pilate, but he will not be a Judas. Mexico's Judases will be found in the long line of disturbers and thieves, who, for selfish ends, have made a mock of the power of the ballot while they appealed to the power of the sword. Two will stand conspicuous at the head of the line: Juárez and Calles.

Only a miracle of statesmanship, a miracle no student of her history may now dare hope for, can save Mexico from becoming a political and industrial slave of the Colossus. It is too much to hope that she will be made a partner. She may retain a semblance of freedom, but it will be a semblance only. Who is not sad to see a once promising nation perish at the hands of her own sons? Do not think, however, that we have statesmen so dishonestly astute as to make such a plan for taking Mexico with no loss of life and treasure to us but much to her. These statesmen of ours who followed the Fathers of the Republic, and especially those of the Polk and Buchanan type, never had it in them to do it.[5] It was all an accident born of their prejudices and lamentable ignorance of the truth about Mexico and Mexicans. All this the intelligent and patriotic Mexicans know. Is it any wonder that they should dislike us? Had we done to Canada one tenth of what we have done to Mexico, her people would have for us a hatred undying.

There is, nevertheless, a word of excuse to be offered for what the rulers and the ruled of our country did to Mexico. We mentioned ignorance. Self-deception would have been a better name for it. In 1810, when Hidalgo raised the first standard of revolt in Mexico, we were at the very summit of our enthusiasm for the republican form of government and, therefore, in no condition of mind to understand the fact that what worked with us need not necessarily work with others. The great truth we forgot was that the application is not the principle, methods of enforcement not the law, a republic only one acceptable form of government. It works where it works. It is not adapted to all peoples. The great desideratum is good government in a form suited to the case. We are always making the mistake of taking the means for the end. We did it in dealing with Mexico. We do it every day in dealing with ourselves. Witness our mistakes about education, now becoming so plain and leading our youth into formerly unsuspected dangers. We so loved what we had, it was so good in our eyes, that we wanted Mexico and all the Americas to have it. There is our one excuse.

So much for the reason Mexico dislikes us. What about our half-dislike of Mexicans? It comes from two sources: racial tradition and religious prejudice. Take them in that order.

English-speaking peoples inherit a hatred for Spain which dates from the reign of Elizabeth of England. It was engendered by a compound of national rivalry and jealousy; by the marriage of Mary I to Philip II, and the attack of the Spanish Armada. When the ships of Philip broke up on the rocks of the British Islands, the reaction to deadly fear on the part of the English crown and people was a hatred strong enough to keep flowing with the blood in the veins of their descendants, disease enough to affect all who, through speaking, hearing, and writing in the English tongue, came into intimate association with them. No reader needs proof of that. If he is honest with himself he knows that he is himself the proof. The Mexican revolutionist too knew this. That was why he kept persistently crying to us that he was fighting the Spaniard, even long after the Spaniard had been crushed and expelled from the colony. The propagandists for Villa and Carranza used this prejudice constantly in dealing with American public opinion. Calles uses it today. The next revolution will use it, not to fight Spaniards but to fight Mexicans. Spain has no power in Mexico. Her civilization has all but passed. Spanish art in Mexico remains only in her monuments. The great Spanish cities that profoundly impressed the traveler from strange lands are no more. The University of Spanish foundation, equal to those of Europe, has all its glory in the past and little hope for its quick return in the future. In Mexico, Spain, except for her language, is a memory. Nevertheless those who have inherited the English hatred for Spain may still be influenced by the thought that she lives in the speech and writings of the educated, and in the values of her culture that still linger in the soul of the Mexican people.

Our success in building a nation, when compared to the failure that is present-day Mexico, is used to deepen our conviction that nothing good could ever have come out of Spain. We see only one side of the picture. Spain's success in Mexico and South America is one of the greatest wonders of history. It was not Spain but Mexico that failed. The Spaniard left a civilization. It is the Mexican who is destroying it.

Turn again to the record. The Visigoth invaders of Spain did not exterminate the Iberian and Celtic natives. They made a kingdom out of them. They mixed blood with them. They became Spaniards. That tradition of dealing with a conquered people they sent across the Atlantic with the Conquistadores. The Spanish did not do with the Indians as did the English colonists. They preserved them, educated them, and founded the prosperity of their colonies upon them. Cortés, cruel in war, changed, as soon as the City of Montezuma was taken, into a wise administrator protecting the new subjects of his King.[6] There were abuses, but local and individual ones. Lummis says:[7] "The legislation of Spain on behalf of the Indians everywhere was incomparably more extensive, more comprehensive, more systematic, and more humane than that of Great Britain, the Colonies, and the present United States all combined."

Spain was being invaded by the French when the first revolt broke out in Mexico. It was put down not by Spaniards but by Mexicans.[8] Every nerve in Spain was strained to save her from Napoleon, while her King was Napoleon's prisoner and his throne was being usurped by Napoleon's brother. Spain had no power to hold Mexico, yet Mexico stayed loyal to her[9] — a fact to be weighed in judging the case. The revolt of Hidalgo was not proclaimed against Spain but as an effort to hold Mexico for Ferdinand VII against Joseph Bonaparte. The loyalty of the Mexican for Spain died hard. It was the new teachings of the French Revolution that killed it in the lowest elements of the Mexican people; and the success of the American Republic helped to do it. What the Mexican failed to note was that our plan of democratic government had been sifted through wise and conservative minds who rejected the dross of the French Revolution. The wise and conservative minds of Mexico were thrust out of the planning there. We had a Washington, a Jefferson, an Adams, a Carroll, a Franklin.

Poor Mexico had nothing but the scum of her semi-educated class.

What happened? Note well the contrast and the result will be well understood. The new Republic of the North was exclusively a white man's nation. The American Indians contributed nothing to the making of it. They were left unschooled and untaught when they were not exterminated. But the white man's nation proceeded to do what the Mexican Republic did not do. It encouraged private enterprise, invited the investment of capital from home and from abroad, asked its citizens to provide for themselves colleges and schools, hospitals, institutions of charity, and beneficent foundations. It allowed churches to possess, own, and control property to that end. It harnessed every good element to its car of progress. All this was far from the thought of the French Revolution. If the American Government had tried to do the things that Church and private enterprise did it would have failed after swamping the country with debt and the people with taxes. There would have been, for example, no Harvard, no Georgetown, and no Yale. Every hand would have been used to destroy, clutching sword and gun rather than book and trowel.

The Mexican revolutionist attacked all this educational and cultural enterprise at its very source. He impoverished the wealthy. He stole the property of the Church. He seized educational and charitable endowments. And not for the nation did he do this, but for the friends of the "cause." The great and flourishing institutions of culture, charity, and learning perished. A tradition of loot was passed on to those who were to follow. Not one, even Iturbide, failed to put it into operation, or to allow it to be put into operation, when the opportunity came.

What then could be expected? Mexico had the start on the English colonies. She rose like a star while she had a mother in Spain. She flourished under tutelage. Her native people were preserved. Mexico was great in subjugation and a failure under what her new conquerors called independence. The American Republic was poor, only a pioneer in subjection but, as was right, great in what really was liberty. And mark this well, for history will bear out the truth of it: the Mexican people were a thousand times freer, as well as many times happier and more prosperous, under Spain, than they have ever been since. Had Mexico's "liberators" been mindful of justice, sane in outlook, unselfish in administration, how different her story might have been. It was not the fact of revolution that makes it the saddest of national disasters. Jefferson was right in fearing the feeble hands of a harassed Spain, which could not have held her American Colonies. The time had come at least to plan for independence. But those who seized the destinies of the Mexican Nation were unequipped, spiritually and morally, for the task. This is no *exparte* statement but the only verdict that the facts and the record justify.[10]

II

SPANISH BACKGROUND

THOSE AT LEAST who hold that Divine Providence, by His inspirations and graces to individual souls, and through these communicated to groups and peoples, rules the destinies and directs the progress of the world, will have no hesitation in accepting the thought that the discovery and opening up of the New World, with all its far-reaching consequences to the future welfare of mankind, was nothing short of a second creation. Only the eastern sun that rose over the cradle of Bethlehem saw an event more important in the history of Christian civilization than did the western sun disclosing on the waters of Santo Domingo the caravels of Columbus. Even individual historical personages have been accepted as children of destiny whose way was prepared before them and whose coming into the world was providentially timed. Chance seems often to have played as small a part in the rise and fall of leaders as it did in the making of the universe. The skeptic may disagree, but the cold logic of reason is against him. Very few of the events that set humanity's feet on great new roads were the result of accidents. Unexpected and unannounced preparation of the ground made them inevitable. Few children of destiny found themselves by a trick of

The altar in the Bishop's residence in Querétaro. The carving is all seventeenth-century work.

the renegades supplied the means of purchasing a luxury for the Moor which was gladly accepted. The Arab language lent itself to a poetry without depth but charming in its musical arrangement of words and images. Contrary to the stories of those who endow the Moorish Kingdoms in Spain with learning, they did not favor it. Of science there was little, of singing there was much. The philosopher Averroes had to stand before the Mosque of Córdova to be spit upon by the passing throng of Mohammedans. It is little that modern writers in English have told of the truth about Moorish learning.

Though French writers forty years ago, before the days of modern historical research, were inclined, many quite honestly, to the idea that the Moor treated his Christian subjects with mildness, the later and deeper students tell a different tale. Even the renegades were oppressed and held in constant supervision. They were given the liberty of useful slaves. The Arab, as he soon was called, chiefly because of language and adoption of Moslem customs under rulers giving tribute to Damascus, did not care for work. The renegades cultivated the land. From the East came artists of all kinds. Bertrand insists that even the Alhambra was of their planning and of Spanish building. The whole history of Arab life in Spain is being gradually rewritten to tell a story other than the popular one.

Ferdinand and Isabella entered the last stronghold of the invader, Granada, on January 2, 1492. Cardinal Ximenes even went to Africa and conquered Oran, in the old territory of the Moors. Spain was almost ready for her golden century. But she had yet to conquer traitors at home, con-

As the traveler student of Spanish history stands before the Great Mosque of Córdova and looks across the narrow Guadalquivir River, he can scarcely fail to remember a ghastly tragedy once played along its banks. In revenge for an insurrection against his authority the Calif Hokam there crucified three hundred, heads downward and facing the Mosque. Nor was he particular about the religion of his victims. Moslem and Christian rebels died in agony that day side by side. One of the most effective of the Moorish customs of the time in excutions was a mockery of the Crucifixion of Christ when the victim expired between a crucified pig on one side and a similarly tortured dog on the other. From the mock-cannibal feast after Algeciras to the last hour of Moslem rule in Spain, beheading, crucifixion, and torture never were for a long time halted. Heads were piled up in profusion after a Moorish victory, stuck on the bridges, and on the walls of cities, even sent to Africa and as far as Damascus, to show all Moslems how their brothers in Spain were dealing with "the infidel dog."

It goes without saying that the Christian did not fail to retaliate in kind. He drew the line at the crucifixions but did not hesitate at decapitations and torture. Neither Moor nor Christian had great need of prisons except for detention. Imprisonment was for both a poor sort of punishment. Both knew better ones, and who can say if these were not, in the state of bloody warfare which then existed, felt to be more effective? A recent news item about the famous Dartmoor prison in England, mentioned the use of the "cat" on escaped prisoners, and on others for certain crimes, stating that as a deterrent its value was far above that of even solitary confinement. The English "cat" and the American "third degree" testify that torture has not entirely been done away with. To their ordinary horrors the Moors occasionally added a policy of general expulsions. After the crucifixion referred to above, Hokam expelled fifteen thousand from Córdova to Africa and destroyed the part of the city in which they lived. Later eighteen thousand more left for Africa, both groups suffering untold hardships in crossing the Sierras.

There was a long wait on the part of the Christians for revenge. The Christian Kings who supplanted the Califs of Córdova sent the Moors themselves on the route of the Sierras and the sea back to Africa. If the Inquisition knew how to get at the truth from the Moriscos by torture, these might take what cheer they could from the fact that they themselves had developed and taught the refinement of what they were made to suffer.

A third imprint on the Spanish character was made by the Moorish wars. Long before the African invader came, the Spanish Visigoth Kingdom had been Christian but, as to morals, especially in its nobles and its clergy, there was much to be desired. Faith for a long time had walked through Visigoth Spain without good works for companion. Not that there were no buildings testifying to her zeal; not that the Christians of the Kingdom failed to produce even saints; but luxury and royal favor sapped the religious strength of the descendants of the martyrs of the Roman period. Under such conditions the weakening of the Kingdom was inevitable. The structure of the State and of the Church was outwardly strong; but, as termites eat from

the center and leave the appearance of the beams supporting an edifice unchanged, so with the moral degradation
of the Spanish-Visigoth Kingdom. The supporting foundation of morality was slowly destroyed in its soul.

The Moors brought with them to Spain the fanaticism of
the Moslem, and his hatred of "the infidel." He had little
of the supernatural in which to believe but he believed it,
as he does today, with all the force of his being. What is
outside the circle of that belief he then hated, as he still
hates, with murderous fervor. He can live in peace with
Christians who govern him, but never without suspicion,
never without hope of one day overcoming and annihilating
them either by war or conversion. The beaten Spaniard who
fled with the cross to the mountains of the Asturias before
the crescent, knew well that the great secret of whatever
Moorish unity there might be was the Moslem religion.
He learned that at the point of the scimitar. Of it he kept
the memory.

Humiliating as it may be to confess it, the spectacle of
the Moor conquering to the war cry of Allah and Mohammed revived and steeled in the Spaniard his faith in God
and Christ. The fact is witnessed not only in the stubborn-
ness of his fighting under the banner of the Cross, but in the
scenes of peaceful pilgrimages to the Shrine of the Apostle
St. James, in the founding of the universities during a time
of greatest danger, in the building of architectural master-
pieces of cathedrals and churches before the fear of their
possible destruction by the invader had passed, in the increase of cultured saints to be successors of Isidore of Seville,
in the establishment of the military religious orders, and

above all in the rise of congregations of men and women pledged if necessary to sell themselves into Moslem slavery as the price of liberation for other Christians. Not only a period of high romance, often the child of mysticism, but a period of Christian religious heroism swept into the life of Catholic Spain. Warfare hardened it. Idealism sublimated it. The soldier had it in his spiritual knapsack and fought on it. The scholar based his labor upon it. The priest preached it. No sacrifice was too great an offering at its shrine. It transformed Spain. It captured Granada. And, when the last victories over Spain's enemies at home saved the nation but ruined her reputation in centuries to follow, Columbus returned with his tale of marvelous new lands discovered. Spain was ready then for more conquest in the name of Christ. The Moors, unwittingly, had much to do with the conquest of the New World. They helped make the Spaniard, who was the only man in the Europe of his day who could be trusted to do it, who really was prepared by long suffering and struggles to carry it on to a successful termination.

The Spanish background of the Conquest of America dates back, then, to Tarek and Algeciras. If the scene could be painted, it would show destroyed churches, looted castles, pyramids of Christian heads, fleeing kings, rising mosques and alcazars, girls dancing while jets of water played in halls of myrtles before drunken emirs and califs, strumming guitars under Andalusian moons, slaves in toil for hard African masters; then sweeping charges of armored swordsmen crying to Santiago, sieges holding for years, toppling crescents, bishops on warhorses, kings who were saints, and saints who did not disdain to think that sanctity and war were not incompatible. We wonder today not a little why it is that the descendants of such people can laugh while they pray, produce sinners who hate sin, and make distinctions impossible to us to show the holiness of the house of God and the fact that it is also the noisy home of His children; who can dance solemnly before the Blessed Sacrament and make carnival in the very heart of the season of penance, who can hate the hand yet love the Sacrifice it offers. We do not grasp the fact that such a man was trained in a logic of his own, by that great teacher called Adversity who is often blind. His major and minor terms are always pain, but out of them came for the Spaniard the conclusion of victory. He had lost when he should have won. He had won when he should have lost. But, winning or losing, he had stood the terrible test that made him ready for anything. He met it again in Mexico, and how he did rise to it!

III

MEXICAN BACKGROUND

CORTÉS LEARNED VERY soon after his arrival in Mexico that his objective must be Tenochtitlán, the present Mexico City, at that time the seat of government of Montezuma II, ruler of the Aztecs, the most powerful of the Mexican tribes. Between the capital and the sea there were other tribes, most of them at heart enemies of the Aztecs. It is of importance, in order to get the Mexican background of the Conquest, to understand that the Aztec tribe in Tenochtitlán was the dominant power. Whatever civilization Mexico possessed at the time of the Conquest at least centered in the court of Montezuma. Nevertheless, Mexico City, as we shall hereafter call it, was by no means the seat of government for the whole country. It was the capital of a tribe strong enough to exact tribute from the others. The geographical situation of the Aztecs, in the very heart of the country, as well as the military advantage of its location on Lake Tezcoco, is one explanation of the power this people exercised over their neighbors. They were, however, a brave people strengthened by religious fanaticism. It will be necessary to consider them at some length since, in conquering the Aztecs, Cortés really conquered Mexico.

The Aztecs had settled on Lake Tezcoco only about two

centuries (A.D. 1325) before the arrival of the Spaniards, and it is quite certain, from a study of existing ruins of ancient monuments, that Mexico was inhabited many centuries before the Christian era. There were numerous tribes in the Mexico Cortés found older than the Aztecs, all heirs to a common culture. He himself chronicles in his Letters a statement on this point made to him by Montezuma: "We have known for a long time," said he, "from the chronicles of our forefathers, that neither I, nor those who inhabit this country, are descendants from the aborigines of it, but from strangers who came to it from very distant parts; and we also hold that our race was brought to these parts by a lord, whose vassals they all were, and who returned to his native country. After a long time he came back, but it was so long, that those who remained here were married with the native women of the country, and had many descendants, and had built towns where they were living; when, therefore, he wished to take them away with him, they would not go, nor still less receive him as their ruler, so he departed. And we have always held that those descended from him would come to subjugate this country and us, as his vassals; and according to the direction from which you say you come, which is where the sun rises, and from what you tell us of your great lord, or king, who has sent you here, we believe, and hold for certain, that he is our rightful sovereign, especially as you tell us that since many days he has had news of us."[1]

Without a doubt this belief of the Aztecs as expressed by Montezuma helped to make the Conquest by Cortés much easier. Andrés de Tápia adds the information that

Montezuma told Cortés how the immigrants referred to had come in ships. It is probable that there was a connection, as claimed, between these early arrivals before the Christian era and the tribes which Cortés found in Mexico. What Montezuma told Cortés was a tradition of all the tribes that had a culture. This general tradition indicates also that the early arrivals were white men with a civilization indicating Mediterranean origin and traditions which we of today could scarcely fail to assign to Phoenicians, Egyptians, and Greeks. There are indeed traces of all these influences in them.[2]

Whence did this people come and when? Sahagún, who discusses in Book X of his History the various existing or legendary tribes of prominence in the native traditions, says: "It is years without number that there arrived the first inhabitants of these parts of New Spain which is almost another world, and coming in ships by sea landed at a port to the north; and because they disembarked there it is called Panutla, as it were Panoaia, place where arrived those who came by sea, and now called, though corruptly, Pantlan. And from that port they followed the shore keeping in sight the snowy mountain range and the volcanoes, until they came to the province of Guatemala." The last close study reaching back to this ancient people is a publication in two volumes of a work called *Prehistoria de Mexico,* by Plancarte. This work has not yet been translated from the original Spanish. It was published in a very limited edition during the comparative peace that followed the Carranza revolution and printed at Tlalpam in the Federal District. Plancarte was the then Archbishop of Linares who was exiled during the Carranza revolution. He had given a whole lifetime to research, doing a great deal of excavating from his home in Zamora, from Cuernavaca, and later from Monterrey. He had a most valuable library of manuscripts and pictures, together with a collection of antiquities known to the Smithsonian Institute in Washington. He had published already a most valuable book on the beginnings of civilization in Mexico, and had another ready for the press when the revolution broke out. The Carranzistas raided his house, stole his manuscripts and antiquities, sold them for a trifle to whoever would buy, and scattered the sheets of his book over the streets. During his exile of five years in Chicago he found good material for his *Prehistoria* in the Newberry Library and in the Field Museum. He wrote it at DePaul University. The author died a short time after his return to Mexico, and a few interested friends put the book in print that it might not be lost.[3]

A most important story taken from the *Historia de los Indios* of Motolinia is as follows: "Aristotle, in the book *De Admirandis in Natura,* says that in ancient times the Carthaginians sailed through the Strait of Hercules, which is our Strait of Gibraltar, toward the west, sixty days of sail, and that they found pleasant, delightful, and very fertile lands. And as that course might be much followed and many remain yonder as settlers, the Senate of Carthage, for fear that their city might be depopulated, ordered under penalty of death that none should come or go upon that course." It will be noted that the voyage from Carthage to the west was sixty days' sail. The sailing time of Columbus from Palos to the Bahamas was forty-nine days. Allowing for time lost by Columbus sailing down the African coast to the Canary Islands, his actual sailing time across the Atlantic would be thirty-six days. There is considerably more than a possibility then that Aristotle's story may be true and that actually a Carthaginian settlement had been made in Mexico. A considerable number of immigrants must have gone forth before the Senate of Carthage was alarmed and forbade further emigration. Mexican traditions insist that some of the visitors went back across the Atlantic. This could only mean that Carthage made an attempt to repatriate its citizens. The traditions say that many of the first arrivals remained. Everything in the story could be used to explain the statement made to Cortés by Montezuma.[4]

Carthage, it is said, was founded about the middle of the ninth century B.C. Spinden, in the *Scientific American* of March, 1928, wrote: "The actual historical era of the Mayas, that is, the time when they began to record every day in sequence in their permutation system, was disclosed as August 6, 613 B.C., the first date in New World history." The striking similarity to the Old World paganism found in Mexico by the Spaniard might be explained by the fact that the water front of Carthage must have attracted adventurers and seamen from all about the Mediterranean. Any vessels crossing the Atlantic from Carthage would be manned by these adventurers from different nations. There must, however, have been settlers in Mexico even before the Carthaginians, if the Aristotle story is true, for the white men who were left after the Senate of Carthage had forbidden further emigration, intermarried, according to

Montezuma, with the natives. Piecing together Mexican tradition with Aristotle's story gives us at least justification for a shrewd guess as to the origin of the certainly notable civilization, not unlike the Egyptian, which had come to an end centuries before the Spaniards arrived, and absolves the latter from the charge that they destroyed it. The pre-Spanish history of Mexico, therefore, is divided into two parts, namely, what Plancarte calls the prehistoric, and what is generally called the Aztec.

Where the Aztecs,[5] as well as the tribes that preceded them, came from is likewise a great deal of a mystery. The principal settlements found by the Spaniards in Mexico were on the high table-lands known as the Central Highlands — *Mesa Central* — though there were also tribes all along the coast. What became of the ancient civilizations no one knows for certain, but we do know that the high table-lands were formed by volcanic disturbances. There is a tradition of a burning mountain, a rain of stones, and fetid gases, killing many and forcing the survivors to depart. It was, however, in our own era — about A.D. 600 — that the cities now deserted in the jungles, such as Palenque, and, by the way, some of them seen by Colonel Lindbergh from the air, were abandoned. A slowly decaying civilization might have left them depopulated and the few remaining inhabitants wanderers. The natives thought that they had found remains of giants, but modern science shows that these are the remains of prehistoric animals. The tribe of the Otomi, still in Mexico, has been confused with these legendary giants. Their ancestors preceded the Naua, the ancestors of the Aztecs.

When the Aztecs came to Lake Tezcoco they were a weak tribe which settled on little islands in the Lake and in the swamps for protection. They were so weak that they were left unmolested. Bandelier, writing in the *Peabody Museum Reports,* explains that the area of dry soil in the Lake was extended by additions of sod: "By scanty artificial foundations of turf thrown into the shallow morass and, erecting upon it their frail dwellings, they lived in poverty until they found out the great advantage which this isolated position gave to them over the surrounding tribes." They then made war on these tribes because they had a safe retreat behind them and their own position was difficult and dangerous to an assailant. Gradually they subjugated the other tribes and made war upon them to secure victims and tribute. It was in this way that the so-called "Empire of the Aztecs" was established, and it likewise accounts for the hatred of the other tribes against them which the Spaniards used to their advantage.

Father Hubbard, head of the Department of Geology of Santa Clara University, in his lectures on his own exploration in the Aleutian Islands of Alaska, mentions the similarity of carvings. He believes, on the strength of these carvings as well as on the strength of the legends of the Eskimo, that all the races of Indians now in America came across Bering Strait from Asia. The totem poles of Alaska have a close resemblance to the carvings found in Mexico. As to the possibility of crossing Bering Strait, he cites a legend quite persistent among the Alaskan tribes which he heard in different forms but all basically alike. These refer to a god so tall and strong that he could fling a mountain from Asia to America. Following the accepted rules of interpretation, Dr. Hubbard believes that at one time the Strait was so narrow that a strong man could fling a stone across it. He holds that it was widened to its present size by some enormous natural disturbance in the Arctic which, throwing a great volume of water across the sands and swamps, swept them down into the Pacific. Judging from the number of Asiatics who must have come across the Strait to form the Indian tribes of America, North and South, the Strait at one time was very narrow. Even had the Strait never been narrower than it now is, that fact would have made no difference. When the Russians came to Alaska they found intercommunication between the peoples of Asia and America quite well established.

It is more than probable that all the Indians on the American continent are descendants of these Asiatic wanderers. Similarity of their traditions, especially those bearing on religious beliefs, is a proof difficult to pass over. Father Desautels, an old-time missionary to the Indians of the Canadian north country, still living, states: "I have gone from tribe to tribe among pagan Indians. I have talked to Indians who never before saw a white man and never had access to the Bible. Legends told by them and other natives at widely separated points are usually the same, yet these Indians could not possibly have talked with each other. Their stories usually parallel those of the Old Testament." He believes that their Asiatic fathers had encountered Jews before they came to America. There are traces of Old Testament stories in the religious traditions of the Mexican Indians, but it is remarkable that only in Mexico is there a

Á Través de los Siglos, Vol. I, p. 233, offers this interesting comparison between ancient Egypt and ancient Mexico. On the left is the Egyptian which in at least one instance will be found on a temple wall dating from about 1300 B.C. The design on the right is copied from the Borgian Codex, p. 8, in Kingsborough.

The so-called Pyramid of the Sun in Teotihuacan. It is about 720 feet on a side, and over 200 feet high. Inexpert attempts to "restore" it have destroyed some of the outer layers of construction.

"Quetzalcoatl was esteemed and held as god, and they worshiped him of old in Tulla, and he had a very high Cu with many steps very narrow without room for a foot." These steps are on the Pyramid of the Sun in Teotihuacan, and were uncovered some thirty years ago. No other similar monument possesses steps answering this description.

legend about white men arriving in ships. That these brought to Mexico a superior civilization which for a long time gave the tribes the "golden age" to which traditions often refer, is fairly well substantiated. The legend of the "Fair God" may also be traced to these bearded white visitors.

It is persistently stated that the Spaniards destroyed the picture writing and hieroglyphic interpretations of the Mexicans and thus left us in darkness as to the origin of the ancient people, as well as of the tribes found by Cortés. The Spaniards did destroy many pagan temples and with them some of the pictures must have been burned; but it must also be remembered that the Aztecs made constant war on the other tribes and that the picture which for them indicated a conquest was the representation of a burning temple. The picture writings were not in the hands of the people but were kept by the priests in the temples. It is also true that tribes ashamed of their origin destroyed the pictures that told the story of their lowly extraction. As a matter of fact, when the Spaniards gave the Mexicans the Latin alphabet they gave them with it the means of writing their native language and therefore of preserving what traditions, legends, and myths they had. The Spanish missionaries became highly proficient in speaking the Mexican language and used it, as well as Spanish, to record the native traditions. Many precious manuscripts were kept in the religious houses throughout Mexico. A great number of these were destroyed in the revolution of the "Liberals" in 1855. This revolution was led by Alvarez, an illiterate mulatto. More destruction was done in 1861 by Juárez, who was an educated Indian. The important manuscript of Father Tello was rescued from the counter of a spice merchant who had purchased it with other papers to wrap his wares. It was the revolutions that did most of the destruction. An example of their work, even as late as 1914, was shown by the destruction of the collection, library, and manuscripts of Archbishop Plancarte already referred to. In that disaster some 25,000 volumes and 700 manuscripts were lost, not counting the antiquities. The destruction of manuscripts by the Indians before the Spaniards came, from motives of racial pride, had its principal example less than a hundred years before the arrival of the Spaniards, when the leading men of the pueblo of Tenochtitlán ordered all the picture writings burned "that they might not fall into the hands of the vulgar and be set at naught." The tribe of Tlaxcalans, who were allies of Cortés, entered Tezcoco in 1520, burned the palace of the King and with it, as an Indian historian notes, "all the royal archives of all New Spain." This statement, however, sounds like an exaggeration. We have enough historical facts in reference to the destruction of the picture writings to know that the Spaniard played a very small part in it. The missionaries certainly did destroy such pictures as were used to propagate and preserve pagan idolatry and the current demonology. The Indians had been warned by the Spaniards to give up their human sacrifices and cannibalism, which might account for the destructive zeal of the missionaries in reference to the idols. That Bishop Zumárraga valued the manuscripts, and the interpretations of them, is shown by the fact that he took a collection of both to Spain in 1532. Sahagún notes of the Indians that "they had no letters or characters whatever, nor could they read or write." Had it not been for the zeal of the scientific minded among the missionaries scarcely anything of the history of the old tribes would be known today. The descendants of the Indians, educated by the Spaniards, produced their own historians.

Some tablets of disputed authenticity have been dug up as far north as Michigan, which, if genuine, might show the presence of Mexican tribes from the south. These tablets tell on slate a pictured story of wars between two peoples, one in dress strangely like that of our own northern Indians, with victory for the Indians and exile for the remnants of the vanquished. Many of these tablets are in the University of Notre Dame. One argument in favor of their authenticity is based on the fact that what are claimed to be tempered copper spears and knives were found in the mounds with them. The art of tempering copper — if it ever existed — was lost long centuries ago. Those who believe the tablets to be genuine records made by an American people, point to the certainty that the copper mines of Northern Michigan had been worked long before their discovery in our own times.

The Spaniards found the Mexican natives with cities, laws, tribal customs, orderly government, dramatic and lyric poetry, temples, houses, and even books, though these latter were the pictures and hieroglyphics already referred to. There were also religious rites and traditions vaguely reminiscent of the Scriptural account of creation and the deluge. Myths regarding the power of the four elements seem almost to touch ancient Greece. They had likewise the idea of the sacrificial as the highest act of worship. But their religion, if it had Christian or Jewish roots, nevertheless had turned into a plant so noxious that, if the uprooting of it were all that the Spaniards had done, they would be entitled therefor to the thanks of mankind.

One might search in vain through all the rest of the world without finding horrors greater than those practiced in the religious ritualism of the tribes found in Mexico—especially in the capital—by the Spaniards. And it was these rites that directed the Aztec relations with other tribes. The "foreign policy" of the Aztec was not to form a peaceful empire. His human sacrifices forbade the very thought of that. Though the first Spaniards believed Mexico to be an empire, because of the central and dominant position of the Aztecs, it was in reality nothing of the kind. It could not be. There had to be a daily sacrifice of hearts, freshly torn out of living human bodies, to the sun. On feasts, frequent enough, hundreds, even thousands, of hearts were needed for the idols. Since not even so degraded a people would have preferred to kill their own rather than others, war for the capture of victims was a necessity. Nevertheless there was a saying among the Nauans that the sun preferred Nauan flesh; and there are records of wholesale sacrifices of the deformed, even of children. But prisoners of war were usually the preferred victims. A peaceful united Empire could supply no prisoners of war. This point alone should be sufficient to prove the falsity of the letters to the King of Spain from Mexico vaunting the Conquistadores as the captors of an Emperor and the winners of an Empire; as it should likewise serve to put an end to the romances and alleged historical writing resting upon them. There was no civilization in Mexico to compare with any in the Europe of the time when Cortés landed. What he found was at best a refined barbarism, marked not only by wholesale murder, but by the most revolting practices of cannibalism. To call this a civilization would be to betray every Christian social ideal.[6]

Prehistoric Mexico had a confederation—more correctly an association—in the central highland of the Nauan, Ulmecan, and Quinamentin tribes. Later on they divided, some passing into the north as far as our present Arizona and New Mexico, and came into our southeastern states; others going to Yucatan and farther south beyond what is now Mexico proper. In the south especially they took with them and developed a culture. They worshiped the sun and the four elements and many gods, built pyramids and houses, and cultivated the ground. They accumulated and correlated much astronomical knowledge to be used in divination, astrology, and daily guidance. Their culture was far superior to that of the subjects of Montezuma. The only confederation the Aztecs made was one with the Acolhuas and Tepenacas — early fifteenth century — for war purposes; which meant tribute and victims. The influence of the Aztecs on other tribes was destructive of any culture these might have retained. The culture of the descendants of the Ulmecas, who lived far from the ancestors of the Aztecs, did develop; as is proved by ruins in Chiapas, Central America, and Yucatan, only to disappear centuries before the white man came. A later revival was found decaying like the Aztecs, from similar causes. The Aztecs, and those tribes influenced by them, degenerated. Bitter hatreds between tribes, due to the wars for tribute and victims, flourished; which explains in part the ease with which Cortés could fling one against another, for, instead of uniting to form nations, the tribes became more and more split up among themselves. Craft and savage force were cultivated to secure captives, and thus the possession of these two evil accomplishments earned the highest honor, and were considered worthy of the noblest reward. There were, in fact, no noble deeds except deeds of bitter warfare. The warrior who brought in the greatest number of prisoners for the sacrifices was always the favored one. The rudimentary science which the tribes had received from outside did not increase. The hieroglyphics that appear in the south, with a suspected tendency to the ideographic, degenerated to pictures in the north. In spite of the fact that the Spanish conquerors found the Mexican tribes the most advanced of all the American Indians, yet, even without the Spanish conquest, these tribes of Mexico would have disappeared by reason of their own degeneracy through the eating of the human sacrifices. "The cult of Mexico," says Orozco y Berra, "was awfully hideous; it required a continual shedding of blood. . . . Our mind rebels and is struck with awe before the human victim; not only the victim gashed to death with sharp knives, but also the one offered up under exquisite forms of a refinement of cruelty. Any religion advocating the suppression of such barbarism would be more acceptable than this. To sweep it out of the world was an immense advantage; to substitute Christianity for it meant a far advance on the way of civilization. This is axiomatic, evident, clear as the daylight."[7]

Such was the Mexico found by the Spaniards; still holding to a shred of its original culture, but rapidly, because of idolatry, superstition, war, and cannibalism, growing weaker and weaker, and threatened with extinction. Cortés found in Mexico the empty splendor that surrounds the deathbed of an expiring race.

This is not the picture of Aztec civilization drawn by many historians, especially Prescott; but they took for their authorities chiefly the letters of some of the Spanish conquerors already referred to, many of them written to exalt their own accomplishments in the court of the King of Spain and greatly overdrawing the picture. Bandelier was the greatest English-speaking authority on American prehistoric civilizations. He it was who wrote the preface to Charles F. Lummis' *Spanish Pioneers*. There he says that he stands behind every word Lummis wrote. Lummis, himself no small authority, has utterly destroyed the romances of Prescott. To show how overdrawn was the Prescott picture, both Lummis and Bandelier proved that the famous "columns of porphyry and jasper supporting marble balconies," of palaces, were nothing more than adobe houses like the houses still used by the American Pueblo Indians. It is from Prescott that most English readers have drawn their information, not only concerning the Conquest but also concerning the ancient tribes. Susan Hale says: "Later explorers, with the fatal penetration of our time, destroy the splendid vision, reducing the emperor to a chieftain, the glittering retinue to a horde of savages, a magnificent civilization devoted to art, literature, and luxury, to a few handfuls of pitiful Indians, quarreling with one another for supremacy;

and sigh to think their sympathies may have been wasted on the sufferings of an Aztec sovereign, dethroned by the invading Spaniard."[8]

Put two pictures together; the Spanish and the Mexican backgrounds of the Conquest of America, and it will be seen plainly how inevitable became the bloody nature of the conflict. On the side of the Spanish soldier was the memory of the Moor, his brutality, his fanaticism, his robberies, his oppressions, his crucifixions. It was not in human nature to forget them. The priest might talk of forgiveness but even he did not forget. When the Spanish soldier saw his ships destroyed by Cortés, his feelings must have been like those of his predecessors who fell at Loja, when the Moor dashed out from his fortifications on the retreating Christian forces, slaughtered or drove them into the river, and almost killed their King. Or what they felt before Malaga when, at midnight, the Moorish yell awoke them to face a shower of arrows and an invisible enemy. There was no Christian army left that day to reach Antiquera. Even the Moorish women had taken starving Spanish prisoners in that terrible retreat, and many a Christian warrior was sold into slavery or perished under the scimitar within Malaga's walls. Here now was the Spaniard in a strange land, all retreat cut off, hopelessly outnumbered, facing new infidels, Moors of a new continent with worse than the old Moor's thirst for loot and blood. The Spanish soldier knew well what failure would mean: the stone idol, the hideous priests with blackened faces and feathered heads, the obsidian knife for an unprotected breast, a torn-out heart, and his flesh sold in the stalls of the butchers. It was the

Moorish war all over again for him, but in this one the Spaniard seemingly had no chance. His supplies were yet to be won from the enemy, and every single loss by death would be a major disaster. There was but one thing to do. Better the poisoned arrow than the altar and the knife. Better death by the hand of the enemy in fight than by that of a butchering pagan priest. There was no choice, with an enemy before him who knew no mercy. The decision thus was easy to make and the Spaniard made it.

IV

THE CONQUEST

AS THE HISTORY of Mexico before the Conquest is divided into two well-marked periods, so the history of Spanish Mexico is similarly divided. The first part is very short. It lasted only from 1519, when Cortés landed, to 1521, when he took the city on Lake Tezcoco. As soon after as 1535 the whole of Mexico was under Spanish Viceregal rule. The second period begins where the first left off, and ends in 1821 when, after the insurrection under Agustín de Iturbide, the last Spanish Viceroy, Don Juan O'Donojú, attached his signature to peace terms acknowledging Mexican independence. The dominant figure of the first period is that of Hernando Cortés. He entered also into the second but in a changed role. In the first he was a conqueror; in the second an administrator. He was also a changed man. Like the sword he carried, which had two sharp cutting edges but at the hilt was shaped like a cross, the first Cortés, the steel part, was a general; but the other, the hilt part, very much of a zealous, though none too wise, missionary. The stern necessity of fighting kept Cortés the soldier, but when the battle was over his heart at least was that of a zealot, for God and Mexico. Even his chaplain, Fray Bartolemé de Olmedo, had to warn him against the fiery zeal with which he tried to reason Montezuma into accepting the Faith. He never forgot his character as Crusader.

The Christians of that day were as a rule more or less like Cortés and the other Conquistadores. They grasped an essential fact about Christianity that we of today often miss; by which I mean that they knew Christianity was not a state of perfection attained, but a way ultimately to attain it. They did not expect to be able to avoid all sins, but did want to commit as few as possible. They recognized the fact that the soul would always be a battle ground while hampered by the body. Goodness was an ideal to them, but ideals often suspend action during a fight.

Cortés has been roundly and vigorously condemned for his methods of conquest. Little, however, is said of his labors, his genuine statesmanship, and his determination not to disappoint those who sent him to Christianize the New World. He was forever offering peace to his enemies, and went to the greatest pains to introduce domestic animals and better methods of agriculture into the new country. His Indian policy put him centuries ahead of his time, and the policy worked, unlike the many adopted by the colonizers of the north.[1]

This "oppressor of the Indians" seemed oftenest to be considered by them as a friend.[2] Though he defeated the Tlaxcalans they became his allies; and when the Spaniards, beaten and broken in that awful *Noche Triste*, fled from the valley before the host of Aztecs, it was the Tlaxcalans who succored them, bound up their wounds, prepared with them for a renewal of the fight, and helped them win the ultimate victory after a three months' siege. The truth is that Cortés was looked upon by the tribes opposed to the Aztecs as their deliverer from a bloody tyranny. No wonder, for the Aztecs were collecting tribute from over 300 Indian towns and villages which they did not pretend to govern.[3] What would have happened had there been no invasion of European civilization into America, North or South, is that the whole continent would have become the home of primitive wandering tribes practicing gross idolatry and cannibalism, until, by the law of "dog eat dog," it finally would have ended as a wilderness, inhabited only by beasts, whose title, as far as decency is concerned, would have been better than the humans who had left it to them.

In the English colonies of the north there never was any question of civilizing or absorbing the Indians. They were to keep going westward as the whites advanced. The English colonists were settlers and nothing else. The Spanish colonial plan was quite different. In the Europe of the day it was admitted that to the Pope belonged the right to assign newly discovered lands to the guardianship of Christian nations so that the natives might be brought into the fold of the Church, educated and civilized. Spain's right in America was not then only that of discovery. It was also an appointment as guardian and missionary, by adoption of the "mandate" idea centuries before the League of Nations invented the term. Spain accepted the conditions laid down by the Pope. Its first obligation under that mandate was to preserve, Christianize, and civilize the natives. The Spanish kings never forgot that obligation, though the Spanish settlers often did.

Out of the fidelity of the Spanish rulers to the obligation accepted by them, and the forgetfulness of it by those of their subjects who thought only of gain, came the seeds of that anticlericalism which has been the curse of Mexico to our day. The missionaries sent by Spain were King's men. They had the right of direct appeal to the royal authority and exercised it—to the annoyance of the gold seekers—from the beginning. Fray Olmedo could with impunity rebuke Cortés, as we have seen, but only Cortés the preacher. He would not have dared rebuke the general. But on the whole the Viceroys admitted the paramount rights of souls, though then, as now, there were struggles by the politicians speaking for the rich and the priests speaking for the poor. It is certain that, with notable exceptions, seekers after gold set themselves against seekers after souls.

It must not be thought, however, that there was always a sharp line of division between the settlers and the clergy. There were priests who came as chaplains to the troops before the arrival of the first regular missionaries, who must be counted with the gold-seekers. There were also other priests who, for the greater part, were half adventurers who had left Spain to the relief of their bishops. These too were of the gold-seeker class. On the other hand the majority of the Viceroys, the disinterested Spanish officials, and many men and women of deep religious convictions, were with the clergy. But the main line of division was there. Both Christ and Mammon were well and numerously represented. The consequences of this early struggle never left the soil of Mexico, nor did the alignment very much change with the passing of the years. If the Moor influenced the character of the Spaniard and gave him a lust for gold, in turn the Spaniard left sad consequences of his failings on the character of the Mexican. Anticlericalism was one of them. But devotion was left as its stronger antagonist. There are today only two classes of Mexicans; the Christian and the hater of the Christian name.

Since this book is not a history but a documented historical study, it does not aim to set down the details of the Spanish Conquest of Mexico which was consummated with record-making swiftness. A study of it reveals some conclusions that hitherto have failed to receive proper recognition.

First and foremost, because of the very swiftness of the process, as well as the small number of soldiers in the army of Cortés, comes the absolute certainty that no Empire existed under the rule of Montezuma, as has already been stated. Second, that because the natives assisted Cortés and, as a matter of fact, supplied the numerical strength without which he would have been lost, the tribes aiding him looked upon the Spaniards as deliverers. Third, that their promptness in joining the stranger shows how desperate they thought their own position to be at the time. These conclusions put a proper value on the statements of the enemies of Spain. If anything were needed to confirm the conclusions, it can be taken from the history of the English colonists. They knew that there could be no compromise with the Indian. Even though their policy with the Indian was radically different from that of the Spaniards, they yet were forced to defend themselves against the native, as well as attack him. Our own high-ranking army officers of 1898, had been trained by active service in Indian wars. The last of such wars is still a vivid memory for not a few living Americans. The history of discovery, exploration, and colonization, in the New World, is always a story of battles and bloodshed. We of the north have no eminence over the colonists of the south on the score of quietly permitting ourselves to be killed and lose our possessions. When Columbus returned to the first colony he left in the New World, he found it a heap of blackened ruins. Dávila lost life and property when he accepted a proffered hospitality that was quickly turned into an ambuscade. The Indians of Yucatan seized fifteen men and two women who had been shipwrecked on their coast, and who, by the way, were the first whites these Indians had ever seen.[4] The women were made slaves and worked to death, and the men fattened and eaten. There were two survivors, one a renegade and the other rescued by Cortés. The very name of the city of Matanzas in Cuba perpetuates the story of another butchery of the survivors of a shipwreck by Indians.[5] Córdova was invited into an ambush in the same Yucatan, and barely saved his company. At Campeche his men, going ashore for water, were all attacked. They escaped but got no water. Later they lost fifty men when on the same errand at Chanpoton.[6] In Florida, where Ponce de León was to meet disaster in 1521, they were attacked while getting water. De Soto attempted to explore without subduing, and discovered his mistake too late; so the Spaniards lost one of the best expeditions they had ever fitted out.[7]

To conquer Mexico, Cortés set out in February, 1519, with five hundred and eight Spanish soldiers, two hundred Cuban natives, men and women, a few slaves, and one hundred and nine sailors; less than nine hundred in all. There were thirty-eight crossbows, thirteen matchlocks, and sixteen horses. For artillery there were fourteen pieces, none too good. The dependence had to be placed on swords and shields. He organized Indian allies as best he could and began his march toward the interior.

The Spaniards had no doubts about the character of the Indians before they left. Bernal Díaz wrote that their Totonac allies every day sacrificed three or four Indians in the usual way to their idols, tearing out hearts, and anointing walls with the blood. The arms and legs of their victims they cut off and ate. Small wonder if, with such a spectacle before them, the Spaniards reached the determination to destroy idols whenever the chance came.[8]

There is no need to go below surface indications above the rich mine of the discoveries and achievements of the last five centuries, to show these centuries witnessing the swiftest development of progress in the history of mankind. Chiefly to the Spanish discovery and conquest does the world owe a debt of gratitude for it all. A library, not a volume, would be required to tabulate and narrate even a part of the reasons for acknowledging that debt. The heroes of Spain doubled the size of the world, opened up a western route to the Orient where Messer Marco Polo sits among the gods of China, gave vast fields to the support of the race and to its progress, and new nations to test the inevitable coming experiments in human liberty. For science these Spaniards confirmed by experiment the truth of the rotundity of the earth, made a vast contribution to navigation, profoundly affected astronomy, added new materials for the study of geology, zoology, and natural history in all

Hernándo Cortés

The street cut through between the church of San Francisco and the Franciscan college in Querétaro. This college, founded in 1693, is now a ruin partly occupied as a tenement.

Another view of the same.

its branches, and took the step that had to precede new inventions of power applied to transportation by sea and land.

It was not in direct, but in indirect benefits, however, that the Spanish Conquest pushed civilization forward. The spirit of the Conquistadores burst into a flame that quickly set on fire other peoples than their own. Portugal caught it first, with Magellan circumnavigating the world. Vasco da Gama carried the flag of Portuguese enterprise as far as the Indies that Columbus died believing he had reached. The fire was lit in England, and with it the torch of liberty that we call our nation. France snatched a light from it and Jacques Cartier of Saint Malo became the true founder of the Dominion of Canada. Even from the forests of Paraguay came a lesson in government as a result of it, where the Jesuit Reductions recalled the Christian communism of the Apostolic age, and gave a first demonstration in modern times of the power of Christian ethics to bless with peace and plenty in justice to all and favors to none. The spirit ran like living light through every land, reaching and enriching every science, profoundly affecting all thinking, and increasing the wealth of all nations. Bertrand[9] called the voyage of Columbus "The Last Crusade" because of his design by it to take the Turk from the rear. Not Columbus but the spirit made successful that Last Crusade. The Great Khan was not entirely a mythical personage, but it was not from him or from India that the real blow came, but from the spirit. On the Bay of Lepanto Don John of Austria,[10] Spaniard, backed by American gold from the Spanish royal coffers, with the united fleets of Spain, Venice, and the Papacy, smashed the Turk's sea power and crippled him, leaving him to await the *coup de grâce* that John Sobieski was to deliver later before the walls of Vienna. Little did Columbus know as he sailed from Palos, what tremendous things would follow his seeking the end of his rainbow. How could Cortés know when he struck the conquering blow at Tenochtitlán, of the fact that the sound of it was to reverberate a challenge to progress in every part of the civilized globe?

V

QUICK RESULTS

THE POLICY OF SPAIN in following up her discovery of the New World by conquest was marked by both wisdom and prudence. She allowed private initiative full steam ahead, and, for the greater part, at its own risk of both life and fortune. The outstanding example of that policy in action was the expedition of Cortés itself. While he had royal authority through the Governor of Cuba, which, when it became imperative to ignore, he shook off, yet the financing was done by himself, aided by those who were willing to send a little gold to find its giant brother. That fact accounts for his insistence on having "a king's share," or a fifth, of all the gold he secured in Mexico. He was in debt for his expedition. The Spanish Government accepted in practice the theory that it is wisdom not to hamper private enterprise. Not only was the New World opened up and settled for a large part as a result of that policy, but it had thus been discovered; for Isabella largely used her own private funds—witness the pledging of her jewels—to fit out the first expedition of Columbus. The Spanish State, exhausted and beggared by seven centuries of the war of liberation from the Moslem, was in no condition to risk much money on an Italian's dream. Not only the lust for gold noticed in Cortés, but the same lust in almost all the other conquerors of New Spain, may find a partial explanation in these facts.

Nor did Spain suffer for the liberty she thus allowed to private enterprise. The conquerors never forgot that they were Spaniards and subjects of the King. What they could claim for him they always did claim. Cortés was prompt to make the three marks of possession on a great tree with his sword when he landed, as Spain's royal seal on the whole territory. He had a royal notary with him ever ready to draw up and attest the King's rights to his discoveries. The King always had his place. Cortés told Montezuma over and over again that he came from his King who was taking the overlordship of Mexico. It is King, King, King, everywhere. Even the Church is second to the King in all things but one. And that became the actual position of the Church when the policy of encouraging private enterprise diminished and more governmental control was inaugurated. With Cortés himself as Governor and Captain General that new policy began soon after the fighting was over and done with. Thus the absolute rule of the court of Spain was extended over all her American colonies and, as these were enlarged by discovery or exploration, each new territory was given its place and its royal representative. The Church went along with the rest. Concessions relative to the choice of bishops enjoyed by Spain herself were, by Papal decree, extended to her possessions in the New World. That right alone was one of Spain's most powerful arms of government, indeed her right arm. What was Spanish became Spanish-American. Some of the Spanish privileges, such as certain exemptions from the law of abstinence, remain in America down to the present time. The royal patronage was all-powerful. Royal permission had to be obtained for the erection of churches, of schools, of monasteries, and convents. The King alone could organize dioceses or set limits to them, asking the approval of the Pope. Ecclesiastical benefices were the gift of the King and, after nomination, action had to be taken by the bishops within ten days. The recipient of such a benefice could even go over the head of his own bishop after ten days and secure official installation by another. The regular orders were not exempt. It was the King who really named their superiors, for all religious establishments came under the jurisdiction of the Council of the Indies, which was the King in action toward his colonies. Indirect as jurisdiction over the religious bodies was, nonetheless it was absolute because of the right of veto possessed by the Crown. Provinces and provincials, visitors, college presidents, heads of chapters, were all included under this head. The very mandates of the Pope, however expressed, as well as instructions from generals of religious orders living in Rome, had to be verified and accepted by the Council of the Indies, acting in the King's name. Salvatierra and Kino, who opened up Lower California as simple missionaries, did not move until they had the royal permission.

This great power on the whole was for a long time well and wisely used. Good ecclesiastical appointments were made. Zeal for souls was encouraged, and education was favored. The royal authority felt its obligation for the spreading of the Faith. It stood firm against complaints that the Indians were being educated and thus made equal to the Spaniards, as will later be seen.

The swiftness of the Conquest was soon matched by the swiftness of development. The institution of slavery had sprung up as soon as the merchandising horde had settled in Cuba and spread to Mexico. Here the Pope interfered. Paul III issued a Bull against it in 1537, but the Council of the Indies had permitted representations to be submitted to Rome. With an alacrity that was a clear manifestation of sympathy, if not connivance, the Council ordered the Bull enforced. We would have no record today of the tales of cruelty and mistreatment of the Mexican Indians by the Spaniards were it not for these Spaniards themselves. The way to the King and the Pope was cleared for Las Casas pleading for the Indians. Even his manifest exaggerations were taken seriously. It is only justice to say that the Spanish Crown did all it could under difficult circumstances to favor and assist the solid growth and development of its American territories.

The Bull of Pope Paul III against slavery was, without doubt, the outstanding and important ecclesiastical and state pronouncement of the day, indeed of any day. Slavery was an inheritance from paganism with which the Christian Church would have to deal sooner or later. There was no place for it in Christianity. But it had gotten itself intertwined with the rights of private property, and a danger lay in trying to separate the tangled threads too fast. In the Early Church it was not hard, considering the fact of persecution from without, to which Christian master and slave were equally liable, to mitigate the evil by the spiritual bond of union between all professing the Faith of Christ. But the Church knew slavery could not last and was watching her chance to strike a blow at a social system she could not accept. Whatever criticisms may be leveled at the exaggerations of Las Casas, they should be forgiven because of his fight against slavery. More than to any other man the credit must be given the heroic bishop for pleading the cause of Indian liberty, not only before Charles V but also before the Pope. There is no record to prove that Las Casas was a messenger of the Emperor to the Papal See, there quietly to inform the Pope that the Emperor was ready to support a denunciation of slavery, but how else can we account for the fact that he went freely to Rome after he had sown the seeds of trouble for himself so widely in Spain? The Papal Bull, issued on June 2, 1537, used no diplomatic language. It was plain denunciation of slavery in all its forms down to forced labor. With it went an excommunication for those who dared disobey. It righted many abuses that military rule had produced in Mexico, though fewer in still-disturbed Peru. But that fact is the one of least importance in the matter. The horns of the Bull pulled out, and tossed into the air where the world might see, a truth about human liberty that humans themselves had thus far failed generally to recognize. Pope Paul III has the distinction of being the first thus to proclaim Christian equality of race and color. He gave the first blow to slavery that was felt around the world. But that blow cost the Church dearly. The Portuguese were deep in the slave trade and proposed to stay in it. So were the English and Spaniards. But the Pope could reason back of the defense of human liberty in America to plain Christian principles. Nevertheless his Bull gave new strength to the anticlericalism that had already begun to show itself in the Spanish possessions. As always the truth could only be spoken at the risk of crucifixion.

The breach between the colonists and the clergy was widened by the move against slavery; but the clergy had now two powerful defenders, for the Pope had strengthened the well-understood attitude of Charles V. The colonists insisted on their side that slavery was a necessity for the development of the new country. Pretexts were used even to extend it, for a compromise had been arrived at that Indians taken in rebellion might still be enslaved. But this move gave rise to new abuses and revived others that had existed even before the Papal Bull was published. There was no place left for compromise in an order that proclaimed the Indians rational beings, even though pagans, humans who must not be disturbed in their liberties or their properties and not under any excuse be made slaves.[1]

The King followed up the Bull with the New Laws, issued in 1542.[2] Both Bull and New Laws were denounced by the colonists. The civil authorities compromised again and delayed action, but the clergy answered by refusing absolution to slave owners. At last the Viceroy, Luis de Velasco, issued an order, in 1551, for the liberation of all slaves. The mine owners immediately threatened the closing of mines and pointed out that such action would result in a loss of revenue to the Crown. The Viceroy answered "that the liberty of the Indians was more important than all the mines in the world, and that the revenues which the Crown might receive from them was not of such a nature as to require the violation of laws, both human and divine." One hundred and fifty thousand slaves were liberated, not counting their women and children.[3] That ended slavery for the Indians, but added greatly to the growing spirit of anti-clericalism. The blame for all was fixed on the clergy.

The problem of the *encomiendas* or *repartimientos* was as knotty and difficult of solution as that of slavery. It arose out of a well-intentioned arrangement for the protection and Christianizing of the Indians. In his capacity as Governor Cortés had issued some most interesting legislation regarding Indian labor. He set a minimum wage, small but still a recognition of the principle. The hours of work were fixed at from sunrise to sunset, with an hour out in the morning for religious instruction and another in the afternoon for rest.[4] In Mexico that meant a ten-hour day, which was a rather remarkable regulation for the sixteenth century. In the England of Elizabeth it was twelve hours.[5] The Indian laborer had to be fed, and his allowance of food was stipulated. He could not be worked more than twenty days at a stretch, nor come to work again until after a lapse of thirty days. No work was allowed on Sundays or Feast Days. Laborers had to be registered with the civil authorities both at the beginning and end of their period of work. These regulations were made especially for the estates called *encomiendas,* and for the government of the Spaniards holding them. More trouble broke out between the colonists and the clergy.

To understand the *encomienda* system it is necessary to consult the Laws of the Indies. The object is there set forth about as follows: "The purpose and origin of the *encom-*

iendas was the spiritual and material welfare of the Indians; their instruction in the articles and precepts of our Holy Catholic Faith; and that the *encomenderos* should have them under their care; and to defend their persons and properties; and to protect them against injury." An earlier law calls this a *repartimiento,* or a partition or distribution for the purpose of "defending them [the Indians] and protecting them, and providing for their religious instruction and the administration of the sacraments."[6]

The *Encomendero* was the recipient of this charge. He was permitted to collect the poll tax (about $2.50 per year per family) which began by payment in products of the soil, later in part cash, and still later fully in cash. He was not allowed to have more Indians in charge than would make up an annual tax of $2,000.[7] He had to build a stone house for himself upon the construction of which the Indian was not to labor. The *encomienda* itself could neither be mortgaged nor sold.[8] Other restrictions made the *Encomendero* pay well for his labor. There are 551 provisions in the Laws of the Indies on this labor matter alone, as well as many incidental clauses in the other 4,951 laws.[9]

This wholesale guardianship of Indians had its abuses, though scarcely as many as the single guardianship plan still in force for the full-blood of North America. It had one outstanding result: it did actually preserve the race. Under it the Indians did not begin to die out. But the abuses set the clergy to their task of vigilance over the rights of the Indian. The plan worked well where it was loyally followed, but there were those who escaped obedience by pretexts. That will easily be understood by those who know

—and who does not?—of the pretexts used even in the present day by so many to set aside the political rights of the Negro in North America.

The clergy again had the whip hand. The King was for the Indian and to him the clergy had direct access.[10] The friars were, of all the clergy, the most insistent in the matter. No opportunity for reporting violations of the law was overlooked by them. They had been charged to report and report they did, not only the lawbreakers but the officials who tolerated their disobedience. To the ranks of the anticlericals were added many of the very officers whose duty it was to enforce the law. Epithets were exchanged in abundance. The bishops, priests, and friars were called "meddlesome disturbers" by one side, and by the other the *encomenderos* were called "inhuman brutes and oppressors." The clergy were charged with being "intent on ruining the colony," while the *encomenderos* were charged with being "intent on ruining human liberties and losing precious souls."

The clergy won. Every Viceroy was held accountable for his Indian charges. He was made subject to an examination on the conduct of his administration, the results of which had to be published so that the Indians "could demand justice for any injuries with entire freedom."[11] Marc Connelly makes "de Lawd" say in *Green Pastures* that, even "being God is no bed of roses." I should not like to go quite that far, but the truth of the statement as applied to the Spanish Viceroys of the day is quite evident. What opportunities were given His Excellency's political enemies!

The *encomiendas* were finally done away with by 1720,[12]

but a modified form of the plan, at least for landed estates, might have been seen, and perhaps may still be seen, in the Mexican *hacienda,* where the workers are grouped in families around the master of the ranch, with a church for all. These, however, are the estates to be divided up by the present revolutionary government; that is, with the exception of such as are in the hands of the reigning powers. How far the suppression of the *encomiendas* hastened Indian decadence is a question for a sociologist to determine. It certainly helped to put an end to the silk industry established by Cortés. The *encomenderos* were supposed to have been compensated by fixed life annuities for their losses. One, a son of Montezuma, made a Count and Grandee of Spain, had with his sisters been given some *repartimientos.* They received pensions in place of them amounting to $24,000 a year.[13] A descendant of this son of Montezuma, by the way, became a Viceroy of Mexico.[14] It will be a long time before a full-blood descendant of Sitting Bull becomes President of the United States.

It may be interesting here to note the career of Cortés as an administrator and to witness the unexpected ability for statecraft shown by one who certainly had in his military genius talents enough for distinction. But we had glimpses of this other talent all through the short campaign by which he won Mexico. He knew then how to outwit Velásquez, in Cuba, who would have taken his expedition from him; and again in Mexico when he took advantage of the law by establishing a legal municipality and getting himself set up as its head, thereby freeing himself of all obligation of obedience to his enemy.[15] His diplomacy in playing with the Totonacs, enemies of Montezuma, meanwhile making no secret of the fact that he was on his way to the capital, was masterly. He knew the value of advance peace offerings to be invoked later when the battles were over. These had their full effect in winning the loyalty of the Tlaxcalans after he had defeated them in a two-day battle. He knew the soft answer that kept his own small force together. A great man was Hernando Cortés. He claimed none too much when he said to his Conquistadores: "You, sirs, tell the truth when you say that even the most renowned generals of Rome have not done such great deeds as ours. Histories telling of these events will say, God willing, greater things of us than of what has happened before." Bernal Díaz, who was with him through it all, was pleased with himself and the others who followed the great general because they gave him counsel "how to do all things in the right way." It was sheer genius in statecraft to advise with others, leaving his councillors to think they are doing everything, and using their self-satisfaction to carry out his own plans.

A military leader turned to the administration of peace and progress, has always a great advantage over a civil ruler without military training and experience in war. He attends to seemingly small but really necessary details. Hence we are not surprised to find Governor Cortés establishing a chain of inns all along the way between the capital and the port of Vera Cruz. We may, however, be permitted to wonder over that attention to detail which prescribed that the pigs and chickens the inns were to have on hand be kept separate from the horses, and that mangers should be kept clean and whole so that corn might not be wasted. Some of his regulations remained in force for three centuries. In 1850 the price of a room in one of these inns was still that fixed by Cortés, twenty-five cents.[16] It was characteristic that he troubled himself about domestic animals and grain, for he gave great attention to his plans for importing from Europe what of them Mexico did not have. He imported fruit also, introduced the culture of sugar cane, built the mills and made the sugar, planted mulberry trees, brought over silk worms and taught the natives how to care for them and make silk. Ten years after the Conquest, Mexico was shipping cotton to Spain.[17] He opened and developed mines while carrying on exploring expeditions. It was Cortés who caused to be built the famous Hospital of Jesus near the spot upon which he first met Montezuma. And by the terms of his legacy to it he protects it to this day against confiscation.

Cortés was a hard taskmaster but on the whole a just one. When he was called later before the royal authority in Spain to answer charges made by his enemies against him, he was acquitted and made a Marquis. He had been responsible for great progress before he had to give up his authority as Governor, but still preferred to live in Mexico. Perhaps one of the best tributes to the works that followed him— he was the first in Mexico and therefore the foundation-builder—comes from the pen of Thomas Gage, an English traveler, writing of the town of Chiapa, in 1625, where there was a Dominican Mission, situated far enough from the capital, considering the slow transportation of those days. "No town hath so many Dons in it of Indian bloud as this.

Don Philip de Guzman was Governour of it in my time, a very rich Indian, who kept up commonly in his stables a dozen of as good horses for publick shewes, and ostentation as the best Spaniard in the countrey. His courage was not inferiour to any Spaniard, and for defence of some privileges of his town sued in the Chancery of Guatemala the proud and high-minded Governour of the City of Chiapa, spending thereon great sums of money till he had overcome him, whereupon he caused a feast to be made in the Town, both by water and land, so stately, that truly in the Court of Madrid it might have been acted.

"This Town lyeth upon a great river, whereunto belong many boats and canoas wherein those Indians have been taught to act sea-fights, with great dexterity, and to represent the nymphes of Parnassus, Neptune, Aeolus, and the rest of the heathenish Gods and Goddesses, so that they are a wonder of their whole nation. They will arm with their boats a siege against the Town, fighting against it with such courage till they make it yeeld, as if they had been trained up all their life to sea-fights. So likewise within the Town they are as dexterous at baiting of buls, at juego de cannas, at Horseraces, at arming a Campe, at all manner of Spanish dances, instruments and musick, as the best Spaniards. They will erect Towers and Castles made of wood and painted cloth, and from them fight either with the boats or against one another, with squibs, darts and many strange fireworks, so manfully, that if in earnest they could do it as well as they do it in sport and pastime, the Spaniards and Fryers might soon repent to have taught them what they have. As for acting of playes, this is a common part of their solemne pastimes; and they are so generous, that they think nothing too much to spend in banquets and sweet-meats upon their Fryers, and neighbouring Towns, whensoever they are minded to shew themselves in a publick feast. The Town is very rich, and many Indians in it that trade about the Countrey as the Spaniards do. They have learned most trades befitting a Commonwealth, and practice and teach them within their Town. They want not any provision of fish or flesh, having for the one that great river joyning unto their Town, and for the other many Estantias (as they call them) or farmes abounding with cattell. In this town the Dominican Fryers bear all the sway, who have a rich and stately Cloister with another Church or Chappel subordinate unto it."[18]

Indian Dons! An Indian Governor! Rich Indians! A high-minded ruler! A banquet to rival the royal table! Sports on land and water! Horseraces! Plays! Industries! Monastery and Church! Out on it. Are these Indians? Yes, but Indians made over. And Thomas Gage went to Mexico 104 years after the fall of the Aztec capital, that is in 1625.

After Gage we are ready for Humboldt. He was in Mexico in 1803. This is what he had to say:[19] "In the intendencies of Oaxaca and Valladolid, in the valley of Toluca, and especially in the Environs of the great city of la Puebla de los Angeles,[20] we find several Indians, who under an appearance of poverty conceal considerable wealth. When I visited the small city of Cholula, an old Indian woman was buried there, who left to her children plantations of maguey (agave) worth more than 360,000 francs. These plantations are the vineyards and sole wealth of the country. However, there are no caciques at Cholula; and the Indians there are all tributary, and distinguished for their great sobriety, and their gentle and peaceable manners. The manners of the Cholulans exhibit a singular contrast to those of their neighbors of Tlaxcala, of whom a great number pretend to be the descendants of the highest titled nobility, and who increase their poverty by a litigious disposition and a restless and turbulent turn of mind. Among the most wealthy Indian families at Cholula are the Axcotlan, the Sarmientos and Romeros; at Guaxocingo, the Sochipiltecatl; and especially the Tecuanouegues in the village de los Reyes. Each of these families possess a capital of 800,000 to 1,000,000 livres.[21] They enjoy, as we have already stated, great consideration among the tributary Indians; but they generally go barefooted, and covered up with a Mexican tunic of coarse texture and a brown colour, approaching to black, in the same way as the very lowest of the Indians are usually dressed.

"The Indians are exempted from every sort of indirect impost. They pay no *alcavala*[22]; and the law allows them full liberty for the sale of their productions."

We hear much about "land for the people" from the present rulers of Revolutionary Mexico. But it was Revolutionary Mexico that brought about the need for land. Of this Mora, one of their own, tells the truth. He states that under the Spanish regime the Indians lived in villages to which there was assigned a territory more or less extensive, a part of which was distributed among the families for their personal use and cultivation, and the remainder served the community for general purposes, part being cultivated for the general expenses of the village. The Indians were not permitted to sell their lands.[23]

It does appear as if the radical rulers of yesterday protested against the very condition their successors say must be restored. Mora complains that the Spanish Government treated the Indians as minors and assigns that as a reason why they have not made more progress.[24] It is too bad he was not with Gage when the latter visited Chiapa, too bad that he did not come north and see how differently our red "minors" were treated. But Mora might have found even a bishop to sing a lamentation with him, for zeal pushed some of the clergy away over on the Indian side. Antonio de San Miguel, Bishop of Michoacán, presented a memorial to the King of Spain in 1795, criticizing all these protective measures as calculated to keep the Indians from progressing.[25] But the record is clear. The Indian could possess land and did possess it. He could secure an education and often did. He was a bit more than the white man's equal since the laws were all in his favor. It was, however, the Indian who accepted his advantages who was the first cause of the decadence of his people. The strong deserted the weak. The Bishop as an advocate was perhaps too much of a churchman. He had perforce to fall into the truth. Before he had finished his bill of complaint, he admitted that, under the system he was criticizing, agriculture and industry increased, and that the method of paying the district officials in fees in place of fixed salaries increased abuses. Evidently there were politicians like our own in those days. The Bishop drew from this fact a significant other: "Hence the constant opposition in which the clergy and the subdelegates live." The anticlerical plant was growing.

How badly were the Indians of colonial Mexico treated? Let us set down an A, B, and a C, to answer the question.

A. The Indians of colonial Mexico were practically self-governing. They elected their own village authorities; allotted their own communal fields; and even in religious matters, due to the scarcity of priests, exercised a character of independence that still causes some annoyances to the bishops.

B. They were treated as minors for obvious reasons. The restrictions consequent to that policy have been proved beneficent and salutary both in Mexico and in the United States, and in the ratio that these restrictions have been relaxed and these laws unobserved, the Indian has suffered. The Ickes Plan of 1934 for our Indians has yet to prove itself. I certainly hope that it will.

C. Don Basco de Quiroga was the first Bishop of Michoacan. He gathered the people into villages and each village was taught a trade. These trades are still practiced in these same villages. In San Felipe, ironwork; Santa Clara, copperwork; Capula, woodcutting; Cocupao, now called Quiroga in honor of the Bishop, painted, figured boxes; Uruapan, varnished gourds, a lacquerware whose varnish is a secret and the envy of the Mexican coachmakers because it preserved its qualities of color and luster in any weather or even in boiling water; in Paracho they make musical instruments; shoes in Teremando; pottery in Patambo and Tzintzuntzan;

and so on for other places. They carry their wares to market where they sell them themselves. They are an industrious and thrifty people.[26]

Does it not strike an American of this depression era that the situation of these Michoacán Indians in days gone by—and in part at least still obtaining—might well be envied by many a village community here at home? Are we not talking of establishing handicrafts for our rural folk? Are we not planning subsistence homesteads? Is not our neighbor Canada trying, with government aid in Quebec, to bring cottage industries to the farms? This very situation, of special village industries, now exists in both Belgium and Holland. It may be that those "ignorant Spaniards" were a century or two ahead of their time.

The history of Spanish colonial dealing with grains will not, however, meet with generous applause from our professional speculators. No board of trade will shower blessings down upon its makers. In view of the present-day troubles of our farmers, however, it is interesting, and, with some additions and much expansion might suggest useful thoughts. I take the whole plan from the Laws of the Indies, but express the substance in my own words. The law is of 1583. Warehouse buildings were erected by the cities as storehouses and markets for grain. They were called *Alhondigas*. The official in charge of each was appointed yearly by the local authorities. He was prohibited from dealing in grain for himself or anybody else, directly or indirectly, and placed under a heavy bond. Purchases of grain in transit were prohibited. All grain was required to be brought to the warehouse for sale, dealing in grain outside the warehouse being strictly prohibited. All those bringing grain to the warehouse were required to submit sworn statements as to how and where they had procured it. The fees for these statements were fixed. Those raising the grain could send it in by their own carts or by professional carriers. Charges for storage were fixed. Likewise the charges for handling by the stevedores. Prices were fixed in the morning before the opening of the market, and could not be changed during that day. As a great many people purchased grain and ground it in their own homes, the bakers were not allowed to buy until noon. The bakers were obliged to declare on oath the amount of grain used by them daily and were not permitted to purchase more than enough for one, or at most two days. If a baker raised his own grain he was obliged to make a sworn statement on the amount of his harvest, and was not allowed to purchase grain until his own had been used. Grain could be stored for twenty days only. At the end of that period it was required to be sold at the price obtaining on the day of sale.[27] A rather remarkable way these Spanish colonial laws had for the elimination of middlemen, speculators, and profiteers. It might not suit our American "big business" of today, but it was not made for the machine age; and it was regimentation, a sound we do not quite like. But all these things were done for Indians, for the natives, and not so long after the time when not one of them except the caciques — not even all the caciques — could be quite sure in the morning that the sun would go down on his still living body at evening; not so long a time after he began to feel safe from the raiders hunting hearts for the altars of the sun god; not so long a time after he had realized that he could look at his children without thinking of a butcher's stall block. The Spaniard may have hurt his feelings by putting him to work, by taxing him two dollars and fifty cents a year, by taking some of his bright children to a boarding school, by teaching him a new language, by telling him the truth about that White God of tradition; but he had not hurt him very much. Now and then the Indian felt inclined to kick against the protecting wall of law this stranger had built around him. When that happened, which was not so often as his descendants kicked and killed one another, his broken toes told him that it was all a bit foolish, that he still needed to go to school; so he went back to his job, and awaited the time when his "saviour" would come, put a gun in his hands, and line him up to shoot or to be shot.

But in the interim some very unlooked-for and surprising things were going to happen to the Mexican Indian. Men of his blood would paint pictures fit to stand comparison with those of many a European master of color and brush. There would arise great Indian orators, novelists, poets, historians, and journalists. Indian teachers would attract to Mexico even the children of the Conquerors and others would go to teach in universities beyond the Atlantic. There would come Indian philosophers and doctors of law, grammarians and prose writers, generals and inventors, masters of Cicero's tongue and scholars in the language and lore of Athens. Two descendants of the Kings of Tezcoco would frame for the future the grammar of Aztec speech. So many books would be inspired by Indian culture as to require volumes to list even their titles and contents.

VI

EDUCATION

IT IS COMMONPLACE to say that Mexico is one of the richest lands on earth in natural resources. The country has everything from grass to gold. Before the Conquest it had a population trained to obedience by fear, with a large part of it already enslaved. Worldly wisdom would have told the Spaniard to make more slaves and exploit the rich resources for his profit as conqueror. It would be necessary only to bring over more Europeans, educate and train them for the purpose intended, and leave the natives in their fear and ignorance, while allowing them to keep their blood-stained idols with rebels against the rulers handed over for victims instead of their neighbors and their own children; all the while shutting official eyes to cannibalism. There would have been no great risk in following such a policy. The Indians had long expected the coming of bearded whites from across the sea to rule over them, as we have seen, and were ready to accept the Spaniards as demi-gods. Whatever suspicions they may have developed after learning that a knife thrust could kill them must have been dissipated after the loss of their great city. As an extra measure of precaution and safety the pagan priests could easily have been purchased by allowing them to continue in their offices and keep their emoluments. It would have been a cheap price to pay for invaluable services.

If such a plan did not appeal to the pious folks at home, especially to Philip II, there was an alternative, later to be adopted by the English. It was quite simple and its operation easy of concealment. It consisted of exterminating the natives by drink or exile into the forests. It would, of course, take a longer time to carry out, but it was sure, and quite safe. True there would always be the danger of revolt. The other plan would do better for quick results. What would our modern world do with such a decision to make? Would business be business? Would that world do on a grand scale what it usually does on a small one?

By every dictate of the god of selfishness and greed Spain made a fool of herself in the New World. Judged by a standard today rather generally accepted, the New World might well be called Spain's Folly. But three centuries of Spanish rule in America vindicates the policy Spain adopted, at least in the eyes of the just. She promised to Christianize, preserve, and elevate the natives, and made a brave attempt to do it as long as the duty remained upon her. What happened after was not of Spain's making.

When the modern man thinks of progress he thinks of schools, and quite rightly. Education is not, of course, all schooling, but schooling is an important part of the educational process. Modern man did not, however, discover that fact. It was known to those of our race who lived centuries ago. Athens, for example, had the same idea. So had medieval Spain. Impoverished and broken by centuries of war Spain yet put that knowledge into practice when, still fighting, she founded her universities. Universities call for colleges, colleges call for schools. Universities cannot live except as capstones on an educational pyramid. Say university, and school is implied. The test of the school, then, is not an unfair one by which to judge at least a major part of Spain's record in Mexico.

Let it be remembered at the outset that everything had to be done. The Mexican Indian could neither read nor write. The pagan priesthood was not a teaching body,[1] as had been the priesthoods of Egypt and Persia to which the civilizations of these kingdoms owed their very life as well as their long preservation. It was nothing like that of the Jews which, though also a sacrificing priesthood, was yet a teaching one as well. It goes without saying that it was far from resembling the Christian priesthood to which our present-day civilization owes not only the preservation of its Sacred Book, but of its classics, its art, its architecture, its first steps in science, and the best in its history. The condition of the Mexican Indians at the time of the Conquest tells us what its priesthood must have been. No reliance could be placed there. For the Spaniard the work of education in Mexico, then, had to begin with the foundation. Even the cellar for it had not been dug.

The Spaniard differed in his educational ideas with quite a large number of the people of today. He was convinced that the educational process concerned not a part of a man but the whole of him; that if it did not reach his heart as well as his mind, it was not education at all. His task was to Christianize the Indian as well as instruct him. With these thoughts in mind he made the school march side by side with the missionary, so that where the mission was, there too should be the school. He had likewise to consider the mentality of his pupils. Obviously he could not at once make scholars out of savages. They had to be given what they could absorb. So the mission schools were simple ones; teaching reading, writing, arithmetic, politeness, and religion. It may here be noted that, even long years after the schools had disappeared, and the reading, writing, and arithmetic had been forgotten — in part at least also the religion — nevertheless the politeness remained. The Mexican peon, untouched and uncontaminated by his instructed neighbor, is still the gentleman, perhaps the only gentleman in rags on earth.

We have seen how complete was the authority of the King over all colonial affairs, even the temporal administration of the Church herself. Because of that, the King stood behind and took the responsibility for education in Mexico. He made his will known to the officials, but he worked through the Church. He is entitled then to share the praise or the blame for success or failure.

As early as 1550 the King expressed himself on the subject of native education. In a letter to the Provincial of the Dominicans he "charged him to see that the Indians were taught the Spanish language."[2] The Church wished every parish priest to "procure with all diligence" the establishment of schools in their towns "where children may be taught to read and write Spanish."[3] The Laws of the Indies followed with the expression of the royal will that "where possible schools must be established to teach them to read and write Spanish."[4]

The Church accepted the task and, knowing the will of the King as well as her own desires, extended it and enlarged upon it. Consequently the two names which stand out among the early educators of Mexico are those of churchmen: one a lay Franciscan brother, Peter of Ghent, and the other a bishop, Zumárraga. Both were interesting characters, but because Peter of Ghent was not a priest and because of his antecedents — he was a relative of the Emperor, Charles V — as well as his genius and devotion to the cause of Indian education, he is entitled to rank ahead of the Bishop.

De Gante, or *of Ghent,* was born in Flanders, but was a subject of the Empire ruled by Spain. He laid the foundation of Indian education in Mexico. His place in history is indicated by García Icazbalceta in his biographical notice on the Friar.[5] It is worth reproducing: "The task was tremendously difficult because the means were entirely disproportionate to the ends. They were confronted not with the education of the children as they arrived successively at the proper age, as in our day, but with an entire and numerous generation, big and little, men and women, who all at once were in urgent need of religious and civil instruction from the very foundations, and without knowing even the language of their teachers. The friars were few and, realizing that if they attempted everything they would accomplish nothing, they decided to divide their time between the conversion of the adults and the education of the children. They endeavored thus to take care of the emergency, leading the adults from their errors, and giving the children, who were docile and not yet imbued with the old beliefs, the new religion with their education. They counted, moreover, that once the little ones were instructed in the Faith they would serve to bring in their elders; and they were not deceived in their hopes."

Regarding the methods pursued he says: "The schools were generally low halls with dormitories and other rooms adjoining. There were schools in all the principal convents, and so large that some of them held 800 to 1000 pupils. The most famous of all was that of Mexico, founded by Friar Pedro de Gante. As customary, it was behind the Convent church, extending toward the north. . . . In this school there were soon gathered a thousand Indians. In the morning they were given lessons in reading, writing, and singing, and in the afternoon were given religious instruction. . . . The little ones were not allowed any communication whatever with their parents, to avoid their contamination by the errors of idolatry. From the more advanced and intelligent, Friar Pedro selected fifty to be catechists, who were given special care and intensive training during the week in what they were to preach the following Sunday. On that day they were sent out in pairs to the towns about Mexico where they preached the Gospel."[6]

To de Gante and his Friars should be given the credit of discovering the fact that the most satisfactory and sure way to instruct an aboriginal people is to catch them young and place them in boarding schools away from even parental influence when that influence is pagan. Our own Department of Indian Affairs knew that, but failed to carry the policy to its logical conclusion; which is one reason for our failure in educating the North American Indian, who, never far from the tepee influence even when in school, goes straight back to it when he leaves. I have seen this result in the State of Oklahoma, and Moffett in his book on the Winnebagoes of Wisconsin notes the same about these Indians.[7]

Zumárraga was the first Archbishop of Mexico. Icazbalceta describes him[8] as "an apostle, poor, humble, wise, zealous, prudent, educated, charitable, a mortal enemy of superstition and tyranny, an indefatigable propagator of the true doctrine of Jesus Christ, a protector of the helpless, a benefactor of the people, materially as well as morally, and eminently practical in all his decisions and advice." General Don Vincente Riva Palacio[9] calls Zumárraga an "indefatigable worker in charity and education"; says that he founded hospitals, established schools for native boys and girls, and "as the editor of many important works for the education of the Indians, he was very liberal minded." The King evidently had used wisdom in nominating him as first Archbishop of Mexico.

It was the petition of the Viceroy Mendoza and Archbishop Zumárraga that brought to Mexico the first printing press which came to the New World. It was procured by one John Cromberger, who must have forgotten, however, that a printing press calls for paper. The Archbishop directed attention to that fact in a letter dated May 6, 1538.[10] Zumárraga gave special attention to the education of the Indian girls. Since the limited number of teaching nuns could not possibly fill the need that he foresaw, he trained and employed lay-women teachers. They disappointed him because other and more attractive careers opened up for them. Matrimony might well be suspected as one of the chief offenders. Zumárraga's letters to the King[11] show the zeal of an apostle in his ambitious plans for the spread of education among the Indians all over Mexico. They involve boarding schools for girls and schools of arts and crafts for boys.[12] He had to fight his way in the interest of the natives. His enemies had him called back to Spain there to answer charges against him, but his account was straight and he returned to Mexico in spite of opposition. Of course, it goes without saying that such a man would die poor and even in debt. One extract from his letters to the King will serve to show his spirit: "That which most occupies my thoughts; to which my will is most inclined and my small forces strive, is that in this city and every diocese, there shall be a college for Indian boys learning grammar at least, and a great establishment with room for a large number of daughters of the Indians."[13]

It was Zumárraga who was accused of destroying the Indian picture writings. To what I have said already on that point, and to a Note in Part II of this book, I need only add, that Icazbalceta traced this charge against him back to a revolutionary propagandist friar named Mier, and the destruction itself to an Indian historian, Ixtlilxochitl, of the seventeenth century. This writer forgot that he had previously accounted for the total destruction of these writings by the Tlaxcalans in 1520, eight years before Zumárraga arrived in Mexico.[14]

It could not be expected that in the early days of the colony, while Cortés was in authority, much could be accomplished in the way of Indian education. To care for the upbringing of their own children under early colonial conditions was no easy task for the Spaniards, and the missionaries only could be relied upon for both teaching and preaching. These came at intervals and were few in numbers. Cortés asked for them early[15] and got twelve Franciscan Friars in 1524.[16] Twelve Dominicans came in 1526. A few days after their arrival five of them died. Four returned to Spain, leaving only three in Mexico. Later came seven and then another group of twelve.[17] In 1533 seven Augustinians landed, to be followed in 1535 by six more, in 1536 by eleven, and in 1539 by ten.[18] In 1723 the number of missionary Friars in Mexico, of three orders, was 2,396. Usually the Friars outside the cities[19] settled in groups of three. Every monastery or church had its primary school. How difficult the task of maintaining these schools was may be judged by the fact that each Friar must have been responsible for about a thousand children. It was of absolute necessity, then, to follow the plan of Pedro de Gante and train the brightest pupils to give part time to teaching the others.

A pastoral clergy — often erroneously called secular in our day — was, of course, being developed. As ordained, they were given charge of souls in the settled parishes. The obligation of opening schools was on them as well as on the Friars. It is recorded that Father Pedro Felipe, who lived in the town of Tezayucan, seventeen and a half miles from Mexico City, had three other towns in his parish, four districts each with a church. He had likewise some twenty villages. For every church there was a school wherein reading and writing were taught to those who could go no farther, but which had other studies for advanced pupils. Padre Felipe could give each congregation only two Sunday Masses a month. Yet 9,888 adult people received the Sacraments every year. The Padre had no clerical assistants but kept ten or twelve native catechists at work. In school they used picture cards to teach the alphabet. The total population of Padre Felipe's little principality was 16,000.[20] There are dioceses in this country with a smaller population. It was a large order Church and King gave to the missionaries, yet Mendieta could say truthfully, after recounting the early difficulty of teaching the Lord's Prayer to the Indians "they now know how to read and write in their own language, and many of them in ours." He adds later the information that in every town there was a school built alongside the church where the children were taught to read and write. Of course, the greater part of all this information has been kept locked up by ancient prejudices away from English-speaking people. These will be still more surprised to learn that trade and art schools were not neglected.

The first institution for the higher education of the Indian was Holy Cross (Santa Cruz) College in Tlaltelolco. The historian Sahagún happened to have had personal experience in the foundation and conduct of it. The idea of a college for Indians was denounced by some of the whites as ridiculous. There were those who held an old theory like one of our own, now happily discarded, about the mentality of the Negro, that the Indians were incapable of learning, and, even if that were not quite true, learning could be of no use to them. Sahagún was not the man thus to be discouraged. The college turned out Indian scholars as finished as the Spanish. He then organized a corps of Indian professors, but made the mistake of turning over the management of the institution to them. It was too much. The Friars had to come in after a twenty-year term of steady decline and reorganize it.[21] It is only justice to say that Sahagún was not the actual founder of the College of Santa Cruz. To Zumárraga should go that honored distinction. It opened its doors for the first time on January 6, 1534, thirteen years after the taking of Mexico City by Cortés. Montes de Oca (see Mexico, in *Catholic Encyclopedia*) notes that this college had among its graduates "native governors and mayors of Indian villages, teachers for the Indians and at times young Spaniards and creoles." No wonder Gage was astonished in Chiapa. In 1553 there were three principal colleges: Santa Cruz, San Juan de Letran, and one for the exclusive Spaniards and creoles. The Augustinians founded the large college of San Pablo in 1575. Soon the Jesuits followed with their College of San Ildefonso. Then came the capstone of glory on the labors of Spain's greatest Viceroy in Mexico. Don Antonio de Mendoza petitioned the Emperor Charles V to found and endow a university. Though he did it, yet he did not see it done. It was not until after he had left for Peru that the University of Mexico came into being, that is on June 3, 1553, 32 years after the Conquest. Harvard did not open its modest doors till a century later.

The wise Mendoza had a splendid successor, Don Luis de Velasco, under whose regency the University actually was established. He saw it endowed from the mines, and given rank with the University of Salamanca. It was called a

Royal and Pontifical University. The language of the Indians had an honored place in its curriculum. The University had, like most of its scattered sisters all over the world, its ups and downs. The worst of the latter was its closing by President Gómez Farías in 1833. This protégé of Poinsett evidently saw no common sense in higher education for Mexicans. President Santa Anna reopened it in 1834, but along came the revolutionist Comonfort who suppressed it in 1857. It was again reopened by President Zuloaga the year following. President Juárez shut its doors in 1861. Maximilian opened them again, but only to shut and bar them finally in 1865. The name is preserved on a half-college, half-high school, now existing in Mexico City; but there is a struggle going on to bring back the glory of former days. It may yet happen, but the fact stands against it that students in higher education are prone to do some thinking, and that those in universities, even as far back as Paris and Oxford, were never easy to manage when they did. Then there is the more practical obstacle that political graft in satisfactory sizes is hard to get out of a university.

The idea must not be left that all this educational activity went on without opposition. The anticlerical element was never inactive and there were always those who believed sincerely that trouble would come out of educating the Indians. On that point at least subsequent happenings in Mexico appear to have upheld them. But it is the long run that tests the racers. Church and King stood firm, even against some of their own supporters. One of these was known as Geronimo López. He flourished, probably as an adviser to the Viceroy, in 1541. It was in that year he addressed a letter to the King which commands our deep interest for two very good reasons: because it indicates opposition in the higher circle of official life to the whole program of Indian education; and because, to readers of this day, it tells the story of success by the pen of an enemy. López was opposed to educating the Indians and hated the Friars in particular for doing it. But his argument is based, not on the charge that they were doing it badly but on the fact that they were doing it altogether too well. His first complaint is that the Friars had taught so many Indians to read and write. "It is a marvel to see them," he said, "there are so many and such good scriveners." But the second charge is a higher tribute to the teaching Friars. He said that they taught Latin to the Indians, and did it so well that they spoke it "like another Cicero, and every day the number grows."[22] It is open to question if López actually knew enough Latin himself to be a competent judge of Cicero's ability, but it surely must have been a terrible annoyance for him to hear these dark-skinned natives, with their imperturbable politeness, try their tongues on the language of the Roman Forum. I do not think that there were many Mexican Indians who spoke such good Latin; though at that I may be in error. I do know, however, as already stated, that there were Mexican Indians who crossed the Atlantic to teach in European universities. These must have spoken Latin, if not with quite the elegance of Cicero, yet with much of the correctness and lucidity of Thomas Aquinas.

The question of the ability of young Indians to speak Ciceronian Latin is, however, of lesser importance than how the Church carried out in general the educational task imposed upon her very willing shoulders by both Pope and King. We may leave the University with a notice of the fact that it opened a medical school two hundred and four years before Harvard, and began the study of anatomy and surgery, with dissection, eighty-six years before William Hunter opened the first school of dissection in England. We have already noted the opening of the first college for Indians — that of Santa Cruz, as early as 1534, and the fact that De Gante began his lifework for Indian education as early as three years after the Conquest. From that time on the dates for the opening of schools look like mileposts along the road of Spanish Mexico's progress. We find them everywhere in the old records.

There are, for example, still some surviving copies of the old *Mexican Gazette* — a monthly — listing important events. Here are some of those chronicled as they happened or merely were noticed in passing: In September, 1728, there is a report of a school being attached to the Belemite Hospital. October of the same year makes mention of the colleges of San Pablo, y San Pedro, and San Juan, in Puebla. The December issue says that the Guardian of the Santiago Monastery and the Commissary General of San Francisco maintain eleven Indian students in the College of Santa Cruz, and that the Pious Work of Juan de Chavarria supports fourteen students in the College of San Gregorio. In the same issue the Gazette's readers are told that the Chapter of the Cathedral of Puebla provides a dowry of $300 each for nine orphan girls. In the issue of June, 1729, a Confraternity of the Blessed

Sacrament is mentioned as supporting thirty in a girl's college and giving to each a dowry of $500. There is likewise a priest named De Figueroa opening a college for girls in Guadalajara. January, 1722, records the opening of a girls' college in Zacatecas by another priest. The Bishop of Durango, who already had opened a hospital in Parral, founded a college which he asked to be permitted to consider as the beginning of a university. That, by the way, was how Harvard got its start. In the March, 1722, issue it is noted that the Archbishop of Mexico, Lanciego y Egilaz, had established Spanish schools in every town of the Huasteca, paying many of the teachers himself. He too was following his pupils by providing $300 dowries for eighteen girls, as well as maintaining them at school, for which latter kindness he paid $150 a month. The Bishop of Durango, already both a hospital and school builder, varies his activities by erecting a reservoir for the town. There is mention in the issue of May, 1728, of six colleges, and the Jesuits ask a license to build a college in Querétaro, but start by constructing a public fountain. September, 1784, has news of a new school in Guadalajara opened by the Bishop; and tells of the return of the Bishop of Sonora, after a visitation of his diocese that took two years, with a report of the opening of seven primary and two grammar schools, and a college for the Yaquis. A college named San Luis is reported in July, 1785. August of that year has something to say about the colleges of San Nicholas, San Pedro, and Santa Rosa for girls, in Valladolid.

Of the founding of hospitals and like works of charity there was no end, but these do not concern us here.[23] What is of interest is the fact that the Daughters of Charity, whose main work was what their name indicates, managed to keep up in the educational procession by opening a girls' school attended by 500 in Silao. There were seven girls' colleges — which really meant academies as we know the term — in Michoacán, with 128 boarders and 2,500 day pupils. I am presuming that the "Missionaries of St. Vincent de Paul" mentioned in connection with colleges in Morelia, Patzcuaro, and León, were really Daughters of Charity. The Jesuits had colleges for boys in Valladolid, Guanajuato, Patzcuaro, Celaya, León, and San Luis de la Paz. In 1560 the Augustinians attached a primary school for some 200 children to their convent. All this is a mere glimpse of early educational activity.[24]

As to results there is considerable that is of interest, but here, too, I must pick and choose from a wealth of material. In 1826, that is, after long years of observation, Ramos Arispe gave a report to Congress on the use made of trust funds in the hands of the clergy. The quotation has a bearing on education because these funds formed part of the general endowment for the public good. He said:

"Few in number, select in origin, and most moderate in their acquisition of large country estates, without compare, they devoted the greater part of the riches that piety had placed in their hands, to the purpose, and in a manner, of public benefit for the encouragement of agriculture, commerce and every industry."[25]

But Von Humboldt, who visited Mexico in 1803, has gathered some facts bearing on the results that are of outstanding interest. Let us have a glance at a few taken from his *Political Essay on the Kingdom of New Spain* (English

Edition, New York, 1811, Vol. I): "No city of the new continent, without even excepting those of the United States, can display such great and solid scientific establishments as the capital of Mexico" (p. 159). "The capital and several other cities have scientific establishments, which will bear a comparison with those of Europe" (p. 130). "It is impossible," speaking of the Academy of Fine Arts, "not to perceive the influence of this establishment on the taste of the nation. This influence is particularly visible in the symmetry of the buildings, in the perfection with which the hewing of stone is conducted, and in the ornaments of the capitals and stucco relievos. What a number of beautiful edifices are to be seen in Mexico! nay, even in provincial towns like Guanajuato and Querétaro! These monuments, which frequently cost a million and a million and a half of francs, would appear to advantage in the finest streets of Paris, Berlin, and Petersburg. M. Tolsa, professor of sculpture at Mexico, was even able to cast an equestrian statue of King Charles the Fourth; a work which, with the exception of the Marcus Aurelius at Rome, surpasses in beauty and purity of style everything which remains in this way in Europe. Instruction is communicated gratis at the Academy of Fine Arts. It is not confined alone to the drawing of landscapes and figures; they have the good sense to employ other means for exciting the national industry. The academy labours successfully to introduce among the artisans a taste for elegance and beautiful forms. Large rooms lighted by Argand's lamps, contain every evening some hundreds of young people, of whom some draw from relievo or living models, while others copy drawings of furniture, chandeliers, or other ornaments in bronze.

In this assemblage (and this is very remarkable in the midst of a country where the prejudices of the nobility against the castes are so inveterate) rank, color, and race is confounded: we see the Indian and the Mestizo sitting beside the white, and the son of a poor artisan in emulation with the children of the great lords of the country. It is a consolation to observe, that under every zone the cultivation of science and art establishes a certain equality among men, and obliterates for a time, at least, all those petty passions of which the effects are so prejudicial to social happiness.

"No European government has sacrificed greater sums to advance the knowledge of the vegetable kingdom than the Spanish government. . . . All these researches, conducted during twenty years in the most fertile regions of the new continent, have not only enriched science with more than four thousand new species of plants, but have also contributed much to diffuse a taste for natural history among the inhabitants of the country" (p. 160).

"The principles of the new chemistry, which is known in the Spanish colonies by the equivocal appellation of new philosophy, are more diffused in Mexico than in many parts of the peninsula" (p. 162). "The best mineralogical work in the Spanish language was printed in Mexico . . . the *Manual of Oryctognosy,* by M. del Rio. . . . The first Spanish translation of Lavater's *Elements of Chemistry* was also published at Mexico. I cite these insulated facts because they give us the measure of the ardour with which the exact sciences are begun to be studied in the capital of New Spain. This ardour is much greater than that with which they addict

themselves to the study of languages and ancient literature"
(p. 163).

I make no apology for drawing out this chapter to an unusual length. The subject justifies it. The fair and honest
historian with these facts before him will allow his thoughts
to turn to a contrast. Naturally the opportunity offered by
the English colonies in North America will be accepted as
a proper one.

In the article on "Education" in *The Lincoln Library* (p.
1623), discussing the history of early methods of payment for
schools, appears the following about our own colonial educational situation:

"There was practically no full community support of
schools until long after the establishment of the present
Federal government of the United States. Indeed, as late as
1873, the last of the northern states to abandon pupil payment was still receiving some support for the teacher from
so-called 'rate bills' paid by the pupil. Even in colonial times,
however, partial support of the school out of the community
treasury had begun. . . ." And for the schools in the early
national period: "The United States Bureau of Education has
estimated that in 1800 the average American was not receiving more than 82 days of schooling in his lifetime. Many
communities had no schools, sometimes because families
were so isolated, and sometimes because teachers could not
be found. The educational situation during the first decades
of American national life was wholly chaotic." The Spaniards seemed to have better luck. Now this: "We find, for example, in a message of Governor Campbell to the legislature

of Virginia in 1839 the statement that 'almost one-quarter part of the men applying for marriage licenses were unable to write their names'" (p. 1636).

In stern contrast with the Spanish policy on schools and colleges for girls, we have the *History of Women's Rights* (p. 168) saying:

"The Puritans, burning with an unquenchable thirst for liberty, fled to America in order to build a land of freedom and strike off the shackles of despotism. After they were comfortably settled, they forthwith proceeded, with fine humor, to expel Mistress Anne Hutchinson for venturing to speak in public, to hang superfluous old women for being witches, and to refuse women the right to an education. In 1684, when a question arose about admitting girls to the Hopkins school of New Haven, it was decided that 'all girls be excluded as improper and inconsistent with such a grammer school as ye law enjoins and as in the designs of this settlement.' 'But,' remarks Professor Thomas, 'certain small girls whose manners seem to have been neglected and who had the natural curiosity of their sex, sat on the schoolhouse steps and heard the boys recite, or learned to read and construe sentences from their brothers at home, and were occasionally admitted to school.'

"In the course of the next century the world moved a little; and in 1789, when the public school system was established in Boston, girls were admitted from April to October; but until 1825 they were allowed to attend primary schools only. In 1790 Gloucester voted that 'two hours, or a proportional part of that time, be devoted to the instruction of females.' In 1793 Plymouth accorded girls one hour of in-

struction daily. The first female seminary in the United States
was opened by the Moravians at Bethlehem, Pennsylvania,
in 1749. It was unique. In 1803, of 48 academies or higher
schools fitting for college in Massachusetts only three were
for girls, although a few others admitted both boys and girls"
(p. 169).

"The first instance of government aid for the systematic
education of women occurred in New York in 1819 (Mrs.
Emma Willard's Seminary in Troy — government subsidy
by Gov. Clinton). This seminary was the first girl's school
in which the higher mathematics formed a part of the
course; and the first public examination of a girl in geometry,
in 1829, raised a storm of ridicule and indignation — the
clergy, as usual, prophesying the speedy dissolution of all
family bonds and therefore, as they continued with remorse-
less logic, of the state itself" (p. 170).

Searching for a striking and informing statement to show
an inquiring foreigner what our country is now doing for
higher education, an American would — quite naturally, if
he knew — answer by giving the total of our university and
college endowments for at least such institutions as had no-
tably large ones. It might be difficult to give the total of all
such endowments because of the rich ones held by Foundations which are allied to but not an official part of our higher
educational system. The figure offered would then by no
means represent the sum of capital behind our universities
and colleges, not only for the reason mentioned, but because
so many institutions of the kind are state schools without
any actual endowment, nevertheless supported from the taxes
of the people. In spite of the fact that the figure offered might

represent perhaps not more than half the actual endowment of our universities and colleges, it would nevertheless be impressive enough to elicit admiration in the questioner and pride in the citizen. According to the *World Almanac* for 1935 the total for university, college, and professional school endowment in the United States is $1,365,635,282. The buildings and improvements of these same colleges are valued at $1,370,680,323. The grand total is $2,736,315,605. The total annual receipts for the same institutions, excluding additions to endowments, amount to $563,631,669. There really is something to stimulate our pride. Can any nation in the world today bring such witnesses into court to prove our interest in higher education?

Let it be remembered that in Mexico all such endowments were classed as Church wealth. It is quite impossible to know how large that wealth was, but President Lerdo de Tejada — I quote from Wilfrid Hardy Callcott's *The Church and State in Mexico, 1822–1857* — "after a detailed study of the various sources of income, not only of the clergy, but of the entire nation . . . estimated the total value of the real property, rural and urban, at $1,355,000,000. Of this a portion worth from $250,000,000 to $300,000,000 was owned by the clergy, making due allowance for the fact that the Church property might have decreased somewhat in value of recent years."[26] The figures are eloquent even if not based on more than an enemy's estimate. If this was all the wealth the Church in Mexico had to support churches, colleges, schools, hospitals, chapters, etc., may we not in all justice say that Mexico was getting the educational and social service that we buy at high prices very cheaply? The Mexican educational establishments alone, if replaced at this time by the State on a par with ours and in proportion to the population of the two countries, would cost the Mexican taxpayer *every year* more than the Mexican State received as a result of Lerdo de Tejada's wholesale confiscations; for the State did not receive anything like what he claimed the property was worth.

A few facts on this subject will help to an understanding of a most remarkable educational record.

First: The wealth of the Church in Mexico constituted, not personal fortunes for bishops or clergy, but endowments for educational, charitable, and social works, differing from our endowments for like purposes only in the fact that they were handled for the people by the officials of the Church.

Second: Investments were made in land and mortgages because (*a*) these were the only investments of the day, and (*b*) in order — see Arispe as above — to constitute a sort of land bank from which people, chiefly farmers, could borrow at a low interest rate.

Third: In comparison with the endowments of our own institutions of higher education *alone* — considering that the Mexican endowments were for all kinds of schools, and for many and different works of charity — the wealth of the Church was small indeed.

Fourth: The blame for illiteracy in present-day Mexico cannot be placed on the Church but justly must be charged to those who confiscated the endowments and, after seizing and closing schools and colleges, did nothing to replace the works these endowments supported.

I give place to Mr. Justo Sierra, a radical and revolutionist, to uphold that last point, which he does in his book, *Mexico, Its Social Evolution* (English Edition), as follows:

"The laws of December 12th and 14th, of 1872, completed the confiscation of the endowment funds which had been created to support the educational institutions of the country.

"The great private foundations, which had accumulated through three centuries, were swept away and no others were created to replace them.

"The wealthy Spaniards had been one of the greatest sources of these endowment funds, and as the Spaniards were expelled in 1828, that fount was definitely closed.

"The attacks upon wealth, and particularly upon the clergy, completed the work of preventing any further donations for the support of educational institutions, and, as the government itself was penniless, the result is obvious" (p. 538).

How the Church tried to repair the damage to education, though she had neither encouragement nor money, may be seen by a fragmentary notice on Oaxaca. In 1880 there were two Catholic societies in the city of Oaxaca, one operating a college and the other a hospital. The college possessed 294 pupils taught by 29 professors *at a total expense of $732 annually*. Only those teaching drawing, music, and primary instruction received pay. The others gave their services free. The curriculum included reading, writing, drawing, music, Christian doctrine, Latin, French, English, logic, mathematics, physics, geography, astronomy, history, and the three professions of pharmacy, medicine, and law.[27]

Mexico was so full of schools and colleges before the confiscations — schools and colleges for boys and girls, for handicrafts, trades, and arts of all kinds — as to justify a sweeping statement to end this chapter: Up to that day there never had been a country on the face of the earth that in so short a time had done so much in an educational way. When the circumstances of time and conditions surrounding the effort and the obstacles to be overcome, are considered, history presents no finer record of educational achievement and success.

The defense rests. But with a court full of witnesses not called because obviously not needed.

VII

THE CHURCH

HISTORY MEETS and often overlaps every other intellectual interest at some point of contact. Political Economy at times becomes an actual part of it. Geography gives it settings. The Natural Sciences help to make clear many of its problems. Romance puts a heart into it. Art and Architecture embellish it. Government marks its periods. Philosophy examines and solves its most difficult problems. But Religion is its very soul.

For two thousand years the Church has been History. She is the one great influence that goes all the way through it, permeating it from beginning to end, and showing no sign of ever leaving it. The historian, informed by experience, is ever on the watch for her entrance upon any scene, always certain that, if she is not on the stage where the human drama of life is being played, she is somewhere in the wings, or perhaps, raising or dropping the curtain. She loves the peaceful and quiet parts, does not disdain even comedy, but tragedy is her very life.

This tragedy in the life of the Church has been played on many stages, with a multitude of different backgrounds, in all the languages of men, and by a host of apparent understudies whose souls were in tune with hers. Chris-

In the eighteenth century Bishop Alcalde (1771-1792) built in Guadalajara some twelve blocks of houses to be rented cheaply to the poor, the proceeds helping to support the Hospital de Belen. Those in this picture are a few that have survived. Juárez confiscated and sold the whole.

Once a Jesuit church attached to a Jesuit college founded in 1625.

Templo de la Cruz in Querétaro. This edifice really consists of two churches side by side. Above the altar is the stone cross made by the Indians shortly after the conquest. The building to the right was once the college of the Franciscans; now a barrack. In the garden to the rear Maximilian made his last stand.

topher Hollis, in his *Thomas More*, has unveiled one for the understanding of men and women of the English tradition. Speaking of the effects of More's execution on the English nation he wrote: "They killed holiness. Before that colossal fact all the excuses and the explanations fade into nothing. It is the mark of a Christian saint that he possesses the imagination that jumps back across a thousand or two thousand years of history. His whole life is lived under an excitement similar to that of the first disciples when they first heard the amazing news that the Tomb was empty. To him that news is so amazing that he never forgets to be surprised at it. He never comes to take it for granted that Christ died for him. And naturally enough to such a man, as to those first disciples, the news, if true, is so important that it is mere madness to give one's mind to any other business and thus neglect it. Such a man was More — a man of the world, indeed, a lawyer and a statesman, but one to whom law and statesmanship were important only in so far as they could be used to further the purposes of Christ. There was not room in England for both such a man and the Tudor state."[1]

No one can write about Mexico without writing the tragedies of many Mores. If there was no room in the Tudor state for even one Thomas More, there is no room in the Calles state for the many of Mexico. If there is no room for them, there is no room for the Church. But she is in the wings. Another arm may lower the curtain but, since history repeats itself, her arm will raise it again. For the Church can never go out of Mexico any more than a mother can go out of the life of her child.

The Prime Minister of Italy has recently given utterance to some wise words well worth remembering: "All history of Western Civilization," he said, "from the Roman Empire to modern times, from Diocletian to Bismark, teaches that when the State undertakes a fight against religion it is the State which will emerge defeated in the end. . . . A struggle against religion is a struggle against the incomprehensible and unreachable. It is a struggle against the spirit in its most intimate and profound form and it is now proved that in the struggle the arms of the State, even the strongest, do not succeed in inflicting mortal blows on the Church which — especially the Catholic — comes out triumphantly from the hardest of tests. The State can be victorious only in conflict with another State. It can then conclude its victory by pressing a change of regime; for instance, a territorial cession, the payment of an indemnity, the disarming of an army, or a determined system of political or economic alliances. When the fight is against a State, the State is confronted with material reality which can be seized, struck, mutilated, or transformed, but when the fight is against a religion one does not succeed in picking out any particular target. Simple passive resistance of priests and believers is enough to render the attack of the State inefficient."[2]

We have looked at the Mexican Church in educational action. But that action was, as it always must be, a secondary activity which is only the extension of her teaching mission. It is the whole mission itself with its sacrificial and sacramental grace that really matters. The other follows.

There have been in the history of the world some outstanding and striking examples of Christian missionary success. One, it goes without saying the greatest, was that of the Apostolic Age. Its effect was to make the world over. Behind it was no worldly power, no scheme of empire, no great body of secular learning, no army, no diplomacy. It was what Benito Mussolini referred to as "the incomprehensible and unreachable," but in attack rather than in defense. Its success stands forever as a sign of the supernatural in the affairs of men. A second outstanding and striking success was that of Francis Xavier in the Orient. Its effects remain only in part, but it left Christian plants in India and Japan for others to cultivate. Granting even to the efforts of Patrick, Boniface, Cyril and Methodius, their full measure of praise, the third in outstanding and striking greatness was the mission of the Spanish *padres* who first brought Christianity to the New World. That mission was great because of the extent of territory it conquered, its immediate and far-reaching influence, and the permanency of its results. It has been studied far less than such a mighty event in the world's history deserves.

To understand these missionaries, men of learning as well as zeal, soldiers who had changed gold-laced uniforms for brown habits, lawyers who took up the practice of a higher law, professors who preferred unspeakable hardships to their chairs, and all ready to die for a supernatural ideal, we of the English tradition must find their spiritual counterparts in such as More, who, though not a missionary, yet exhibited the spirit that makes missionaries. He helps us to understand. But the *padres* had a story all their own, and were of a type all their own.

The type is admirably shown in De Gante who, though only a lay brother, yet refused the Archbishopric of Mexico so that, to his last hour, he might labor for the education of the children of the Indians. Nothing kept such men back from the untraveled wilderness but the arm of the King. They were permitted to go only as far as the soldiers and chafed under the restriction. But when the indomitable Jesuits came, they broke through, gave Lower California to Spain, the Faith to the yet unreached Indians, and opened Upper California to Junipero Serra and the Franciscans. The whole work of the conversion to Christianity of the Mexican Indians was done in such an heroic and kindly way as to hold for the missionaries, especially the Franciscans, the deep affection of their converts. In 1568 the lack of Friars was such that a number of missions had to be abandoned, among them that of Tehuacan. The Friar Pastor in charge was notified to remove his books and leave without attracting attention. This, however, was impossible, for the Indians seemed ever able to ascertain in advance what he contemplated. Indian carriers from another town came at night for the books, but were caught and the books seized before they could leave the place. The Indians, now thoroughly aroused, proceeded literally to wall up the exits of the church and mission, a small door only being left as entrance to the church, and a small hole through which an Indian might enter on hands and knees into the mission itself. As a special precaution against the escape of the Pastor, the men kept guard at night, and in the daytime the women brought their grinding stones, their looms, and their babies to the church courtyard where they combined their domestic duties with keeping a watch over him. Every letter coming to him was read. If from his superiors, it never reached his hands. At last, by a subterfuge, a communication was smuggled in to the Pastor ordering him to suspend all religious services. At this the Indians surrendered and permitted him to leave; a tearful procession a league long accompanying him for many miles.[3]

It would be impossible within the compass of this book to follow the *padres* who, with Mexico City as their hub, passed out along unmarked roads to every part of the new country. But, as to their methods and the results of their labors, we may catch a glimpse from one of the last and most distant of them, that of the Upper California already mentioned. It may be taken as a type of all the others.

The establishment of the California mission was begun by Padre Serra in 1769. From the standpoint of the natives to be evangelized it was among the most hopeless of all prospects. The natives of California were low down in the scale of human advancement; wanderers, almost shelterless, subsisting on the bounties of wild nature rather than on their own industry. The Faith was preached to them. They were gathered together and taught to live as human beings, to till the soil, raise grain and vegetables, plant and care for vineyards and orchards, breed cattle, sheep, hogs, and horses, cure and tan hides, as well as gather the wool of the sheep and weave it into blankets and cloth for their clothing. Likewise were they shown how to work in wood, clay, stone, and metal. From the California deer they developed a thriving industry in buckskins. Nineteen missions, with buildings erected by the Indians themselves, were established in California. In 1810 they had a population of 18,780 Indians served by 39 Franciscans as pastors and teachers.[4]

I cite the California example because, as its territory is now a State of our Union, the facts about it are more familiar to Americans than those which refer to the older efforts in the South. The California missions have been a favored theme of American writers because of our very wide interest in them. The remains of their buildings, some still quite well preserved, have had the effect of awakening the romantic as well as the inquiring spirit. They have now a place in song and story, even in the drama; and the scholars of California, such as Dr. H. E. Bolton of the University of California, and the late Father Englehardt of Santa Barbara Mission — himself a Franciscan — have painstakingly dug into their records and uncovered their past. The same is being done for the Texas missions by Fr. Francis Borgia Steck, of the Catholic University of America. A great fertile field of historical interest has thus been opened.[5]

The California missions, however, are only the greatest to us. From one end of Mexico to the other greater ones were scattered. These had their colleges and higher schools, orphanages, hospitals, and other institutions of religion and charity. The California missions did not cover more than half the territory of the present state. The others covered all of Mexico, went well down below it, and were duplicated in the Spanish possessions of South America. The California missions came into being only at the end of a long apostolate as the crown on a multitude of similar triumphs.

It has been charged that, with its first successes, the Church relaxed her missionary zeal. It would be more correct to say that the Church, well founded in Mexico, turned her attention to consolidating her gains by arranging for the normal spiritual life of a convert people. There were fewer new lands in sight to conquer then. The California missions were undertaken when the beginning of a decline in Spanish influence was in sight. They show that the Church fought against ignorance and barbarism to the last minute and down to the last man who had any fight in him.

The Franciscans were driven from California in 1834. Their churches and schools were sequestered and closed. All were abandoned to ruin and the new Christians dispersed to live again as had their savage forefathers. The ruin of these missions was one of the greatest crimes against civilization ever perpetrated by civilized man, but it was only one small part of a greater crime. We still have the monuments of the effort, to keep us reminded that even civilized man can, under the temptation of greed, degenerate into a blind fool.[6]

The record of the services of the Church to the Mexican

people is so splendid, so full of merit, so astonishingly effective, that even her enemies must ask themselves why she is now being slandered and persecuted. The answer must be the same for Mexico as for other countries. Perhaps Bossuet has given it in the fewest words: "It is a law that the Church cannot take a step forward but what it costs her the life of her children. To establish her rights she must let her blood flow in streams. Her Spouse has purchased her with His blood, and she must purchase His grace at a like cost." We must note that Bossuet in that answer was doing no more than paraphrasing warnings uttered by Christ Himself.

There is a kingdom of thought over which truth rules and against which theory is always a potential or actual rebel. The mission of Christ was to announce and establish that truth. The Church was founded by Him to continue His saving labors by making revealed truth available to all men in every age. The Church has no other right to existence. Where and when the truth rules a golden age follows. Christian civilization is a product of Christ's truth. The truth of Christ is life. It cannot be destroyed, but it may, in limited territories and at certain times, be overcome and seemingly disappear. That has happened over and over again in the history of the world. The destruction has always come about through the success of a false theory masquerading as truth. The Church deals with theories to examine and test them. Without the test she does not accept them. She treats them as things of potential value but not yet as laws. But the theory, only too often, is the pet of personal vanity which demands its acceptance as truth. To secure that, the theorist is often unhampered by any code of morals. To hold it within its proper bounds the Church is hampered, as far as the world is concerned, by the fact that the truth has a decided code of morals. The rebel theory can lie. The truth cannot. The rebel theory can steal. To theft the truth cannot resort. The rebel theory can appeal to man's lower passions. The truth can appeal only to his virtues. The rebel theory can kill. The truth must save even her enemies. Everything of the world favors the rebel theory. Nothing that is of this world favors the truth and the Church which keeps it.

No honest student of history can fail to see the battle-grounds upon which this never-ending warfare between God and Mammon was fought in the centuries past. The battles themselves may have had other pretexts alleged to explain or justify them, but all explanations and justifications come back to the one thing — the theory passing its bounds; which is one of the surest signs that as a theory it was false from the beginning. The more viciously it fights the more certain becomes the appearance of its error, for when its authors, committed to it as a truth, know that it is an error, their vanity steps in to urge them to impose it by force. That is exactly what is happening today on both hemispheres. It is the explanation of present-day Russia. It is the explanation of present-day Mexico.

Nothing is more according to the nature of a false theory than that it should fight the one institution which claims to possess Divine truth. It makes no difference that the force of the latter is spiritual. Does not the spiritual overlap the temporal everywhere? Is not the temporal a flying globe surrounded by the spiritual? The Church answers that it is so; but she adds that the spiritual and temporal are nevertheless on different levels. The temporal has its own life based on the free will of man. It is no tyranny to give it the truth. The Church then asks only one thing — her freedom to offer what she has to give. The false theory dares not grant that, since it cannot live in the atmosphere of the truth.

When then it is asked how the Church can live in the United States of America at peace with the State, and not in present-day Mexico, the answer is simple: There is no false theory so far as the State itself is concerned which forces the Church here to voice protests. The truth she holds about government is a fundamental one which is not denied by that form of it called popular or democratic. The fundamental is concerned with the highest values, as those of justice and right. These are attainable under the popular form of government. Its slips and accidents, its confessed or unconfessed failures, are what they are — only slips and accidents, confessed or unconfessed failures. When they are named as such the great values are not threatened, but admitted and proclaimed.

When it is asked why the Church in Mexico cannot live at peace with the State, the answer is just as simple and logical: The truth cannot live in the atmosphere of the lie. It is no mystery to the Church that she is persecuted in Mexico since even the fundamental truth about government is persecuted; and the government in Mexico is not for justice and right but for the exploitation of all the people for the benefit of a few. The Church might tolerate that condition for a time in the hope of betterment. But her very existence is a protest against it. The false theory knows that and takes steps accordingly. What the Church can neither stand nor tolerate is the subjection of the Gospel of Christ to the spirit of the world. She can let her churches go, her schools, her plan of action in places, her very physical existence itself. She cannot let her soul go. She cannot give up the Divine mission confided to her. She neither asks nor wants to force the minds of men. But she both asks and wants the right to speak to them. She neither asks nor wants to condemn any theory unheard, but she does insist that it shall not, before it has been tested, masquerade as the truth. That is her attitude toward Socialism.

To a thoughtless world an objection will be suggested: "Does not such an attitude constitute an obstacle to progress? Has it not frequently retarded progress?" The answer is that the opposite is the case. It was the false theory that retarded progress. In principle it is better to advance slowly over a sure road than to take every *cul-de-sac* and side path, and be obliged to return back from each. An outstanding example is found in medical science. Of the thousands of "cures" annually offered it, none are accepted without careful test and few pass its searching examination. Theories which affect the life of the world are much more dangerous than those which affect only the health of the individual.

I am well aware of the fact that this statement of the fundamental cause of antagonism between the Church and the present Mexican Government may encounter an argument against the authority of the Church to claim the exclusive possession of the Christian truth. To attempt an exposition of the claims of the Church to possessing such authority, would lead me beyond the scope of the present study. What is important here is to understand that the doctrine of spiritual authority makes it inevitable that those who base a theory of government on the necessity of State supremacy over soul and body, must find themselves in opposition to her, and will most probably seek to destroy her. Indeed the difficulty is not alone that of the Catholic Church. It is present in the conscience of every man who believes himself to be the possessor of a supernatural faith. No more than the Catholic Church can that man accept the theory of State absolutism. We are well convinced that it is the most dangerous theory of the day, and not only to religious freedom but to all human liberty. Pushed to its logical conclusion, it is a universal danger. Dr. Robert R. Milliken, "one of the half dozen foremost leaders of American science," was reported in the news dispatches of December 29, 1934, as having said to the American Association for the Advancement of Science, in Pittsburgh: "If the present craze for the new regardless of the true, in art, science, society, and government goes much further, the remedy may be found in the prospect that a nugget of sober uncolored truth may become the most exciting news there is just because of its rarity. I venture the prediction that our present age, because of its craze for the new regardless of the true, will be looked upon by our children's children with more amazement and ridicule than we ourselves feel because of the credulity of the middle ages or the smugness and hypocrisy of the Victorian age."

Regardless of the acceptance or rejection of the Church's claim, the fact stands that it was its rejection that left the mind of the modern man a victim to the theorist in "art, science, society, and government."

The Church civilized Mexico. The process of decivilizing, under the rule of the theorist, is now going on.

"All this is nonsense. The past is dead. The Church is out and will never come back." I have heard that answer. Any student of history lives in the past as well as the present, for it is part of his duty as a student of history to contrast the past with the present. It was as a student of history, even within my narrow limits, that I heard the defiance before. I heard it in the England of Cromwell, in the France of the Revolution, in the Italy of Cavour. I heard it in Ireland, in Scotland, in Germany, in Portugal, and — quite recently — in the little province of Spanish Asturias. Where have I not heard it? Nero said it brutally. Diocletian said it regally. Marcus Aurelius said it learnedly. Julian the Apostate said it as it is said today. Who has not said it? And I know that wherever, whenever, or by whomsoever it was said in the past, the future gave it the lie. The answer of mankind to it in the end is always the same. I am not forgetting what men want me to say. But what I am telling them is the truth.

VIII

RETURN TO SPAIN

THREE CENTURIES SEEMS a long period to pass over with the slight attention of a few paragraphs, especially since, during that space of time, Mexico enjoyed prosperity in industry, mining, and agriculture, as well as advancement in civilization and culture, of the most remarkable kind. The country was in comparative peace, not a peace of fear but of content. Spain had few of her own armed forces, but enlisted native-born soldiers to take their places, and entrusted the guardianship of her colony to them.[1] The Spanish Viceroys were as such rulers go, good and bad, but with the good decidedly predominating. The natives, even Indian, were given positions of importance and responsibility as they advanced in education and experience. Prominent and even wealthy families were rising out of the native population. Those who remained on the lower stratum of society were as a rule contented and happy. The decrees of the King, and later the Laws of the Indies favored them. It is true that there were restrictions on foreign trade and strangers were not made welcome; but it must be remembered that for a long stretch of time in those three centuries, Spain was the first and wealthiest nation in the whole world, jealously watched and feared by all the others;

and her ships and coast lines were subject to constant attack
by their privateers and pirates. Her American coast line was
long and hard to defend. Naturally the stranger was regarded with suspicion. But through Spain, Mexico had a
flourishing, even if restricted, trade. There was marked development in the arts, especially in architecture. Mexico's
churches and public buildings erected during these three
centuries are still a source of pride and glory to the nation.
It is quite true that the first *Audiencia* was corrupt and inflicted great wrongs on the natives, but it is also true that
it was soon supplanted by a near-model one. Abuses inevitably arose because of the great distance from the Kings
who held tenaciously to their absolute power over the colony. In great and important matters which had to be decided in Spain, regulation was slow, and often, passing
through the hands of colonial administrators, badly applied.
It did not take England very long to make her rule impossible in her American Colonies. That of France in Canada
was often the object of bitter criticisms by the settlers. No
marvel, then, that there were criticisms of Spanish rule in
Mexico. But, in spite of it all, that rule did last for the three
centuries without once being threatened seriously, or up to
the time when the power of Spain to continue her guardianship was weakened, not in Mexico, but at home.

The Church suffered from the handicap of the Royal
Patronage. By far too much was she an arm of the Spanish
State. She had little independence beyond her doctrinal
mission. It was dangerous for her clergy to attack what
they knew to be abuses. One Franciscan had to flee for his
life for having made a pulpit assault on slavery before the

The *Sagrario Metropolitano* (the Baptistry) in Mexico City is a separate church although attached to the great cathedral. The fountain in the foreground is dedicated to Fray Bartolome de las Casas, Padre de Los Indios, the famous "Apostle of the Indians."

—Publishers' Photo Service, N. Y.

Agustín de Iturbide, the first Emperor of Mexico.

Church was able to have it abolished. The attack was, however, by a mob and not by the courts. There was no liberty given the Pope or the bishops in the matter of filling vacant sees. Even the ordinary rights of bishops in pastoral appointments was greatly limited by the necessity of consulting the Viceroy. To the credit of the Court of Spain, however, it may quite truthfully be asserted that on the whole, especially in the early days of the colony, the nominations to episcopal sees were excellent. Montes de Oca mentions the names of such distinguished men as Zumárraga, Julian Garces, and Vasco de Quiroga. "With few exceptions," he adds, "the bishops of New Spain were scholarly men, zealous for the salvation of souls."[2] The generosity of the King was an offset to his ecclesiastical domination. All the Spanish Kings took their responsibility to the colonies seriously. They poured out money lavishly for the schools and churches, aided the missionaries to make their journeys into unknown regions, and supported their foundations even out of their personal resources. No one can say truthfully that the Royal intentions were not of the best, nor that they failed more often than the circumstances might well have been expected to justify. The fact most eloquent in favor of Spain in reference to Mexico is that the three centuries of her rule saw little use of force in maintaining it. Sylvester Baxter, quoted by Bertrand, sums up the case for Spain in Mexico in one pregnant paragraph:

"New Spain never experienced the long period of colonial simplicity of the English possessions. The land was transformed as though it had been illuminated by Aladdin's lamp. Thanks to the startling energy of the conquerors, greedy for wealth and power, animated at the same time by a profound faith, the new Spain became flourishing within a few years, and was metamorphosed into a marvellous kingdom, whose immensity was dotted with splendid cities which arose suddenly in the midst of the desert, or occupied the site of an old native town."[3]

Safely the case may be left there, for events in Europe were busy weaving the fate of Mexico, all unknown to herself.

Spain's "Golden Century" was dominated by the influence and rule of Philip II, son and successor of the Emperor Charles V. He died in 1598. During his last illness he said: "God, who has given me so many kingdoms, has denied me a son capable of ruling them." Ominous words, bordering even on the prophetic. Not yet was the legacy of Charles V to fall from Spanish hands, but the hour of the disaster was marked on the clock of the years. Philip III inherited a Kingdom outside Spain proper that put a Spanish ribbon nearly all the way across the breast of Europe, but the ribbon did not support a decoration. It was a sword that hung from the end of it. Besides Spain, the new King governed Sardinia and Sicily in the center of the Mediterranean, and the southern half of Italy. He commanded the rest by the stopper of Milan. North of Switzerland he held Franche Comté, and north of that, touching the seacoast, the Spanish Netherlands. The ribbon then ran from Sicily to Flanders. Through the influence he could exert with intervening States he held a line between France and the Empire. His American possessions made him the dominating factor across the Atlantic.

Philip's father had ruled that kingdom as few men with such vast authority could do. Philip II was a man of detail, conscientious and scrupulous to a fault, the type of man who makes blunders only because he tried to do everything himself and fails at points because he is neither omniscient nor possessed of a hundred heads, hands, and eyes. He acted as if his reign was, by the grace of God, to go on indefinitely in the same way, even through others. But when he died its responsibilities fell on weak shoulders. Philip II failed by not placing some power on the one who was to inherit it all, so that his shoulders should become both strong and willing. His was the mistake that Porfirio Díaz was going to duplicate on the other side of the Atlantic centuries later. The trouble with these "men of destiny" is self-inflicted blindness. It is not an exclusively royal defect, and is always the hardest of all defects to discover in one's self.

To understand why the slow decline of Spain meant the quick decline of Mexico, it will be necessary to recall that Mexico was across the Atlantic, far away from Spain. Only echoes of news could pass between them at a time which depended for transportation on slow-moving ships. And by this time Mexico was not really a colony but an actual part of the Spanish Kingdom. The scheme of "The British Family of Nations" was, in some respects, the scheme by which Spain ruled. There was one King and many Viceroys. To that King Mexico was like Naples, Sardinia, Flanders, and the other European possessions. The only difference between the Spanish and the British idea was in the fact that the Spanish King had more power over his

"Family of Nations" than the British King has over his. Under such circumstances what happened to the Spanish possessions in Europe had to happen also to those in America, but the latter were more slowly affected thereby.

It is not necessary here to follow closely the chain of historical events that weakened Spain. All that is required is to recognize and interpret them and their importance in affecting the fate of Mexico. The great Spain took the whole of three centuries to pass into the place of a second-rate power. The causes for that decline may easily be read in the history of those three centuries.

First and foremost was what some men call Fate and others the Will of God. Nations rise to the peak of greatness and decline. It was always thus because every great nation rose to that point through the genius of a very few men, if not of One Man. Our own country is not, as popularly supposed, an exception. One man made it, Washington. One man's genius established its plan of government, Jefferson. One man saved it, Lincoln. The greatest of national successes cannot get far away from the One Man. Isabella made Spain. Charles V established it. The reign of Philip II was only a time extension of the reign of Charles, who failed in his great objective of reuniting Europe only to win his second objective by gathering together his Spanish Family of Nations. The thing, however, was too big. Only genius could hold it in one hand, and governmental geniuses are rare. How rare they are we of today know. There may be one or two in all the world of today but of that we are not yet quite certain. The first reason to assign for the decline of Spain is that she had no genius to save her. But France had one, Richelieu, to oppose her.

The second reason, the one that hastened the decline, was the rule of incompetent favorites in the Royal Court. Lerma, Olivares, Valenzuela, and Godoy were, with trifling variations, of a kind. They were precursors of the modern grafter, though God knows that they had many precursors themselves. To hold power for rule by genius is a triumph. To buy immunity from a fall by jobs is a crime. One favorite lost Portugal to Spain. Another, who ruled the Queen's bedchamber, lost not only his reputation, which was not at the time very precious, but Spain's opportunity, which was. Had he, Godoy, done what Charles III had failed to do, viz., establish each of her possessions as a Kingdom grouped around an Emperor, with rulers from the Royal family itself, thus capitalizing growing national sentiment, her decline might have been retarded for centuries, and Mexico's subsequent history rendered less shameful.[4] Portugal dealt more wisely with Brazil.

The third reason for the decline was the Royal policy which aimed at making Spaniard and Catholic mean the same thing. For it the Moor was in part responsible. It was unity in religion that saved Spain from the Moslem. Spaniards had become so accustomed to fighting as Christians that in their souls they coupled together the names of Spaniard and Catholic. When, after the victory, they had to fight treason from within, it was the "Infidel" and the Jew who were the Spaniard's enemies. To the romantic Spaniard the Church became his "Lady." When he boasted of being Catholic he meant that he was the perfection of a Spaniard. The Kings were even as their subjects. Ferdinand's Queen was Isabella the *Catholic*. His Most *Catholic* Majesty was the highest title of the King. Such it remained down to the last King of Spain. If the future brings back the Kings it will bring back the title. But beneath the fair exterior of that confession of faith was a danger that made it very un-Catholic. The Faith is universal. Spain had come to hold that it was Spanish, almost exclusively so. Thus spoken, it was nationalistic rather than patriotic. The nations that went over to Protestantism and hated Spain took the hint. England especially saw the force of the idea and bound her new religion in abject slavery to the State. Worse still was it for Spain herself in that, by her assumption of semiexclusive perfection as a Catholic nation, she managed to take over ecclesiastical powers to which no State has a right. The logical end of such an attitude could be nothing less than an attempt to tie the cause of Christ forever to the fortunes of a man-made State.

A fourth reason for the decline was the expulsion, and later suppression, of the Jesuits, which struck an almost fatal blow to Spanish education at home, changing the task of imparting it from one of sheer devotion to one of self-interest. This helped alienate the colonies where the Franciscans had the love of the Indians but the Jesuits the admiration of the élite and of the educated mestizo. Nor was the Jesuit unloved by the multitude. Where he went as a missionary he had gained affection for his unselfish and enlightened devotion. The very closeness of the bond between Church and State made any hurt to one a hurt to the other. The ingratitude of the act made it, to thoughtful men, inexplicable. It was the Jesuits, writes Sir Charles Petrie (p. 350) "who modernized teaching, by giving a larger place in it to the humanities and by reviving the study of classical antiquity. Colleges of theirs were established in the principal cities in the Kingdom. In Spain, as elsewhere, they educated generations of humanists." Before the expulsion of the Jesuits, even during her political decline, Spain had advanced in culture. The loss of such teachers now doomed her likewise to a cultural decline. As far south as Paraguay the blow inflicted a deep wound. Mexican education certainly tottered under the force of it.[5]

A fifth reason is one greatly to Spain's credit. As she had borne the brunt on her own soil of the Moslem attack on Christian Europe, thrusting the Moor back into Africa, so she bore the brunt of his attempt to regain his foothold on Christian territory by treason. Spain alone had the Morisco problem to deal with. The expulsion of the Moriscos was a national necessity. Those who were in league with them likewise forced the expulsion of almost all the Jews. But Spain paid a high price for safety, since thousands of acres of her farming lands which had been cultivated by the Moriscos were abandoned, and with the Jews went industries highly profitable to the country.

I stop at a last reason for the political decline of Spain, and a second one to her credit. She had been overgenerous in gifts of manpower to her American Colonies and to her other European possessions. The defense of the latter took a heavy toll of soldiers from home for the armies. The development of the former drew as heavily from her educated, merchant, and laboring classes. The strain was becoming too great, especially since Milan did not pay its own way but forced the mother country to support it with revenues from others which were needed to repair the damages at home. Add to it all the drain on the Royal purse for the missions in America, and the loss of so many of the nation's most learned men to staff the colleges and universities constantly expanding in Mexico and South America.

Meanwhile in America disaffection was spreading as the new ideas of the French revolution—prepared for by the success of the English colonies in gaining their independence—took root. This latter was England's greatest, though most unwillingly given, revenge on Spain. Not arms but storms had twice saved England from defeat and perhaps subjugation at Spain's hands. Neither was forgiven. English pirates had harassed her old enemy but could not inflict irreparable damage. England's great American misfortune did. Her loss of America lit the fires that ran from Canada to Patagonia. When, in 1821, the last Spanish Viceroy signed a recognition of the independence of Mexico, all the land Spain held in the colony proper was what was under the feet of the last defenders, the tiny island entirely occupied by the castle of San Juan de Ulloa.

The last King of the three centuries was Ferdinand VII, who came into power in 1808 only to be deposed by Napoleon in favor of his brother Joseph Bonaparte. Ferdinand was restored in 1814. He lost Mexico in 1821. The immediate causes responsible for the loss—those already mentioned were the remote ones—are not hard to find. Before Ferdinand returned to Spain after the liberation of the nation from Napoleon, central government was difficult and, after many attempts to make it effective, power was assumed by a parliament which had no legal foundation for its existence. A majority of its members were radicals affected by the ideas of Rousseau and the French revolutionists. They adopted a constitution to the "liberal" liking but unacceptable to the majority of the people. Ferdinand rejected it. There were riots in its favor and, because of these, matters went from one state of confusion to another. At last Ferdinand agreed to accept the Constitution in spite of its illegality. The "liberals" proceeded to go further and attacked the Church. This aroused Spain and made a clean-cut dividing line between them and the royalists. In all Spain's European possessions the revolutionists were active. A minority, the "liberals," seized power. A series of disorders followed which have for us only the interest of its effect on Mexico, already in a ferment of anxiety, loyal to Ferdinand, but harassed by radicals. Ferdinand knew of the danger, but for want of ships could not send troops to the aid of his Mexican supporters. The Mexican radicals knew what they wanted. To gain it uprisings were necessary. They had begun in 1810 under the flag of King and Religion. No matter, they must be encouraged, since any disorder was good for radical hopes. Secret societies kept fomenting trouble till, at last, an army officer named Agustín Iturbide, not a radical, struck the blow that won independence. The clergy had been with him, and had drawn the people to his side. The radicals had not won his victory, but they set out to win one of their own by crushing the Liberator.

An interesting contrast may be made between the Mexican war for independence and our own. Mexico had no definite grievances against the mother country. Sentiment was worked up first against Napoleon and then against the Spanish residents. Only at the end was disloyalty shown to the King. It was the Spanish Constitution of 1812, the illegal one, with later attacks on the Church, that stirred the Mexican people to action. But the stirring was done chiefly by the propaganda of the radicals, whose plans were to take advantage of it when the time came. It would have been dangerous for them to show an anticlerical bias before they had secured arms and power with which to defend themselves against the people. Our revolution was based on a definite grievance. Its proposals and demands were well understood and popular. The English King was disliked. Loyalists were few, in spite of Trevelyan's assertion to the contrary. Of real radicals there were almost none. Jefferson's liberalism was not of the French kind. He was a statesman who felt his responsibility to the people. Above all, the secret-society menace to independent and patriotic thought was practically nonexistent, for Masonry in the English colonies was social and conservative. Above all loomed the serene, able, and patriotic figure of Washington, silent in his retreat at Mount Vernon when his work was done, but with the shadow of his genius and sagacity walking before every man who had to do with changing a war for liberty into a Constitution to keep it.

IX

THE FIRST REVOLT

PUT A TURBAN on the head of the leader, scimitars in the hands of his followers, raise a crescent flag over all, and you have a fairly good counterpart of a Moorish raid on the soil of the New World. Or, change the clothes of the mob, put feathers on the heads of its leaders, give them spears and bows, offer them the bodies of the slain to eat instead of looted food, and you have a close resemblance to a war for victims to the Mexican sun god.

The first revolt of consequence—there had been only spasmodic riots before—was totally unexpected, though the germ of it had been born. The preparation had been the work of the small minority of radicals, Spanish, mestizo, and out-and-out foreign. All, however, was French by influence. The Bonapartists had been helping to sow seeds of discontent during the struggle to place Napoleon's brother on the Spanish throne. Their American headquarters, from which they reached Mexico, was Baltimore. With the overthrow of the Bonaparte cause in Spain their work in Mexico ceased, but the seeds they had sown could not be gathered up.[1] They had no interest in gathering them.

The methods of the radicals in advance action were the same as those used by their successors over all the world even up to the present time: breeding discontent and describing nonexistent Utopias. But it was not possible to breed any general discontent in Mexico that was based on hatred for the Church. The Church was loved. Nor was there much more than passing discontent among the people. Some other source of trouble had to be found. Bustamante, an intellectual of a later day, explains one as follows: "We discerned the dawn of our independence, and the possibility of obtaining it, when we first read the writings of the learned Baron de Humboldt, and we one and another asked ourselves, 'How is it that our country contains such riches and abounds in resources enough to make it one of the first nations on the globe? By what trick of Fate have we ignored that we were the possessors of so much wealth?'"[2]

All that went well for the white or for the educated mestizo. But, as Mora says, numbers were required, and numbers the Indians alone could supply. We shall let him tell how it was done in his own words. That he will not be biased against the movement is assured by prefacing what he has to say with this, his own sentence: "The revolution that broke out in 1810 had been as necessary to the attainment of independence as it has been pernicious and destructive to the country." Mora was anti-Spaniard and anticlerical. He writes: "The fallacies propagated by it [the revolution]; the persons who directed it or took part in it; its long duration and the means adopted to secure its triumph; all have contributed to the destruction of a country that, in all the years that have passed since then, has not yet been able to repair the immense losses that it suffered. As it was impossible to do away with an established government and the habits of submission and obedience, fortified by hundreds of years, without opposing *numbers* to *power,* it was necessary to interest the masses in the revolution, all of which could not be done in Mexico by the simple announcement of distant benefits little understood nor of abstract ideas about the necessity, utility, or justice of independence.

"It was, therefore, necessary to excite the prejudices of the multitude, and to inflame the passions of the people, to secure their co-operation. The Indians were very numerous at that time, and this meant that they should be made to join the revolution; and the manner in which this was done was so plain that it could be hid from no one. The atrocities of the Conquest and the destruction of the ancient Sultanate of the Aztecs were shown to be a calamity and the beginning of all the evils suffered by the Indians. This event, therefore, to which the colony owed its existence, was converted into a pretext for revolution, and from it was deduced the justification for independence for a people who possessed nothing in common with the destroyed nation nor with the rights of the ancient Sultan of Tenochtitlán.

"A multitude of persons supposed to be intelligent, but who were certainly little educated, took it upon themselves to revive all the fables about the grandeur, prosperity, and culture of the ancient Mexicans, as had been related by those interested in magnifying the difficulties and the glory in conquering them. All this was for the prime object of exciting odium against the Spaniards, which from the beginning they hastened to propagate and convert into popular sentiment, and to make this a powerful factor in the revolution. This double error, the greatest of the revolution, took root so profoundly that it exists even yet among the generality of Mexicans, to the extent that nothing else is heard, among the commonalty that pretends to be educated, than 'The Barbarity of the Conquest; The Three Hundred Years of Slavery and Chains of the Mexican People,' and other similar phrases that are repeated *ad nauseam,* maintaining, with the odium against the Spaniards, the belief that they are conspiring against independence, and that this cannot be safe whilst they remain in Mexico."

All this ought to make enlightening and thoughtful study for the civilized world today, since the philosophy of it seems so familiar to its ears. Radical political change, amounting in practice to the complete destruction of all anterior forms of government, as well as the whole social structure, is demanded by a handful of people out of millions. The one justification is the fact that the handful want it at all costs. The masses of the people do not care for it, do not understand it, do not desire it. Few of them even try to study it, nor could if they would. But the change cannot be brought about without them. Therefore they must be excited to a revolt which those who do want it will be glad to lead. What matters the means? What difference the lie? Why hesitate about the blood-letting? We have had all these under our own eyes for the last fifteen or twenty years in both hemispheres.

There was in Mexico, however, another condition that played into the hands of the few propagandists for revolution. It is still there. Perhaps in a milder form we have it ourselves. It might be called the White-Collar Menace. For the year 1810 Mora describes it thus: "It already has been said that the persons, under whose direction it [the revolution] was forged, were the least suited to organize and lead it in an orderly manner. Not one of them possessed the least understanding of, nor experience in, affairs: of what is a government and much less of the aims and results of a revolution, something until then unknown in the country. Many of them were without any prestige whatever, and some of them knew nothing beyond the towns or cities where they lived. As nearly all were unknown, the sphere of their influence was extremely small, and perhaps even smaller than their very slight prestige. Although there were a few among them that lived in some sort of comfort, still their fortunes were insufficient for even the first steps in such an enterprise. Because of this it was necessary to procure funds at all costs. This compelled them to adopt the most ruinous measures, seizing the wealth of the Spaniards; attacking property rights by various means, but always ruinous; and outraging the owners when they refused to give what had been asked of them, or when they hid it, or when in reality they did not have what had been demanded."

He goes on to relate some of the consequences: "These immeasurable damages inflicted during ten years, in which the equality of the forces engaged prolonged the struggle without a decisive triumph by either of the belligerents, made of New Spain a field of desolation and a heap of ruins, in which were buried both victors and vanquished; but it produced a total change in men and affairs. The monotonous succession of sieges, battles, surprises, and defeats; the repeated execution of prisoners by both parties;

the blood that was shed in torrents; and the conversion of all Mexico into a field of battle, spreading death and destruction far and wide; make exceedingly difficult the narration of all these horrors by the writer, and tires and disgusts the reader of them.

"In 1810 New Spain was mined throughout and covered with tinder, ready at the least spark to burst into flame and become a general conflagration. These conditions, nevertheless, were entirely unknown, to the extent that the Spanish authorities, as well as the leaders of the revolution, were amazed when they saw the rapidity with which the fire spread throughout the country. The former feared, and the latter counted upon, the elements for an uprising, but neither of them was prepared to believe what experience proved them to be."[5]

I have not hesitated to make these long quotations, not only because they put the situation before us most graphically, but especially because they were written by Mora. No enemy of the revolution could have exercised greater frankness than does this friend. From his statement certain facts are plainly discernible: The revolt of Hidalgo, and those of his followers who continued it as guerrillas, was unwanted by the people, a fraud perpetrated on those who took part in it, a murderous orgy destructive of all sense of justice, and a devastating evil to the whole country. Yet Mora said that it was "necessary for independence."[6]

Hidalgo himself needs some explaining; and, because he was a priest, the explaining of him may well be prefaced by a paragraph about the state of clerical life at that time in Mexico.

In a previous chapter attention was called to the fact that the Church in the whole Spanish Kingdom, but especially in America, had only her doctrinal liberty. In the domain of faith and morals she had little to complain of. Outside that domain the union of Church and State had long before taken the form of the subjugation of the administrative side of the Church to the State. This in part involved also the disciplinary side. As already pointed out, Spanish Kings, like the Emperor Charles and his son Philip, had done a great deal to make that situation tolerable. Their usually excellent nominations for episcopal sees, as well as their care in selecting Viceroys, had given the Church influence enough to avert evils which, under such conditions, might well have been expected to show themselves early. With the dynastic troubles of Spain and her European conflicts such good influence gradually lost its hold. Unfortunate appointments were made. Certain priests who were failures in Spain were sent to Mexico with directions for placing them. Even at the beginning Cortés had warned against this policy. These men had a bad influence over some of the native clergy, for the Church had followed her custom of trying to raise up a clergy from among the people, even the Indians. In 1810 there was a small percentage of unsuccessful and ambitious priests in Mexico, but more than ever before—or since. It had not, however, greatly affected the whole body. These men were exceptions. To them was added annually a small number of poorly trained young natives. Even at that time Mexico did not have a sufficient number of priests to care properly for the people. In truth she never has had.

Hidalgo was of the native white class. He had studied at the Seminary in Valladolid. Mora, with beautiful inconsistency, said that he made his course "with great credit as a famous scholastic," and later that he was "very mediocre."[7] Perhaps that latter remark was, however, intended to apply only to his military career. To those who know what is required in a priest, Hidalgo was one who had missed the elemental necessities of a spiritual, if not an intellectual, training. His student associates were aware of it and called him, "The Fox." Alamán, the historian, who knew Hidalgo personally, and who secured intimate details of his life from personal friends and relatives of the priest, does not paint a very attractive picture of him. As a graduate student the Cathedral Chapter of Valladolid gave him $4,000 with which to pay his expenses while studying in Mexico City for a doctor's degree, presumably at the University. He lost the money gambling. After serving in a number of parishes he finally secured enough political influence to secure for himself the parish at Dolores. At once he gave half his salary to an assistant to look after his pastoral duties and plunged with the rest into several unclerical pursuits to which he was attracted by their novelty. He tried vineyards, silkworms, bees, a pottery, a brickyard, a tannery, a crafts shop. All failed. Money slipped through his fingers but made him popular with the common people. It is to his credit that he was generous.[8]

What drove Hidalgo into starting the first revolt? In justice to him it may be that he had at least an altruistic reason born of his generosity. Mora says that he had been reading the books used for radical propaganda and had often dis-

cussed their ideas with others of the clergy who had imbibed ideas similar to his own.[9] If that were true, however,
he would have been only a potential follower, not a leader,
certainly not The Leader. Something compelled him when
he was over seventy to take a place for which he must have
known himself unfitted. What was that something? The
record is there to read. For ten years the Inquisition had
been watching Hidalgo and noting his utterances. Dávalos
says that it had numerous affidavits about his talk and
doings.[10] Without doubt he feared what did actually happen
on October 13, 1810 — a month after the beginning of the
revolt—when he was cited to appear and answer charges
based on these documents. He knew this was coming[11] and
entered into a plot with several residents of Querétaro and
Captain Ignacio Allende, an officer of the Queen's Provisional Regiment.[12] The plot was discovered, but the plotters
had been warned. It was then do or die for Hidalgo. On a
Sunday when his people came to the church for the usual
Mass, the trapped priest sent up the famous "Grito de
Dolores."

There is a magic in words. There was and still is magic
in these three. Dolores was only the name of a town, but it
seems to carry the thought of an overwhelming burden of
sorrow upon a downtrodden people. *Grito* means a shout,
but it may also mean a heart-rending scream. If Hidalgo
coined the phrase he was more than a poor visionary who
had blundered into mischief and misery. He was a poet.

There was little of a Washington about Hidalgo. The
contrast between the two men is distressing, yet many try
to make it. There is a real appeal to the imagination in the

story of the Liberty Bell, but only an appeal to pity in Hidalgo's rushing to the prisons to gather to his cause the riffraff of the bull pen. Whatever justification Idealism had to be on Hidalgo's side in the picture of the church bell ringing at Dolores and the first recruits coming from the fast-gathering Indians, is lost in the mad events that followed. For an hour Hidalgo was The Leader. When he opened the prison he was The Led. He could no more have prevented what followed than a boy with a spoon could stop Niagara. Hidalgo was willing to be a traitor, but he soon became a thief, a robber, a murderer; and all in spite of himself.[13]

No one, least of all men who, like Hidalgo, had discussed the "new ideas" learnedly in cozy conversations with so many other precursors of "parlor pinks" and "college socialists," could possibly have realized how deep they were sinking. No one, least of all Hidalgo, knew how frightful would be the mad answer to his scream of terror, his appeal to have others save him. "Superficial to an extreme," writes Mora of him, "he abandoned himself entirely to the force of circumstances, limiting his plans and foresight to what was to be done on the morrow. He never took the trouble, and perhaps never even considered it necessary, to reflect upon the result of his efforts, nor did he establish any fixed rule to systematize them." But Mora thinks that the three conspirators had been reached by the Bonapartist influence coming out of Baltimore.[14] Strange then that Hidalgo should have proclaimed loyalty for Ferdinand VII, putting the King's name on his standard. In his manifesto he proclaimed that he intended to preserve the country for the rightful King and turn it over to him when his own work was done.

From Dolores the mob of ranchmen, released prisoners, deserting militia, and Indians, swept toward the capital. At Guanajuato they found rich loot, but they had not waited for Guanajuato. They swarmed like locusts and left only the waste of locusts behind them. The corn in the fields was ripe. They cut it down with a stroke. Domestic animals were carried away with them. Dwellings were stripped even to the doors and window frames. The Indians had taken with them their women and children to help carry off the loot. Loaded down with plunder, many of them went off and others, nothing loath, took their places.[15]

Out of Guanajuato they made a shambles. Two massacres occurred there, at the market, the Alhondiga. More than five hundred were killed. The red terror swept on through San Miguel, Guanajuato, and Celaya. Alamán himself saw the sacking of Guanajuato and drew a dreadful word picture of it. Hidalgo's old seminary home, Valladolid, was on his way. He sacked it. He had now 80,000 men. At Las Cruces he defeated a government force of 3,000 sent out to stop him. Yet he turned and retreated, fought a battle at Aculco which he lost to the Royalist Calleja. Nothing daunted, he marched on toward Guadalajara. He had now 100,000 men and 95 pieces of artillery. On the Bridge of Calderon near the city he met Calleja again with an army of only 6,000 men that swept Hidalgo's 100,000 into irretrievable disaster. With his lieutenants and 1,500 of his mob, mostly military deserters who knew their fate if captured, Hidalgo tried to reach the Rio Grande and safety—perhaps

Baltimore. In the desert he was caught. In September, 1810, he had left Dolores. In July, 1811, at another Dolores as wide in extent only as his vision, he stood before a firing squad, he a priest degraded from his office, and in blood paid the price of blood.[16]

There were priests and friars who joined Hidalgo,[17] Evidently it was on the strength of this fact that Mora based his statement that the revolt was the work of the clergy.[18] As an historian he had to give the facts, but as an anticlerical he had to charge it to his self-selected enemies. But the revolt was in reality only the result of one ill-spent priestly life facing retribution and stumbling into unknown conditions. The priests with Hidalgo, if we are to judge by the best known of them, were men of the same stamp as himself. Dávalos does not spare the old man nor some of those who were with him. Mier was a schismatic radical with a lecherous tongue. We find him later on in Philadelphia posing as a bishop to stir up strife during the Hogan schism. Navarette was concerned with the killing of thirty-odd Spanish prisoners. Jiménez was a drunkard. Torres was a thief, killed later in a drunken quarrel. In some there may have been good faith and patriotism. In none was there the obedience they had vowed. It is hard to find an excuse for any of them. The burdens of many bishops must have been lightened when they died or were scattered.[19]

The written confession of guilt made by Hidalgo before his execution is a pathetic document. For once the worm of worldliness that during the whole priestly career of this old man — as stated, he was past seventy when he began the revolt—had been destroying his peace, hid itself in the sincerity of his repentance. In that document he sat in judgment upon his own case, and no court on earth could have been more searching and severe. Such a judgment could never have been forced. There are too many signs of disgust for himself, as well as of the sincerity with which he now felt it, to sign it by any other name than the poor old sinner's very own.[20]

A much more attractive figure carried on after Hidalgo's capture, his old pupil at St. Nicholas College in Valladolid, a priest too, José Maria Morelos. That he was a student at St. Nicholas while Hidalgo was its Rector justifies a sad comment on the spiritual training then being given the students of that old college. In truth it would seem as if the "new ideas" out of France had attracted at least the curiosity of a number of priests who considered themselves an élite group of intellectuals. Valladolid had more than its share of them. Morelos joined his former Rector at Charo, and, luckily for himself, was at once sent out to raise recruits and capture Acapulco. He succeeded in getting together 3,000 men and seizing arms from the militia. Morelos reversed the record of military inefficiency made for the revolt by the ignorance and stark madness of Hidalgo. There was much of military genius in him. While Hidalgo with 100,-000 had been defeated by Calleja with only 6,000, Morelos could win against trained troops with only half their number. He was clever as a military leader but equally so as an advocate, finding always the best answer from the legal and ecclesiastical standpoint to the accusations of his judges. Bad as his priestly life had been—he admitted that at his trial—yet it must have been a fairly studious one. When charged with treason against the King of Spain, he retorted that since there was no King in Spain there could be none to claim his loyalty. He condemned Ferdinand for the very act that had done the King's cause the greatest damage, his failure to stay in Spain. But the intervention of the Inquisition in the case of Morelos was thoroughly illegal. That court sat in its revived form and was more than ever the State institution it always had been. It now assumed jurisdiction to take over a case after another State court had judged it. But it would have been fortunate for Morelos had he had nothing to suffer but the punishment of exile and penance the Inquisition pronounced on him. He was shot by authority of the other court on December 22, 1815. His lieutenant and friend Matamoros had been killed in battle. With the passing of these two, the rebellion simmered down to guerrilla tactics and banditry, which gave those who would live by the sword encouragement to pass on the tradition of loot as far as the days of Porfirio Díaz, who suppressed the custom — for a time.[21]

Morelos was degraded from his priesthood by the Bishop of Oaxaca before being turned over to the secular arm. He bore himself with dignity during most of the ceremony, and was not moved by the copious weeping of the Bishop whose tears never ceased to flow. But when his consecrated hands were scraped, as if so far as possible to do the impossible and remove from them the unction forever a part of them, great tears rolled down his cheeks. Perhaps these were more efficacious than the silver scraper. It could only play its part in figure. Welling up from a repentant heart the tears could touch the poor hands and cleanse them from the guilt of blood.

It is not easy for most people to understand such priests as Hidalgo, Morelos, and Matamoros. They do not fit into the popular conception of what a priest should be. They scandalize Catholics, puzzle Protestants, and rejoice the unthinking. But it is not really difficult to understand them, once we have learned even a superficial something about human nature and remembered the times and circumstances that produced them. The scandal such men give is a testimony to the fidelity of the great body in which by choice they made themselves exceptions. Within that body such men form everywhere a small group that simply will not fit in because they never ought to have come in. They are men who, without, perhaps, even knowing it at the time, were attracted rather to place than to spirit; and place here may mean opportunity, ambition, vanity or even as with Hidalgo, plain curiosity. The humdrum work of the care of souls fails to satisfy them. They have a yearning for "big things." Even learning, as learning, does not interest them; while learning as display does. They never secure a mastery over themselves and never, therefore, can understand the fertile virtue of humility. Before the Revolution, France had groups of them in every large city, attending the salons of Madame This or Madame That!, superficially discussing the political theories of the hour. Some were very brilliant men, and of these Talleyrand was, perhaps, the outstanding light. They usually won admiration—to that end their cloth helped—but no one would even dream of asking spiritual direction of them. When theories became responsibilities they had not the courage to retrace their steps and find safe ground again. For them the mob had taken the place of God, and so they rushed straight into spiritual desolation and ruin. Such priests are one of the intimate family worries of the Church. Their special talents might be directed into channels leading to the true objectives of their state, but, since the responsibility for them is one of the burdens of their superiors — and since not all superiors are possessed of the combination of wisdom, patience, and sagacity needed to help, the type still keeps on producing a handful of Wolseys within and of Sieyès without. My sigh is for poor Lammenais.

The Mexico of the pre-revolutionary era produced by the troubles of the reign of Ferdinand VII and the French "new ideas" does not make a very attractive picture, but to the student of her history it explains a great deal. In Mexico the State was walking with very uncertain steps; still ruled by Viceroys from Spain while from Spain no help could be expected in the event that their rule might be threatened. They were strangers relying on native loyalty to a King who was not a King. The people were worried by the present and apprehensive of the future, harassed by a handful of radicals who knew quite well how to keep them in a constant state of bewilderment. The bishops were still semi-State officials as well as spiritual leaders.

Seminary training had become in some centers a machine process, with fidelity to the clock but little to the spirit. The missionary spirit itself had gone to the Californias and other far-away places. With prosperity in the valley of Mexico, churchmen were forgetting the zeal that made it, in the new responsibilities and comforts it brought. The flock was faithful, but distressed and in fear of the rise of anticlericalism in Spain, more than fearful that the conquest of Spain by France would bring religious persecution to America. This was the fear Hidalgo and Morelos took advantage of to recruit men and sympathy. Both proclaimed their intentions of protecting religion and it was good popular diplomacy to do so. Fear in the people deepened after the first revolt. The "liberal" Spanish constitution of 1812 was re-established in Spain in 1820 and the radicals in Mexico rejoiced. There was satisfaction, too, among the White Collars. But the mass of the people of Mexico were against it. The very elements that had opposed Hidalgo and Morelos came soon to want independence. These included the clergy. It was not the provisions of the Constitution that were the source of the hatred against it, but its origin. The danger of its being put into force in Mexico seemed—and in that the people were good judges—to be the terrors of the French Revolution. They knew that the liberty it promised was only the forerunner of tyranny.[22] How right the people were in this the future would prove.

To make matters worse the Spanish Cortes, in the October of 1820, passed a decree suppressing certain religious orders. It went into force in Mexico. The Jesuits who had been re-established were again to be dispersed. In Pueblo the authorities did not dare carry out the decree by daylight, but had to await the cover of darkness to avoid a popular uprising. Primary schools, orphanages, and asylums for the insane, were closed, or bad management of them substituted for good. The army was losing its morale. The native troops were left unpaid, while the Spanish troops were cared for. "Indianism" was preached more than ever, and the idea, as was stated by Bustamante, was gradually accepted that Spain had taken riches and power from the native races. The Spaniard, always thrifty, had become wealthy. The Indian, always thriftless, had become poor in spite of the advantages offered him. Mexico in sentiment was ripe for trouble.[23]

In spite of the defects of Hidalgo, however, the credit of striking the first blow for independence, though it is not quite clear that independence was his real objective, must go to him.

X

AMERICO TRIUNFO

THE WASHINGTON OF Mexico was Agustín Iturbide. He was shot for his pains. Iturbide had been an officer in the royalist army and, as such, had fought against Morelos. Selected by the Viceroy Apodaca he took command of the royalist army of the West, but by this time he was no royalist. Gradually his convictions as to the ability of Spain to manage her American Colonies had changed, and he had inclined to independence. There were in Mexico by this time three parties: Royalist, Independent, and — much under cover — Radical. The party for independence had become the strongest. For the time being, it was in the radical program to play with it. Iturbide could be taken care of later. The radicals in Spain had procured the re-adoption of the Constitution of 1812 with the thought in mind that it would please the Mexicans. It did nothing of the kind. It frightened them, because it was the shadow of Rousseau and Robespierre over them. The shadow was enough. Spain had betrayed Mexico to the enemy. She could no longer be trusted. Iturbide knew that what he saw the best people in Mexico saw. He had made his decision to move for independence before he left to assume command of his troops. With much native support lost, he knew that the Viceroy could not defend his position. If independence had to be, this was the moment to strike for it.[1]

From his headquarters in the town of Iguala, Iturbide sent forth his proposals for an independent government in Mexico. These proposals are known in history as the Plan of Iguala, which called for a monarchial government to be offered King Ferdinand on condition that he come to Mexico. In the event of his refusal of the crown, it was to be offered in turn to the Princes Carlos and Francisco. At home inequalities were to be abolished between citizens. The Catholic would be the state religion. A Congress would be called to put the Plan into constitutional form.

It will be noted that the Plan was in substance what two Spanish Kings already had rejected. Had either of them acted on the proposals at the time they were made, it seems quite certain that Mexico would have been saved long years of bloodshed. The country was not, even in 1820, ready for democratic government. The attachment of the people was to monarchy with a constitution, but not the one of 1812.[2]

As expected, Iturbide had an open road to power before him. The people were with him. The Viceroy could not muster military strength enough to oppose him. There would be little fighting. Iturbide went about attaching the rest of the country to the party of independence. Old insurgents came to him. Generals Guerrero and Victoria joined his forces. Even the royalist army gave its share of deserters to the popular cause. Iturbide was a soldier on whose military judgment reliance could be placed. His army was not a mob of looters, but was, the people thought, worthy of the cause. His arguments convinced O'Donojú, the new and last Viceroy, when they met at Córdova, on August 23 and 24, that he should sign a treaty acknowledging independence under the Plan of Iguala. After all it gave the throne to the family of the King. The army of independence took possession of the capital in September, 1821.[3]

The first objective gained, Iturbide became the President of a Council of Regency which he set up in accord with the Plan, consisting of four others and himself. Thus he began well by sharing power and pleased the people. Here was one to be trusted. On the outside all was peaceful. On February 24, 1822, the Congress assembled. Two parties in it were for the Plan of Iguala but differed about calling a King from Spain. The other party was for a republic. Through it the radicals would try a second step in forwarding their designs. Spain came to their aid by rejecting the pact made at Córdova. It was the last of the Spanish blunders because it was the one that ended all hope for the continued attachment of her richest colony to Spain. The division now, so far as the Congress was concerned, was between an out-and-out republic and a monarch of some sort. The people of Mexico City settled the matter by a demonstration demanding that Iturbide be made Emperor.[4]

A story is told by Alamán of the anxiety of General Victoria to secure the crown for himself. He wrote to Iturbide in camp suggesting that choice for Emperor be made of an unmarried insurgent leader who had never been pardoned by the Viceregal government. After mounting the imperial throne, this Emperor would marry a girl from Guatemala and thus unite the countries. General Victoria alone could have filled the specifications.[5] Victoria's real name was Juan Felix Fernández. He assumed the name Guadalupe Victoria, as he told General Teran, because he thought it a great piece of political strategy. Teran, seeing the absurdity, agreed gravely and said that he himself would change his name to Americo Triunfo.[6]

Iturbide, turned Emperor, lost no time in making mistakes. He began them by trusting the radicals, thinking that they were Mexicans first when in reality the interest of Mexico was a poor second to the triumph in America of their ideas. The United States of the North had given these ideas a cold shoulder. Now the radicals were going to plant a real revolutionary government at her door. Agustín I invited the old insurgents, who were the hope of the radicals, to come in. They swarmed. The Viceroy had pardoned them and they were now well represented in the Imperial army, thus constituting a horde of irresponsible vagabonds and criminals in the armed forces of the nation. The Emperor soon found himself with a half-bandit organization on his hands. Thus the "army of liberty" became so vile no respectable citizen could think of enlisting as a common soldier. Without private means he could not even live honestly as an officer. It became inevitable that the army should become an agent of oppression in the hands of any group that could bid for its support. The bid need only be what the old insurgents had come to love — pillage. That tradition had by this time fastened itself firmly on the armed forces of Mexico, to be invoked even up to the present day. The radicals had made their step, even if for a while — and a short while as it proved — they had to tolerate an honest Emperor. In the meantime Victoria was awaiting his chance.[7]

The Emperor was soon beset with troubles from the Congress. He arrested some of the makers. A young general, looking after Vera Cruz, named Santa Anna, showed signs of making more. He was removed. The Emperor dismissed the Congress and set up a Council of Government. Santa Anna revolted. Off went the regally minded Victoria to join him. The Emperor abdicated. He had not enjoyed his royal state while he had it. His reign lasted less than a year. The spelling of reign so far as his was concerned might well be changed, for it was all a rain of miseries.[8]

The radicals were ready for step three. Victoria would do while Santa Anna waited. As for the ex-Emperor, he went to Italy. When the news of fresh miseries in Mexico came to his ears, he decided to return; and when he did, he was captured. On September 27, 1821, the Liberator had entered the capital of the Independent Mexico he had created. Two years and ten months later he fell before a firing squad at Padillo. He had served his purpose and, at least, had died like a soldier.[9]

The reader has already had some swift glimpses at the causes of Iturbide's failure. An attempt will be made to gather them together into one picture.

Mexico was utterly unprepared for independence. The mass of the people accepted the idea with reluctance when they had no alternative under the conditions that ruled the political situation in Spain. To Iturbide's misfortune the foundation stones of preparation were lacking. Even the mortar of popular sympathy was a weak mixture. The people had been frightened into independence by the re-enactment of the Spanish Constitution of 1812. Fright was a poor support for so great a change. The radicals had no intention of keeping the Empire one day longer than they felt safe in moving to get rid of it. They did not enter the Congress to help but to hinder. The Bour-bonists were a bitterly disappointed group when they realized that no King would come from Spain. They did not want a mere Mexican to be their royal ruler. They had the natural superiority complex of their day. A Mexican Emperor, "bone of their bone and flesh of their flesh," seemed nothing short of the ridiculous. The change was too swift for the man. Iturbide was a general used to quick and uncomplicated decisions which found ready obedience from his troops. As Emperor he became a man pulled this way and that, trying to harmonize differences so radical that no possibility short of bloodshed could bring them into any sort of unity. The minority made up in shouting, as is usually the case, for its lack of numbers. Iturbide either mistook the shouting for power, or decided that the majority, if only because it was a majority, ought to be generous in making concessions for peace to a group that did not want peace. These concessions ought never to have been made, for they were well calculated to destroy the objective of establishing an effective and satisfactory government. Even a rapid review of the measures taken by the Council of Regency, the Congress, and the Emperor himself, will verify the truth of all the above points.[10]

There is more. On taking possession of the capital the Regency was set up in accord with the Plan of Iguala with Iturbide at its head, but the new Spanish Viceroy, Don Juan O'Donojú, strangely enough, was one of its members. The names of the others are of no importance. What is of importance is the fact that there was much political dynamite in a group supposed to represent all parties. The very first act of the Regency was to set up a power greater than itself, for Iturbide was made Commander-in-Chief on land and sea for life, and assigned a salary of $150,000 a year. O'Donojú was taken care of with a pension of $80,000 a year, the why and wherefore of which is hard to find since O'Donojú was not a Mexican. General promotions were made in the army. A Lieutenant General was named with three Field Marshals. In addition, one of the new Field Marshals, Guerrero, got the honorary title of Captain General of the Army. Of Brigadiers there were many, all on the active list. Although Alamán stamps the proceeding as a tactless measure and an evil sure to create distinctions, nevertheless it might not have been so bad if only titles had been concerned, but it was also giving money away with lavish hand before the Regency knew where the money was to come from. The Council then proceeded to cut off its own source of revenue. It promulgated a war-time, but also propaganda, decree of Iturbide, issued while in the field, cutting off half the taxes imposed by the Viceroys. Two taxes were put on all imports from abroad: one of 25 per cent and one of 8 per cent. Importation of raw cotton was prohibited. Worse resulted in the case of the Indians. They had paid, as wards of the State, only a small tribute. The new government made them full citizens and declared their equality with the whites, all of which had a good sound which the Indians liked at first. They did not later like so well the fact that their new dignity brought with it a place on the general tax list. Nor did they enjoy the loss of their hospitals which had been supported out of their small tribute. These were now forgotten and had to be closed, since the community treasuries were soon empty.[11]

The Regency was brave, however, when it took up the question of the Royal Patronage, which, in effect, was the union of Church and State. Here was dynamite indeed, for the radicals wanted such a union of Church and State as would permit them to kill the Church; while the moderates wanted ecclesiastical as well as civil patronage. The Church wanted only her administrative freedom. No one seemed to think of adopting the American plan as a compromise. It would have prevented the radicals from seizing Church property for themselves, cut patronage off from the politicians, and dissolved entirely the union of Church and State.

What at bottom was the Patronage question? It was the old bargain entered into between the Spanish Kings and the Church by which the State agreed to take over the care of certain temporalities of administration and expense in return for the right to nominate the administrators of these temporalities and collect — and tax — the tithes for the support of the Church. Pope Julius II, in a Bull dated July 28, 1518, conceded to the monarchs of Castile and León the right of nomination to all ecclesiastical benefices on condition that they erect and endow all the Cathedral

and parish churches. By the same Bull they were granted
the tithes. It looked like a good bargain, since the only
interest the Church had in the matter was the upkeep of
her work and, after all, the Pope could see to it that the
nominations of the monarchs supplied at least worthy
bishops. His interest was less in the persons than in the
offices. As I already noted, the Spanish Kings left little to
complain of in reference to their part of the bargain,
especially in the early days. It was because of this Patronage
that the Church in Mexico had been enabled to start, almost
from the beginning, with a full and complete ecclesiastical
hierarchical establishment and all the temporal requirements for her missionary, educational, and social work.

Alas! even in Kings and Queens human nature is human
nature, and the spirit of human nature is greedy. As time
went on more concessions were asked for and had to be
granted. The monarchs were so good that it was hard to
refuse within reason. Other concessions were assumed, like
that of preventing Pontifical decrees and letters from reaching the bishops before passing through the Council of the
Indies, the prevention of provincial councils without royal
sanction, etc. There was quite a terrifying list of these un-
authorized infringements on the liberty of the Church.

The new government of Mexico seemed to have had no
shadow of doubt but that it had inherited in full all the
rights and the assumptions of rights of the Spanish Kings.
Nevertheless it went gingerly about acting on them. A
feeler was sent to the Archbishop, not asking for his
opinion as to the rights of the new government to the
Patronage, but to inquire how they should be applied

while the matter was being readjusted with the Holy See. The Archbishop played for time. Here was a vital question. What it finally would involve was the whole union. He could have had no hallucinations at the time about its possible, even probable, consequences to the Church. If the new and hungry "politicos" had the Patronage, it would be to their interest to maintain the union of Church and State to protect their own pocketbooks. Few of them were altruistic or holy. On the other hand, the Archbishop must have known, by certain signs that had already shown themselves, that without the Patronage these gentlemen would find it hard to keep their hands off the property of the Church. Principle was against Patronage. Worldly wisdom was with it. The Archbishop called the bishops into conference. They told the Regency that the Patronage days were over. They also told it that, pending adjudication by the Holy See, which they well knew would uphold them on the principle, the Church would do her own appointing.

To those acquainted with this episode in the history of Mexico, the constantly repeated assertions of American agents of Carranza, Obregón, and Calles, that they were not persecuting but only trying to dissolve a union of Church and State, become ridiculous. It was the bishops themselves, against all their own temporal interests, who gave the union its mortal blow.[12] And that was more than a century ago.

The Plan of Iguala had attracted royalist support chiefly because of the assurance therein contained that a Bourbon prince would be invited to occupy the Mexican throne. Nothing officially was done about it. It was rumored that

Don Francisco, son of Ferdinand VII, had expressed his willingness to accept the crown; but the matter was dropped there as far as the Regency was concerned. Small wonder the royalists looked with suspicious eyes on the Regency and questioned the good faith of Iturbide. It was a blunder, and one of major proportions, since it made a breach between Iturbide and the most respectable elements. With the mass of the people, however, he was still The Liberator, loved and revered. He did not long remain so, for the old insurgents turned on him. In the race for place they found themselves disqualified by his Decree that rewards would be given only to those whose services postdated March 2, 1821. These old insurgents were of the mob, part of the people, and could talk. That they did with effect. The press fanned the flame of dissatisfaction. We think our Soldier Bonus troubles here are peculiar to our own situation. Let us be reassured. Mexico had them over one hundred years ago and they helped dethrone an Emperor.

The money specter walked again. There was none to establish the planned tobacco monopoly; the Spanish troops had to be paid according to agreement and the Mexican soldiers wait — were they alive they would still be waiting; public employees were only about half paid; producers lost crops or sold contraband because they could not export them; bills of damages for military destruction were coming in sheaves; there was a deficit of over seventy millions made by the Congress. The Empire was in the pawnshop. The California Mission, called the Pious Fund, was put up as security for a popular loan, but the loan was none too popular.

The gainful but business-sustaining Spaniards soon began to depart for Spain, and the radicals thought it time to put out another feeler in the shape of a conspiracy of the old insurgents for a republic. Victoria, who had been sent to jail, escaped, aided by two congressmen; and in hiding adopted a policy of watchful waiting. He would not have long to wait.

Of almost equal importance with independence itself had been the anger of the people over the expulsion of the Jesuits and other religious orders. By it the best schools had been closed and hospital services crippled. The Regency was flooded with petitions for the return of the orders, which the Plan of Iguala had announced as a policy of the revolution. These petitions were shelved on the ground that the matter was "not urgent." This was done by the Bourbonists, but it reflected on Iturbide.[13]

In the meantime Chiapas and Guatemala joined Mexico, and more of Central America seemed willing to follow suit. Honduras and Nicaragua were for the Empire; Costa Rica and San Salvador for separate independence. This was encouraging. But when Iturbide made a brave attempt at organizing a permanent legislative body, he was not successful. He wrote from exile later on that it was "the managers of the machine" who were responsible. A deputy, Bocanegra, wrote later: "It is necessary to confess that the deputies from the provinces were all of us victims of our own inexperience and lack of knowledge of the management of an Assembly, and of our good faith, and on the other hand the prearranged partisan combination of those comprising the party called Bourbons." There it was, the

Hidden Hand. The radicals were not asleep and they had a royalist name.[14]

When the Congress met, the deputies had taken an oath of fealty to the Plan of Iguala and the Treaty of Córdova. After the swearing they had listened to an address suggesting that both might be ignored. The leader of the Bourbons proposed and carried the proposition: "that the National Sovereignty resides in this constituent Congress," which meant overboard with plan, treaty, and oath. Then Congress placed executive power in the Regency and judicial power in the Judiciary. Thus was the oath thrown a life-preserver, but carefully out of its reach. The fact was that the true constitution of the nation was the Plan of Iguala.

Iturbide is censured by Wilson, in his *American History*, for not having been "guided by the counsels of prudence," and for not allowing "his authority to be confined within constitutional limits." The truth is that he knew perfectly well of the electoral frauds mentioned by Bocanegra and that the Congress had been rigged by his enemies. It was his Plan of Iguala and himself the people wanted. The Congress was against The Liberator, but the deputies had no desire to get down to work. They neglected the making of a constitution but arranged for many agreeable civic celebrations and fiestas. To embarrass Iturbide it was proposed to honor Hidalgo and his followers against whom he had fought. One annoyance like this after another the deputies proposed. Money swilled through their fingers. Even a trust fund for the Holy Land was mortgaged and the mint was exhausted. There was constant confusion in dealings between the Council of Regency and the Congress. Unpaid troops were deserting, much to the glee of the Bourbons who wanted to weaken Iturbide. Forced "loans" from Church institutions were ordered and, these being insufficient, the Congress went out hat in hand, metaphorically, to solicit the financial aid of private citizens; offering already mortgaged property that did not belong to the State as security. It would be tiresome to sketch in all the details. The only satisfied ones were the Bourbons. It suited them to have matters go from bad to worse. When they put the ermine of an emperor on Agustín Iturbide they were only decorating a special victim for the sacrifice. Old Huitzilopochtli in Hell must have licked his chops and shaken his fat sides laughing. Here indeed was a great heart to eat and more coming. Old Huitzilopochtli did not bother about souls. But he loved bruised hearts.[15]

XI

THE HIDDEN HAND

"NO ONE CAN swing the sword of truth around in a crowd without hurting somebody" was the way a pulpit orator of my acquaintance lyricized an unhappy fact. And no one can swing history around in a crowd without hurting many. This book has been quite frank in dealing with the clergy. It will be quite as frank in dealing with the Hidden Hand of Masonry, which plays a part, and no creditable one, in the Mexican tragedy. That there are likely to be many Masons among my readers ought not, and will not, make me any the less frank in telling about that part. The truth is that, from the arrival of Spanish officers, civil and military, in Mexico, during and after the Napoleonic wars in Spain, down to the advent of Benito Juárez in Mexican politics, Freemasonry kept the unfortunate country in a turmoil of troubles, including revolutions, skirmishes, and riots. Nor am I forgetting what came after Juárez; but whatever that was concerned individuals and what passed for Freemasonry. My concern now is only about what was visible on the surface, well known to everybody at the time.

Let the Mexican historian speak first. I quote from Alamán—he is dealing with what I have called Spanish

Background: "Masonry had been increasing on the quiet, in spite of the vigilance of the Inquisition which had conducted to its prison a number of persons accused of belonging to it. In their favor the King, who was held certain to have joined the society in France, caused the dictation of certain measures of leniency at a session of the tribunal in which he took part, and in which he acted as Inquisitor. This society, little known and much concealed in Spain previous to the French invasion, had been propagated during the war by the officers of the troops of that nation, and, in distinction from what it was in England and other places where it had become a fraternity for mutual assistance, had assumed an entirely political character, and truthfully could call itself a permanent conspiracy. It had made rapid progress in the army, and by means of it the conspirators in all the provinces were in secret communication, working under a single plan and moved by a common impulse."[1]

That paragraph relates to Spain. Another from Bancroft makes the connection: "There were but few masons in the country [Mexico] before the coming of the expeditionary forces, and these had preserved strict secrecy from dread of the Inquisition. The field and nearly all the company officers of those troops, as well as of the navy, were members of the order, and it was whispered that Apodaca [the Viceroy] was one of them, though this was not divulged. He was, however, sure that the masons had effected the revolution in Spain, and feared that those in the army of Mexico had been directed to promote one in the colony."[2]

Alamán asks attention again: "The arrival of O'Donojú

in Mexico gave a great impulse to Freemasonry, for, though he himself lived but a few days, the persons that accompanied him joined the existing lodges and formed new ones, all under the Scottish Rite. One of the latter was named El Sol [The Sun] to which belonged a periodical bearing the same name, edited by Manuel Codorniú, a doctor who came with O'Donojú, whose purpose was to support the Plan de Iguala; to propagate the liberal principles established in Spain, and, among these the fundamental point, to exclude the clergy from all participation in the education of the young, so as to mold them with an education devoid of any religious foundation, leaving religion an incidental matter until it could be suppressed entirely, from which has come the persecution of the Jesuits and the development of the Lancastrian schools. Thereupon the Freemasons became a powerful influence, which we will see in action in all the succeeding events."[3]

In these three quotations are revealed the source of the power of the radicals, the secret of their unity, as well as their political objective. The Scottish Rite was the party of Rousseau, of French and Spanish "liberalism"; the advance guard of Juárez, Carranza, and Calles.

There are, especially among English and American Freemasons, some who will object that blame should not be attached to the whole body for actions by one branch of a Rite, and some who would go farther and claim that true Freemasonry consists of only three degrees, Entered Apprentice, Fellowcraft, and Master Mason; and that therefore the so-called Rites are nothing more than a string of societies recruited from the true Master Masonic body.

Into that question I need not go beyond noting the possible objection. So far as this study is concerned I have to deal only with the record of two Rites.

As Alamán has said, the Scottish Rite was introduced into Mexico from Spain, and Spain received it from France. In Mexico it does not appear that Scotland had anything to do with it. But its Scotch name did, nevertheless, become that of a political party in Mexico; while York, near enough in England to the border of Scotland, gave its name to another and a rival party. A revolution was fought in Mexico between these two, with not a known Scotsman or Yorkshireman on either side. The story of that revolution, with its approach and its effects, ought to have in it enough of the uncommon to be classed as news.

Once the Scottish Rite had formed a foothold in Mexico it began to grow rapidly, and for the same reasons that it had spread widely in Spain. It offered an opportunity to plot unseen and unheard. The secret signs, the lodge, the oath, the bond of unity, were all seemingly designed for political connivance. Those Spaniards who wanted to overturn everything, but had no majority to rely upon, had been quick to see. It worked, as the Constitution of 1812 and the suppression of some of the religious orders testified. For the French and Spanish the Scottish Rite was anti-royal and anti-Church. With many of its members it was anti-God; perhaps with almost all of them. Thus it was presented to the radicals of Mexico, not only by the Spanish army and navy officers, but by civil servants, the entourage of arriving Viceroys, and the returning Mexican members of the Spanish Cortes. It captured the Mexican White-

Collar class and some of the "literati," while accepting recruits also from the ranks of the lax and politically minded clergy.

There is a bare possibility that some of these clergymen became members of the Scottish Rite without knowing of its affiliation with the Freemasonry condemned by Clement XII in 1738 and by Benedict XIV in 1751. This bare possibility may be admitted but not seriously urged. A small group has already been noticed among the clergy who, since they did not stick at the irregularity of bloodshed, would not be likely, at least while in good health, to bother much about incurring an *ipso facto* excommunication. There was no great danger of their lodge brothers informing on them, since these knew as much about the ecclesiastical censure as did the clergy. Besides, it was quite unlikely that any priest could be ignorant of specific orders he had been instructed to follow. Then the gate to the Rites is the Master's degree. The Scottish Rite clergy were simple skeptics masquerading as faithful priests to hold their benefices and make sure of a living. What they did not know was that English and American Grand Lodges had refused, a few excepted, to recognize those of France and Spain. A whole volume could be filled with denunciations, dating back to prerevolutionary days in France, from English and American Freemasons, against the tenets held by the Continental Lodges. Even to this day, in spite of attempts during the Great War to bring about a *rapprochement,* these Continental Grand Lodges are still unrecognized; that is, at least so far as is known to the rank and file of Master Masons.

The Scottish Rite in Spain left its members in no darkness as to its ultimate objective. It was frankly revolutionary; willing to tolerate Brother Ferdinand VII but very unwilling to allow him to be more than a royal figurehead. It wanted certain "liberal" concessions, such as immediate ousting of the Church. After that it would see. For Mexico the idea was the same, with Brother Ferdinand VII not so necessary a part of the picture. Independence under a controlled President would do. The big thing was to get rid of the Church. So far as Iturbide was concerned, he might be used for a time. After him—well, we shall see what we shall see. The old insurgents were unwanted riffraff. The Scottish Rite lodges were for White Collars, uniforms, and the like. The rest might be used but not admitted. After all, there were plenty of them and, when the hour came, numbers would be needed. As to bloodshed? *C'est la guerre!*

The policy of the Scottish Rite in Mexico was then quite simple: elect friends to Congress; see that they covered strategic points in the Councils and in the Army; if all the legislators could not be of the lodges, arrange to "elect" young uninitiated men without much knowledge of their duties. These could be influenced easily by the initiated. One of the deputies, too late, however, told the story. Señor Bocanegra of the Iturbide Congress explained that the Scottish Rite lodges arranged everything in their meetings that was to be proposed to the Congress and what of the proposals were to be agreed upon by the majority. That makes it quite clear why the Rite wanted, from outside its membership, only men with no experience in government.[4]

The thing worked. The lodges had Iturbide surrounded. He could not put his Plan of Iguala into effect. He could not recall the religious who had been expelled nor reopen their closed schools and hospitals. Religious liberty was something to be seen about later. This business of being an Emperor was all well and good, if he did what he was told. But the trouble with Iturbide was that he had to be dragged along when he wanted to walk the other way.

Now this state of affairs did not please the Colossus of the North who desired no Emperor in the New World, not even a little controlled King such as Don Francisco or his brother certainly would have been. Besides, the United States Government looked with no favor on the ideas of the radicals, even those who wore white collars. Less did it want European influence to control the trade of Mexico. So, while the Colossus of the North was not likely to be a friend of the Emperor, no more would it be a friend of the Scottish Rite—that is, in Mexico. With these suspicions in mind, Joel Roberts Poinsett, of Charleston, South Carolina, was sent by the American Government as its agent to Mexico. Though after his recall he served as Secretary of War, he is best known to fame as the Dr. Poinsett who introduced the flowering shrub called Poinsettia into the United States. It still lends a rich tint to our Christmas celebrations. These plants have even a physical resemblance to Dr. Poinsett, as may be surmised from a fact about them to which the *Encyclopedia Americana* calls attention: "They must generally be grouped with other plants to conceal their bare crooked stems." It may also be noticed that when they flower the color shown is red.[5]

Now, Poinsett's political ideas were, of course, those of the then American Government and had nothing of the monarchial about them. He interviewed Iturbide at once and took occasion to inform him on the views about Mexico entertained at Washington. They were practically those of Jefferson. James Monroe had been even more frank than Jefferson in stating them to one Bernardo Guttiérez de Lara, who had fled from Mexico to the United States in 1811. He called on Mr. Monroe, then Secretary of State, and left in a huff after hearing his proposals for extending help to a revolution in Mexico. Mr. Monroe's words are reported by the Spanish Minister to the United States in a letter to the Viceroy of Mexico: "Mr. Monroe told him [de Lara] that the United States would aid the revolution in the Mexican provinces with all their power and that they would sustain it to the point not only of furnishing arms and ammunition but in addition with 27,000 good troops which they would soon have for the purpose. But that Col. Bernardo [de Lara] and the other revolutionary chiefs should arrange for the establishment of a good Constitution to assure the happiness of their countrymen. To this end he laid stress on that of the United States and gave him to understand that the American Government desired that the same Constitution be adopted in Mexico, and that they would then admit these republics into the Union and that with the addition of the other American provinces it would become the most formidable power in the world. Col. Bernardo [de Lara] who had listened serenely to the Secretary of State, until he proposed his plan of joining the Union, now arose from his chair in a fury at hearing such a proposition and left the office of Mr. Monroe much angered at such an insulting insinuation."[6]

Iturbide's reception of the views of Mr. Poinsett was more polite than that of Mr. de Lara. Besides, Poinsett may not have been quite as frank as Monroe. He mentioned a Constitution for Mexico like that of the United States. Iturbide pointed out the difference in the two peoples and the fact, rather plain at the time, that the American plan of government would not serve in Mexico. In that, judging from subsequent events, I think Iturbide may have been wrong. At any rate, things could not very well have come out worse than they did under the series of constitutions Mexico drafted for herself.[7]

Poinsett was a practical man. He remembered the adage about fighting fire with fire. He resolved to fight Freemasonry with Freemasonry. In his pocket, according to R. A. Wilson—*Mexico, its Peasants and its Priests*—he carried a charter for the establishment of the York Rite in Mexico, and proceeded to put it to use. The York Rite established by him would, of course, be republican and proletarian. He got down to real work.[8]

Though rivals—to the death as it proved later—the two Rites had something in common. Both were against the Emperor. Both were also against the Church. But on no other points did they agree. The Scots wanted aristocratic control, they being the aristocrats. The Yorks wanted to weaken Mexico by throwing control into the hands of the irresponsibles. Neither saw the agreement in the two seemingly antagonistic policies. Naturally it was in the word *irresponsibles*. But that word was not spoken by the clever

Poinsett. He became a Mexican patriot for the nonce, as well as the real founder of our strange Mexican policy of constant and inconsistent meddling in the affairs of our southern neighbor. He went so far that there were riots against him in Mexico City. He was venemously hostile to the religion of the Mexican people. He assisted the group of radicals who ousted Iturbide, thereby becoming the real leader of a force containing a few "intellectuals" like himself, but in the main made up of mulattos and mestizos, mixed breeds intent on pillage, unfortunates trained by years of revolutions to know no other way of making a living. Poinsett was all this time only an American Government agent. It was after Iturbide had been shot that he came back as Minister, to be accurate in 1825. He brought his policy of stirring up hate back with him. In 1827 the Grand Lodge of Mexico in collaboration with him adopted a resolution — *"acuerdo"* — suggesting that the York Rite should immediately "redouble its efforts" to make its principles effective in Mexico "in accordance with the terms in which it is conceived," namely: . . . "Improvement in the moral condition of the people by depriving the clergy of its monopoly on public education, by increasing educational facilities and inculcating social duties by means of the foundation of museums, art conservatories and public libraries, by the establishment of educational institutions for classic literature, science and morals."[9]

How much like Calles that sounds! And how often has the recommendation about the clergy been carried out! But where are the schools and the libraries? The books in the valuable library of the University were packed in boxes and then "lost." The old and successful "educational institutions for classic literature, science and morals" that won Humboldt's admiration, have been destroyed and never replaced. In truth they never could be replaced. The loss of the manuscripts alone is irreparable. It is hard to hold to even a mild and pleasant vein of sarcasm in writing the truth about such things. But I have it not in heart to blame overmuch the probably quite respectable professional and business men of the American lodges. What did they know about Mexico beyond what they had been told? What did they know about the Church beyond the errors in a load of inherited prejudices? How could they have known that what had been said to them about both came from a Brother with the mentality of a slaver and the social instincts of a guttersnipe? Can anyone fail to note, in this connection, how straight is the line by which such calumnies have come down even to the present day? The revolutionists who fought for radicalism in Mexico did not fight for any idea of their own. Neither did they fight for Mexico. All they fought for was the idea of Joel Roberts Poinsett. They continued his plan to weaken Mexico and, thus far, it has been succeeding.

Poinsett had two Mexican assistants in organizing his rival Rite: Lorenzo Zavala and José Maria Alpuche. Both of these were of the Scots. The latter, when deputy to the Spanish Cortes, had been initiated in Spain. When he began to take an interest in the York Rite, his old lodge expelled him. But he was a valuable recruit for the Yorks because Senator for Tabasco, and one of the secretly most influential little band of political priests. Zavala had been in Lou-

isiana to make Poinsett's connections there. But Poinsett had
also a powerful adviser in Arizpe, a priest who was Minister
of Justice and Ecclesiastical Affairs. Between them they got
five lodges organized and started thus a rush for membership. The rich Colossus of the North was supposed to favor
the new Rite, so the job was an easy one. Congressmen,
senators, generals, ecclesiastics, governors, merchants, and
every other class of influential men flocked in. Had not the
Yorks the power to save? The proof? There was Colonel
Ayestaran who had been indicted for short accounts. He
joined the lodge and behold, the indictment was turned
around on his enemy. But the enemy, too, was wise, for he
joined also. Both went scot-free. It was good to be in the
same lodge with the Minister of Justice. Excitement increased and so it came about that there were but two political parties in Mexico, the Yorks and the Scots.[10]

The next election was all disorder. A conspiracy to bring
back Spanish rule was unearthed, and the Yorks charged it
to the Scots who thus lost some favor. To offset this it was
decided to expel Spaniards. That gave the Minister of Justice and Ecclesiastical Affairs an opportunity to get at the
California Missions which were manned by Spanish Franciscans. He did and it was the end of Father Serra's great
work. The ruins are still to be seen along the Camino Real.
The expulsion was hard on the Spanish who had fought
for Iturbide and independence, especially since the soldiers
had married and had families in Mexico. The expelled
men, women, and children were dumped on American soil.
The bodies of many who died of yellow fever are in the
cemeteries of New Orleans. Out of the mess of pronounce-

ments, riots, and recriminations, the fact stood out that the Scots and Yorks were about ready to get at each others throats. There was another mocking laugh coming to Old Huitzilopochtli in Hell.

Opportunity came over a presidential "election." General Bravo, Scottish Rite Grand Master, had had assigned to him the second highest number of votes, which made him Vice-President; but the Yorks knew well what "elected" had come to mean in Mexico. The word "assigned" tells what that was—and still is. They protested in the usual way. Bravo decided on a revolution to get rid of Poinsett and all secret societies. It was not hard to see the incalculable harm these were doing in Mexico. The revolution failed. General Bravo was captured. The Scottish Rite went to pieces. Promptly the York Rite split into two camps each with a presidential candidate. When Gómez Pedraza was counted in, the defeated candidate, General Guerrero, called out his braves for another fight, which meant that the split in the camp of the victorious Yorks was made unbridgeable.[11]

Poinsett's friend Zavala had never been out of the picture. Now he came to the front of it by suggesting the sacking of the Spanish commercial establishments. The idea, taken up enthusiastically, put Mexico City for several days in the hands of a mob, which fact presented an excellent opportunity to get at political enemies. Zavala was not a bit squeamish. When he caught his he killed them. He even tried his own hand at assassination by attempting to kill a judge of the Supreme Court. But while his intention was accurate his aim was bad. At any rate, Guerrero became President. Alamán declares that he personally saw a copy of a communication from General Guerrero, as Grand Master of the York Rite, to the United States lodges, announcing the triumph of one Masonic body over another, but Bancroft casts doubt on the statement. At any rate, out of the welter of blood Guerrero rose by the simple process of declaring an election null and void—which was probably quite true. It would be quite as true the other way around. A new law of expulsion urged by the York Rite followed. It drove the remaining Spaniards out of the country, in crowded American vessels. They were robbed of their money and effects, and finally thrust ashore in the United States or Cuba, penniless, to die like the others. It is interesting to note that Bancroft says that Poinsett's York Rite party was, "to a great extent made up of ignorant, ambitious and unscrupulous men to whom the national welfare was of no consequence." It would appear that the Scottish Rite had at least signs of some outward respectability; just enough to make Poinsett want to kill it.[12]

The expulsion of the Spaniards had the effect of hurting the industry and commerce of the country. There seemed nothing left now for the radicals to loot but the Church. But, alas! between the miseries of confiscation and the miseries of forced loans, there did not seem to be much hope for deserving Yorks even in the Church.

Spain, having achieved a period of comparative rest, made an attempt to recover Mexico in 1829. The expedition was defeated by General Santa Anna. That fact is important to this narrative only by its introduction of a new player on the central stage, Santa Anna himself.

General Bustamante had been made Vice-President by a schismatic branch of the York Rite. He joined with the defeated Scots and headed a revolution against Guerrero to restore the Constitution of 1824. Guerrero, leaving Bocanegra in charge of the capital, went out to meet Bustamante. Santa Anna promptly started a revolution to support Guerrero, but his men deserted him and joined Bustamante, who took charge of the country on the first day of the new year, 1830. It looked bad for the Scots, especially after Guerrero had been captured and shot. But Bustamante became a conservative, and the Scottish Rite once more respectable. The York Rite followers now represented not American but all radical interests. They kept on going with guerrilla warfare marked by atrocities; but they had little experience, bad organization, and no funds. The officers could not prevent the atrocities even if they had wished to do so.

Revolution was deep in the Mexican blood by this time. Colonel Landero, commander of the army at Vera Cruz, was found short in his accounts. He tried to get ahead of a trial by starting a new revolution and seized a large sum of money awaiting transmission to Europe as a settlement on a foreign debt. General Santa Anna saw an opportunity in this revolution and proceeded to take it, and the money, out of Landero's hands. Though he had opposed Pedraza for the Presidency, he now recalled him and gave him the job. A new election was called and this time Santa Anna secured the supreme power, with Gómez Farías, the famous York Rite friend of Poinsett, as Vice-President.

The radicals were back. They did what might be called their level best to exterminate the leaders of the other party, so there was another orgy of executions.[13]

This Gómez Farías has been written up as one of Mexico's great men. His full name was Valentín Gómez Farías. In 1831 President Bustamante had sent a certain Inclan to Guadalajara to check a threatened revolution. He used such severity that an effort was made to oust him. The leader of that effort was Gómez Farías. In spite of that fact we find Gómez Farías soon joined with Inclan in a revolution against Bustamante. The atrocities committed under his leadership and encouragement led Santa Anna to raise a revolution against himself for the purpose of ousting the Vice-President, who sought refuge in New Orleans. There he conspired with Lorenzo Zavala to effect the independence of Texas. Santa Anna later had to go into exile himself; but he returned in 1846 to Mexico, at the suggestion of our own President Polk, to promote the plans of the Southern slave holders to extend slave territory. His agent in Mexico for that purpose was Gómez Farías. There can be no doubt about the deal with Polk, for Farías wrote to Dr. Mora, the historian, from the United States, explaining the plan in full. Gómez Farías certainly deserves a place in Mexican history, for he lost a full half of his country. He also has the distinction of having been the cause of the first open and really vigorous attack against the Church. He placed the appointment of parish priests in the hands of civil authorities, did away with the tithes, freed monks from their vows—which freedom was not accepted—barred the clergy from participation in education, attempted to seize Church property and funds—which, of course, meant all the institutions of charity and education—closed the University of Mexico which soon had a low-down liquor saloon located in the chapel. Mora adopted the anticlerical ideas of Farías and handed them on to Juárez and Lerdo, to whom, in large measure, the famous radical Laws of Reform are due. In 1831, during the rule of Bustamante, the State insisted on the right to appoint bishops and canons. It was ordered that preference in such appointments must be given to revolutionist clergymen; which provision shows the hand of the lax and ambitious clerical gentlemen already mentioned. There need be no comment as to the kind of bishops and canons they would have made. The Church, of course, protested.

By this time education was in a bad way, and the Government had no money left, after paying off the graft and war expense, to do anything about it. All the clergy could do was to urge peace and to counsel the faithful to respect the rights and properties of others. The revolutionists did not like it, and immediately started a cry against "the unwarranted interference in politics by the clergy." Efforts to oppose attacks on educational and charitable activities and property made these attacks all the stronger. Whatever protests came from the clergy were turned into the charge of meddling in politics. Some of the bishops were sent into exile. This exodus of bishops forecast those under Juárez, still later under Carranza, and in our own day, under Calles.

All this was too much for Santa Anna. When he came back to power he recalled the exiled bishops and priests, reopened the University, and tried to bring about a general restoration of business. The Congress elected in 1836 approved. But the radicals were not satisfied. Down went the York Rite. American Masons supporting it did not know what to think. They were still mystified in 1919 when an investigation of Masonry in Mexico was ordered, and a report was made to the Grand Lodge in Alabama which concluded: "Owing to the unsettled condition in Mexico both from the Masonic and political point of view, not to speak of any other reasons, we do not recommend recognition of any of the Mexican bodies claiming to be Masonic." To the credit of the Masonic bodies in America it must be said that few of their Grand Lodges had at any time recognized the Mexican lodges. With the passing of Poinsett, Mexican Masonry was thrown back on its own counsels and The Hidden Hand rested for a time.[14]

For how long a time? So far as the Mexican lodges were concerned only while there was nothing left to steal and while Díaz was their real head. After Díaz they began again, and are now active. An American, employed by the Mexican Government as a guide for tourists in Mexico City, said to a visitor — he did not know that he was talking to an American priest: "The Masons are in the saddle in Mexico. They hate the Church, and will drive her out as they have done in other countries." But there is a schism in the Mexican lodges headed by Cárdenas. For Mexico there is no peace, even in the dark.

XII

THE GREAT STEAL

NATIONS ARE FOND of using the heraldic lion for an emblem, since the lion is called the king of beasts and looks every inch of it. Besides being brave, both in attack and defense, when in a satisfied mood he is the picture of watchful benevolence. No wonder he has imposed himself upon heraldry. Taking thought of the Catholic Church there are those who would assign to her the emblem of the lion, and that in all justice. But for herself the nearest the Church comes to accepting any heraldic emblem, is by tolerating the use of a pelican feeding her young with her own blood as a symbolic ornament in religious decoration. The symbolism is most exact when it relates to the glory and martyrdom of the Church in Mexico.

With revolution following revolution, presidents swept out and sweeping in, constitutions torn up and new ones adopted, wholesale executions, bandits enlisting and going back to their lairs, the whole history of Mexico between 1810 and 1876, when Díaz became President, is a confusion of flashes. In the very center of it all, bewildered, bedeviled, and betrayed, was the Church, trying, with only the consciousness of her mission and the love of a helpless majority, to save civilization for the unfortunate country.

All these institutions by which the culture of a nation is made and preserved, because by them protected, were the work of the Church. Whatever education the leaders of the revolutions in Mexico possessed she had given to them. Without her labor, devotion, and influence, they would still have been in savagery, exploited by gold-seekers backed by foreign men-at-arms. That their forefathers had been spared, taught, and protected, was because she had caused it to be so. The University, the colleges, the libraries, the arts and architecture, the hospitals and asylums, all the works of charity and benevolence, all the advances of civilization, were of her making and still under her direction. She had saved even the great burden of their cost to the taxpayers, always depending, first on the charity of the Kings and then on that of those who could afford to help and give of their own free will. All the wonderful signs of progress that had so charmed visitors from other lands were of her making or of her inspiring. For the sake of the people she had lost much of her liberty and tolerated many unjust impositions, given sons to martyrdom and daughters to danger. If ever an institution on earth merited the gratitude of a people it was the Catholic Church in Mexico.

What the Church saw as she stood looking out over the scene of the bloody years' making was the threatened ruin of the work of three centuries. The nation's treasury was bankrupt. Business and industry were all but wrecked. A peaceful people were being made over into snarling and scratching tigers. Robbery and murder had become habit. The government was on horseback and rested only to destroy. The people were being used like mongrel dogs in the hands of the vivisectionist — human beings for Marxian experimentation.

What folly held the minds of men who, through their own history, could follow the story of their nation's progress from savagery upward is hard to understand. What madness seems often to possess the mind of the modern world is likewise simply inexplicable. It is like unto that of a man who, having gained more than half his objective, and with the other half in sight, allows those who had learned nothing from his example to persuade him to destroy what he had won and begin all over again. In the whole foolish world Mexico was and still is the outstanding example of such folly, and America the outstanding example of blind sympathy for it. What the Mexican revolutionists wanted was what would destroy the gains of three centuries at a blow. So began the Great Steal.

To no man more than to Gómez Farías, the friend of Poinsett, is the discredit due for the actual beginning of a process that could have no other result than to throw the Mexican Indian back into barbarism and beggar the rest of the population. In 1823 a loan was made in England for $16,000,000. The bonds were sold at 50 per cent discount, and all the Mexican Government received from them, after expenses and commissions had been deducted, was $5,698,-300. A few months later another loan for a like amount was floated. It netted $6,094,590, which, however, was paid partly in military equipment. In 1837 the principal and interest on these two loans amounted to $46,239,720. The financial state of the Mexican treasury may be judged by these examples.[1]

When Iturbide was overthrown the government took the Poinsett advice in part, and adopted the American system of a union of states by creating nineteen separate legislative bodies. Each of these had to be financed. At once the State of Jalisco adopted a constitution which declared the Catholic the official religion of the Commonwealth, but immediately proceeded to declare that "the State shall fix and pay all expenses necessary for the cult." Though the clergy have been charged over and over again with a desire for the union of Church and State, it is to be noted that they protested against this law. Other States followed the Jalisco example: Tamaulipas attempted to regulate parish fees; Nuevo León to forbid donations; Durango to seize the incomes from trust funds; Jalisco to interfere in Church finances and lay hands on endowments; Vera Cruz to take the properties of religious orders; Coahuila and Texas to forbid endowments for charitable purposes, seize those already established, interfere in the tithing, and forbid the bishops to issue pastoral letters; San Luis Potosí forbidding "visita de testamentos";[2] Puebla closing the College of San Pablo; and Zacatecas establishing a bank with trust funds to be taken from the Church. All these, and many more, joined clergy and politicians in a conflict that was to become more and more bitter as the former were determined to defend what the latter were as determined to steal. The efforts of the Church to appeal to the federal powers, in these circumstances served but to infuriate the local authorities and inspire them to make charges against the clergy of setting an example of disobedience to the laws. That trick still works.

Under Gómez Farías followed a series of federal decrees calculated to bring about a practical union with the State and thus enslave the Church. By them the pastors of parishes were made virtual State officials; members of religious orders were declared free from their vows; the clergy were barred from all participation in educational work; and steps were taken to seize all properties and funds of the Church. This last could have but one result for the educational and beneficent institutions of the nation, since it meant their abandonment. It was then that the University was closed, and part of it turned into a grog shop. These were the decrees that finished the California Missions.[3]

A roar of public protest met the decrees. Gómez Farías and his crew had to hide themselves from popular fury, as Santa Anna came back to power, recalled the bishops who had been exiled, reopened the University and nullified, but without repealing, the Farías decrees. Then the whole question was reopened, even as to the Patronage. If the Church could not be robbed in one way another might be tried. Only the Texas revolt saved Santa Anna. He raised an army to fight it, won a worthless victory at the Alamo, and was defeated two months later at San Jacinto. What a mercy for Mexico it would have been had Sam Houston dealt with Santa Anna as Santa Anna would have dealt with him! The Texas revolt brought out another forced loan. Santa Anna fell.

In 1837 General Bustamante, now a conservative, took the presidential chair. Besides the financial mess, he had to face a threat of invasion by the French, seeking payment for alleged damages suffered by French citizens in the many revolutions. The radicals seized this opportunity for a new revolution led by Gómez Farías. On July 15, 1840, they seized the President in his office. He escaped and subdued the revolt, but with the help of Santa Anna. The year following, Bustamante paid for the help by being driven out. Santa Anna came back to power. But he was reduced now to small pilfering, as for example taking silver plate that netted only $7,000 from the Cathedral of Puebla.

The Great Steal was on again. The Dominicans and Augustinians of Puebla were mulcted for $25,000; the Archbishop of Mexico was forced to accept drafts for $170,000; and another forced loan was ordered for $2,500,000. The personal property of those not paying was seized to satisfy the demand. The California Pious Fund was transferred to the management of the government and then confiscated. All these exactions were less on the Church than on the only educational and beneficent institutions Mexico had.[4]

A revolt followed, the radicals taking advantage of the anger of the people aroused by the confiscations. Herrera was made President. Again a foreign war intervened. It was with the United States. How well Mexico was prepared for it may be judged by the report of Slidell, the American agent, to President Polk: "The country, torn by conflicting factions, is in a state of perfect anarchy; its finances in a condition utterly desperate. I do not see how any means can be found to carry on the government. The annual expense of the army alone exceeds twenty-one million dollars, while the net revenue is not more than ten or twelve. While there is a prospect of war with the United States, no capitalist will loan money, at any rate, however onerous. Every branch of the revenue is already pledged in advance. The troops must be paid or they will revolt." It was then that Polk squandered $2,000,000 on Santa Anna who was in Cuban exile, ordering American warships to permit him to land at Vera Cruz. When the actual President, Paredes, left to fight the Americans, Santa Anna got back to power by the simple expedient of a barrack revolution in the capital. Of course Gómez Farías was in it. Santa Anna had himself again "elected" President. The Church authorities were ordered to endorse notes for $2,000,000, and sell them. Santa Anna proposed raising $25,000,000 by pledging Church property. It did not work. But Gómez Farías cut it to $15,000,000 to be raised by selling the property at auction. This was the confiscation that had always been the radical plan. There was a storm. State governments protested. How the Church that had no taxing power could raise money when the government had failed was not explained. But the money was secondary. It was the radical plan that came first. Everyone knows how the war resulted, but the victors did not care to discuss what history tells them was little to their credit.[5]

American occupation forced Mexicans to forget their own differences and divide over the question of annexation. Gómez Farías, so eager to help Texas out of Mexico, seeing now that annexation would give a death blow to radicalism, wanted to continue a guerrilla warfare on the Americans. Against this was the growing sentiment for annexation. President Polk knew it, but only after he had indicated the territorial settlement he was willing to accept. When he learned the truth he wanted to temporize with annexation in mind. Peace and security were the only temptations to exhausted Mexicans. The Americans got out as soon as the settlement was made, and none too soon. Polk wanted Mexico. The excitement of military success had incited a general demand in the United States for annexation. In response to this he recalled Trist, but the latter ignored him and signed the treaty, to the embarrassment of Polk.[6]

Arista became President in 1850. He also tried to float a loan with the Church properties as security. It failed. The security by this time had become practically valueless because of all that stood against it. Three years more and Santa Anna the Irrepressible was back again. He was now a conservative and opposed to the Church property loans. He declared himself Perpetual Dictator with the title of Most Serene Highness. Gadsden, the American Minister, did his bit in encouraging the radicals to reform and fight. It was an easy job, for the people wanted to see the last of Santa Anna, who had been playing for his own benefit during a space of thirty years, an unstable and unreliable failure and the very king of betrayers. Since he, with Gómez Farías, did most to pave the way for the finish of the Great Steal, it will not be out of place to throw a quick flash of farewell over his dubious exploits.[7]

An officer in the royalist forces, Santa Anna joined Iturbide to effect independence. After supporting Iturbide as Emperor he betrayed him by joining the radicals. He then revolted unsuccessfully against Victoria whom he had aided in destroying Iturbide. With the election of Gómez Pedraza to succeed Victoria, he aided Zavala in his revolt to overthrow Pedraza and place Guerrero in power with

Bustamante as Vice-President. After the revolt which disposed of Guerrero and made Bustamante President, Santa Anna revolted against the latter and recalled Pedraza from exile to act as President while he arranged for his own "election." Being "elected," with Gómez Farías as Vice-President, he left the latter in power to try his hand at radical lawmaking while he retired to his estate of Manga de Clavo. After Gómez Farías had run amuck for a year and aroused universal indignation, Santa Anna ousted him. This earned him a popularity that might have been profitable had he not thrown it away in the Texas debacle. Bustamante then became President again, and, in spite of his previous overthrow at the hands of Santa Anna, left the latter in charge of affairs for a short time. Shortly after that Santa Anna helped to subdue the attempt by Gómez Farías and others to oust Bustamante. Then he turned on Bustamante and drove him out. Again he retired to his estate, leaving General Bravo in charge. Being "elected" President again, he once more retired to his estate leaving Canalizo in charge. A revolt ousted Canalizo and compelled Santa Anna to leave the country. He returned, with the aid of Mr. Polk, to oust Paredes who had ousted Herrera who had ousted Santa Anna. Having lost the war against the United States he resigned and retired to Jamaica whence he was recalled in 1853 to take a last fling at bedeviling his unfortunate countrymen, after which effort to be driven in 1855 permanently from the stage of Mexico's militant politics.

With Santa Anna out of his place in the sun, the more advanced radicals seized the capital. Their ostensible military leader was a bandit named Juan Alvarez, but in truth the intellectual leader was Benito Juárez, a new actor in the tragedy. It was he who chose the illiterate mulatto bandit, known for his savagery, as military commander. Once in power and faced with an urgent need for money, in spite of violent protests from all parts of the nation, it was decided to seize the educational and beneficent institutions of the country already loaded with mortgages for revolutionary loans. Alvarez was the man for that job. The son of a negress, he had learned the trade of blood and loot in the revolt of Hidalgo. After independence he found a mountainous stronghold suited to his purposes and from there became a bandit or revolutionist according to the pay. His forces there were a band of diseased Indians. Every government had been obliged to buy him off, his regular stipends running from $10,000 to $25,000 a month. He never rebelled unless the money failed to come; from radicals or conservatives, Yorks or Scots, made no difference to him. One thing to Santa Anna's credit was that he refused to deal with him. Alvarez had a long list of murders to account for, but no one dared call him to that account. At Teloloapan he murdered all the men and distributed the women among his troops. This is mentioned only as a sample. One other will do: a young woman who refused his personal advances was stripped naked and tied to a tree. Alvarez entertained himself lashing her at odd intervals. This was the monster Benito Juárez made President of Mexico when Santa Anna was ousted in 1855. Over the unprintable atrocities his followers committed in the capital on arrival, decency demands that we draw a veil.

Alvarez appointed Juárez Minister of Justice and Ecclesiastical Affairs. The new Minister was an educated — by the Church of course — Zapotec Indian, fullblood, who had his mind made up to annihilate all opposition, take and hold power on any terms — even treason. He knew that Alvarez was impossible and preferred his mountain lair to the still civilized-appearing capital. So it turned out. Alvarez went away leaving Comonfort in his place. There was a revolt at Puebla. Comonfort crushed it. Because the Bishop and the foreign consuls advised the city to capitulate to save bloodshed — though they actually did save bloodshed — the clergy were accused and an excuse thus found to proceed against them. Comonfort ordered all the Church property in the diocese, which comprised the States of Puebla, Vera Cruz, and Tlaxcala, to be seized and sold as indemnity to the government for the expense of putting down the revolt. To criticize this decree meant terms in prison of from two to five years.

On July 25, 1856, Comonfort ordered the property belonging to all civil and religious corporations confiscated. This meant the end of foundations, whether owned by the Church or not. Many of these had been established and endowed during the colonial regime. A new constitution was made and a decree drawn up directing all public officials and employees to take oath to obey it. Refusals came in volleys. The bishops at once pointed out articles to which they could not in conscience subscribe since they made the Church a creature of the State. The radicals still wanted the union in some "practical" form. The bishops would not secede from Rome, and Rome would not agree to give the "politicos" what they wanted. The radicals were still a small minority. Their only hope to hold power was to maintain it by military usurpation. They were determined this time to accomplish that end. Troops were assembled in the capital and battles took place in the streets. The government forces melted away and, as Comonfort fled, Juárez claimed his office. Zuloaga took it from him by force. Juárez fled to Guanajuato and issued a manifesto. By bribery he escaped after defeat and reached the west coast where he took ship for Panama. He crossed the Isthmus and went, via Habana, to New Orleans. The radicals still held Vera Cruz. Juárez and his friends slipped in there.

For two years Juárez fought out of Vera Cruz. Zuloaga refused to make concessions of territory to defeat him by gaining American recognition. But Juárez was willing, and so the American Government supported him. Armed intervention was the prize. Juárez signed up, but the American Senate refused agreement to the Treaty made by McLane and Ocampo, a refusal that stands to the Senate's credit by declining to make the United States a receiver of stolen goods. But Juárez received aid from the American President. All he had in Mexico was Vera Cruz. Miramón was ready to attack it from the sea. By executive order his two ships were seized by the American Navy and handed over to Juárez. That practically ended the fight. It was

an American victory for what American principles repudiated. It was also our second war, but unacknowledged,
with Mexico.[8]

The last obstacle to the Great Steal was now removed.
The Government of the United States had so decreed.
Higher education ceased. Hospitals were closed and the
sick-poor left without care. Orphans and aged were driven
into the streets to find shelter where they could. As a sample
of the result, we find fifty-two houses in the City of
Mexico, belonging to various institutions, and assessed for
purposes of confiscation at $525,528, sold for $1,832.40 in
cash plus government-due bills that cost $40,077.90. That
deal was the foundation of a millionaire family fortune.
And all the government got out of "the fabulous wealth
of the Church," which meant in reality charity foundations,
the colleges, hospitals, etc., of Mexico, was a similar percentage of cash on a total property valuation of $62,365,-
516.41. That was the sum and substance of it up to 1866.
How much was unaccounted for in the provinces is a
matter of conjecture. The University of Chicago alone
could produce more than double that amount in cash or
bonds, and, if our government decided to seize the endowment of Columbia University, there would be sad
disappointment if the invested endowment, not the actual
buildings, did not bring three times the whole loot of
the Church in Mexico.[9]

Nor was all this "Church property," as already pointed
out. It was that of educational and charitable foundations
chartered by the State. The act of Juárez duplicated here

would mean the seizure, not only of the property of all the churches, but of the endowments of the Carnegie, Rockefeller, and other foundations.

Was it any wonder that the Mexican people turned hopeful eyes to Europe? That they welcomed Maximilian? Or, for that matter, since the noisiest thing on earth is a radical minority, that Maximilian betrayed their hopes? But before Maximilian came, as he did in 1864, the Great Steal had been consummated.

What became of the property? That which could not be sold for cash was left empty or used for State purposes. Maximilian found the great Hospicio de Pobres (asylum for the poor) covering more than eleven acres — it included an orphanage with an industrial school and a maternity hospital — in a state of abandoned ruin, in whose warrens some three hundred unfortunates found scant shelter at night, begging their sustenance in the streets by day. The great Hospital Real became a tenement and its printshop was sold; its chapel given to an American missionary. The Terceros hospital became a hotel. The college for girls, founded by Gante in the sixteenth century, became the German Club. The great Girls' College of Belem became the unsavory city prison housing some fifteen hundred malefactors. A boys' college near by became a barrack. Hundreds of similar institutions all over the country met a similar fate when not abandoned altogether to ruin, as many were.[10]

Were these institutions not replaced? Foolish question! How could they be replaced with the money received for them squandered and the nation bankrupt?

One wise judgment is recorded for Poinsett. It tells us a great deal and helps us to an understanding. For that little at least the student of history may thank him. He recognized the presence in the Mexican population of the element let loose by Hidalgo and encouraged to grow strong by the revolutions that followed; even by those he made. "Under strong governments," he wrote, "they turn to crime; under weak governments to revolution."[11] Porfirio Díaz must have let that sink into his soul. When he assumed power in 1876, after defeating Lerdo, the successor of Juárez, he quickly gave Mexico a strong government — too strong in fact to suit the radicals.

Americans committed an egregious blunder in assuming that the Great Steal did not affect us. It did. Our part in the Great Steal was — and still is — the support given to a succession of thieves. They saw a strategic business position in that alliance. All wrong! It is the people who do the buying, especially the women. That error has fostered a growing hate for a century. Through Mexico our whole Latin-American trade has been affected. We may rest assured that Latin-Americans, other things being equal, will avoid contacts with those they know to be hostile to, and even contemptuous of, that which they hold most sacred. Europe might well congratulate itself that the Atlantic keeps it out of Mexican politics, but does not keep it out of markets controlled as to buying power by the mass of the people and not their tyrants.

XIII

SEMICOLON

MR. CARLETON BEALS, in a preface to a translation of the memoirs of José Luis Blasio, secretary of the Emperor Maximilian, writes a significant sentence about the latter: "His thought is shot through with borrowed French revolutionary sophistry." And another: "His brief rule in Mexico stands devastatingly condemned by his own youthful yardstick of idealism." At once the question springs up in the mind of the puzzled student of Mexican history: why was a ruler selected for Mexico who carried in his own mental luggage the bullet to slay him? Maximilian firmly believed that Mexico could be governed only by a monarch. Surely he was not fool enough to think that the crown made a monarch. Yet the "borrowed French revolutionary sophistry" kept showing itself during all the three and a half years he spent as Emperor of Mexico. Unless furnishing palaces, directing court etiquette and functions, and making Haroun al Raschid visits to the bakeries — and the slums — was governing, Maximilian did little of it. He was brought in as a savior to a nation that badly needed saving. He was not able to avoid the mistakes that made it impossible for him to save himself. What he did for Mexico was to pave the way for a monarch without a crown, but a real monarch, Porfirio Díaz.[1]

Maximilian, Emperor of Mexico, 1864-1867.

Porfirio Díaz, "Don Porfirio."

What gave rise to the highest hope in Mexico after it had settled down to be ruled by Don Porfirio, as Díaz was called, was the popular conviction, accepted without close examination also by Americans, that the Mexican era of revolutions had ended with a full-stop. Everyone now knows that the wrong mark of punctuation was used. It should have been a semicolon — with a long dash after it, a dash of 35 years. The era of revolutions did stop, but the element that made them stayed around under cover, while a goodly part of the dream of Maximilian became the actuality of Díaz.[2] Not that Don Porfirio was troubled with any "yardstick of idealism" after he became convinced that the presidential chair under him was not likely to break and let him down. He may have had that when he fought with Juárez against Zuloaga. A lot of youthful idealism must have been lost when he fought Lerdo, and what "French revolutionary sophistry" he may have had, must have turned quickly into a determination to look after himself in the future.

Maximilian had done this for Díaz: taught Mexicans how peaceful and restful it was to be ruled. In addition the Emperor had taught them, at least those living within the influence of the capital, to become accustomed to the show of ruling. His Serene Highness Santa Anna had tried to do that and failed. A little one-legged Highness made a poor show of majesty. But the handsome Austrian giant with the long blond beard, the dignified kindliness, and the well-decorated front, could carry it off magnificently, and did. All Díaz lacked was the crown and the ermine. He took to the rest, including the receptions, the court etiquette, and the decorations. But behind them was a fixed determination to stand no nonsense. He is the long dash of 35 years after the Maximilian semicolon.

A contrast helps and a contrast between Maximilian and Díaz is there. The Juárez-Lerdo interval was too short, nine years, to let it be forgotten. Maximilian gave the government form with little force. Díaz gave it force with little form. Maximilian made of himself a sort of living Field of the Cloth of Gold for two bitter enemies of each other, conservative and radical, who could not by any possibility be friends; Díaz made of himself a wall to keep them comfortably divided. Maximilian wanted to be thought religious and concealed his illicit amours; Díaz did not want to be thought religious and had no illicit amours to conceal. Maximilian, as a Catholic, was a member of a forbidden secret society, yet wanted his Mass and Sacraments; Díaz was the whole secret society himself — or thought he was — and would wait for Mass and the Sacraments till he felt urgent need of them. Maximilian kept his place with the aid of foreign soldiers; Díaz kept his by making the people afraid that foreign soldiers might come. Maximilian felt that he could hurt friends to win enemies; Díaz had only one friend, Don Porfirio. Maximilian forgot many promises; Díaz did not make enough promises to put a strain on his memory. Maximilian at the end was shot like a gentleman; Díaz at the end did not think that a gentleman should let himself be shot. The contrast fades into the grim reality that both failed.

It did not seem for a long time that Díaz could fail. Consider the method he took to weaken radicals, now called

Liberals and in dress suits at his receptions. There never were more than a small minority of them, but their strength lay in the horde of bandits they could call in for pay.

The Díaz organization of rural police—the famous *rurales* —had taken nearly all of that bandit-class that could be relied upon as intelligent followers out of the Liberal influence. Many of these were ranchmen reduced to poverty by revolutionary raids, or by loss through bad management of their farms. Others were mere revolutionists with nowhere to go in peace and nothing to do. These latter had no taste for honest labor, but experience had taught them how to give a good account of themselves in a fight. The Díaz policy of making disciplined police out of such potential dangers was a hard blow to the Liberals, and a most discouraging one. No soldiers, no generals! Then there was so little to loot. The "intellectuals" could get over that, but what could they promise their followers? Obviously the Church had already been looted. The actual buildings for purposes of worship had to be left open, though nominally government property; but as government property they could not be taxed. Besides, to close them, in the villages and rural districts especially, would be an empty gesture. The people had only to knock the seals off the doors and take possession, which was exactly what they would do. To destroy them would make hundreds of small counter-revolutions which always invite the danger of a general one. There could be no more Indians enlisted on the pretext of saving their religion, since they were not openly being deprived of it. Díaz had not taken the Comonfort-Juárez-Lerdo persecuting laws off the statute books. He had the Liberals there.

But he was ignoring them whenever he could, only now and then raiding a Catholic school already warned in advance to have the building clear of evidence when the police arrived. He had the Church there. She had settled down, and was doing her work in poverty, even rebuilding. Díaz could not replace all the religious with state schools. The condition of the national finances forbade that, so only here and there was such an effort made. The Church was trying hard to take up the educational slack—it was mostly slack—and succeeding fairly well. The people were too well satisfied to be deceived, sick of bloodshed that not only got them nowhere but ruined them. It was not long after Don Porfirio had made his policy understood that the people simply accepted it as best and refused to budge. Hard times indeed for the disturbers.

Still they had made progress. Starting in Spain they had come near to ruining their country. Banishing business and industrial forces across the Atlantic they had left Mexico a desolate waste. They had stripped the Church of all temporal goods, driven her out of official education, and stopped the charities that had brought her close to the hearts of the people. Officially the Church did not exist. Officially there was no God. That was something to the radical mind well worth seas of bloodshed to secure. True, the people were still Catholic. But out in the wilds there were fewer priests, and the Indians would surely sink back into barbarism so that they could be handled again. Had they not already done that very thing in both Californias? And the old mission schools were no more. How much easier to deceive unlettered Indians than de Gante's and

Zumárraga's classical scholars, even than the reading and writing Indians of Serra.

Don Porfirio was too much for the radicals. He had modern equipment for defense, could and did out-general them in policy, had made a happy marriage by which he suited the conservatives as well as himself. He had built up the finances, could borrow money at a low rate of interest, and was now actually driving, with Mexican labor, railroads toward the American border. Down over them would come Yankee business, investments, and industrial leaders to replace the expelled Spaniards. The radicals knew that Don Porfirio was no intellectual. They had thought him an illiterate. He was anything but an illiterate.[3] Carmelita, as the people always called his aristocratic and beautiful wife, had been seeing about that. Her husband read nothing except State papers, but he was a good and silent listener. He somehow absorbed a lot of knowledge, put his surroundings and visitors unconsciously under contribution to his quietly won little stock of learning, welcomed scholarly bishops and let them talk, and, above all, just watched his world and everything that had even a remote point of contact with it. But whatever he got from Carmelita's influence over him, and his associations, was as nothing compared to his knowledge of the value of authority, how to use and enforce it, the necessity of obedience, and his natural gift of common sense. In nothing was Don Porfirio an enthusiast. He himself could issue no thunderous and flaming manifestos such as Santa Anna and Juárez had done. They were, however, all right in their day, but the day was over. The Díaz job was to make jobs. Hungry Mexicans were not the kind who made revolutions, but they certainly were the kind who joined them. The radicals had not much to hope for while Don Porfirio held the executive power in his hands. He was determined thus to hold it as long as he could. He held it until it fell out of those hands when they were trembling with age.

That Díaz gave Mexico peace and prosperity no one can doubt. Outwardly all was well. The surface signs were all excellent. It had not taken the Spaniards long to make Mexico a show place for the world. The thirty-five years of Díaz could have settled Mexico down to independence. It looked as if they had, but they had not. Lauded as one of the greatest of nation builders, Díaz was nothing of the kind. He found a toy balloon that many grown children had blown into, only to have it snatched away from them by other grown children while it deflated in a scream. He had it all to himself. No one dared to try to snatch it away. He blew it up. There was no scream. It exploded.

This was wrong: the two tasks most vital and fundamental to the continued existence of the nation, Díaz did not even try to do. One was the permanent and just settlement of the land question, created by the laws of Juárez, which always had been camouflage for the revolutions; and the other was the Church question which had always been hidden beneath the camouflage. Daniel Webster was not wrong when he said: "When tillage begins, other arts follow"; nor yet when he did the odd feat of finishing an utterance of 1840 by one of 1820: "Whatever makes men good Christians makes them good citizens." Culture finally rests on morality, but there are beautiful carvings on the way down to the foundation. Díaz did not see, nor have other Mexican politicians seen, nor have many writers on Mexican problems noted, that these two tasks are intimately connected. Mexico cannot rise to nationhood until they are taken up in all sincerity and settled without blare of trumpets or flash of steel. The doing of them calls for peace, not war.

One of the demands of the revolution which the United States won for Don Francisco Madero, Jr., was "land for the people." The dishonesty of the demand as made by the Madero family was well noted by Edward I. Bell writing of an interview between Don Francisco, Senior, and José Ives Limantour, Finance Minister to Díaz, on March 16, 1911: "It was with difficulty that Limantour restrained a smile at the thought of Francisco Madero, Senior, one of Mexico's great land owners, advocating a plan which contemplated dismemberment of estates at government condemnation rates."[4] A testimony to Limantour's frigid diplomacy was in the fact that he did not laugh outright. Not one of the suggestions made by Mexican revolutionists for a division of land has been honest. Obregón advocated it; but he had more of it than any other man in Sonora, and, through his monopoly of the *garbanzos* output, had a hold on much more. Calles is the great "agrarian," great because he shouts loudest for division; but he grabbed all he could for himself. The truth is that none of the schemes put forth for the division of Mexico's land have been based on any idea of justice. Each one has been the design of either a hypocrite, a thief, or a man ignorant of the facts of the situation. In justice to individuals the land cannot be stolen even that good may follow. In justice to the nation the peasant must have his land. Díaz could have solved the problem. At the end he said he would. Perhaps a key to the solution could have been had either in the United States or Canada. Both countries had used it, though neither had had a better opportunity to do so than Mexico.

There is no dearth of land for the people of Mexico, even now; and it is good land, better land than can be found anywhere in the North. The one trouble about settling the land question in Mexico as we settled it here, or as Canada settled it—both acting in advance of trouble—is that in Mexico the vacant lands are not reached by railroads, and the Mexican peon is not a pioneer. He loves company. But Díaz had power and credit. He could have had a plan worked out to overcome the peon's dislike for solitude by providing for settlers on vacant land the conditions these settlers had left. The key was the railroad. A practical rail-road magnate, according to the story told by Mr. Bell, had offered that key. That is what Bell reported Edward H. Harriman saying to Mr. Limantour in the latter's house in Mexico City: "Under existing conditions, none of the railways could be operated with efficiency or made to yield the profit which modern methods could extract. Until these methods should be applied the development of Mexico's resources must be greatly retarded. Mexico with its millions of acres of untilled land was importing wheat and cotton; its manufacturers of woolen and cotton fabrics were hampered by excessive costs of raw material. Flour was an untasted luxury for nine-tenths of the population. Native sugar was supplied in great cones unrefined. Many rich mines were remote from transportation. Stock raising, except in the northern states, was haphazard and unremunerative; and within fifty miles of Mexico City native farmers were plowing with a crooked stick. The remedy lay with the railways."[5]

The United States never had a land problem because railroads were driven out into the vast territories where there was land in plenty. As it was taken up more railroads were built or new branches were opened. Canada did the same within the memory of men not yet old. The Spaniards could not have done it, save at the end when Spain was too poor and weak to carry out any policy of importance. Had Spain held out for a few years, there can be no question but that her colony of excellent business leaders in Mexico would have done it. The revolutionists never wanted railroads. They were much too afraid of peace and the Colossus. Neither the United States nor Canada were worrying over Rousseau's social and political theories. Europe's folly was Europe's own. They were not trying to kill the goose that laid the golden egg for them; but only wanted the goose to be diligent about production. When these two northern countries started with nothing, and the parent was not only the provider but the schoolmaster for the family, Mexico, as we have seen, had a system of education that went as far as the Spanish pioneers themselves had gone. Mexico then had the equipment for turning out her own engineers, scientific experts ready for the coming of the engine. She preferred to smash her own chances to smithereens by smashing her schools. It was not yet too late when Díaz came; but he did nothing more than build his railroad lines to the border through a desert, and consolidate them to leave fruitful pickings for his dishonest successors. Was there any earthly reason, with the unlimited credit he had built up, and the untold richness of Mexico's land and mineral wealth, that he could not have done what his northern neighbors had done and were doing?

The Church question is the ignored question so far as American writers on Mexico are concerned. It was and is too big for them, too dangerous, too—let it come out—dark for prejudiced minds to think on. Their general conviction, unjustified by study, is that Mexico was right in trying to get rid of the Church. The fairest American editorial comment thus far offered is the ambiguous and unintellectual statement that "perhaps there has been fault on both sides." Even at this late date let us be fair. Christian civilization is not a dream. We are its product. And it was and still is fundamentally the gift of the Catholic Church to the race of man. That is no theory. It is a tangible and living historical fact that no educated man or woman can in honesty deny or ignore.

There was no fundamental difference between the Church in Mexico and the Church in Spain, yet in Spain she was the steel band of unity that kept the Moslem from overrunning Europe; and in Spain the Church was not at her best, since the State had so much power to control her administration. But the band of steel held nevertheless. Lecky could write: "Catholicism laid the foundations of modern civilization," and Canon Farrar adds in his Hulsean Lectures of 1870: "From the fifth to the thirteenth century the Church was engaged in elaborating the most splendid organization the world has ever seen. Starting with the separation of the spiritual from the temporal power, and the mutual independence of each in its own sphere, Catholicism worked hand in hand with feudalism for the amelioration of mankind. Under the influence of feudalism, slavery became serfdom, and aggressive was modified into defensive war. Under the influence of Catholicism the monasteries preserved learning, and maintained the sense of the unity of Christendom. Under the combined influence of both grew up the lovely ideal of chivalry, moulding generous instincts into gallant institutions, making the body vigorous and the soul pure, and wedding the Christian virtues of humility and tenderness into the natural grace of courtesy and strength. During this period the Church was the one mighty witness for light in an age of darkness, for order in an age of lawlessness, for personal holiness in an epoch of licentious rage. Amid the despotism of kings, and the turbulence of aristocracies, it was an inestimable blessing that there should be a power which by the unarmed majesty of goodness made the haughtiest and the boldest respect the interests of justice and tremble at the temperance, righteousness and judgment to come."[6]

Nevertheless, in all justice to Díaz it must be admitted that the Church question was not at that time an easy one to settle; no easier than an attempt on the part of a policeman to convince a man who had been robbed by a bandit that he ought to let the poor fellow off with a goodly part of what he had stolen. Carlton Beals compares Maximilian to "a lamb among wolves" and gives as an example of one wolf "the narrow bigotry and greed of Archbishop Labastida and other Mexican prelates." Perhaps it would have been better had Labastida simply offered to let the bandit go with all his stealings. But, after all, the whole incident was fresh in memory, and even Mexican bishops are human. Neither was it money and property that was uppermost in these episcopal minds. It was something Mr. Beals may not be able to grasp. The spiritual interests of the people were at stake. Maximilian may have been "an enlightened Catholic," as Mr. Beals thinks, but the bishops had the strange idea that such a Catholic would know enough about laws to keep those of Church discipline and enough about the Ten Commandments to avoid the sin of adultery. After Maximilian, who could blame the bishops if they hesitated to settle with Díaz on the basis of considering him "an enlightened Catholic" with little proof of the assertion? Mr. Beals has, to his great credit, implied that he was wrong in some of his early opinions about Mexico. Is it asking too much to request him to give thought now to the bishops' side? American bishops at this time would probably advise their Mexican brothers to ask nothing more than simple liberty, and suggest beginning all over again. Mexican bishops at this time would probably accept the advice. But we are looking back to the time when the wounds were still fresh and bleeding.

Besides, the loot had gone both into the hands of the grafters and into the coffers of the revolutions. The latter were empty, and the former would not disgorge. And there was the inherited hate, spawn of the French and Spanish lodges. What if the bishops were willing to give all—and that is what they would have done in the end—in exchange for the liberty of the Gospel, would that have sufficed to satisfy the radicals? Ask Portes Gil and Calles.

But Díaz did not try. He tolerated. He was glad to see the Church working to help the country beat back. But he would not repeal the unjust decrees. He left the two great questions untouched. Perhaps that was why he shook his head so sadly when he boarded the train ready to carry him to Vera Cruz and exile. He had not had boldness enough even to try to do justice. The radicals would have killed him if he had tried. On his deathbed the stubborn old Church pronounced her absolution over him and left the rest to God. She is an easy debtor in the end, that stubborn old Church.

I have the jeweled pectoral cross of Labastida. It looks like a blaze of sapphires set in green gold; but the green gold is copper and the stones are glass. His "greed" certainly could not have had much that was personal about it. The cross is worth about two dollars and fifty cents in money. It is worth in reverence for devotion more than money can buy.

XIV

DON PANCHO

WHO IS THE ENTHUSIAST? He is the conqueror and the King, the leader in every movement, whether good or bad, the blazer of every trail, the pathfinder into every jungle. His keel has furrowed the unknown seas, his alpenstock has marked the sides of every mountain and glacier, his spade has dug deepest into the earth, his mind has tried to encompass every problem, his zeal has converted millions to truth or perverted millions to error. He has done all of the world's things yet done that were worth doing. He is Progress personified. Yet, over the desert his bones have whitened. The kindly moss has covered his dead body in the great forests, to hide the ugliness of its decay. The sea gives up neither its treasures nor its dead—so he is sleeping forever in the peaceful depths. He has encrimsoned the world's battlefields, and has found graves deep down where men take gold and silver from the bowels of the earth. Yet he lives and never learns. It is well it should be so. Progress would cease were he to think too deeply and learn too much from what he has suffered.

When I wrote that paragraph eighteen years ago I had no particular person in mind. Now I see how well it fits Don Pancho.

Don Pancho was Francisco I. Madero, Jr. The pet name was used first by his family and then, out of very sincere affection, by nearly everybody in Mexico. He was the grandson of Evaristo Madero, head of an old family rich in land, in mines, in vineyards, in banking. The chief estates and industrial holdings of the family, all operated as one, were in Nuevo León and Coahuila. The agricultural holdings especially ran to millions of acres, always expanding by new purchases. Don Pancho was the idealist of the family, who became likewise its enthusiast. He attended a Jesuit school in Saltillo and wished to enter the Order. His father, very angry, removed him from the school and sent him to France. Here his opinions changed. He acquired his revolutionary enthusiasm, and became a spiritist. He had been at school for a short time also in the United States where he learned to speak English.

Don Pancho did not have the business ability of his family; his ambitions running along another line. He yearned to be the savior of his country. He was not, however, a politician, and still less a soldier. But his family was of the old *hidalgo* type in which there is a great deal of unconcealed pride. Without doubt, Don Pancho desired to carry high the banner of the local Madero name. He would make it national, even international. There was a family tradition to justify his entrance into the field of politics, since his grandfather had been, though most unwillingly, once Governor of his state.

Political ambitions did not blaze up at once in Don Pancho. It is more than likely they were lit by the spark of a fancied success in the dangerous field of political au-

‧thorship. He had written a book, not much of a book, for he was neither a writer nor a close reasoner. *La Sucesión Presidencial* shows signs of assisted authorship. But it married the idealism of the boy to the enthusiasm of the ambitious man. When Political Idealism is married to Political Enthusiasm the child of the union is often Disaster.

The book shows that, at the beginning at least, Don Pancho was not undiplomatic. When it was published General Díaz was in office and, perhaps, it might have been unhealthy not to be diplomatic. The book praises the sincerity of Don Porfirio, his record as an administrator, his unquestionable honesty, and his unblemished private life. "My family," Madero says, "is among the most numerous and influential in the state. Neither I nor any member of my family has the least complaint to offer against General Díaz or against his Ministers, or against the governor of the state, or even against the local authorities." He goes on to say: "General Díaz has rendered two great services to the country: ended militarism that in thirty years lost its false brilliance and prestige; and erased the hatreds that divided the great Mexican family, by means of his able policy of conciliation." I think Don Pancho was sincere in what he wrote about Díaz. He was no lover of revolution — in fact he hated it — and did not even dream that a revolution could be successful against Díaz. Nevertheless, that book was the actual preparation for a revolution, a revolution against Díaz, and a revolution that succeeded.[1]

If Don Pancho had kept the ideals that he imbibed in France he would have become the ordinary type of radical. But three influences fought these ideals in him: his aristocratic family, his Jesuit training, and his exposure to American thought. His book, therefore, had nothing in it to startle Americans. Boiled down to essentials it advocated the policy of no re-election, land for the people, and for the country a system of democratic government much resembling our own. It was, in a word, an appeal for democracy. The author could and did quote in its favor the very words of Díaz himself. Don Porfirio had given an interview for foreign papers to George Creelman. In that interview he declared his intention of retiring at the end of the term of office he was then serving, when he would have reached the age of eighty. He said that he would welcome then an opposition party, provided it appeared in good faith, intending to govern and not to exploit. He assured such a party in advance of his protection and support, and added that he would be proud to see his country become a real democracy.[2]

Don Pancho believed Díaz and took him at his word. It is interesting to speculate whether or not Díaz believed himself. I incline to the thought that he did. He might well have judged, from surface signs, that Mexico had gotten over her revolutionary sickness. The country was prosperous and in general quite well satisfied. Díaz had given it 35 years of peace and prosperity as preparation for a change without disturbing tranquillity. He himself, after he became President by revolution, never any more mentioned revolution. He may have felt that it was at last safe to rely upon ballots rather than bullets. The Creelman interview might then have been given out in perfect good faith; but it might also have been a feeler. As a feeler it was a success. The politicians at once busied themselves at the old game. Díaz had given them a glimpse of paradise and sweet memories came back, romantic dreams of "battles, sieges, fortunes," as well as the loot that gilded it all. The interview told them that Don Porfirio was weakening. In a little while he would be dead. They could wait, but in the meantime organize in the old way. For them happy days were dawning in Anauhuac.

Don Pancho was doing none of these things. Being an idealist he naturally would not do them. He was sticking to what Díaz had outlined in his few, terse words. Don Pancho wanted democracy, a free ballot, a free state, and even — his own later acts proved it — wonder of wonders, a free Church. He dreamed of political and social reconstruction on the altruistic foundation of nothing less than the Declaration of Independence. He felt himself to be, not a conqueror, but an apostle. So he went around making speeches, even in the capital, advocating an Independent Party. He wanted a convention representing the opposition that Díaz said he would welcome, but demanded that Don Porfirio himself be the party's candidate for the Presidency, with a Vice-President, quite evidently himself, to handle the power; thus leaving the President the *otium cum dignitate* of honorable rest. In that way he thought power would pass quietly from the dictatorship to the people. Don Pancho foresaw the Dictator training his young and inexperienced Vice-President in the details of government while not himself governing. The plan was a good one if it could be made to work, but no one believed that it could. Fundamentally there was something wrong about it. Ostensibly it was a democratic plan, but here was Don Pancho, the democrat, telling the Convention what it had to do. That was a bit undemocratic for a start. He was likewise assuming that Díaz would let the Vice-President rule. That seemed to ignore the unchangeable character of Don Porfirio. Above all, the politicians by this time were fighting over their own chances, since the threat of the Díaz whip had been removed. They were not a bit interested in Don Pancho's dream, but deeply interested in the question of what was in it for them. It became apparent to every practical politician that for the new Moses there would only be a glimpse of the promised land. The milk, honey, and grapes, the politicians were going to enjoy themselves.

Don Pancho had his Convention even while Díaz was still in power, but it did not nominate Don Porfirio for President. It nominated Don Pancho himself; which is to say that the Convention graciously permitted him to go out and get killed. The politicians knew quite well that when Díaz went there would be only two practical possibilities: a new dictatorship, or a revolution ending in a dictatorship. The only open question was how the dictatorship would come about. Don Pancho must have glimpsed the truth when he wrote his book, for he had said: "These two possible contingencies the Independent Party necessarily will attempt to avoid. The first by directing the energies of the people in a path as yet new to them; by a democracy. The second, contending at the polls, even without hope of success, so that the public will be awakened and strengthened sufficiently to enable it to contend with the successor of

General Díaz and recover our liberties one by one."[3] Splendid! But if the successor of General Díaz proved to be a man able to fill his ample shoes, he, being the challenged party and in power, would have the choice of weapons. The little idealist from the North was relying only on what was right. Perhaps in his American school he had heard the verse:

> "For right is right since God is God, and right
> the day must win.
> To doubt would be disloyalty; to falter would
> be sin."

Don Pancho had no drop of disloyal blood in his small body and there was enough of the Jesuit training left in him to fight the thought of wanting to be a sinner. He did not know what a difficult position he was in, what an impossible position. He really wanted to be a political saint, but of the confessor kind. Fate was good to him — or was it God?—He became a martyr.

Martyr to what? The answer is important, for in it is the highest eulogy that can be paid Don Pancho. He was to be a martyr to the only honest declaration of policy in accord with the wishes of the Mexican people made since the days of Iturbide. He was to be a martyr for the only solution of Mexico's political problem short of absolutism. If the Constitution was not a planned deception, for what other cause could Don Pancho be martyred? He was an honest man. He not only took Díaz at his word, but he took Mexico at its word. Its Constitution called for a democratic form of government. So did Díaz. If that form of government was impossible, why not change the Constitution and set up a form that would be possible? The trouble with Don Pancho was a trouble that afflicts half the world. He took democracy for the principle when it was at best only one means to an end. He again, like half the world, did not think of the support below the beautiful carved stones of democracy in the building. Government is for the happiness and welfare of the people; consequently the form to be adopted in any country must be that suited to the people. Don Pancho's syllogism was imperfect, but so, for that matter, was that of everybody else he had ever heard talk about it. Had he remained a little while longer with the Jesuits, and gone as far as to secure an education, he would have learned how to reason and would have known that a syllogism does not work back from a conclusion.

The situation in Mexico was not what Don Pancho thought it to be. What the politicians wanted was to keep the bugle blast of democracy in the Constitution and then ignore it. The battle that Don Pancho saw was a clear fight between absolutism and democracy; but to him absolutism was a heresy and democracy the truth. The fact is that neither are heresies under all circumstances and neither are truths under all circumstances. If Mexican experience were to be called into court as a witness it would be forced under oath to testify in favor of absolutism, since that was the only form of government it knew had worked. Díaz absolutism had returned to the people a prosperity that Spanish absolutism had given. On the side of absolutism were the peaceful farmers, the open mines, the oil wells, the industries, the higher wages, and the demand for labor. On the side of democracy there was a Constitution that had never been obeyed, and that was all. But Don Pancho saw clearly that the Constitution was the law. He knew that the Mexican people wanted to have it, at least in form, so he was the only man in Mexican public life who dared to say with uncrossed fingers what, under such circumstances, ought to be done. He did not see the obstacles, which were all human ones. He thought others were going to be as honest as himself. There were some statesmen in Mexico quite as honest as himself who could not see how a people could be ruled by nothing but sentiment. Don Pancho was quite determined to be logical. When he started his political campaign he even encouraged the formation of a Catholic party. The last thing the politicians wanted was a Catholic party, or any political party guided by Christian principles. The idea of such a party getting into power was a nightmare to them and they knew quite well that the voters would put such a party in power and keep it there if they were allowed to vote. Democracy was all right on paper, but for practical purposes, so far at least as the politicians were concerned, it was both delusion and snare.[4]

In connection with the interest of the United States in Mexico were trade considerations. We have seen that the thought of Jefferson, continued down through Monroe and Polk, was to take over Mexico. Díaz and Limantour had changed that when they built railroads to the border, for these railroads brought down American capital, and American capital had told the United States that trade annexation would serve better than political annexation. Don Pancho did not see what the railroads had done to him. As a matter of fact they had seen to it that any Republican administration at Washington would be against him. The Mexican railroads ran their biggest engine right over Don Pancho's democracy. He won the Presidency in the only fair election Mexico ever had. He lost it through a gesture by the practical politicians that had always proved successful in solving their personal problems — and Don Pancho was a personal problem.

There were other but minor reasons for the ill-success of Don Pancho. He had promised too much; for example, land to the peons. The peons now wanted the land all at once. Don Pancho could not deliver. To settle the land question would take study, time, and an acceptable plan. Don Pancho would have to find students he could trust to work out such a plan; the peons would not give him the time. An acceptable as well as politic plan depended on both. Then Don Pancho had stressed the need of education. But for that teachers would have to be found. Time was an element there. Calles later had to employ teachers who could barely read and write. Obviously only the Church could help Don Pancho in this education matter; and the Liberals would be on his back if he dared ask help from that quarter. In a word: Don Pancho could not begin with a clean slate. Whatever plans he made would have to take into account existing situations, hatreds, and prejudices. He was like a physician treating a bad case of intestinal obstruction with an operation barred. If he found no way to remove the obstruction by the use of internal medicine, he would simply have to lose the case. Don Pancho lost his. As a matter of fact, he had already lost it when he took over the Presidency from De la Barra.

If he had only seen it, that same De la Barra might have been Don Pancho's life preserver. What Don Pancho had advised in his book was that Díaz be left in the Presidency with himself as Vice-President and heir-apparent. That was unsound so far as the senile but still stubborn Old Dictator was concerned. It would be sound with De la Barra in the place of Díaz. Don Porfirio was no longer popular, no longer efficient, had made too much of a concession in the Creelman interview. His day was done. To keep the nation on a respectable footing before the world and increase its prestige, an educated, cultured, and trained statesman was needed. Don Pancho had none of these qualifications. All he had was a sound theory of government, as judged by the Constitution, which, as was plain, Mexico was not yet ready to use. That and popularity. To join his popularity with De la Barra's brains and experience would have made an ideal combination to hold the fort, especially strong because De la Barra was *persona grata* in Washington. Taft's whole official family recognized De la Barra's ability. Besides, he was also *persona grata* to the bishops, who trusted him and would not want to embarrass him. He was one of those rare men with that personal charm so marked in Maximilian, who always won those with whom he came into personal contact. De la Barra knew the American political system perfectly, and was therefore the best man available to smooth the way to securing its ultimate adoption in some form suited to

Mexican conditions. Above all, De la Barra knew the politicians and, by relying on getting Washington friends to
frighten them into common sense — with covert threats of
intervention, for example — he could force them to leave
him alone. It was quite safe to assume that there never
would be any American intervention while De la Barra
was known to have the direction of Mexican affairs. And
De la Barra was modern. In his short term of office as
Provisional President he appointed a Board of Labor looking to a study and solution of a burning question on just
lines. Don Pancho had his political savior right in the
National Palace, but never knew it. In fact, Mexico was
not so badly provided with able men. No cabinet is all
good. Mexico had De la Barra, Limantour, Gamboa, and
Lascurain. A clean slate, a strong hand on the financial
helm, and De la Barra might have remade Mexico — and
saved Don Pancho.

Why a clean slate? Are not the traditions of a people
always to be considered? Yes; the good ones! But where
were the good traditions of Mexico? They had been lost
in the revolutions, or destroyed by the revolutionists with
their "Plans" and their lootings. The nation had become
an experimental farm for every noxious weed on the face
of the political earth. Don Pancho may have pointed out
the right way, but it would have been foolish to assume
that it really was the right way. President Wilson later had
assumed that it was the right way for the world, and the
world now knows that he was wrong. To find the right
way for Mexico it would be necessary to go back to the very
essentials of government. A thought expressed in one of

Mr. Henry L. Mencken's most ironical paragraphs might have helped: "Democracy came into the Western World to the tune of sweet, soft music. There was, at the start, no harsh bawling from below; there was only a dulcet twittering from above. Democratic man thus began as an ideal being, full of ineffable virtues and romantic wrongs — in brief, as Rousseau's noble savage in smock and jerkin, brought out of the tropical wilds to shame the lords and masters of the civilized lands. The fact continues to have important consequences to this day. It remains impossible, as it was in the eighteenth century, to separate the democratic idea from the theory that there is a mystical merit, an esoteric and ineradicable rectitude, in the man at the bottom of the scale — that inferiority, by some strange magic, becomes a sort of superiority — nay, the superiority of superiorities. Everywhere on earth, save where the enlightenment of the modern age is confessedly in transient eclipse, the movement is toward the completer and more enamoured enfranchisement of the lower orders. Down there, one hears, lies a deep, illimitable reservoir of righteousness and wisdom, unpolluted by the corruption of privilege. What baffles statesmen is to be solved by the people, instantly and by a sort of seraphic intuition. Their yearnings are pure; they alone are capable of a perfect patriotism; in them is the only hope of peace and happiness on this lugubrious ball. The cure for the evils of democracy is more democracy!"[5]

Protestant churches in American small towns used to have revivals quite as a matter of habit every winter. None of the revivals were unsuccessful in gaining converts but, somehow, the congregations of the churches did not show evidence of the growth a year later; and the revival work had to be done all over again. Wise old residents who could not be reached by the revivalists used to say of the converts: "It's all right in winter, but lots of them will never summer their religion." Alas! the great reason for Don Pancho's failure was that he could not summer his democracy. When the real test of it came he could not pass it. Not only did he himself secure the Presidency by a fair election, but the Congress elected was, in the main, the actual choice of the people. When the votes were counted the Catholic Party Don Pancho had encouraged was found entitled to over ninety seats after only a few weeks of organized effort. The Liberals were panic-stricken. This practical business of democracy must stop. They rushed to see Don Pancho and, with him, cut the Party representation down to less than thirty. Over sixty members saw their seats given to the Liberals. One ousted member sought the office of the gentleman who had the handling of the matter, and asked to see the votes from his district. The package was still unopened. The indignant Deputy asked how then could the returns have been checked and a decision given ousting him on the ground that his opponent had a greater number of votes. His question in no way embarrassed the Liberal. He replied that political reasons were to be considered above all others. The Catholic Party had been allotted a few seats and that was all there was to be said on the matter. Presumably the packet, if not destroyed, is still unopened. Don Pancho's democracy was having hard sledding. Had he taken thought of the popularity lost by

Maximilian because of his concessions to the Liberals, perhaps he might have avoided the mistake of cheating Dr. Vásquez Gómez out of the Vice-Presidency in favor of their candidate, Pino Suárez.[6]

It was on February 4, 1912, fatal date, that the railroads ran the engine over Don Pancho's democracy. The war between European and American interests had come to a crisis. American troops were sent to the Mexican border. Let Mr. Bell, who was in Mexico then, tell what happened: "Within a fortnight the hundred and eighty correspondents of the newspapers under my management reported brigandage on the increase in all sections. The marauders had been operating on a small scale, except the Zapata bands in the State of Morelos, south of the capital, and the Zalgada brigands in the State of Guerrero in the Southwest. Many others now appeared with magical suddenness, the obvious suitability of the occasion to their special industry stimulating them to deeds of unusual atrocity. Murders for loot, murders for no assignable motive except cruelty gratified by indescribable tortures; crimes against women, the invariable accompaniment of Mexican brigandage — all these in a few days began to stain more broadly the page of history."[7]

The temptation to let Mr. Bell picture Don Pancho at that time is too strong to be conquered. Remember, he is telling what he saw: "How painfully Madero was affected by his situation I had abundant means of knowing from persons in Madero's office and members of the Chamber of Deputies, but more than a week passed before I saw the President himself at close range. The interview took place

in the innermost of the presidential reception rooms of
the National Palace. It happened that as I entered, there
appeared at the opposite end the undersized, frock-coated
figure of Madero coming from his private office. In my
mind was the impression of the immense and ponderous
building stretched across the Plaza's eastern boundary; of
the great stone stairway, its steps hewn for giants so that
the knees of an ordinary person are lifted almost to his chin
as he climbs panting in that rarified atmosphere; of the
long corridor, and dwindling series of reception rooms; and
it seemed to me that I had walked down the diminished
vista which one sees through a strong field glass reversed,
and in the vanishing point of this perspective stood 'the
little man,' dwarfed by his huge responsibilities, so desper-
ately circumstanced, so pitifully doomed to failure and extinction. All illusions aside, he was greatly changed from
that enthusiast who was my neighbor so little while ago,
and taught political economy to his curbstone pupils in the
Calle Berlin. His cheeks which used to curve smoothly
from his broad forehead to his narrow chin were now
sunken and lined; his brow was wrinkled; a dozen years
had been added to his apparent age, a fair half of them
in the last seven days. He showed loss of sleep and was
extremely nervous, with the impatient manner of a man
who is trying to do too many things at once, and knows
in his heart that they are none of them done well, but he
had not lost a grain of his courage nor an atom of his
essential self-respect."[8]

The temptation is still strong. I am being led on with
Mr. Bell by a bit of color needed for the full picture: " 'I

do not want to kill my people to make them good,' he declared in a shrill voice, at which a knot of Mexicans awaiting audience in a far corner of the room turned questioning eyes upon me as one who was being roughly lectured in a tongue they did not understand. 'I could have controlled them,' he went on. 'I am preparing to open lands to them. I am arranging employment at good wages for all Maderista soldiers and many other men, on public works. Does your government suppose that I have given no thought to conditions here, or that extensive plans such as mine can be carried out by magic in a day? I ask of no man or government anything but a reasonable chance. Why is this unfriendly effort made to force me to violate my pledges against the shedding of blood? What influence is at work secretly to accomplish this injustice? Surely the United States has nothing to gain by making me a tyrant and a madman!' "[9]

"What influence is at work secretly to accomplish this injustice?" Without knowing, the little man had there put his finger on the great question.

Don Pancho was neither tyrant nor madman. He was really trying. True, he had made mistakes. But who in his position would not have made them? He had meant every word he said. He had yielded only under the pressure of necessity. There he stood clutching the last remnants of his democracy, trying to save it from the jaws of the snake. Bewildered, confused, half-sobbing in disappointment and anger, Don Pancho, who did not know how to fight, was fighting an enemy unseen. It first had made him weaken. Now it was ready to destroy. The enemy was not radicalism this time, but a brat that radicalism had spawned. It was Greed.

On the night of February 22, 1913, Don Pancho's dream of democracy died. It was assassinated — with him.

XV

FIRST CHIEF

DURING THE DÍAZ regime a benevolent and bewhiskered man named Venustiano Carranza occupied a seat in the Senate. He had ambitions to become Governor of Coahuila and succeeded in satisfying them. There he became very friendly at the Jesuit College in Saltillo, the state capital, attending commencement exercises, and delivering addresses. He extended his interest likewise to the Christian Brothers school for poorer children, including orphans. The Governor, learning that the municipality of Saltillo was paying the Brothers only five dollars a month for the care of some dependent children who were charges on the city, expressed his mortification and surprise at the smallness of the stipend—not half the cost of maintenance —and voluntarily offered to have the State more than double the amount. He was on the friendliest terms with the Bishop of Saltillo and the clergy. In fact, no matter what happened in other parts of Mexico, as long as Venustiano Carranza remained Governor of Coahuila there seemed to be no doubt but that religious peace would prevail there.

All this would seem to indicate that Governor Carranza was not an irreligious man. His addresses to the students stamped him as anything but that. While he made no claim to sanctity, neither did he seek to shine as a sinner. His appearance was striking. He was tall and well built, with grave eyes that gazed through statesman-like glasses. He spoke with gravity and bore himself with dignity. Altogether he had about his person the marks and signs of an excellent official who desired in all outward things to do credit to the great office he held. His perpetual senatorship, and later the governorship, proved that he was held by President Díaz to be one of his warmest friends and most ardent supporters.

When Madero came into power with the success of his revolution no change was made in the governorship of Coahuila. There appeared to be no necessity of making one. Like other governors in northern Mexico, Venustiano Carranza constituted himself a barrier between possible insurgents there and the Federal capital. He was allotted money from the Federal treasury to maintain an army for that purpose. Díaz had left enough, some 63,000,000 pesos, or 31,500,000 gold, as a needed nest egg for his successor. The egg did not remain long in the nest. Gustavo Madero had raised over $300,000 to help his brother "by ways that were dark and tricks that were [not] vain." This loyal brother of Don Pancho now feared scandal and arrest. He had been near to both in the United States. The money had to be replaced to save him from jail. Naturally it was chipped off the gold nest egg. But governors had to be placated to keep their loyalty, and an excellent way to do that was to make allotments to them for the support of troops to put down possible local revolutions. An old tradition in military life is the padded army list, which illustrates one of the many time-honored ways by which a calf may be skinned, a goose plucked, or a dignified human bribed. All this was, of course, known to the hungry political horde in Mexico City. But even after dividing with them, a tidy sum still remained for the Governor of Coahuila—and the Etceteras who ruled other states.[1]

Trouble arises easily between gentlemen who follow the avocation of political grafting, even those who make inspiring addresses to students. They are usually sensitive to an extreme, not to say suspicious of one another. It is unfortunate for the profession, rendering the practice of grafting dangerous even on the inside. The danger is increased when there is at the head of public affairs someone not familiar with the code of ethics recognized by the membership. Such was Madero. I mean Don Pancho, not Gustavo. He was by no means enthusiastic about tipping governors to encourage them to do their duty. Neither did he like the idea of their thieving. Since others of his followers did not like the Governor of Coahuila, the decision was made unanimous.[2]

When Madero fell Carranza agreed to recognize Huerta on condition that he remain Governor of Coahuila and that the stipend from Mexico City be restored. Huerta demurred about the money. The Maderistas had left no gold nest egg, and the Díaz one had been chipped out of existence. Nevertheless Carranza notified Mr. Holland, the American Consul in Saltillo, that he accepted the government of Huerta. But on the first of March Huerta wired Carranza for an explanation of the latter's seizure of 50,000 pesos from the banks. That plainly was an insult. It was Carranza's business to deal with the banks, not Huerta's. He revolted, and the dead Madero, who was to have been attacked by his revolution, became its patron saint. Though the revolution did not seem to have any chance of success, being nothing but a badly supported guerrilla affair, nevertheless the Carranza luck held. The American Navy bombarded Vera Cruz and shut up the port from Huerta. Carranza could get all the arms he wanted from over the border. President Wilson was against Huerta and could be counted on to help his enemies. Carranza's troops began to march south to the capital. Villa, a bandit criminal, had joined up. Between the grafting governor, the bandit, and the Government of the United States, Huerta was crushed.[3]

When the Carranza revolution began there was no sign in it of enmity to the Church. Indeed, as stated, Carranza had always, as governor, been friendly—even kind. Villa might do anything to get plunder, but not Carranza. All at once there was an astonishing change. The clergy was made the object of persecution. The first step was, of course, to charge them with complicity in the assassination of Madero, who had, in fact, been their one hope for peace and better days. Proof was not needed. Shouting would do the trick and did. The orgy of stealing, torture, and murder was on.

What started the persecution so suddenly and unexpectedly was for a time a puzzle. As stated, no one would have wondered much to hear that Villa had committed outrages of any kind. Villa was like that, a fairly good duplicate for the long dead Juan Alvarez who had killed his way into the Presidency—and out. The persecution broke out all at once and everywhere in Constitutionalist territory. It was quite evidently an arranged affair—arranged with someone, somewhere.

While the success of Carranza's revolution was still in doubt there was in Vera Cruz the headquarters of a society called the Casa del Obrero Mundial, known to us as the Industrial Workers of the World. It did not share the democratic views of Don Pancho. It was not likely to appeal greatly to Don Venustiano. But it had a following among people "of the lower class" that gave it some importance to the Carranza eyes, now already black and swollen and becoming difficult to use for seeing purposes. Its importance to Carranza grew as his hopes for success diminished. He made terms, part of which was the persecution. Whether Carranza agreed to it himself or whether his generals agreed for him is one of the secrets of revolutions that may never be known. Carranza did not himself seem enthusiastic about it. But, on the other hand, he kept silent while it went on.[4]

If any doubt existed as to the culpability of the Workers, it was dissipated by their doings in Yucatan. This state was close enough to the Vera Cruz headquarters, and distant enough from the First Chief, to make a record all its very own. The military leader of the Carranza forces, afterward the Governor, was General Salvador Alvarado. He brought an army with him, and started in the usual way by closing all the churches. He was a good business man, far from the influence of altruistic clubs, so he decided to handle the business of Yucatan as well as govern the State. The Cathe-

(Left) The church of Guadalupe where Carranza's daughter was married. He was living at the time in the house at the left whose owner he had dispossessed. (Right) The church of San Francisco in Querétaro.

The Church of Tepozothan in the State of Puebla. This is one of the most beautiful churches in Mexico.

dral would make an excellent warehouse for his barrels of
salt pork, kentles of fish, and other household necessities.
He moved his stores in. He then assessed the customary
"loan." Two brothers who were planters objected. That
they were MacGregors did not bother him. He probably
did not know that it was no hanging matter for Scotsmen
to hesitate about lending money on terms that precluded
the possibility of getting it back. Alvarado hanged both
MacGregors on a wire clothesline. He was strong on hang-
ings. He even hanged ten of his own policemen because
they did not like the idea of dirtying their new uniforms
handling pork barrels. After that Alvarado had a comparatively smooth passage to his main objective. He did two
outstanding things: took control of business and finished
with the Church, both in the joint names of Constitution-
alism and the Workers of the World.

Alvarado went about the business part of his governorship very thoroughly and began at the bottom, obliging
everyone to give up all coin and banknotes in exchange for
the scrip he issued. In Yucatan it could not be said that
there was peace but soon there was plenty of money, such
as it was. There was "lashins and lashins" of it. Why not?
Alvarado had printing presses not in use. He had stopped
the publication of the newspapers he did not like, and
their plants had nothing to do but print money. Mortgages
were paid off when wheelbarrows rolled the scrip to pay
them right up to the doors of the lenders. If any debtor in
Yucatan owed anything, after Alvarado had gotten down
to real work turning out money, it was by an oversight.
The Governor had all the good money and sent some, pre-

sumably, to the First Chief. But he needed more. How Alvarado proposed to get it, and did get it, is a most interesting story of sheer business ability. The man was great—in the sense that Lucifer is entitled to like distinction.

The State of Yucatan lived on one product—henequen or sisal, out of which is made the binder twine used extensively by American farmers. It is a stubborn sort of plant which refused to grow at its best anywhere but in Alvarado's State where it was called the Green Gold of Yucatan. Alvarado took over control of the entire crop, and doubled the price; paying the planter in his own money, but getting good coin out of the American farmer who simply had to have his binder twine. The only trouble Alvarado had was with the Workers. They had to have jobs at good wages. Stevedores at the port got as high as $35 a day. Alvarado, to make more jobs, destroyed a railroad and built another. But the planters were almost ruined by the Workers' agitators. The business of Yucatan began to go down as the American Harvester Company found new land elsewhere on which to grow sisal. What difference? Alvarado had his, and Carranza got some—presumably.

As for the Church, that was easy. The Governor sent a mob out to do that part of the job; tearing down altars, breaking statues, ripping up paintings, and smashing furniture. They even went hunting for religious objects in private homes. The mobs could act freely since the Governor gave them a military escort. Sixteen churches were thought to be too many for 80,000 people so, when things settled down a bit—folks do get tired—seven were taken for warehouses. The Workers got a few for meeting halls. Two were given over for Protestant use, though the entire Protestant population could easily have been accommodated in Mr. Brisbane's famous taxicab. The 80,000 Catholics were left two, with nothing in them.

The thoroughness of the Workers in authority for persecuting purposes might well have offered a warning of what they could be expected to do elsewhere. Two priests landed at Salina Cruz from Peru on October 24, 1914, to cross the Isthmus of Tehuantepec and take ship at Coatzacoalcos for Spain. They were arrested, all their baggage and money seized, kept in jail for sixteen days, and subjected to every variety of insult and abuse. The ingenuity of their tormentors was taxed in doing this. On several occasions they were taken from jail to headquarters through the streets on pretext of being examined. On these occasions their escort was mounted and the horses were ridden at a trot while the priests, on foot, were compelled to run, to the lively satisfaction of the socialist rabble. On November 9 they were sent to Vera Cruz with only the clothes they stood in, which, because of the manner of their treatment, were far from presentable; and not a penny in their pockets. These were only visitors passing through the Workers' territory.

Carranza was appealed to. He answered: "It is impossible to control an army." Surely not when it is an army of "high-minded patriots," friends of such noble idealists as President Wilson. Ah! Surely not. Friends of so many noble people in the United States, who had spoken for that army before the Senate Committee! "Impossible to control an army?" If that was so, is it not strange that so many are reading what was done with a kind of shudder they never knew before? And not one-hundredth part of the tale was ever told. We may find relief in shifting the scene, but nothing could be worse than Yucatan.

The experience of one Archbishop will illustrate what happened elsewhere. He was arrested, his house and cathedral sacked, and then he was sent from door to door with a guard of soldiers to raise half a million pesos from the faithful under penalty of death for failure. Seeing their chief pastor in so distressful a position the people gave freely, but no such amount could be raised. The Archbishop was, however, permitted to leave his city for another. Word was sent ahead of him and the performance repeated. Disguised, he left Mexico to save, not himself from death, but his people from robbery. He is still alive, which is the reason for withholding his name. Incidentally, this story and expulsion explain why the Mexican bishops went into exile.

Some of the bishops were not so fortunate as to get a chance to tramp across the desert to the United States; the Bishop of Tepic, for example. There was a paper in his diocese which published an editorial condemning the revolution. Although the unfortunate Bishop was neither its editor nor owner, he was arrested and given a sentence of eight years in the penitentiary. Soon there were priests in every prison. What happened to nuns need not be mentioned. It was one of the most awful revelations ever made about a "civilized" army.

In Monterrey no harm was done to churches and clergy at first; but when the change of policy came—three days after the taking of the city—the churches were closed and a "loan" of half a million pesos put upon the clergy. When they truthfully stated that they had no money, they went to jail. Later those who were not Mexicans were released on demand of their national consuls, while the Mexicans remained in jail. The Archbishop's house—the house of the scholar already mentioned—was entered, his library scattered, his scientific manuscripts destroyed, and the diocesan archives seized. On June 7, church furniture was publicly burnt, statues were shot at as "Huertistas," and sacred vessels unmentionably profaned. In other towns of the State, such as Tanquecillos, Margaritas, Cerralbo, and Los Aldamas, the profanations were repeated. In Saltillo eight priests, after imprisonment, were made the subjects of mock executions. Villa, by the way, improved on this system, which was that of a firing squad, by half-hangings to extort money. After robbing an official of the Diocese of Zacatecas, Father Velarde, he was taken outside the city and killed. Two Christian Brothers, teachers, and their chaplain, Father Vega, were shot on Bufa Hill. The other teachers went to jail. A "loan" of a million pesos was assessed on the clergy. To get it they were starved for three days, not even being allowed water. From door to door the priests were conducted by soldiers. They raised 100,000 pesos, and were then sent into exile. A priest at Villa de Guadalupe opened a temporary hospital to take care of the wounded. He was fortunate enough to escape, but another, Father Alva, not so fortunate, was shot.

The same story, with local variations, is told of Aguascalientas, San Luis Potosí, Querétaro, Guanajuato, León,

Irapuato, Silao, Celaya, Zamora, Toluca, Puebla, Tepozot-
lan, Jalapa, Córdova, and Orizaba. American troops protected Vera Cruz, which became a safe refuge, though star-
vation threatened there. All the records were made by affidavits from exiles, many in my own presence. Only a very
few have been referred to here. The persecution was as
general as the Carranza occupation. The former benevolent
Governor of Coahuila had made a long step from his kindly
attitude to the teachers and clergy of Saltillo to become the
responsible leader of butchers and thieves.[5]

On August 20, 1914, Carranza entered Mexico City and
took over the government, not as President, but as First
Chief. On September 23 following, Villa was in arms
against him. The First Chief had to leave the capital and
set up his own at Puebla. There were quick changes of
Villista and Carranzista rulers. On January 28, 1915, Carranza again took over Mexico City. Driven to it by repeated
charges that he was nothing but "Wilson's Man," Carranza
began a series of notes and statements aimed at restoring
Mexican confidence in him as one free from American dictation. His statements were insulting, but President Wilson
understanding his position was patient. The First Chief
was having a hard time between the treason of his former
Mexican friends and the necessity of insulting his new
American ones. It was only a question of the length of
time he could hold out; but during this year he succeeded
in having Obregón join him in a promise of religious
liberty for all Mexican citizens, a promise Obregón was
soon to forget.

Carranza was forced to call a Constitutional Convention,

but for the supporters of his revolution only. In 1917 the Convention met at Querétaro and, in spite of the First Chief, adopted articles of persecution. The Convention by its First Article restricted the rights of the Mexican citizen to those "which are granted him by this Constitution"; thereby reversing the democratic order that makes the people the source of rights and the Constitution the declaration of the people's sovereignty. In the Querétaro Constitution the people receive only what is conceded to them by a party, a theory which was to have its effects outside Mexico.[6]

Carranza was chosen by the President of the United States, Woodrow Wilson, to be the President of Mexico. When the Turks massacred the Armenians the Christian world shouted its protest. When the Russians murdered the Jews the shout was repeated. No people shouted louder against the massacres than the Americans and the English. About the horrors perpetrated against the Catholics of Mexico few voices were raised. President Wilson told an Indianapolis audience that he would allow the Mexicans to shed all the blood they wanted. He told me in his office in the White House that, as the inspiration of democracy had come out of the French Revolution, which had shed as much blood as Carranza and his men, perhaps *something good* would come out of the Mexican debacle. His words were offered in consolation. I thanked him and withdrew.

Years before I had read with a thrill a noble-sounding line written by a poet: "For the dreamer lives forever but the toiler dies in a day." How many times I had quoted that line in speech and writing! What a fool John Boyle

O'Reilly had been to write it! What a fool I had been to believe it! I had enough of dreamers since my heart had first begun to reach out toward the poor bruised heart of Mexico. In her story I had seen dreamers in action, trying to turn their visions of power, of wealth, of fortune, of fame, into ignoble reality; and ever I saw that they were building their palaces out of the corpses of the slain, cementing them together with mortar mixed in blood. I had enough of dreamers; wild-eyed patriots spouting poetry over things that never were and never could be; crazy theorists in the grip of some vague inspiration to make marble statues out of cloud banks; philosophic dabblers in attics moaning over a god of their imagination when the One God stood clear in the light of His creation; ambitious madmen in palaces thinking they saw imperial glory when it was red iniquity they were beholding; fools in hovels idealizing their rags and all the while longing to change them by theft for ermine; fighters on the battlefield rising to a murderer's heaven on the miasma of death. I have had enough of dreamers, for I have seen their devastating work, the base end of their imagining, the dissolution of their visions into red mist.

Let the dreamer go. Carranza had never really been one. He had been a very practical Governor and wanted to be a practical President. It was no longer the Liberals with whom he had to deal, for they were scattered in exile all along the American border. Anticlericalism had passed out of their hands and was now in the possession of the out-and-out radicals in communication with Russia. The Casa del Obrero Mundial was changing its name to the Confederacion Regional de Obreros Mexicanos. It would soon be popularly known as the C.R.O.M. The old Liberals had merely wanted to control the Church, so that if she ever had anything again they could take it away from her. Only the men were anticlerical among the Liberals. They were particular about bringing up their children Catholics, often sending them to Catholic schools in the United States or Europe. They wanted their wives to practice the Catholic religion. It was different with the C.R.O.M. which wanted nothing short of the complete destruction of the Church. Carranza had promised that but he could not keep his promise. Without President Wilson he could not reach the Presidency of Mexico. That Wilson had explained to Carranza how difficult his own position was can scarcely be doubted. Agitation among Catholics in the United States over the persecution was increasing all the time. Catholic Democratic leaders were urging the President to say something or to do something to quiet it. Mr. Wilson decided to make a statement. He addressed that statement to me in a letter signed by William Jennings Bryan, Secretary of State, and dated March 20, 1915. The letter, however, was written by the President himself. An abstract from it will show how it became a death sentence to Carranza:

"Not only the United States, but all the world, will watch with the greatest interest and concern the course now to be pursued by the leaders of the Constitutionalist cause in effecting a transfer of power at Mexico City. This Government feels that the critical time has come when the choice which is now to be made by the Constitutionalist leaders will practically determine the success or failure of the government they mean to set up and the reforms they hope to effect.

"We venture to say this because of our earnest sympathy with the main purpose of the Constitutionalists and our desire to be of permanent service to them in bringing Mexico out of her troubles. We have been forced by circumstances into a position in which we must practically speak for the rest of the world. It is evident that the United States is the only first-class power that can be expected to take the initiative in recognizing the new government. It will in effect act as the representative of the other powers of the world in this matter and will unquestionably be held responsible by them for the consequences. Every step taken by the Constitutionalist leaders from this moment on and everything which indicates the spirit in which they mean to proceed and to consummate their triumph must of necessity, therefore, play a very important part in determining whether it will be possible for the United States to recognize the government now being planned for. In the most earnest spirit of friendship, therefore, this Government wishes to call attention to the following matters of critical consequence:

"First, the treatment of foreigners, foreign lives, foreign property, foreign rights, and particularly the delicate matter of the financial obligations, the legitimate financial obligations, of the government now superseded. Unless the utmost care, fairness and liberality are shown in these matters the most dangerous complications may arise.

"Second, the treatment of political and military opponents. Unless there is to be a most generous amnesty it is certain that the sympathy of the whole world, including the people of the United States, now the real friends of the Constitutionalists, will be hopelessly alienated and the situation become impossible.

"Third, the treatment of the Roman Catholic Church and of those who represent it. Nothing will shock the civilized world more than punitive or vindicative action toward priests or ministers of any church, whether Catholic or Protestant; and the Government of the United States ventures most respectfully but most earnestly to caution the leaders of the Mexican people on this delicate and vital matter. The treatment already said to have been accorded priests has had a most unfortunate effect upon opinion outside of Mexico.

"You can not too earnestly urge these matters upon the attention of those now in the counsels of the Constitutionalists. It is obvious to us that the whole future of what the Constitutionalists are attempting will depend upon the way and the spirit in which they deal with these questions. Nothing ought to be overlooked or dealt with hastily which may result in our being obliged to withhold the recognition of this Government from the new government to be created in Mexico City as we withheld it from General Huerta. Our ability or inability to serve them they must now determine. . . . The Mexican leaders will certainly know that in order to command the sympathy and moral support of America, Mexico must have, when her reconstruction comes, just land tenure, free schools, and true freedom of conscience and worship."[7]

That letter put the First Chief between two fires. Obregón

had deserted him and had made an agreement with the C.R.O.M. Carranza had given Wilson pledges which he had to keep. He went before the Mexican Congress on December 23, 1918, to ask that provisions in the Constitution of Querétaro be modified: "Without flinching I have come before the Congress suggesting amendments to our Supreme Law. In doing this I have no motive other than a sincere desire to restore harmony between the word of the law and the universally accepted principles of common justice. In suggesting that you enact into law the bill I herewith submit, I cherish the hope the Congress will understand that my motive today is that which it has always been, namely, to give more weighty consideration to the welfare of the people as a whole than to the demands of any group no matter how honorable it may claim to be.

"The bill I now enclose would amend Article 130 of the Constitution adopted at Querétaro, to insure respect for liberty of conscience that has been so highly esteemed in Mexico as an inalienable human right, removing provisions which abridge that liberty to a degree not consistent with correct morality and not in the public interest, which provisions moreover are not in harmony with the postulates of modern civilization, are a denial of true liberty and violate the statute itself under which the political organism of our country functions. . . . Those who adopted the constitution of 1857, had no hesitation in admitting that in Mexico there should be liberty of worship and liberty of conscience. If they did not embody it in the constitution it was through an excessive devotion to the complete separation of Church and State by which they denied their own jurisdiction in any religious matter. The legislators of that day were so scrupulous in this matter that they refrained from even the mention of religion. This was due doubtless to the fact that the delegates to the 1857 Constitutional Convention had entered into an agreement not to introduce any provision that would place any restriction whatever on the liberty of conscience which itself is guaranteed by the constitution they adopted. . . . Not before the promulgation of the 1857 Constitution did civil administration in Mexico take on a purely secular character. Confusing the law of the church with the law of the state a mystical character was given to government, and it would have been altogether natural for the legislature to regulate matters of worship. Nevertheless legislatures scrupulously abstained from doing so. . . . The abridgment of the liberty of the human conscience as is done in the Querétaro Constitution has no antecedent in our national legislation, no precedent even analogous is to be found for this provision which I ask you to amend. I have searched our national record in vain, I have examined every effort made to curb the alleged abuses of religion, I have found nowhere anything that even had the faintest appearance of a mandate from the nation for any law that interferes with worship. Even in the Reform Laws, enacted at a time when laicism was firmly in the saddle, there is no clause which interferes with the details of worship. . . . I hold that, even if we take nothing else into consideration, the very fact that in our civil law there is no basis for any act that would prescribe or regulate the internal affairs of any religion without violating the principle of non-intervention which is traditional in Mexico, you cannot fail to see the justice of the recommendation I make that Article 130 be amended."

What Carranza said threw down the gage of battle. The Congress would not act on his recommendation. The capital became too hot for him. He loaded his "government" on a special train and started for Vera Cruz. When the train came near Córdova it was found that the road ahead of him had been torn up. The party deserted the train and took refuge on the ranch Tlaxcalantongo. With three others Carranza went to sleep in a hut. There was now no possibility of his reaching Vera Cruz. Before retiring he had decided to try to reach Tampico. Sadly he said before lying down: *"Dios nos ayude esta noche*—God help us this night." He never saw the morning. Shots were fired between the wattles of the hut as if an attack had been made upon his party. But though there were four sleeping in the one room of the hut, only Carranza was killed. Some of his own men must have been bribed to do the job. Later, when his portfolio was received by his family, they found in it a crucifix and a little religious medal. On the latter was the inscription: *"Madre Mía Salva Me*—Mother mine save me." He had done a brave thing to go before the Congress with a request to change the provisions of the Constitution and end the religious persecution. He must have known that it was a brave thing to do with enemies all around him, and Obregón, backed by the C.R.O.M., in the field against him. It can be said for him that he kept his word to President Wilson at the cost of his life. Perhaps the memories of the old days in Saltillo when he had respected religion, though he did not seem to practice it, had helped him to be brave. Certainly no revolutionist who understood the situation would have advised him to do what he did. Perhaps he felt that the end had come and that he could at last tell the truth. Perhaps he realized that since his own hand had unloosed the whirlwind, he had no right to complain if it sucked him into swirling death.

XVI

WILD GOOSE ASTRAY

SINCE THE DAYS of King Brian Boru who won the Battle of Clontarf in Ireland, the name of the family has suffered many changes. In America it became Bryan, Brine, and even Brin. In France one meets it as Aubrien. In Russia, if my memory for strange spellings holds, it is Obrutcheff. In Spain and the old Spanish colonies we find it sometimes as Obregón. A list of officers, in the various Irish regiments in the service of the King of Spain in 1803, has six O'Briens followed by two Obregóns. The descendants of the "Wild Geese" are all over Europe and Spanish America, though the Irish in the blood cannot, after more than two centuries, be much larger than one last fighting drop.

General Alvaro Obregón enters this story on July 7, 1914, when, after defeating Federal General Mier, he took Guadalajara. The battle was small potatoes even for an O'Brien (Mex.). Mier did not make a strong stand. He had no great army and the city made no resistance. After hearing the atrocity stories of Villa's conquests the citizens were pleased, since the city had to fall, to have Obregón take it. His first word to them was reassuring; but he lost no time in shooting General Mier. The citizens were informed that they would soon be convinced that the Con-

stitutionalist cause was one of peace and justice. The
Juárez motto was ordered inscribed over the door of every
school: "Respect for the rights of others is peace."

It would seem, however, that one of the rights of others
was not the possession of an automobile. The army confiscated every one in the city beginning with that of the
Archbishop. General Obregón took that for himself. Fine
horses and carriages were put into the same category as
automobiles. Very soon the officers extended their depredations to the houses of the wealthy, camped in them, and
parceled out among themselves, their women, and their
friends, what they wanted of the furniture, table service,
even the clothing. They then searched out officials of the
Federal Government, employees, and members of the Catholic Party. A number of these were shot. Nothing was done
about the depredations of the officers, but General Obregón
tried to restrain the individual outrages of the private
soldiers. He did not succeed very well. Though there was
a barrack for soldiers in the city the General decided to
make an end to the institutions of learning by turning
them into barracks. One of the finest buildings consecrated
to learning in Mexico was the Jesuit College in Guadalajara.
When I saw it years after, looted and empty, especially
its splendid library without a single book left in it, I was
amazed at its size and beauty. General Obregón's followers
— he came from Sonora — were mostly Yaqui Indians still
bedecked in feathers. They camped with their women in
the elegant lecture rooms while Colonel Calderón took
possession of the President's quarters. The soldiers, for
want of something better to do, destroyed the scientific

instruments. As the school was under the protection of the Government of France, the French flag hung over the door of the building, but that made no difference. It was soon occupied by a mass of filthy bodies, men, women, and children, cooking their meals on the stone floors, washing their garments, and bathing in full view of everyone. Around them were piled their arms, accouterments, and family possessions. Dogs, of course, had equal rights and behaved accordingly. For a while the President of the College was allowed to lodge in the barracks. He accepted the lodging in preference to the street, and was kept prisoner for a few days. Perhaps it is just as well, because he might have been taken for "Don Clero." The Yaquis had been told that they were fighting "Don Clero" and not their beloved priests; but they showed respect to the Jesuits who continued to live among them. To the credit of the Indians it may be said that they did not destroy scientific instruments until some of the officers had given the example.

The Seminary was one of the finest buildings in the city. It too was taken for a barracks and there was no delay about sacking it. Soldiers said to be fighting for a new deal, with education as part of it, threw the books out the windows, or sold them for a few cents a volume to anyone who would buy. A worse fate was in store for a women's college, an English establishment. The British consul protested in vain, but the flag of "the Empire upon which the sun never sets" had a chance that day to see the sun setting in Guadalajara. The most shameless of Obregón's troops, with their women and their horses, took possession of the beautiful gardens. The soldiers' women went into the sleeping apartments, stole the clothes of teachers and pupils, dressed themselves in what they wanted, and sold the rest. The furniture went too, for a pittance. They destroyed what they could neither use nor sell, and took over the infirmary for the sick and wounded, though there was plenty of room in the hospital. The soldiers and prostitutes occupied the private rooms.

The Governor was General Diéguez. He had once been a miner, and had served a term in prison for communistic rioting in the mines of Cananea, Sonora. He was now advancing civilization and spreading the sciences in the Constitutionalist way. General Obregón was his friend and permitted him to go ahead on his own account. People who had a grudge against others pointed them out to Diéguez as anti-Constitutionalist. A number of leading citizens, including priests, were apprehended. The courts were closed. Means of communication were destroyed so that no one could appeal, even to Carranza.

A woman of the underworld, a notorious character called Ataila Apodaca, was told to proclaim a war unto death against the clergy. Her friends issued three sheets containing vilest attacks and calumnies. They were the only papers permitted to circulate in the city — a preparation for what was to come after. After faking a plot of the clergy to make the people rise, an order was issued to arrest all priests and take possession of the churches. Soldiers were let loose in detachments of fifty. They made a clean job of it, and included with the clergy the sextons and the people they found praying in the churches. They arrested also Marist Brothers in their College, as well as boys playing on the grounds, and the servants. The prisoners were stripped of everything, money, watches, books, even their glasses. That was on July 21, 1914.

The next day the prison housed 120 priests of all nationalities, as well as Bishop Plasencia who was visiting in the city. Improvised courts were assembled while the prisoners were kept isolated in the dungeons for six or seven days before they were let out. Naturally the people of the city were in consternation. There were no religious services on Sunday, for the churches had been profaned. Everything of value was stolen from some of them. Even graves were opened and desecrated. Thirty or forty old guns, which had been bought for 25 cents each by the Marist Brothers for the military drills of their students, were found, and it was immediately reported that a cannon and a number of dynamite bombs had been hidden by the Brothers. In the meantime General Obregón had gone to Colima. He had set the priest prisoners free — the money found in their pockets had already been freed — and permitted them to leave the city. But the colleges remained closed. On August 3 the Jesuit College was confiscated. As already mentioned, it was still empty when, during the presidency of the General, I saw it.

There was one protection for the clergy and teachers of Guadalajara, the fact that there were many foreigners among them. The Marist College was under Italian protection, and, as mentioned, the Jesuit College under French and the Womens' College under British. The Constitutionalists made up their minds that it might be dangerous to interfere too much with these, so they decided to banish foreigners in order to make it easy to deal with the Mexicans, who had no protection. The foreigners were gathered together. A representative of the Governor made a speech and told them that, for political reasons, they would be banished in three days from Mexican soil. No attention was paid to appeals. The prisoners were ordered to leave by the port of Manzanillo, still occupied by the Federals, and where there was no certainty that ships could be found. The unfortunates asked to go to Vera Cruz where they might find ships, but no such permission could be had. They were allowed five days to get out of Guadalajara as best they could. But a train was provided later, and a military band played revolutionary airs as it left for the coast.

The Governor of Colima was kind. He knew that the way to the port was not open and that to abandon the exiles was to condemn them to death. He gave them permission to live within the city limits. As soon as Manzanillo was taken, however, they had to go there. By this time the British, German, and Spanish consuls were among the exiles. These pointed out that at Manzanillo there was neither food nor ship. For eight days the exiles waited, all the while living on charity. On the 29th of August, still no ship. Although the exiles by this time were suffering from the heat and were indescribably dirty, they were not allowed to bathe even in the sea. Fifty nuns arrived in the same hell-hole. There was no way known of getting out of the awful climate. At last for $6,500, part to be paid by begging on arrival in the United States, the exiles managed to leave. They still had about half enough money concealed on their persons to pay the fare. The captain trusted them for the rest until they got to San Francisco.[1]

That is the record by which General Obregón, or O'Brien if you will, first gets into this story.

It is not necessary to the purpose of this book that I should go deep into the history of General Alvaro Obregón. No more than the other three or four hundred generals connected with recent revolutions, or appointed because of them, was he a trained soldier. At his home in Sonora he had been engaged in business in a small, unsuccessful way. Not till 1910 did he begin to interest himself in Mexico's militaristic politics. It is quite unlikely that he had any hatred for the Church or the clergy. His wife was a pious lady and, even after his term of office as President, it was known that Mass, at which he himself assisted, was said in his Sonora home.

To relate here more than the sad events following the capture of Guadalajara would only take space from the real reason for bringing Obregón into this story at all. That he was then carrying out orders based on an agreement with the Workers seems certain. The assurance given to the citizens of Guadalajara, and the sudden *volte face* that followed so soon, upholds that opinion. No one meeting Obregón — at least none with whom I talked — carried away the impression that he was either a hater or a bloodthirsty person. The harangues and abuse he showered on the citizens of both Guadalajara and Mexico City might be accounted for by a loss of head through his sudden rise to power and pride. I am not excusing Obregón, but only trying to state what I believe to be the truth about him; which is, that officially he was like the other sons of the revolution, but personally a man who liked to be well thought of, even taken for a gentleman.

What is important to my purpose is to note in Obregón what we already have seen to be a rule in studying the revolutionists from Hidalgo to Calles. The makers of the revolutions, bad in action, hoped to be decent at the end, even to the point of compromising with the Church. Take them one by one. Hidalgo was appalled by the forces he had let loose and in the horror and confusion lost control over them. He proclaimed that he was fighting for the religion of the people. Morelos kept better discipline but his idea was the same. Santa Anna wanted the Church patronage but not her life. Maximilian, who must be placed among the revolutionists, had the same desire as Santa Anna. Comonfort, Juárez, and even Lerdo, tried to enforce an anticlerical Constitution which hampered but did not destroy the Church. Díaz held to that Constitution but did not enforce it. Madero was openly and avowedly for religious liberty. Huerta did nothing to indicate a change from the plans of Díaz. We have seen Carranza struggle to change the Constitution of Querétaro. The point of greatest interest for us in Obregón is that he actually took steps to bring about an understanding with the bishops. All that must be a surprise to many readers. I confess that, as I followed the vein whenever it showed, and I seldom lost it, I too was surprised—and agreeably.

No one wrote so hard against the Carranza and Obregón revolutionists as I. No one scored their brutality more. No

American was so hated by them. No citizen of the United States drew upon his head to a greater degree the dislike of President Wilson and his Secretary of State because of the blame for bloodshed in Mexico I publicly attached to them. Not one word I then wrote or spoke do I now retract. But today I have the whole picture before me, and I cannot but see, in each successful Mexican revolutionary leader, a fear of the consequences of the loss of religious influence over the lives of the Mexican people. They could shout maledictions and rob without remorse but, when safely in power — or unsafely as it proved — they all cast longing eyes in the direction of the bleeding Christ as if begging Him, in spite of their sins, not to leave their country and themselves to the mercy of the evil forces with which they had been playing.

Obregón was like the rest, afraid of some power that had a grip on him, and hating it. While the Mexican bishops were still in exile he sent a friend to see them. That man, Mestre Chigliazza, a Tabascan lawyer, came on his behalf to Washington and there consulted with the Archbishops. The Obregón agent told them frankly that Obregón wanted them back and assured them that the Church would be restored if he could bring it about. While Obregón was still President he arranged to meet me in Mexico City to discuss the Church problem, in the hope of an understanding, although the bishops had all returned and most of the churches had been reopened. Through a mistake of a church official the interview did not take place. When Obregón went to Mexico City in 1926 he expressed his regret that the conferences of Archbishops

Ruiz and Díaz with President Calles had failed. At seven o'clock one morning he himself held a conference with Bishop Fulcheri. President Calles caused it to be broken up. Obregón had already at that time restored two confiscated churches to the Apostolic Delegate, Msgr. Filippi, and was about to restore even the house of the Delegation. This I knew because I was on the ground, and what I learned was confirmed by the Apostolic Delegate.[2]

With the same suddenness that marked the outbreak of persecution in the Carranza revolution came a change. On a Sunday in 1928, in Guadalajara, I gave Communion to hundreds of men in the Church of San Francisco. A few days later I was present, on a week day, when thousands of people went to Communion as a spiritual gift to me. On the Sunday following I saw a parade of Catholic workmen that never seemed to end. I assisted at a ceremony in the Cathedral with a congregation that overflowed the great building as far up as the steps of the Archbishop's throne. Three days later, in Mexico City, I read denunciations of it all in the radical press, and on the Sunday following a group from the radical labor unions in Guadalajara, small but determined because protected, broke into the office of a newspaper, smashed the presses, and scattered the type over the street. They then went to the square before San Francisco Church and waited for the congregation to come out from Vespers. Twelve Catholics were shot before the sun went down. How many of them died I do not know. A short time after the Apostolic Delegate was expelled.

The dreaded power had acted. I had seen the love of

the people for their faith and for their pastors. I had even shared it. I had talked with men whom I knew had great influence with the President. It was not the people. It was not the educated laity. It was not the President. What I had seen and felt was only a small part of the mystery. Woe to any President of Mexico who does not think and act with that Mystery.

When Alvaro Obregón was in Mexico City for his second inauguration in 1928 a young artist fired five bullets into his body as he sat at table with his friends looking over sketches the same young artist had made of him. With his friends! When his body was examined after his death there were fourteen bullets in it. The poor fool of a boy was executed of course. Innocent persons were also executed. The Mystery had accounted for a President it feared would not carry out its orders, and glutted its hatred for the Church that it knew could not. The plot was cleverly made with both purposes in mind.

XVII

THE IRON MAN

IN THE OPENING CHAPTER of his fine study of Richelieu, Hilaire Belloc has this illuminating statement: "It perpetually appears throughout history that one man achieves and is the true creator of a capital event. This event will not have the ultimate consequence he would have expected. He may have produced that event without any design beyond the immediate limits of his action, but produce it he did. In military history the thing is glaring. The genius of Foch never expressed anything more truly or tersely than when he gave us the sentence: 'It was not an army that crossed the Alps; it was Hannibal.' The truth is equally apparent in every other form of human energy. The interest excited in us by the prospect of great genius may make us exaggerate the part which one will can play, but it is an error on the right side. We are safe in saying that in all notable achievements, but especially in the case of the highest, one man stands at their origin."

Although Mr. Belloc laments the tendency of historians to forget this fact, and speaks to correct an error, following "the depreciation of the individual human agent, and the conception that history was a process blind, necessary, and even mechanical," nevertheless, in the average man there is no ignoring of the fact that great changes are made by great men, usually by one great man. Mr. Belloc's own popularity as a producer of biographical studies is a proof of that. No matter how the actual historian treats his task, his reader, perhaps intuitively, keeps the correct thought. He finds the human center, places the point of his compass on it, and draws the circle of the great man's influence.

In the different studies produced from the history of Revolutionary Mexico, however, it has not been easy to select The Man. Hidalgo is out of the running. He antedated the real struggle by twelve years. Had Morelos been successful, lived to enlarge his objective and to rule, without doubt he would have been The Man. Matamoros was only an able camp follower. Iturbide did not get time enough to show his mettle. Alvarez was saved from being ridiculous only by the fact that his depravity overshadowed everything else about him. Not before we reach Juárez do we even hesitate. But his fame is transient and overestimated. He was a creature, not a creator; a creature of the none-too-wise American Government of his time. The reign of Díaz was an unannounced selection played by the whole orchestra. Madero was a well-intentioned dreamer of dreams. Carranza was a grabber, who hoped to develop into a statesman. Obregón's presidency was a march on the fife and drum. I forgot Maximilian. His part was an interlude played on a piccolo. I stop before the figure of Plutarco Elias Calles and — wonder if.

Mr. Belloc makes of Richelieu the creator of the halfimbecile and wholly divided thing that is Modern Europe. The one who brought the French statesman's work to completion — and inevitable disaster — was Otto von Bismark. In the events following the efforts of these two men the details of their acts and the records of their private lives are forgotten or ignored. Plutarco Elias Calles is at this time very generally taken as the Iron Man of Revolutionary Mexico. I do not agree, but must take the selection as it is.

In consequence of this title, the details of the acts of General Calles, as well as his private life, must largely be ignored. It is what he stands for that counts. All the constitutional and legislative acts which gather around him, and which he accepts by making them part of himself, are his responsibility; as well as all the creatures of his making that he uses to carry these acts into effect. That he has an atrocity record equal to, even surpassing, that of his predecessors is quite true. The murder of Father Pro is only one of them. That his private life makes his criticisms of others a mockery is likewise quite true. But the importance of his public policy is too great to allow anything to draw us away from it. What counts in the Iron Man are not his personal sins but the ideas he represents in public action. These are two: the Constitution of 1917, with the extension of its Articles made or commanded by him; and the persistency with which he enforced, and is enforcing, them. On public documents, decrees, and dictatorial commands, must the Iron Man of Mexico be judged.

It must be remembered, and that is why I repeat it here, that the revolution of Carranza, in which Obregón and Calles were leaders, was fought for the Constitution of 1857. That Constitution was not, however, satisfactory to the radicals. Before Carranza was certain of success he

enlisted the aid of the Workers of the World and gave
them charge of securing the support, not only of their own
members, but of all the Mexican workers and of others not
Mexicans. It goes without saying that only through an
agreement to carry out the radical program could Carranza
have secured that help. It must also be remembered that,
whatever concessions Carranza made, they could not have
been in accord with his own views unless absolute hypocrisy
be predicated of him, since three months after his treaty
with the radicals he issued the following statement: "The
Constitutionalist Laws of Mexico, commonly called the
laws of the Reform, which establish the separation of
Church and State and which guarantee to the individual
the right to worship God according to the dictates of his
own conscience so long as in doing so he does not disturb
the public order, shall be strictly observed; therefore, no
man shall suffer either in his life, his liberty, or his property by reason of his religious belief. The temples shall
continue to be property of the State, in accordance with
laws already enacted; and the Constitutionalist Government
shall renew the authority to use for purposes of worship
such of these as may be found necessary."

That statement was Carranza's protest against such men
as Calles. It raised a storm among the radicals, who had
determined to change the Constitution to suit themselves.
Inasmuch as no revolution in Mexico had ever been supported by the mass of the people, but always represented
a minority, the Querétaro Convention could not in any
way be considered representative. The new Constitution
was imposed by that Convention. It was not a civil but a

military document. It never was submitted for ratification to the people of Mexico. For that the Iron Man must accept his share of the responsibility.[1]

The Convention met in 1917. Its first Article, as already stated, limits the rights of citizens to those it grants, as if the military dictators who wrote it had become the source of all law. This Article alone kills the very first principle which the Liberals had enunciated. Other clauses call for a complete union of Church and State, a union better referred to as absorption, because they put the Church entirely under the jurisdiction of the State, denying her all rights and liberties.

The need for schools was quite evident and the Constitutionalists had proclaimed it, but the new Constitution prohibited any minister of religion from teaching in a school, public or private. Article 3 prohibited religious corporations or ministers of any religious creed from establishing or directing primary schools. Article 130 went further and ordered the confiscation of any school erected for the purpose of teaching religion. It provided likewise that in all primary-school matters the curriculum, teachers, etc., be under the direction of the Federal government. Not only were clergymen forbidden to teach, but they were even forbidden to maintain any institution of scientific research. Nevertheless Article 3 begins with the words "Instruction is free." All this too falls heavily to the blame of the Iron Man.

Well understanding that, so far as the Catholic schools were concerned, religious orders gave the lives of their members to education without salary, Article 5 forbade the establishment of such teaching orders "of whatever denomination" — thus striking at other than Catholic schools —"for whatever purpose contemplated." The educational provisions of the Constitution of 1917 not only give the State a monopoly of education but throw the whole burden upon it. Not even the United States could bear such a burden. It would bankrupt most of our large cities if the private schools were closed and the State had to bear the expense of purchasing buildings and maintaining public schools for their pupils. This would be true of New York, Boston, Philadelphia, Chicago, Detroit, or any other large city in the north or east. How then, could Mexico hope to solve its educational problem if forced to start from the foundation? It is for the Iron Man to answer that question.

No legal status was given to any church. The Constitution of 1917 states, in Article 130, that "The law recognizes no juridical personality in the religious institutions known as churches." They were the only institutions singled out for such treatment. For most of this sort of thing the Iron Man was responsible, as the chosen friend of the radicals who wanted it—as the man behind it.

Dr. William D. Guthrie, a former President of the American Bar Association, in a written professional opinion,[2] shows that this Constitution deprives churches of all means of redress and protection, because they cannot appeal to Congress or to the courts to enforce their property rights. This, he says, "is in direct violation of long-established principles of international law, or as it is termed in Europe, Africa, and Asia, the law of nations, or the *jus gentium* of the Roman law." He further shows that if the Church authorities even petitioned against the confiscation, they thereby lost their citizenship: "Citizenship shall be lost: . . . by compromising themselves in any way before ministers of any religious creed or before any other person not to observe the present Constitution, or the laws arising thereunder" (Art. 37). This again, he says, "violates international law among all civilized nations under principles of universal acceptance 'both in the law of continental Europe and in the common law of England,' as has been emphatically declared by the Supreme Court of the United States." In support of this statement Dr. Guthrie cites an opinion of the United States Supreme Court delivered by the late Chief Justice Fuller. In that opinion the Chief Justice said: "The Spanish law as to the juristic capacity of the church at the time of the cession merely followed the principles of the Roman law."

My statement that the Constitution of 1917 provides for a union and not a separation of Church and State is upheld by Dr. Guthrie as follows: "The Mexican Government is not attempting in good faith to bring about the separation of Church and State as Americans conceive the substance of such separation, nor is it attempting merely to prevent alleged ecclesiastical intervention or interference in politics or in matters of state. On the contrary, both the Mexican Constitution and the Presidential Decree now in question are calculated and, indeed, deliberately intended to bring about a more entire domination by the State over the Church than has ever existed before, and to place under the absolute control and supervision of the Mexican Federal

and State Governments every church in Mexico, and pre-
eminently the Roman Catholic Church and her temples,
which, to repeat, represents the religious faith of more than
nineteen twentieths of the population. The membership of
other churches, it is understood and counsel has been so
instructed, may be reasonably asserted to be comparatively
almost negligible so far as numbers are concerned; but
they, of course, are equally affected and interested and
will inevitably be equally subjugated and oppressed if they
ever attempt to free themselves from governmental control
and direction, though unhappily some of their spokes-
men do not seem to perceive this and prefer to join in the
attacks on the Roman Catholic Church in Mexico."

With regard to confiscation of church buildings, he says:
"It would, as it seems to the undersigned American
counsel, be simply preposterous to claim that these provisions were intended to produce or promote in good faith
the separation of Church and State in Mexico. On the
contrary, a more complete subjugation of Church to State
could not be devised by the wit of man. Certainly, no precedent of any such complete absorption of church control
and regulation or governance of divine worship even in
state churches by the State has ever before been attempted
in modern times except in Soviet Russia and Jacobin
France, and no such precedent can be recalled in the
history of Christianity or Judaism."

After quoting from the 1st, 4th, 6th, 7th, 8th, 10th, 13th,
15th, 17th, 18th, 21st, and 22nd Articles of this Constitution,
and commenting on them, Dr. Guthrie writes: "Paraphrasing the noble words of our Declaration of Independence,

the Roman Catholic Church is advised that, whilst, of course and pre-eminently, first 'appealing to the supreme judge of the world for the rectitude of [her] intentions,' she now appeals to the advised opinion of mankind throughout the world and in the form of fair and honest public opinion in every country, to the end that all may appreciate that her policy in Mexico is proper, wise and just, and that she would have been untrue to herself and her traditions if she had submitted in our age to the arbitrary, brutal and subversive persecution now being enforced in Mexico, which is so plainly incompatible with the crudest notions of religious or personal liberty."

In Article 130 of the Querétaro Convention — the one Carranza was shot for wanting to change — it is forbidden that any person not a Mexican by birth be a minister of any religious creed in Mexico, but if a Mexican by birth does become a minister of a religious creed, by the same Article he loses his vote as a citizen and becomes ineligible to hold any office. A Calles Minister of Education was a Methodist clergyman. He therefore held his office illegally by permission of the Iron Man. Article 82 forbids the President of Mexico to belong to an ecclesiastical state, which could easily be interpreted as forbidding membership in any church. Article 130 prohibits a minister from receiving a legacy, or even being a trustee for a legacy, if it be destined for religious purposes. "Ministers of religious creeds are incapable legally of inheriting by will from ministers of the same religious creed or from any private individual to whom they are not related by blood within the fourth degree." All the provisions in Article 130 are protected by this extraordinary clause: "No trial by jury shall ever be granted for the infraction of any of the preceding provisions."

In spite of the fact that at the time of the writing of this chapter, the Iron Man was himself a patient in a religious hospital in Los Angeles, Article 27, Part III, of the Constitution which he pushed through, says: "In no case shall any institution of this character [for the sick and needy] be under the patronage, direction, administration, charge or supervision of religious corporations or institutions." The Dictator of Mexico, its former President and the man who helped to place the Article in the Constitution, in his distress rushed to the care of a religious institution in another country. But this is not looked upon as illogical. The close relative of President Rubio, killed by peace officers near Ardmore, Oklahoma, in 1931, was returning from a religious college in Atchison, Kansas, when the unfortunate event happened. Two little daughters of the Iron Man attended a Sisters' school in Mexico City. I personally knew and spoke with one of their teachers who was then in exile and poverty.

Article 24 of the Constitution of 1917 reads as follows:

"Everyone is free to embrace the religion of his choice and to practice all ceremonies, devotions, or observances of his respective creed, either in places of public worship or at home, provided they do not constitute an offense punishable by law." But to make sure that no one in effect will be thus free Article 130 provides that as the law is now enforced, family prayers at home constitute an illegal religious act.

"The Federal authorities shall have power to exercise in matters of religious worship and outward ecclesiastical forms such intervention as by law authorized. All other officials shall act as auxiliaries to the Federal authorities."

Calles himself as President enlarged on Article 130 and has been doing so through others ever since. He is the author of the six-year plan. Catholics have appealed to courts, to legislators, to Federal executives, to governors, but all to no avail. They have been insulted, jailed, tortured, and murdered for having dared to do so. The number of priests has been cut down by decrees of the Iron Man's governors to a point where it has become impossible for the people to have pastors at all. One State decreed one clergyman for every 100,000 people. The Archbishop of Puebla, who was allowed one priest for every 4,000, appealed to the legislature to examine into the needs, adding that one priest for 4,000 was insufficient. There is no place in Mexico, except perhaps in the capital, where there are 4,000 Protestants of all denominations put together.

To show the impossibility for religion even to exist under such laws it is only necessary to quote from testimony given before the Senate Committee investigating Mexican Affairs as follows:

"The best answer to the charge that Mexico is priest-ridden is to give the figures. Some of them were given by Navarro y Noriega, published in the *Boletín de la Sociedad Mexicana de Geografía y Estadística*, 2a Época, volume 1, pages 290–291. He places the number of clergy in Mexico in 1810 as 7,341. Of that number 3,112 belonged to orders devoted to teaching, hospital, and other public service.

There were 2,098 sisters, most of them teachers. The Mexican population in 1810 was 6,122,354. The proportion of the clergy to the population was then 1 to 834. Now, in 1917, according to the account of the United States Census Bureau, the number of Catholic clergymen in the United States was 20,287, and the Catholic population was 15,742,-262, a proportion of clergy to population of 1 to 776. But in the whole United States in 1917 there were 191,722 clergymen of all denominations, and 42,044,374 church members. So that in the United States in 1917 there was a clergyman to every 219 church members, while in Mexico in 1810 there was only one clergyman to 834 of the entire population. If you consider only the clergy of the United States other than Catholic, the proportion is one clergyman to every 153 church members, and in some of the non-Catholic bodies the clergy are as numerous as 1 to 35. Of course, these latter are very small denominations." The figures for 1810 were used because that year saw the largest number of clergy in Mexico. It has diminished since that time.[3]

Statements made by citizens of Querétaro, who had under their eyes the Convention of 1917 and its members, say that the sessions held in the Iturbide Theatre were riots of drunkenness and open immorality; that, even though the delegates had been selected only from among the revolutionists, nevertheless the chief anti-religious clauses were held back till the end; that they were voted on at two o'clock in the morning when the delegates, overcome by loss of sleep and by drink, not only were unable to discuss them, but even to know for what they were voting. Naturally the names of those making the statements cannot be published, but that they were made, and by many, was testified to by an American who lived in Querétaro for years after the Convention and knew the people who gave the information as reputable citizens.

To Dr. Guthrie's legal opinion I owe the knowledge of a paragraph from Chancellor Kent's *Commentaries,* which by its clear statement of a fundamental legal truth, merits quotation at this point: "The free exercise and enjoyment of religious profession and worship may be considered as one of the absolute rights of individuals, recognized in our American constitutions, and secured to them by law. Civil and religious liberty generally go hand in hand, and the suppression of either of them, for any length of time, will terminate the existence of the other."

The American doctrine is also stated clearly by the late Mr. Justice Miller of the Supreme Court of the United States, called "one of the ablest and most scholarly justices who have ever sat in that great court": "Freedom of religious profession and worship cannot be maintained if the civil courts trench upon the domain of the church, construe its canons and rules, dictate its discipline, and regulate its trials. . . . It is as much a delusion to confer religious liberty without the right to make and enforce rules and canons, as to create government with no power to punish offenders. . . . The civil power may contribute to the protection, but cannot interfere to destroy or fritter away."

What would be the result of the practical application of the Mexican laws to a Protestant religious denomination were they in force in the United States? For illustration I select the Methodist-Episcopal Church, North, out of others because of its large membership, and set down the effect these laws would have on both institution and membership.

1. The denomination would not be permitted to own any building — church, parsonage, club, or school — nor to hold property of any kind in its corporate name for endowment.

2. If such property were held in the name of an individual, or other juristic personality, the simple opinion of the Attorney General would be sufficient, without trial of the case, to authorize the confiscation of that property by the State.

3. All Methodist-Episcopal universities and colleges, such as Northwestern at Evanston, Illinois, would be confiscated and closed if (a) the actual title were in a Methodist-Episcopal board of trustees, or (b) if it could be *suspected* that the Board was in any way under the control, even honorary, of the Methodist-Episcopal body, or (c) if any kind of religious lectures or classes were given in the institution.

4. Endowments for scientific research possessed by any Methodist-Episcopal school, college, university, or society, would be confiscated; and it would be a criminal offense to use the same for the purposes of the foundation.

5. No Methodist-Episcopal body, even though not operating in its own name, could receive any legacy for the support or expansion of its work.

6. No Methodist-Episcopal clergyman, no matter what

his educational training or experience, could direct or even teach in a university, college, or school.

7. A Methodist-Episcopal church for foreign-speaking congregations could not employ a minister unless he were a native-born citizen. Nor could a visiting Methodist-Episcopal clergyman from abroad hold a religious service or preach even once in any church of the denomination.

8. The very fact that a citizen might be a Methodist-Episcopal clergyman would preclude the possibility of his inheriting anything from persons not within the fourth degree of kindred to him.

9. If in the family of a Methodist-Episcopal clergyman there was a son also a clergyman, he could not receive a legacy left him by his own father.

10. No Methodist-Episcopal newspaper or religious magazine would be allowed to comment on any of the political affairs of the nation, or even give information to its readers on the acts of the governmental authorities.

11. No burial services could be held at the grave of a dead Methodist.

12. No religious services for a dead Methodist could be held in his home or at a funeral parlor.

13. No Methodist-Episcopal minister or layman could give an invocation or pronounce a benediction at a meeting, no matter how small, a banquet or other gathering of the people, public or private. The prayer itself would make the whole meeting illegal.

14. No Methodist-Episcopal clergyman, if a religious form were used, could officiate at a marriage, either in his

own home or in that of one of the persons being joined in wedlock. The religious act would render even that gathering illegal.

15. Prohibition, or any other matter that involved a law passed or proposed, could neither be explained nor discussed in a Methodist-Episcopal church.

16. There could be no Methodist-Episcopal preparatory seminary or theological school to train and educate candidates for the ministry.

17. The Order of Deaconesses would be illegal and its property subject to confiscation.

18. All Methodist-Episcopal hospitals, orphanages, or other charitable institutions would be confiscated and closed.

19. All new Methodist-Episcopal churches, even if for the building of them the necessary permission had been granted by the government, would become the property of the State when built.

20. The number of Methodist-Episcopal ministers in any State would be fixed not by the bishops or even the people. but by the Governor.

21. Methodist-Episcopal ministers, by the fact of ordination, would at once lose their right to vote.

22. A State official would have charge of every Methodist-Episcopal building to report to the government if the laws were violated in it, or if any of the furniture purchased, paid for, and installed by the people, was being treated as though they owned it.

23. In the event that a Methodist-Episcopal college taught secular subjects, such as arithmetic or algebra, no

credit could be granted for them to students in preparation for professional studies.

24. Violations of such laws would be criminal offenses punishable to a degree equal to, and often greater than, theft or arson. Fines would range from $250 to $2,500, or jail sentences including confiscation of any property involved.

25. The Epworth League, as a society of young people promising to do certain acts of piety or religion, would not be permitted. To resign and re-enter the society would be punishable with from one to two years in prison. This would apply also to deaconesses, except that as women the punishment would be one-third less than for men.

26. Advising a minor to join the Epworth League or the Order of Deaconesses would be a major criminal offense involving a jail sentence.

27. To advise others in a public address to protest against such laws would subject the offender, clerical or lay, to six years in prison and a fine.

28. The same offense given in a private address would draw a fine and from one to five years in prison.

29. No prayer meeting could be held outside a church building, not even at home.

30. No Methodist minister might wear in public any article of clothing or insignia designating him as such.

31. For violations of most of the above laws no trial by jury would be permitted.

32. All children born to Methodist-Episcopal parents would belong, not to them, but to the State, to do with as the government desired.

The educational property and endowments of the Methodist-Episcopal Church, North, is valued at more than $138,414,751, according to the U. S. Census for Religious Bodies of 1926. The value of property used by this denomination for charitable purposes in 1926, was $40,233,520 with $6,550,720 endowment. The value of church edifices and parsonages is about $500,000,000. These figures do not take into account the publishing societies, the missionary organizations, or those universities and colleges to which title is held by boards of trustees.

As General Calles was married after the laws and decrees covering this long list of possible "crimes" were passed, and the ceremony performed, as is usual in Mexico for such cases, in his own house by a priest, he himself became subject to punishment and to the confiscation of the building. He had assisted likewise at the religious ceremony of the baptism of two children born to his sister, and was cognizant of the fact that the rosary was said in his house around the deathbed of his first wife. These acts were violations of his own laws.

It is a terrible truth to add that if a priest gives a last absolution, or says an audible prayer over a Mexican soldier dying on the field of battle for his country, that act is criminal before the law and punishable as such. Read over the Articles of the Constitution, the Presidential decrees that interpreted and enforced them, as well as the court decisions that uphold them, and see if in any way I have exaggerated their import.

For the existence of these persecuting laws Plutarco Elias Calles is chiefly responsible. It requires the most hopeless condition of blind hatred in anyone — American, Mexican, even Moslem — to restrain him from asking if the passing and enforcing of them took place in the twentieth century of the Christian Era, and if the present government of Mexico is not really being conducted by madmen rather than by civilized human beings.

The answer of a Calles apologist might be that the laws are intended to set up a socialist government, and not to persecute. I have heard that answer given. No comment on it seems necessary. The National Revolutionary Party, of which General Calles is the head, is behind an amendment to Article 3 calling for "socialistic education" instead of "laical instruction." In the discussions by the Party it was made plain that "socialistic education" means atheism in religion, communism in economics, and materialism in morals. When general objection was made against all this by the people, the government immediately attributed it to the clergy, charging them with "fanaticism and prejudices." "Fanaticism" is believing in God and "prejudice" is keeping the Commandments.

In the State of Michoacán sixty public-school teachers resigned rather than teach as prescribed. In Aguascalientes all resigned. Resignations likewise marked opposition in other parts of Mexico. But the number of them may make it difficult for the government to proceed against the teachers in the criminal courts. The resignations, as acts which may be interpreted as critical of the government, place all protesting teachers in the criminal class.

Under retired President Rodríguez the Minister of Education for a time was one Bassols, a close friend of General

Calles. His particular educational fad was sexual instruction. He sent out indecent pamphlets to the teachers and others about it, and the consequences of them cannot be described. The people at last spoke. Bassols had to resign in order to quell a riot of protests. President Rodríguez, while accepting the resignation, made public a letter from Bassols charging the clergy, and in particular the Archbishop of Mexico, with fomenting the agitation against him. He was immediately appointed Minister of the Interior. That was flying into the face of public opinion with a vengeance. No one doubts but that the Iron Man, and the Iron Man alone, had taken the risk of doing it. Would he have done it only for the sake of a political nonentity and liability? There was more than the Bassols nonentity behind his act —the power that owns General Calles.

Men who, by the strength and force of their character, exercised for right or for wrong, merit the title of "Iron," appear, if not often, at least often enough, in the world, to give us rules by which the type may be known and measured. Is Plutarco Elias Calles one of them? Let us see. The true Iron Men stand alone. They may be aided by other men — indeed they must be; they may even be influenced by other men, but never against their own deliberate choice of objective; in small matters they may allow the advice of others to modify their methods, but never their ends; they are supremely self-confident and admit to themselves the existence of no master, even though outwardly they may seem to give allegiance to one; they never allow any person or any party to become strong enough to menace their power, but carefully play such potential enemies against each other, while seeming to be for both a friend; if one party, by slip or accident, becomes dominant over its rival the policy of the Iron Men in its regard is always the same — to destroy it, for the Iron Men are ruthless, and in most cases self-convinced that they are right; they do not fear to lie, or at least to allow those with whom they deal to deceive themselves — but they attach no self-reproach to falsehood of that kind; they believe that, as exceptions to the general run of men, all things that concern their ambitions are likewise exceptions; they may have certain high standards of personal morality in some things, but even in these, such standards are flexible and subservient to the central objective which they make an integral part of themselves.

Is Plutarco Elias Calles an Iron Man? In the fact that Iron Men must stand alone he is not. All through his public career it was plain that the power he exercised was not of himself. Twice to my own knowledge he made attempts to conciliate the religious forces and, though perfectly satisfied that he had made an acceptable and cunning compromise, he broke his word and retreated to the old ground; but not like one who had succeeded in fooling an opponent, rather like one who dared too far without a master's approbation. Calles does not stand alone. He is not his own master. He has not the freedom to play one outside force against another. The issue is clearly drawn between radicalism and religion and on it he has no choice because he has no freedom. Calles is only a nominal head. His party is ostensibly of his own creation; but in fact it is only a name for something many long centuries older than he and it rules him. Outwardly he has no rival — that is, no personal rival — but he has worse than a rival, for he has a master in that red group he fears to disobey.[4]

In only one sense, then, is General Calles an addition to the short list of the Iron Men who have appeared in history — the Richelieus, the Cromwells, and the Bismarks — and that one sense gives him only an appearance of independence. He is Iron in the sense that he is a mechanical man, moved by a current of power to which he must be attached. The strong levers, pulleys, wheels, and wires are his. The current is not. It is the idea of Weishaupt, of Rousseau, of Marx, generated in the laboratory of the foreign radical, and sent to him over the wire of the Mexican lodges. If ever it happens that another force from outside attempts to move in a different way any part of the Iron Man's mechanism, a short circuit will result and he will blow out and blow up.

XVIII

THE AMERICAN FRONT

IT WAS A DESPERATE Germany that sent Lenin into Russia. Mr. Winston Churchill, in the British House of Commons on November 5, 1919, said: "Lenin was sent into Russia in the same way that you might send a phial containing a culture of typhoid or cholera to be poured into the water supply of a great city, and it worked with amazing accuracy. No sooner did Lenin arrive than he began beckoning a finger here and a finger there to obscure persons in sheltered retreats in New York, in Glasgow, in Berne, and other countries, and he gathered together the leading spirits of a formidable sect, the most formidable sect in the world, of which he was the high priest and chief. With these spirits around him he set to work with demoniacal ability to tear to pieces every institution upon which the Russian State depended. Russia was laid low. Russia had to be laid low. Russia was laid low in the dust. . . . Her national life was completely ruined; the fruits of her sacrifices were thrown away. She was condemned to long internal terrors, and menaced by famine. . . . Her sufferings are more fearful than modern records hold, and she has been robbed of her place among the great nations of the world."

I have no wish to do more than cite that passage as one of the most significant extracts from a parliamentary debate in modern times. Germany was fighting for her life at the time. Lenin came within an inch of saving it then while he ruthlessly destroyed all before him in his own country—this "high priest and chief" of "the most formidable sect in the world." Who could understand better, and weigh more accurately the words he uttered, than a Cabinet Minister of the British Empire with the files of the Foreign Office at his service?

Germany's act of sending Lenin into Russia was carrying propaganda to its most vicious and ignoble end. But all nations have used propaganda. They believe that they are fully justified in so doing. Ludendorff said "from the military point of view his [Lenin's] journey was justified."[1] The moral point of view he of course ignored. Our own nation has used propaganda in Mexico. All diplomatic representatives are of course, in a way, propagandists. But we sent Poinsett, Gadsden, and Lind into Mexico as agents: two for Mexico's ruin and one for her perversion. Morrow, not a trained diplomat, was really a banker's propagandist sent to collect debts under another name.

Mexico, ever since Hidalgo—it began with him in a weak way—has recognized the fact that its front line of defense against all comers is not south but north of the Rio Grande. In "all comers" the Colossus himself is included. So Mexico keeps men on the American front, a propaganda army. Some of these—most of them in fact—are volunteers who serve without pay: parlor pinks, uplift societies, clubs, anybody or anything that can be impressed by sentiment and shallow talk. Others are paid. The propaganda bill of the Mexican Government is a large one. North Americans get most of the money. The New York *American* published on December 2, 1927, a letter signed by Aaron Saenz, as Mexican Minister of Foreign Affairs, authorizing a bribe of $50,000 for an American chain of newspapers to "control the press in an effective manner." This propaganda thing is common.

But Mexico uses very few Mexicans on its American front line, and for a wise reason: apart from the universal power of the bribe they are worthless in the United States. They have not the approach. They cannot learn it. Their mental processes are radically different from those of Americans. They have the "Latin" rather than the "Saxon Mind." This last statement calls for an explanation.

Behind the Latin thinking there are centuries of that philosophy of which Cardinal Mercier was the outstanding modern master. It is an inexorable logical process of thought which affects not only the student exposed to it, but even the races influenced by it. Sir Thomas More had it in England and, in spite of the common fall of his countrymen before the false theory of the all-inclusive authority of kings, he found himself in the position of being forced by the logic of his knowledge to die for it. The thing is an inheritance from monastic learning, medieval in its development and precision but Greek in its origin. It is the immortality of both Aquinas and Aristotle. Essentially it is religious because with "being" it begins. It is the one thing on the face of the earth that admits of no compromise. One can be only logically with it or illogically against it. There is no solid standing ground in the middle. It means the Catholic intellectual position or nothing, and explains the remark of a witty Frenchman who confessed to the loss of his faith. Being urged to become a Huguenot, he said: "Sir, it was my faith I lost, not my reason."

The "Saxon Mind" is not at all like that, as its many and varied philosophies show. It begins to reason right in the middle of things and goes backward or forward without being sure where it is going. It can accept compromise. It can accept God without bothering about His attributes, creation without troubling itself as to its why and wherefore. Truth for it is often relative and not absolute. It sees no intellectual need of authority and repudiates it in consequence. It elevates liberty of thought to the vacant throne of authority and makes a royal virtue out of dissent. Its highest life is one of seeking and searching. Its highest abstract intellectual virtue is tolerance, though in the concrete tolerance is not always thus honored.

Send the Latin Mind that has decided against God to meet the Saxon Mind that sees no need to decide at all and hate meets indifference which does not understand it. The Latin Mind cannot be indifferent—the Saxon Mind can be and is. The Latin Mind clings to unity. The Saxon Mind sees actual disadvantages in unity. In a word, the Latin Mind simply cannot comprehend the mental processes of the Saxon Mind.

Apart entirely from the disadvantage of his lack of knowledge of the American's language, which in many cases could be overcome, the Mexican atheist is in no condition to fight his own battles on the American front.

He must have there men who can appeal to Americans along their own line of thinking. The attack on American public opinion by Americans on behalf of Mexican revolutionary opinions does not, then, laud atheism and try to force Americans, who abominate it, into accepting it as progress. There really are few avowed American atheists. Americans understand the skeptic but not the atheist. They simply refuse to believe that there are any atheists; taking a few professions as gentle aberrations or foolish boastings. But even in this few there is no enthusiasm for their own atheism. To fight for it, to legislate in favor of it, to go out and kill for it—Americans would consider the idea sheer lunacy. In that they are logical enough. So the American fighters for the Mexican revolution conceal its atheism, minimize it, or deny its existence altogether, as the only way out of the problem it raises; or they try bringing forward strongly the idea of liberty of conscience—which they know the Mexican atheist would never think of—to cover up from discussion that which they know they cannot defend. On that part of the front their problem is one of effective camouflage.

They have another problem on the score of democracy. The real Mexican revolutionist does not believe in it and never did. He talks about it, puts it in his book and then ignores it. Democracy would be the bitter end of him. Give Mexicans the ballot and a fair count and there would be no real revolutionaries in power. No one knows that better than those now in power who can only keep themselves there by force of arms. Alvarado in Yucatan gave the outstanding example of their methods. I outlined what they are when I referred to him. He made sure that the people had no money, no free press, no pastors, and no arms. Then he was set and could govern as he pleased, which he did to the ruin of Yucatan. Yet his apologists on the American front made a great democrat of him, a lover of the common people, and an administrator *par excellence*. In the United States he would have been a murderer, a tyrant, a thief, and an anarchist. I have never yet met a Mexican, except a priest or a bishop, who believed that democracy could ever work in Mexico. Even the conservatives are a unit in doubting its efficacy for Mexican rule. When they had the chance to try it they promptly became open and avowed royalists. The radicals, on the other hand, set up the forms of democracy to cover up the fact that they have an uncrowned czar on a shaky throne. In a vague sort of way Americans know all this in their hearts, but allow themselves to be persuaded to forget or excuse it. They excused Carranza's pre-constitutional rule on the ground of political necessity. President Wilson said: "There is one thing I have got a great enthusiasm about. I might almost say a reckless enthusiasm, and that is human liberty." It was a typical shot from the biggest Big Bertha on the American front. And at the time that exactly was what President Wilson was.

Labor has a battalion on the front, though not so large as the one that was there under the command of the late Samuel Gompers. He it was who kept President Wilson on the front. His motive, as already stated, was to tie the Mexican labor movement in with the American Federation at home and in Canada. He did not succeed in Mexico, but he did succeed by his activities there in consolidating opposition in the labor circles of Quebec against the American Federation; thus saving what he would have swallowed, the Catholic National Unions of that province. Mr. Gruening, who has devoted so much time and work to a study of Mexican labor conditions—a respectful bow to him for that —ends his study on a hopeful note not entirely justified by the composition, yet has this to say about Mr. Calles' boss: "The head of the Mexican labor movement, Luis N. Morones, has become a man of wealth. He owns many properties including a textile factory—though not in his own name. He lives lavishly. He sports not less than a half dozen automobiles. His parrandas[2] staged every week-end in the suburb of Tlalpam are notorious for their orgiastic extravagance. In a retreat, intended not for any considerable group of workers but for the inner clique—the Grupo Accion—a great steel-girdered fronton court, swimming pool, bowling alleys, tennis court, and three dwellings with a retinue of servants lift this club to a plane of luxury unequalled except by millionaires' country clubs in the United States. Comrade Morone's diamonds have become famous and, while neither as large nor as numerous as cartoon and satire present them, were deemed worthy of a defense in the C.R.O.M.'s official publication. Harmless in themselves, they have become a symbol of contrast with the hundreds of thousands who still wear huaraches, and of dissatisfaction within the movement."[3] But the leaders on the American front never fail to laud "the ideal conditions of Mexican labor."

Protestantism was once well represented on the American front. Like the labor battalion it is far from being so well represented today. Carranza had Protestant American friends always glad to go to the front for him, men like Dr. Tupper, Dr. Inman, Bishop Cannon, and, though he came into prominence on the front a little later, Bishop Creighton.[4] Before the Senate Committee of 1919–20, some of them appeared. They came early but did not stay late. Dr. Inman stated that "50 per cent of the leadership [in Mexico under Carranza] ranging all the way from members of city councils to governors and secretaries and senators, have been educated in American schools in Mexico, or schools in the United States." We have had a chance to observe the work of these distinguished graduates of missionary schools in the cause of Christianity and are not enthused. One part of a general letter to heads of Protestant mission boards in Mexico, dated July 31, 1919, written by Dr. Inman, and found in the Senate Report on page 42, might give thought to its author today: "When the Mexican revolution began Protestant churches threw themselves into it almost unanimously because they believed that the program of the revolution represented what these churches had been preaching through the years and that the triumph of the revolution meant the triumph of the Gospel." Well, the revolution did triumph. It waded through blood to its goal. So many of those delightful graduates of the mission schools are in their graves. No Protestant American minister or teacher may officiate in Mexico today, not even Dr. Inman. I suppose he is still on the American front, though I do not know. Bishop Creighton certainly is, to the distress of some of his own church editors. Dr. Tupper in 1919 had never heard of the religious restrictions of the Carranza regime as they are set forth in Article 130 of the Constitution. Bishop Cannon was quite surprised over the same Article. Both reverend gentlemen had preached in Mexico after its adoption. Mr. Carranza said it would be all right —to violate the law. In 1926 the Protestant battalion was working hard for Mr. Calles. Arthur Sears Henning gave an outline of activity in his favor during the Coolidge administration, in an article in *Liberty* published on April 6, 1929. He stated that the Federal Council of Churches circularized 75,000 ministers to save the Calles government from the annoyance of being forced to withdraw laws confiscatory of American properties. The excuse was "arbitration." The Rev. Hubert C. Herring actually went to the Mexican government to negotiate, contrary to American law, Mr. Henning asserted. Arbitration won its case but the American property owners are still awaiting action about their properties. The Protestant battalion is no longer large. The anti-religious laws made to kill Catholics but relaxed in favor of Protestants are now applied to the latter, though far from as murderously as to Catholics. But the battalion did effective work in its day, and the Mexican persecutors might well show more gratitude for it. Dr. Herring in particular wasted enough friendly co-operation on them to win him the Grand Cross of the Legion of Honor had he done as well by France.[5]

There was always a Liberal battalion on the American front. During the Carranza days it was extremely active, sending some representatives before the Senate inquiry of 1919–20. The names of its leaders are now more than half forgotten, but Mr. Carleton Beals was one who is not forgotten. How he feels about it now is best told by himself. Mr. Montavon quotes him in a place of honor, right on the cover of his timely and accurate brochure *The Church in Mexico Protests*. Mr. Beals knows well how to express himself, so well and so to the point that I have no hesitation about reproducing his actual words: "I have stood unflinchingly on the side of the Mexican Government in their theoretical position regarding the Catholic Church, but I was almost deported from Mexico because I dared to speak of the personal abuse of Catholics in that struggle. Every personal right of every Catholic was violated. They were held by the police, they had no legal protection, no protection whatever from the courts of Mexico. Often a Catholic was arrested and fined; and if he could not pay his fine he was sent to Islas Tres Marias, the Pacific Coast penal colony. It was a glorious moment for arbitrary robbing of Catholics in Mexico. They were jailed and mulcted of their properties without due process of law. If you can take away the personal liberty of a Catholic, you can take away the personal liberty of everybody else." The American Liberals have been sadly disillusioned about Mexico. They once thought that what they meant by liberalism was what the Mexican Liberals meant. Now most of them know that the two ideas were poles apart. The Radicals of Mexico have snatched away the Liberal fire leaving American Liberals only a choice between following the torch of destruction or sulking in their tents.

The Masonic contribution was never more than a company of scouts seldom seen on the front itself, but doing effective work. Mr. Samuel Gompers mentioned its "way in and way out" in his autobiography (Vol. II, page 312),[6] when he tells of the visit of a fellow Mason from Mexico to him in Washington. It is still working but very much in a haze of doubt because of President Cárdenas' dissenting body. American Masonry is of too mild a type in general to suit the Latin Mind. But there are American Masons on the front, and through their Washington headquarters, they are always active.

All the battalions on the American front work most earnestly to keep its most powerful body in line, the Government regiment. As long as that force stays, the front is powerful and holds. It works along a simple but effective line, that of neighborly, peaceful friendliness. To all intents and purposes every American administration since Wilson's has been held as an ally of every Mexican administration by the fact of an embargo on the shipment of arms to others than the Mexican government. The National Revolutionary Party and the C.R.O.M. can get arms. No other Mexican organization can. The Mexican Government remains in power, and snaps its fingers at opposition at home as well as abroad, because the United States Government by its embargo on arms gives it the courage to do so. The Mexican Government has also its pull on American business interests to influence Washington. There are always Americans anxious to get favors for the companies they represent and quite ready to come home and pull wires. In fact, they are forced to do it. A few months ago, before his inauguration, President Cárdenas — who was not particularly favored for the place by Mr. Calles — conceived the idea of bringing President Roosevelt to visit him. It was a grand idea. If it succeeded it would put the official stamp of American approval on the religious persecution, the socialistic schools with their sexualistic instruction, and the dictatorship of the proletariat; besides putting Mr. Calles, who is not of the proletariat any more than Mr. Morones — both being millionaires — in his place. It was a beautiful political plot. If President Roosevelt came to enjoy the hospitality of President Cárdenas, the latter would be the big man of Mexico. What difference about the effect of the visit on the political fortunes of Mr. Roosevelt at home? The game was started through a business corporation that needed the Cárdenas support, and action followed on the American front. I happened to be around when the march arrived at a long and deep ravine. The engineers could not bridge it. The infantry and cavalry could not get around it. The artillery could see nothing to fire at over it. Yet it was nothing more than a revelation of the purposes behind the march.

Failure on the American front brought Mexican Head-quarters into action. The Latin Mind went north to meet its Saxon brother. Ex-President Rodríguez called on President Roosevelt and the news was given out that he had succeeded. The Mexican Government press trumpeted it all over the nation; but the sound also went over the border. The President of the United States issued a denial, and it is possible that the Iron Man's features somehow were twisted into a smile.

Though depleted, the American front is still active. Its volunteers beg us to mind our own business and let Mexico do as its government pleases with people who are fools enough to think that it matters a bit whether there be a God or not. Some of them are quite sincere. But behind it all is the shadow of the Jefferson hope: Mexico a colony for the Colossus; one flag flying as far down as the Canal. And all to be brought about in the easy way: let Mexico commit suicide.

There is a warning well known in Mexico uttered by Luis Cuevas some seventy years ago. I can quote it only by paraphrasing it from a memory that caught its meaning but not its exact wording. It is taken from his book *El Porvenir de Mexico*: "Mexico under the regime of Liberals will go to its own ruin and the time will come when the Mexican people will be forced to stretch their arms toward the United States, crying: 'Save Us.'"

XIX

INTERNATIONAL ASPECT

TWO EVENTS HAVE transpired of late in Mexico which show that its present government is by no means at ease over the international aspects of its persecution of religion. One is an address by the Minister of Foreign Affairs to the diplomatic corps at a banquet given in honor of the inauguration of President Cárdenas,[1] and the other the publication of an historical and legal essay by Emilio Portes Gil, Attorney General of the Republic, entitled *The Conflict between the Civil Power and the Clergy*. It happens that both the address and the essay are attributed to one man, for Emilio Portes Gil was transferred, before the address was delivered, from the portfolio of Justice to that of Foreign Affairs in the Cabinet.

As Minister of Foreign Affairs Mr. Portes Gil in his address makes a surprising sort of appeal to a diplomatic corps; nothing less than solicitation of the individual interest of each member to explain to his government the reasons for such an extraordinary condition as religious persecution in Mexico. Hitherto the attitude of the Mexican Government on the matter was of the "mind your own business" type. But in his address the Minister complains petulantly against "high Church authorities" in other nations who, he stated, were trying to discredit the government of Mexico, because of its "new policies regarding social and religious problems," confessing that these new policies were hurting "created interests" as well as "deeply rooted traditions." He asked the diplomats to beg their governments to consider, not these policies themselves, but the reasons for adopting them. The address was liberally quoted from by the American newspapers.

As the reasons offered the diplomatic corps for the existence of the "new policies" were a summary of those given in the essay written when Mr. Portes Gil was Attorney General, I shall treat them when I consider that document. What must strike the reader at this point will not be the reasons themselves but the character of the strange address. The occasion, the audience, the speaker, made it nothing less than an official pronouncement of the Mexican Government to the other governments of the world, assuming before them that the government of Mexico is, on the face of things, doing an unusual and blamable thing, not at all in conformity with accepted ideas of right and justice. The address is then in effect an admission of guilt with an appeal to extenuating circumstances.

I question if a more strangely remarkable official pronouncement has been made by any government within the century. It is a clear manifestation of the untenable character of the "new policies" before the court of international public opinion, an admission of acts against the accepted and admitted rights of private citizens. Either that or an alternative almost as ugly. If the Minister meant only to hold an unofficial chat over the acts of his government with his guests as a gesture of diplomatic courtesy, he implied that his nation is bound to other nations by no bond save that of politeness; that what Mexico does is simply none of their business even though it may — as it does — affect unfavorably their own citizens residing in Mexico. Such an attitude can be taken only as a rejection of International Law, a denial of rights not acquired but inherent in man. At the same time the Minister forgot that, while serving as President of the Mexican Republic, he said, on June 21, 1929: "I am glad to take advantage of this opportunity to declare publicly and very clearly that it is not the purpose of the Constitution, nor of the laws, nor of the Government of the Republic, to destroy the identity of the Catholic Church or of any other, or to interfere in any way with its spiritual functions." He forgot likewise the agreement he entered into with the Holy See as represented by the Apostolic Delegate, by the First Article of which the "hierarchial superior of the religious creed in question" was recognized, and by the Third its right of petition. It was President Portes Gil who then forgot that a non-juristic personality can have no superior because it has no legal existence, and no right of petition because it has no juristic personality. Nevertheless President Portes Gil recognized the juristic personality which Minister Portes Gil is supposed to deny.[2] Between his address, his book, and his treaty, Minister Portes Gil is in a tight place.

I mentioned the rights of foreign residents. Judge Manton, in an able brochure,[3] calls attention to the fact that Mexico ratified the Havana Convention of February 20, 1928, on the rights of foreigners. It contains this clause:

"States must recognize in domiciled or transient foreigners in their territory all the individual guarantees which they recognize in favor of their own nationals and the enjoyment of the essential civil rights." Mexico's interpretation of the clause is indicated by an anterior Decree of March 12, 1828, reading: "Aliens . . . are under the protection of the laws, and enjoy the civil rights which they (the aliens) grant to Mexicans."[4] Did Minister Portes Gil, in his address to the diplomats, think at all of the fact that none of the citizens of their respective nations resident in Mexico enjoy the rights that are enjoyed by Mexican citizens resident in their countries? There was good reason why the Mexican Government should be far from easy over the feeling abroad in reference to its "new policies."

Minister Portes Gil asked of diplomats that their respective governments should be persuaded to accept expediency as an excuse for setting aside, not only International Law, but the moral law of nature, or that expediency be the law itself. The "new policies," are constitutional. He then invokes a man-made constitution as against a higher law — that of human liberty.

There was another element of surprise in the Minister's appeal. Seated around the table at the famous banquet were diplomats representing other Latin-American republics, the citizenry of each made up of peoples very much like the people of Mexico. None of these nations have any such "new policies." In the face of this fact the Minister could only mean that his country is a notable and very evil exception among the Latin-American States. As Mexico looks upon itself as a potential leader of the Latin-American republics, the appeal of the Minister must necessarily be taken as the abdication of that claim, and therefore a public act of apology for a condition both shameful and humiliating. It is known that the overwhelming majority of the Mexican people are being proceeded against by the "new policies." Does the Minister consider an overwhelming majority unfit to judge for itself? If so, how can he claim to be part of the government of a civilized state? By a virtual concession of inferiority this Minister of the Republic of Mexico puts his nation into the class of states needing a Mandatory to guide it. I am not saying it, but Minister Portes Gil has implied it. What he thinks of his own people must be as terrible as what his own people think of him.

But Minister Portes Gil was quite right in recognizing the interest of foreign nations in the Mexican "new policies." Judge Manton in that justifies him when he writes: "Can these glaring abuses against the traditional religion of the Mexican people be justified merely because they are sanctioned by the Constitution? Certainly not. In the international order of things, the rights of foreign persons, whether natural or moral, and the rights of humanity, cannot be violated with impunity by any Municipal Law. The Code in Private International Law adopted at the Sixth Pan-American Conference held in Havana in 1928, reflecting the current position of International Law, says: 'Constitutional precepts are of an international order'; which is to say, that they are not beyond scrutiny in order to determine if, in violating the rights of foreigners or of humanity, they violate the requirements of International Law. . . . Is there no specific relief for this state of things?

Must the Church, in order to survive, depart from her pacific mission and urge her adherents to a course of civic disobedience? Fortunately, there is a specific remedy for these wrongs, namely, Intervention. But we do not mean intervention, whether diplomatic or violent, by this or any other single government. The intervention we have in mind is that which the Covenant authorizes the League of Nations to undertake. . . . Intervention in the interest of Humanity in the internal affairs of another nation is a practice generally recognized — and we so hold also — as entirely consistent with and sanctioned by International Law. Christianity, in its ethical and moral aspects, is, as we have seen, the basis of that law. But it is more than an ethical system for the guidance of nations; it is, in its essence, a religion for the individual. It engages man's personal responsibility to God and to his fellow-men."[5]

The authorities cited by Judge Manton in support of his contention are so many, as well as so distinguished, that I must ask my readers to procure the brochure for themselves and read them. I am glad to be in a position to add to them some information which must strengthen the force of their authority.

In the Spring of 1919 when the Conference of Peace was sitting in Versailles, which really meant Paris, there was no little discussion about a proposed Article for the Covenant of the League of Nations barring from membership States failing to grant "liberty of conscience and religion" to their citizens and residents. It was supposed that the Article had been suggested by the Jews, who were then holding an International Congress which met daily in the city. I was interested in this proposed Article, and went to Paris to do what I could to have it made part of the Covenant. President Wilson was supposed to be greatly in its favor.

The proposed Article, so much in accord with American principles, was discussed at a meeting of "Friends of the League" held in London. Whatever this body represented or whoever called it together — it seemed to have no real official standing — its recommendations were being taken with respect in Paris. Decidedly it had influence. On the day this body took up the proposed Article on religious liberty for discussion in London, the Hon. Mr. Thomas, then an English labor leader but later a member of the British Cabinet, presided. When the Article was read, as I was informed in Paris, Mr. Thomas said: "Here is one Article that will be accepted without discussion." The entire meeting seemed to be strongly in favor of it. Nevertheless it was tabled and, as a result, cut out of the draft of the Covenant submitted with approval to the Conference in Paris. I tried in vain to learn who had caused the Article to be dropped. One informant hinted that it was the Premier of Greece, Venizelos. I failed to secure corroboration of that information from any official source and gave up asking, feeling that here was one of the secrets of the Conference.

One day, after it was made known that the Article on religious liberty was definitely out, a distinguished international lawyer drew my attention to Article XXII, Sections One and Five, of the Covenant, remarking: "Your Article seems somehow to have crawled back." I was astonished to find that it had. Under the heading "Mandatory System" I read: (Sec. 1) "To those colonies and territories which as a consequence of the late war have ceased to be under the sovereignty of the States which formerly governed them and which are inhabited by peoples not yet able to stand by themselves under the strenuous conditions of the modern world, there should be applied the principle that the well-being and development of such peoples form a sacred trust of civilization and that securities for the performance of this trust should be embodied in this Covenant"; and then: (Sec. 5) "Other peoples, especially those of Central Africa, are at such a stage that the Mandatory must be responsible for the administration of the territory under conditions which will guarantee freedom of conscience and religion, subject only to the maintenance of public order and morals, the prohibition of abuses such as the slave trade, the arms traffic and the liquor traffic, and the prevention of the establishment of fortifications or military and naval bases and of military training of the natives for other than police purposes and the defense of territory, and will also secure equal opportunities for the trade and commerce of other Members of the League."

The important word in Section One is "principle," referring to "the well-being and development of such peoples" as "a sacred trust of civilization." The outstanding words of Section Five, when taken in connection with Section One, are "freedom of conscience and religion."

I looked inquiringly at my legal friend. He said: "The full intent and force of Article XXII could be brought out only by court interpretation; but the intent is there and cannot be hidden. If the Mandatory is obliged to act thus in favor of the people of his Mandate, it must be presumed that he is similarly bound to his own citizens — *Nemo dat quod non habet.*[6] I am quite sure what the decision of an interpreting court would be."

The Permanent Court of International Justice has never been asked to interpret Article XXII, at least to my knowledge, or to that of the better informed persons I have consulted. It should be asked.

The American Declaration of Independence is based upon the doctrine that man has certain fundamental civic and social rights as man; going as far as to call them "inalienable." These rights constitute the foundation of what has for centuries been known as International Law. But that law itself is made with the strong stones of the moral law of nature. Without that moral law of nature, the existence of which the Creator has made known to the conscience of man, no sanction would exist for any covenant or contract, small or great, between individuals or nations. Blackstone, in his *Commentaries,* wrote: "These are the eternal immutable laws of good and evil to which the Creator Himself in all his dispensations conforms; and which he has enabled human reason to discover, so far as they are necessary for human actions. Such among others are these principles: that we should live honestly . . . should hurt nobody and should render to every one his due; to which three general precepts Justinian has reduced the whole doctrine of law. This law of nature being coeval with mankind and dictated by God Himself, is of course superior in obligation to any other. It is binding over all the globe in all countries, and at all times; no human laws are of any validity, if contrary to this; and such of them as are valid derive all their force, and all their authority, mediately or immediately from this original."[7]

In setting down — as the League does in Article XXII — a summary of the rights that must be granted to peoples under a mandate, and which in any just interpretation, *must* be taken also as rights of the citizens of the Mandatory itself, no more was done by the League Covenant than to repeat what already had long been accepted as a human right included in the summary of the Declaration of Independence by the words: "life, liberty, and the pursuit of happiness."

Judge Manton does not quote the provisions of Article XXII, but relies, in a brilliant setting forth of his thesis, on a wealth of citations based both on the fact of natural human rights and on International Law. But he does point to another article of the Covenant as a means of bringing the case of religious persecution in Mexico before the League of Nations, namely Article XI, which reads: "It is hereby also declared and agreed to be the friendly right of each of the States Members of the League to draw the attention of the Body of Delegates or of the Executive Council to any circumstances affecting international intercourse which threaten to disturb international peace or the good understanding between nations upon which peace depends."[8]

Judge Manton then answers a question which will be uppermost in the mind of the reader: "What could be the judgment of the Court as applied to the case of the Catholic

Church in Mexico? Briefly, the Court may declare the religious provisions of the Mexican Constitution of 1917 to be inconsistent with the obligations of Mexico under International Law; it may find, as a matter of fact, that certain acts of the Mexican Government with respect to the Church are violative of the international rights of the Church; it may decree reparation, which may take the form of restitution of Church property used for essentially religious purposes, and the payment of indemnity for such property as is not essential to religious worship. It may also advise the League to inform Mexico that it should cease putting into effect such legislation as is in manifest violation of the rights of humanity and of the Church."[9]

Interesting as was the Minister's address to the diplomatic corps his essay is much more so. It has been taken as an official White Book. The genesis of the work was the dispatch to the Attorney General of certain letters — pilfered from the Mexican mails — alleged to have been written by Mexican bishops in exile, with a request from the President of the Republic, Mr. Rodríguez, for the examination of their contents and a legal opinion as to their value as proofs of sedition.[10] This examination, however, does not seem to have been necessary, in view of the fact that the President himself informs his Attorney General, in his accompanying letter, that "The Catholic clergy have undertaken a campaign of open sedition in which they have clearly revealed their intention of going as far as rebellion." All the Attorney General really had to do was to agree with the prejudgment of the President. The question of the innocence or guilt of the alleged authors of the letters had been settled. If the President merely wanted a brief to uphold his judgment, and the Attorney General had had the time to occupy himself with that quite useless work, the latter might at least have given his answer legal form and thus kept extraneous matter out of it. The Attorney General does neither. The brief is not in legal form, and of its 135 pages at least 107 of them, if not more, are made up of extraneous matter.

The real legal meat of the Attorney General's book is in Title Second, which begins on page 115, and contains his agreement with the President as to the guilt of Archbishop Leopoldo Ruiz y Flores and Bishop José de Jesus Manrique y Zarate. The letters upon which the indictment is based are reproduced.[11] What do they tell?

The alleged seditious letters do utter a clear protest against the persecuting laws of Mexico, but in no way do they offend against the law. The letters do not call for a revolution. Archbishop Ruiz y Flores, as Apostolic Delegate the ecclesiastical superior of all the bishops of Mexico, specifically advises against revolution in his letters. No one can mistake his words as quoted by the Attorney General himself on page 123, as follows: "We must desire, advise and pray God that Catholics may not engage in the adventure of a revolution." Again on page 129 a quotation from Archbishop Ruiz y Flores runs as follows: "Others delude themselves with the idea that everything depends on an armed movement that would overthrow the revolution, and fail to see that two wrongs do not make a right, and that no government, however good, can be established unless founded on an educated, respectful and righteous people," etc. Surely these words both strong and clear show that when the Apostolic Delegate urged organization he meant one of the kind he could with whole heart endorse, one of peace and legality.

I defy any prosecutor to get from such letters the slightest justification for "exercising criminal action" and ordering the arrest of their writer. The attitude of both President Rodríguez and his one-time Attorney General is unjustified by any law, besides being petty and undignified.

The historical side of the essay attempts to cover a period of about four centuries in order to justify criminal action against two living men by citations from the history of other days and accusations against the dead. How any lawyer could make a case against living men from letters and documents having no reference to the present, written by people long since passed away and presumably at peace — since no matter what their eternal fate may be they have ceased to live in Mexico — is a puzzle. How historians, like Mora and Mendieta for example, can testify from their graves against two bishops on the definite charge of present-day sedition, is equally a puzzle. What the history of Mexico during four centuries has to do with a few letters written yesterday does not legally appear. If such a brief as that alleged to have been prepared by the Attorney General were submitted to any American judge it would probably be found next morning in the alley behind His Honor's chambers.

The whole First Title of the book is a tirade against the Church and the clergy based on such quotations. As a legal document it is without form. As an historical essay it is only void. It shows research by someone, but research to no purpose. A few points will make these facts clear to any fair-minded person, certainly to every lawyer.

The argument of Minister Portes Gil, as stated, is a general one against the Church in Mexico. It is intended to show that the government is justified in deciding "to suppress altogether the temporal activities of the clergy in Mexico," as well as to arrest two bishops. The evidence is drawn from the alleged evil conduct of individual members of the clergy who lived at different times during the last four centuries, as well as their, equally alleged, interference in the politics of the nation. As to the latter charge, one answer suffices: the clergy of Mexico were Mexican citizens. As such they had the same legal rights as other citizens. The law did not deny them the right of free speech, the right to express opinions, the right to vote, the right to protest. Even if the clergy in Mexico did interfere in politics that fact in no way justifies their condemnation by persons who, though not members of their body, freely exercised the same rights. The thing is as ridiculous as would be an accusation of murder against a descendant of the Puritans on the ground that his great great great grandfather was once suspected of playing cards on Sunday in Salem.

Let me now, but only to make the issue clear, take it for granted that in every case cited against these dead members of the clergy they were guilty as charged. What follows?

Since the Attorney General covers four centuries, a long period of time in human history, his showing is pitifully small. Does he suppose that the Church, with her well-known anxiety for the good conduct of her clergy, expects perfection even from one generation? Has Minister Portes Gil himself escaped affliction, even in accord with his own atheistic standards, from the small group of his own relations? Or what do his own relations think of Minister Portes Gil? I know little of the history of the Portes and the Gil families. I am only surmising that their records may be in general somewhat akin to the records of other families. I have seen children brought up carefully by highly respectable parents and some of them turn out to be "black sheep." But in all my life I have never heard anyone say that, because of the presence of a small number of "black sheep" in any family, the other members should be exterminated. Nor have I heard anyone say that, because "black sheep" were produced within family circles, the human race should become promiscuous and do away with the family relationship altogether.

Frank Tannenbaum quotes Portes Gil himself as saying in an address: "The Revolution has had individuals who have enriched themselves while in power; it has had to lament those that were frightened by the truth; it has had to mark on its dark pages some of its members who through vandalism and arbitrariness have become rich, some of them fabulously rich. But it has not been sidetracked by these events. On the contrary, the fact that the Revolution has been able to swallow so many of its children merely proves its greatness as a reconstruction movement."[12]

Very good! But where do these words leave the Attorney General's indictment of the two bishops, which is based on charges against a handful of dead priests who do not in any way enter into the question as to whether or not certain private letters pilfered from the mails are seditious? If the fact that "the revolution has been able to swallow so many of its children merely proves its greatness as a reconstruction movement," what is proven for the Church as a reconstruction movement by the fact that she could not only swallow but digest a number of her own clergy who had been false to their mission as well as to her moral teachings? The Attorney General shows a tendency to recognize a principle when it suits him to do so, but a lamentable tendency to forget its acquaintanceship when it no longer serves him — a bad fault in a lawyer, a worse fault in the chief of all the nation's lawyers.

Mr. Herbert Gruening, who wrote what really is a much more effective propaganda book for the Mexican Government's "new policies" than that to which the Attorney General has attached his name, speaks with great severity of two generals whom Minister Portes Gil knew, Serrano and Gómez. The Attorney General may remember that they were murdered for political reasons at a dinner party, and their guests with them. Mr. Gruening maintains that they deserved their fate.[13] Both these men were of the Attorney General's political party. There is a rumor that he had something to do with the denunciation that led to the private executions. Would he suggest that the alleged criminal actions of these generals should be used to justify the massacre of *all* Mexican generals?

In bringing evidence of the sinful lives of some dead priests against the whole Church — evidence for the most part supplied by the Church — the Attorney General has to admit that it is rather shop-worn and ancient. Suppose I took any group, religious or secular, that had been active in a limited way for only half a century instead of for four, and that never had had a membership at any time of more than one hundred persons, what could I do with the reputation of the whole group by using the Portes Gil tactics? Probably slaughter it. If I were to take merely what has been published in newspapers for the past fifty years about scandals amongst the clergy of any religious denomination in one State — I could a thousand times easier work on lawyers, physicians, merchants, even judges, and certainly politicians — what would be shown? If I were to accept as true what has actually been recorded in print about the moral conduct in Washington of the leaders of the Republican party during the Harding Administration, I would have enough — again using the Portes Gil tactics — to demand the extermination of the party everywhere. True, the idea might be received by the Democratic party with three rousing cheers — until I began digging into the Democratic record. Then there would be a great silence.

Did it strike the Attorney General as strange, if the Church and the clergy of Mexico had been all corrupt for four centuries, that the fact has not damaged the Church utterly in the eyes of the Mexican people? The clergy in Mexico have always been, and still are loved by the mass of the Mexican people, loved to such an extent indeed that the holy and pure sons of the revolution have always needed an army to protect them — take the Red Shirts as example — whenever they attacked the Church or the clergy.

And why is it necessary in Mexico to hold fake elections in order to keep the Portes Gils in office? Why must the people be denied the right of the ballot? Why was it deemed advisable to suppress the Catholic party under Madero and refuse seats in Congress and Senate to most of its elected representatives? Why does the present government of Mexico, of which the Minister is a member, have to impose its will in reference to the destruction of the Church by force? If the Church was so corrupt, how does it happen that, with her organization almost completely destroyed and her clergy scattered or in hiding, her enemies still remain so fearful of her? Why do the people still seek the services of the few priests left in Mexico? Why do even revolutionists make an attempt to die Catholics? Thoughtful men will pause to consider. On the other hand, if I, a stranger with access to only a few scattered records, were to do what the Attorney General has done and compile such charges against his revolutionary friends as he has compiled against the clergy, does he think that I could do it within the limits of a book of 135 pages? He knows as well as I do that the compilation would run into many volumes, and that his own admissions would aid me to do the useless labor thoroughly and truthfully.

Over and over again the Minister refers to the wealth of the Church, to her land holdings, to the salaries of her bishops and clergy. He would have his readers believe that the average episcopal income in Mexico ran to about 100,-000 pesos a year. That would be about $50,000 in our money. Knowing how many dioceses in Mexico were always poor, I cannot agree with the estimate, but I can readily admit that there were bishops in Mexico who must have had a *diocesan income* of well over $50,000 a year. As a matter of fact, if the monies passing through my own hands, as the bishop of an American diocese far from rich, were considered personal income, they would amount to more than $50,000 annually. The trouble is that all that money is ear-marked before it reaches me. Part of it has to go to the education of my clergy, another part to the care of orphans and the poor, another to the support of needy parishes, etc. When all the ear-marking has been honored it is often quite a serious question as to whether or not enough will be left me to purchase a suit of clothes. Granted that the Mexican bishops in times of prosperity may not have been troubled by so much ear-marking, the whole country shows what happened to the surplus of diocesan incomes. I myself have seen the public works, hospitals and colleges, buildings for philanthropic purposes, that tell the story. The only rich bishops of any nationality I have met personally were three in number, but none of the three were millionaires and all owed their wealth to family inheritance. One of these is now dead. His wealth went to charity and his diocese. A rich priest, in the estimation at least of Catholics, is a man who dies with one fifth of the Attorney General's *annual* salary as the savings of his *whole lifetime.*

Like others the Attorney General is careful to charge the Church with the wrongs of the Díaz regime. What power had the Church under Díaz? She had nothing to do with keeping him in office, nor with shutting out of place and opportunity the younger element of educated and ambitious Mexicans. The hacienda system that broke up certain com-

Querétaro and its aqueduct.

Chapel erected on the spot where Maximilian was executed. The Hill of
the Bells, near Querétaro.

Seminary library in Guadalajara. Scattered and destroyed.

Laboratory of Seminary in Guadalajara. All this was wantonly destroyed.

munal holdings under Díaz was not only not of the Church's making but against the time-honored plans she had worked out from experience for the care of the Indian. She had always respected and upheld the right of private property and her desire is to increase the numbers of those who possess it. The conditions under which she did her best work have always been connected with home-owning farmers. It is so today. Her most stable as well as pious parishes are in the rural districts where the religious family idea forges a bond between people and pastor. The Church had nothing to say about bringing foreigners into Mexico to develop or take over Mexican industries. Her natural reaction to such a move would have been against exposing her flock to foreign influences likely to introduce heresy. The whole body of the friends of Díaz were either her open or secret enemies, members of the lodges she held to be either heretical religions or propagators of atheism. Díaz himself was not a Catholic. He could not be for he was a Mason. Emilio Portes Gil puts Huerta down as a Catholic. But since, after his fall, Huerta was expelled from a secret lodge, is it not plain that, if he died a Catholic, he had to return to the faith by conversion? Every friend of Díaz I met, with the exception of De la Barra, was in favor of the Laws of Reform so abominated by the Church. I argued against these laws with a distinguished exile who had been a Cabinet Minister. Exile or not he stuck to his false gods. The Church in the days of Díaz could work only as and when he permitted her to do so. The popular and honest elections, desired but not granted, would have pleased the Church, since they would have substituted freedom for repression. Díaz actually issued new decrees to hamper her. On no one point, then, can it be urged that the Church was responsible for anything Díaz did, except that she kept on living and working as best she could, making a virtue out of necessity. But the full measure of persecution has been poured down on her because of Díaz; while those who hated her made terms for themselves, or escaped with fortunes founded on lootings from her. It is a sad fact that many an otherwise decent man, whose conscience would reproach him were he to accept goods stolen from another mortal, nevertheless has no hesitation about profiting by thefts from God.

I shall have to recall, because of what is to follow, that Mr. Portes Gil as an author offers an official "White Book" intended to be an international apology for the persecuting laws of the government of which he is an official. It is distributed free of charge to foreign statesmen as such publications are always distributed, and it bears the imprint of the "Press of the Ministry of Foreign Affairs." I have thought it necessary to recall that fact before I proceed to cite and comment on one of the most extraordinary of his many extraordinary charges against the Church and the clergy by the making of which the Minister descends to the level of the trickster. Only the blindness of revolutionary hatred could have permitted him to charge both with the awful "crime" of building and sustaining schools and institutions of charity in a country that had lost almost all she had of them. The accusation he makes might be applied to any civilized country on earth, launched against any and all Christian denominations, not only in America and England, but as far as the heart of darkest Africa. Here are the exact words of the accusations; kindly note them well:

"The clergy . . . tried to exploit the people by means of their education and to that end it founded rural schools in the Indian villages as well as primary, superior and preparatory schools in various centers, in the capitals of the States and in the Federal District. As was to be expected the education imparted in these schools was deficient as a consequence of their religious sectarianism, the text books used being in accordance with their religious ideas and practices, and in those establishments the pupils were obliged to carry out their religious practices including auricular confession.

"The State of Mexico was one of the States of the Republic in which those educational centers were established in the form of eight colleges, forty of these were established in the State of Michoacan, forty in the Federal District, eight in the State of Oaxaca, twelve in the State of Guanajuato, eighteen in the State of Jalisco and thirteen in the State of Puebla. Seminaries with the sole object of training youths for the priesthood were established in those States also and in other States of the Republic.

"In the matter of public charity the clergy took charge for the purpose of speculation, of asylums, hospitals, foundling hospitals and foundations placing these institutions in charge of nuns and members of different orders and thus we find two of these institutions in the State of Puebla, a hospital and an orphanage in the State of Mexico, eighteen asylums, a lying-in hospital and two poor houses in the Federal District, twelve asylums and an orphanage in the State of Michoacan, nine asylums, three hospitals and a lying-in hospital in the State of Jalisco and two hospitals in the State of Oaxaca."

Before commenting on the "crime" itself, let us glance at one or two of Mr. Portes Gil's unjustified assumptions in reference to it. He claims that "the education imparted in these schools was deficient." Why? Because they were "sectarian," used religious textbooks, and demanded that their pupils practice their religion. Every Catholic and Protestant school in the United States, Canada, the British Islands, South America, France, Italy, Germany, and all the rest of the world, does the same. Yet when the pupils of such schools come into competition with the pupils of schools that have not such "defects," and in secular subjects only, the average of their success is admitted because it is notable. It was so notable in Mexico that whenever many Liberals — even Radicals for that matter — could find religious schools for their children, they sent them there in preference to the schools of the State. Two little daughters of Mr. Calles went to a Sisters' school on the Avenida Chapultepec. With them there were children of leading government officials. A boys' college not far away was full of pupils, sons of anti-religious revolutionaries. That information I gathered on the ground. The parents were following their heads. Juárez studied in a seminary. Madero was a pupil of the Jesuits. But — and here is perplexity — Mr. Portes Gil himself, I am informed, had near relatives educated in Catholic schools. The wife of Mr. Portes Gil is a practical Catholic who, therefore, goes to confession. He himself acted as godfather for at least one baptism in Tampico. But to cap the pyramid of the "crimes" of Mr.

Portes Gil, he attended the Escuela Libre de Leyes, the Free School of Laws, established by Catholic lawyers to teach their accepted legal principles as opposed to those of the law school of the government. Why did he himself pose as a practical Catholic in order to stand as godfather for a Catholic child and thus take upon himself the obligation of rearing that child in the Faith should it be left without parents? If he has so good an opinion of State instruction as he says he has, why did he not attend the government school of law? What terrible indications of "crime" has he noticed in his wife because of her religious practices?

Mr. Portes Gil sets it down for the information and admiration of statesmen, especially in the United States, that he holds the Church guilty of establishing charitable institutions "for purposes of speculation." Does he not know that hospitals very rarely are even self-supporting, and that orphanages have to be maintained by the bishops? Where do the "purposes of speculation" come in? What ridiculous turn of thought possessed him to attach "purposes of speculation" to poor houses? What kind of "speculation" is that of the Little Sisters of the Poor who accept no endowment, gift, or legacy, that might take from them the high and holy honor of begging from door to door in Christ's Name for the old, the feeble, and the deserted, under their care?

Let us take up the "crime" itself in all its hideousness. When Díaz came to power the revolution had pretty well done the schools and charities of Mexico to death, and the impoverished nation could not restore them. President Díaz knew that. The Church stepped in and did what Mr.

Portes Gil truthfully alleges against her. In her name I plead guilty of giving Mexico schools and colleges when they were most needed, of opening rural schools in the Indian villages, of establishing "primary, superior and preparatory schools in various centers, in the capitals of the States and in the Federal District." The Church and clergy stand convicted on their own proud confession. I likewise plead guilty for them on the hospital, orphanage, and poor-house charge, but not to the "purpose of speculation." If Mr. Portes Gil wants more I shall gladly plead guilty for them also to the "crime" of establishing newspapers, magazines, reviews, and other signs of base degradation and cosmic ignorance. But Mr. Portes Gil as a prosecutor understates his case: the Church was guilty of opening schools for both boys and girls before the revolution in every parish of the Central States of Mexico — Puebla, Mexico, Tlaxcala, Querétaro, Guanajuato, Jalisco, Michoacán, Aguascalientes, San Luis Potosí, Tepic, Colima. There was not a single city, town, or village, having a parish, that did not also have these two schools. And a fortunate thing it was for Mr. Portes Gil and his fellow revolutionists that the Church opened schools and colleges; for if she had failed to do so most of them would not today know even how to read and write, and, instead of living in palaces, would be eating beans and chili with a twisted piece of *tortilla* for a spoon and sleeping in the corner of a one-room adobe hut — as better though poorer men do.

Suppose the Church and clergy had not been guilty of doing all this educational and charitable work, what would now be the charge of the revolutionists against her in the court of international public opinion? Simply that she had made no effort to do her duty. They would now be laying all the blame for an eighty per cent of illiteracy, for which the revolutions alone were responsible, against her; saying that the poor neglected people, anxious to educate their children, were being forced to send them abroad because of the failure of Church and clergy to meet their noble obligation. They would be saying that the Church and clergy did not try to help the little Indian children, accusing them of heartless laziness in the face of the national danger of appalling ignorance. They are adepts in arguing for the side that pays.

Does Mr. Portes Gil think that the people he expects to read his book are unreasoning fools? What must be his opinion in particular about the United States senators, congressmen, and governors to whom he was careful to send it? He must believe that they are blindly bigoted enough to accept all the imbecility on his simple "say so." He does not seem to know that more than Mr. Calles have had experience with hospitals managed by nuns. He forgets that right under the eyes of the senators and congressmen are two Catholic universities, and that these same senators and congressmen have dealings with their distinguished graduates almost every day. Does he not realize that even though our elected representatives may have to run many a gauntlet of criticism they are far from being unthinking prospects for puerile propaganda?

The legal mind is supposed to be a logical mind. Does it lose its logic when joined to the radical mind? It would seem so, for, in his book, the Attorney General exhibits the mind of an infant who only wants things because he wants them. Minister Portes Gil takes the letters and admonitions of ecclesiastical and civil superiors, written to guard the people from the scandals of a few sinners, as proof positive that the Church, thus trying to protect her people from these few sinners, was herself a sinner. In the name of common sense why then should bishops have troubled themselves about the sinners? The fact that they complained about them and tried to suppress them or keep them out, only proves that they were unwanted exceptions in a body properly conducting itself. And Minister Portes Gil makes his modern revolutionary and radical standards those by which the thoughts and acts of men who lived and ruled under entirely different conditions long years ago are to be judged in the present. It is like criticizing the senators of Ancient Rome for not joining triumphal processions in battered and disjointed "tin lizzies"; which is to say, in cars that did not then even exist and would have spoiled the procession if they had.

The Attorney General's book has another surprising side to it, but one in clear accord with the ideas of President Cardenas about certain ideals of democracy, a side I hope will be noticed by the American statesmen to whom the English translation has been sent. It stems right up from the root of a thoroughly bolshevist hatred of free speech and popular rule. Opinions are wrong because they are not those of the Attorney General's party. Therefore it is wrong not only to think them in the present, but those who thought them in the distant past are to be condemned. Discussion is out of order. Lenin's dictum is the only one worth heeding: "The dictatorship of the proletariat is nothing else than power based upon force and limited by nothing, by no kind of law and by absolutely no rule."[14] Does an Attorney General expect American statesmen to accept that as gospel because he covers its rottenness with what he thinks is the attractive shroud of anti-Catholicism? Upon what rock is Mr. Portes Gil's party built? Who said that the gates of heaven should not prevail against it?

The Attorney General makes what has been a universal mistake among Mexican revolutionists from the days of Juárez; he hopes to win sympathy for his cause through an appeal to what he believes to be the innate religious bigotry of the American people. He does not know that this bigotry is white-haired and feeble. Fifteen millions of Americans voted for a Catholic candidate for the Presidency in 1928. There are not more than seven or eight million Catholic voters and many of them did not vote for the Catholic candidate because they were not of his party. It safely can be said that millions of non-Catholics cast their votes for Governor Smith; and, inasmuch as many who did not merely followed their party allegiance without reference to the religion of the candidates, it is plain that the strength of anti-Catholic bigotry is not only waning but has for a generation been grossly exaggerated. It is because the Attorney General did not know this that he perpetrates the following indecency: he states that the clergy had control over publications, "what books should be published, what theories would be practiced, and what trend public thought would take, etc." He asks: "Can a greater despotism or domination of the spirit and conscience be imagined?" Yes, I am quite sure that it could. Indeed, I know it could. Apart from the fact that the Minister is careful not to document his statement, and that even if true the clergy were acting within the law, it is unnecessary to use the *imagination* to find "a greater despotism of the spirit and conscience." It exists in the flesh. Let anyone try to get books, newspapers, or pamphlets against the Minister's party over the Mexican border and the uniformed despotism will step into plain view. In fact it is now in full operation in Mexico under the rule of the National Revolutionary Party, and everyone knows it. Will this book be admitted into Mexico? It will *not*. Even the Minister's own book is based on letters pilfered from the mails by the government of what is called a free republic. Did that shock the Minister? Not noticeably. But why charge such a condition to the clergy when in the second paragraph following, the Minister says: "The Spanish monarchs had in Mexico an ecclesiastical patronage, and unlimited rights. *Therefore they manifested their predominance over the Church.*" So it was not the Church that did it at all but the State. Perhaps a dispatch of the Associated Press, dated February 13, 1935, will help Mr. Portes Gil to find the despotism without burdening his glowing imagination. Having read it only in the Spanish paper, *La Prensa,* of San Antonio, Texas, I give a translation:

"Mexico, D.F., (Feb. 12). A reform in the postal laws was decreed today to prevent the circulation in the Republic of all printed matter except that containing affairs of 'positive social interest.' According to belief, the said law is directed principally to prevent the circulation of those publications opposed to the government. According to the clauses of the law, publications from foreign countries and containing forbidden matter in the judgment of the government, will be returned to their place of origin, and Mexican publications found in like condition will be confiscated by the Department of Communications."

Mr. Portes Gil's opinion of eighty-five per cent of his fellow citizens may interest them. "The Indian continues to profess his own religion, and if some parts of it have been suppressed, such as sacrifices, that is so because he is socially and politically obliged to do so." Which is to say that if the Mexican Indian were socially and politically free, as Indianism in Mexico would wish him to be, he might return to human sacrifices and the cannibalism that was part of them. What pleasant reading for President Cárdenas who is said to be an Indian! He is not a cannibal because he is not allowed to be one?

It is recorded by Alamán that, even as late as 1811, near Tula, in the southwestern part of the present State of Tamaulipas, the Indians cooked and ate a prisoner. Suggestions are even now being made by some close friends of the revolution, that Indianism should be revived and promoted. How distressing it would be for the Minister for Foreign Affairs, comfortably filled out, were his Indian Excellency to accept that idea too literally!

XX

SOLUTIONS?

SOME FINE DISCOVERIES, especially in chemistry, have been made by accident; but accident is not the rule in chemical experimentation, for chemistry is an exact science. Nations, too, have profited by accidents, but no nation dares rely on their repetition. There are natural laws governing civic and social development which, if violated, throw the whole mechanism of government, first into danger and, if the warning be not heeded, into ruin. When any State is in such a danger it is wisdom to start repairs with an open mind and attention to first principles. A dynamo badly gone wrong in an electric-light plant, to be set right again calls for consideration of the fact that its primary purpose is to furnish illumination. A State badly gone wrong can be set right only by recognizing the fact that its primary purpose is to serve its people by giving to them law, order, peace, and opportunity. The expert who would set it right must start, then, with the people it is supposed thus to serve. "The State exists," writes Dr. Husslein, "for the good of the community and the protection of all legitimate social, domestic, and individual interests. It answers to a human need and makes possible that greater natural perfection which men cannot otherwise acquire. It offers both safeguards and opportunities of cultural development which neither individuals nor families could by themselves procure. It is, in fine, the expression of man's efforts to satisfy more fully the social demands of his human nature and so goes back for its origin and justification to that nature itself, which is but the reflection of God's divine plans in the Eternal Mind."[1]

The essential preliminary to a consideration of solutions for Mexico's ills is, then, that the whole problem be considered dispassionately, without recourse to preconceived and unproved theories, and in a spirit if not of patriotism at least of humanitarianism and generosity; as if there was nothing in it for anybody but the good to be accomplished. That condition certainly is one hard to find, for the political theorist is so sure of his theory that it enrages him to have it set aside, even though it may have nothing behind it save novelty. The wealth of experience gained through the centuries he would have ignored.

The important — even all-embracing — headings under which the ills of Mexico must be studied are these: government, land, labor, education, and religion. All are factors now present, and will always be found present no matter what the future holds for Mexico. They are the essential parts of the dynamo which primarily is for illumination.

Government is for the benefit of all the people. It is badly out of order when it exists for the benefit only of the few. I think I have shown clearly enough that, as it exists today in Mexico, it is for the benefit only of the few. Whatever the platitudes, the fact remains that the people of Mexico never were as unhappy as they are today. By the confession of Mr. Emilio Portes Gil himself, many of the "liberators" have become enormously rich at the people's expense. But as things stand, only one solution of the government problem can, under the Constitution, be considered fundamental at this time — the democratic form. In spite of the Constitution — of many constitutions —that form of government in Mexico has been tried only once, that is in one federal election. The result was hopeful.

Can Mexico succeed under a democratic form of government? Why not try? True, Mexican experience, as already shown, is against it. But experience is against it only because absolutism was successful. Mexico has really known little but absolutism. The strong hand did keep order and gave the only comparative prosperity and peace the people ever knew. Democracy has been a name. Why not try to make it a reality? Why not use the spiritual forces of the nation to instruct the people in the use of it, without party bias and with but one objective — their welfare? With proper instruction, based on the citizens' spiritual as well as temporal responsibility, the handicap of illiteracy need be no great obstacle. After all it is the spirit that counts. There is no magic in literacy. Education is above it. Many a man in our own country of the pioneer day could neither read nor write, but was nonetheless an intelligent man, a successful man, and a good citizen. Besides, the condition of illiteracy is not really a difficult one to overcome. To conquer it, taking advantage of available forces, is not beyond the power of a few generations. The Church in Mexico was conquering it when she was forbidden to keep on trying. Since Mexico wants a democratic form of government the people should be given it but, at the same time, they should be given the assurance that their efforts to rise to its obligations will not be nullified by the abuses that were universal in the past and that still exist at the present day.

The land question has furnished both excuse and attraction for every Mexican revolution. But none of the revolutions found the answer to it. Perhaps some day it will settle itself. Troubles have a way of doing that. "The best friend of the statesman," remarked one, "is the certainty that Death will solve so many human problems for him." It would appear as if, for the last hundred years, Mexican statesmen had the same idea. There was a land question. There is a land question. There will be a land question. But Mexico is not the only country that has had one. The plaints of those who worry about it in its Mexican form are reminiscent of Cobbett's stinging tirades against the English gentry, and the impassioned speeches of the Irish Party of pre-Sinn Fein days at Westminster. I myself was born just in time to escape a Tenant War in my native province. Man wants his own bit of land. He may be happy enough as a slave or a tenant. But so is the bird in its nest. His wings are for use nevertheless, and he would fly about in his kingdom of the air unaided.

The solid citizen is the independent farmer. He has a stake in the country and therefore has something to defend. The Church maintains the right of private property. She can do it all the easier if those who have it are the many rather than the few. She has lived and worked in every civilized, half-civilized, or savage country on earth. So she has good reason to know about land hunger. But she knows that, while the hunger may be stayed by stealing, the soul cannot digest the sin. To solve the problem of land distribution justice as well as cleverness is needed.

The land problem in Mexico is old. It would have arisen Spaniard or no Spaniard by the simple fact of an increased population and the desire of the Indian to stay where he was born. The Mexican Indian is no pioneer. He will not leave home alone. To get him far away either hunger must drive him — as it does those who come north — or home conditions must be reproduced elsewhere for him. The root of the Mexican land trouble is deep in the soul of the Indian man. It is questionable if he would accept ownership at the price of breaking the bond that binds him to his *compadres*. And that condition of soul and body long antedates the coming of the Spaniard.

When he did come the Spaniard found no Indians personally possessing land.[2] The mass of the people worked the common land of their towns and villages, which they were not allowed to alienate. They had councils which allotted to each the part he might plant. There was other land never allotted to anyone as an individual, common land for game, for building materials, for fuel.

Limits to the communal lands of each town or village were not well defined. If more land was needed the people took it, sometimes by fighting, often preferably that way because in the fighting victims for the temple and human meat for themselves could also be won. The tradition of the common land never passed out of the Indian mind. Even today the Indian will fight for the common land with more determination than for his own individual holding. One great mistake of Juárez was the breaking up of so many *ejidos*. The Spaniards never dared do that in a wholesale way. What the Spaniard did do was to give unoccupied land to Spaniards, as the United States and Canada did for homesteads, thereby setting up the *encomienda* or, later, the *hacienda* system. With the land — though that was not intended — he gave likewise the desire to invade or overlap the *ejidos* of the Indian towns and villages. The Spaniard got his land from the King on condition of taking care of the Indian, teaching and Christianizing him. The King made regulations to protect the Indian even as to his pay, food, hours of labor, and rest. They were wise and good regulations, but not always obeyed. When they were obeyed, the Indian was by no means badly off; but he had no land of his own. He had the *use* of what he could cultivate of the land his kinship group occupied.

When, later on in independent Mexico, the towns and villages wanted to extend their communal lands, they frequently found the *hacienda* in the way. Since some *haciendas* had intruded on *ejidos* they just swept over that particular one, and took what they thought, sometimes rightly, really belonged to them. Then alongside the *hacienda* there began to spring up the ranches, usually owned by creoles or even advanced Indians. The masters of these were really independent farmers. By their ostentation and general desire to be around with the people these ranchmen helped to make the Indian of the *ejidos* desire his own land. So Mexico came to the days of its independence with a land question which had the *hacienda,* the *rancho,* and the *ejido* on one side, facing the vast population of landless workers such as share-croppers, renters, and laborers on the other. The revolutions drew some of these latter away to the armies and eased the pain for a while by blood-letting. But fighting done, the landless came back and another kind of fight was on.

I have already pointed out how the hunger for land was alleviated in the United States and Canada by the railroads. But the Spaniard could not have solved the land question in Mexico that way. Railroads had not been invented. He could have helped with roads, but did not. The Central Mesa was too attractive in its fertility and climatic conditions for him to bother about other parts, and he needed labor. All the inhabitants of the Mesa hated, and still hate, the thought of living in the hot countries along the coast and to the south. They group together where life is pleasant and the tropical bugs not there to annoy them. The early revolutionary governments, however, could have done as did the north but missed their opportunity. So the land problem was always left for posterity to solve. Posterity thus far has failed to solve it.

The Mexican people themselves are divided over the question. Some of the *haciendas* have been cut up and their lands distributed. But there are troubles left about water rights, machinery, and above all the fact that in many places the land must be worked in great tracts to pay. Then there are those of the people who do not want to take ownership risks but prefer the old and tried regular wage. There are likewise those, well-treated by the master of the *hacienda* — looked upon indeed as his personal responsibility — who do not care to be forced to shift for themselves. By no means do all want land.[3] To make matters worse there is a species of racketeering going on conducted by armed bands who secure easy money from the new owners or the old masters. Attempts to allay the land hunger have in only too many cases made matters worse. The broken-up *hacienda,* which once employed thousands, can no longer take care of these thousands. The cities are growing, but also groaning with refugees from the country, out of work.

Where the *haciendas* were large one-crop farms, as in Morelos for sugar, or in Yucatan for sisal, the system of land distribution is a failure. Mr. Herbert Gruening, American friend of the revolutions, admits this. In 1925 he found land and people in Morelos in a sad condition, the latter saying: "What was called prosperity for the State is not for us"; and this: "In the *hacienda* days at least you were paid regularly; now you weren't sure of anything and if the *hacienda* came back, the old abuses probably would not." In Yucatan Mr. Gruening noted that the distribution of land "netted the people little economic benefit."[4] How could it where so much land is needed for its one-crop condition, especially now that the State has lost so much of its American market — once a veritable monopoly — and is in competition with so many other countries raising sisal? General Salvador Alvarado's grasping red hand ruined Yucatan. The hemp-growing region is not adapted to the needs of sustenance farming.

When the endowments of religion, education, and charity, were all in land — by ownership or loans — it was always possible for a thrifty and shrewd Indian or creole to become a land owner by purchase. The loans especially were helpful, for the interest charge was reasonable and the Church as always an easy creditor. Now the interest charge is high and the creditor hard. But, in spite of the assertion of President Calles that much property "still is in the hands of Catholic priests and religious institutions or orders of the Catholic Church,"[5] I know to an absolute certainty that no religious institution or order in the Catholic Church has land in Mexico. Even if President Calles were right, at that, the endowments were pitifully small for the works they had to support, for the Indian gives little or nothing to the Church.[6] But today there are none. If poverty is freedom, then the Mexican Church is free.

Anyone who knows the complications of the Mexican land question and offers a solution for it is treading on very uncertain ground. Titles go back for centuries to a fragment of paper with a seal on it, to a dried-out scrap that cannot even be deciphered. Tradition or prescription is sometimes the only title. Grants by one Government have been annulled by its very successor. Large *haciendas,* without change of title, are worked by many descendants of one original owner. Acres held as *hacienda* property really belong to the *ejidos.* These *ejidos* are often in possession of property stolen from the *haciendas.* Former Church property is held on morally doubtful titles. Land distributed to agrarians is left uncultivated or abandoned and thus the contract by which it was acquired is broken. New *haciendas* are in the possession of revolutionary leaders or governors who received them for the people but kept them for themselves. Above all, the racketeers and the government officials have pretty well driven out all thought of honesty in attempts to bring order out of chaos. A strong government aided by a free Church invoking honesty and peaceful patience, alone can find the answer to the Mexican land problem. While Mexico has neither it is impossible of solution except by plain robbery, which will leave the last case worse than the first.[7]

The labor question should not be hard of solution on the basis of the encyclicals of Leo XIII and Pius XI. These suggest simple justice to the three classes involved in it: the worker, the capitalist, and the consumer. All three should have their organized groups meeting together from time to time to discuss problems common to all. Nowhere in America is there less labor trouble than in Quebec, and nowhere in the world have these principles been better applied and put to work for peace in the kingdom of labor. They are fair. They are honorable to all. Why experiment with Marxian dreams which experience shows offer no hope to labor but only such misery as that of Russia?[8]

The religious problem is the easiest of all to solve. In Mexico it is not complicated by divisions among Christians. The one sure and safe way, even under present conditions, is to consider the American plan. Let the Church alone. Give her her freedom. She wants nothing from the State but that. Dry up the old stream of talk about State control. The Church can take care of her own nominations and thus insure no return to State slavery. If the Mexican Government is honest about wanting religious freedom here is the tested plan for obtaining it. And that plan would be accepted gladly. It is obvious that it would work, for it does work, not only in these United States but in many countries just as Catholic as Mexico.

Present-day Mexican Government officials have been insistent in proclaiming that the Church in Mexico is different from the Catholic Church anywhere else in the world. "If we had such a Catholic Church in Mexico as you have in the United States," their sympathizers have said to me over and over again, "there would be no religious trouble in Mexico." Well, here is the way to have it. Moreover, even with the solution suggested there would remain in Mexico for a long time the necessity of finding a sufficient number of priests for the parishes. Let other nations volunteer help to solve that part of the problem. If the officials of the Mexican Government really want what they say they want, there will be no difficulty about giving it to them. The Mexican bishops, once freedom is accorded, will need the help.

Education is no less an easy problem to solve, though one calling for more time. If the Mexican Government wants to do only what ex-President Calles stated and "take possession of the consciences of the young, because they do belong and should belong to the Revolution," there is absolutely no solution to the educational problem in Mexico. The Revolution does not own the consciences of the children. The children of the nation do not "belong to the community, to the collectivity." They belong first to the parents who brought them into the world. But if the Mexican Government wants education, it can have it. If the dynamo is for illumination, it can be set to work and the united forces for light will labor to the end desired. The Ontario plan, the Quebec plan, or the American plan, all offer a start for negotiations on the question. I venture a guess that these negotiations, so far as the Church is concerned, would not occupy all of twenty-four hours, even allowing for sleep and rest. And if the Mexican Government really does desire to have the Catholic Church in Mexico conducted in worship and labor as is the Catholic Church in other countries, it can have all the effective guarantees it needs to be fully assured that it will be given exactly that. If, on the other hand, the Mexican Government wants only to destroy religion, it must not complain if its appeal for world sympathy be rejected in the light of its determination to rule or ruin.

XXI

THE ARK AND THE FLOOD

THE COMPLICATED AND SWIFT action of the tragedy of Revolutionary Mexico has made it difficult for many people to grasp the relation of the different scenes to the plot as a whole. Indeed it all looks like a confusion of characters having no legitimate place in a play of the kind. In struggles for liberty we expect the actors to fit preconceived notions as to who and what they should be. The whole world, for example, is prepared for the "embattled farmers," the blacksmith forging ploughshares into swords and pikes, young Nathan Hales, experienced and daring Marions. The trained military leader like Washington is no surprise, especially since even before the beginning of his military career he was of the soil. We understand a Cincinnatus. Pious mountaineers have their places. Even young poets are natural performers in every scene. But in all this confused Mexican revolutionary action are people who do not fit in: priests under Church censure, military renegades, traitorous diplomats, bandits from mountain lairs, released prisoners, ruined ranchmen, ne'er-do-wells from good families, all mixed up with the unwashed mob. The Mexican revolutions seldom seemed to touch the people themselves. In truth the people never

334

fought in them. They were being fought over, to plunder and oppress. Whatever interest the people took in the early struggles diminished as these gave way to the new. Always, however, history tended to repeat itself. The revolutions, whatever their proclamations, ended by presenting victims for the sacrifices to greed in the capital. And the victims were, as of old, the people themselves. There were always the blood-drenched altars. Someone well phrased it: "The revolution devours its offspring."

This repetition of history never was so strongly revealed as it is today, for the Mexico of today is much like the Mexico of the Conquest. There is the same very loose bond of union between the different parts of the country, a tie of force but not of central government. The State governors are very like the old Indian kings and chiefs: none too loyal, all anxious to keep power within their own boundaries, all suspicious of their nominal Federal rulers. The people are the victims of both. If not destined for the knife in the great *teocalli* they are for the smaller ones in the provinces. The hatred of the people for the Federal Government is the one real strength of these State governors. There are those of them who do not obey but rule as they please, one or two who will not even persecute. The "tribes" outside are ripe for rebellion, aching for a chance, and cursing the Colossus of the North for refusing them the right to buy arms for their defense. Given a Cortés from anywhere ready to sink his ships and he need have no more men with him than the old Conquistador had, present-day Mexicans would fight his battles in exchange for promises of relief. The only salvation of the Mexican Republic as it today exists is that very Monroe Doctrine which it so cordially hates. Without the Doctrine and the certainty that the United States would fight to sustain it, Mexico's existence as a nation would not be worth insuring at the highest possible premium for the short period of one year. Let an army land in Lower California, and its chiefs need only back a revolt for independence with their promise of protection. Then that army might stay. The same could be said of Yucatan. Mexico has not one Achilles heel, but is the living miracle of a nation with as many heels of the kind as it has States. If Mexico's worst enemy were asked to suggest a policy and plan to bring absolute ruin and subjection to the nation, there would be no need of deep study to find it. Both plan and policy have long been in operation, and the end is delayed only because of present neighborly inconvenience, with possible bothersome but not insuperable complications to follow.

It is precisely the weakening of religion in Mexico that has brought about this condition, and may soon bring about the ruin. The people are losing hope. Their old patriotism is weakening under affliction. Francis McCullagh, a London correspondent who scooped the Russians for his paper, saw that during a visit to Mexico: "I think," he wrote, "that the religion of a Christian people is a more important matter than all these things put together; and when I speak of religion I do not mean that artistic sentimentality which floods the souls of sensitive and cultured travellers when, guide-book in hand, they walk through ancient churches: the religion I have in mind is a binding force, a stern discipline, and many things else, but a mere sentimentality it certainly is not. Even from a temporal point of view, Christianity is good for a nation. Misled by anti-Christian theories, mostly Marxian, the present rulers of Mexico are fighting against religion. They may overcome it in Mexico, but they will lose everything else as well. 'First seek the Kingdom of God,' etc., is as true in the negative as in the positive form. First abandon the Kingdom of God, and you will lose everything else. Mexico is losing everything."[1]

Mr. McCullagh said, "mostly Marxian." His pen point there touched the Mystery; the explanation of it all. Yet not all, only the source. Greed has played a great and important role in Marxian success. Hatred has not failed to lend a hand. But back of it all the Red Hand of Communism is plainly seen.

The greed devil has been so prominent in Mexico that he did not even take the trouble to remain an invisible ghost. Always he was on the stage in flesh and blood. As Easy Money he beckoned many to come in and enjoy the loot. The "general" who managed to get off the stage alive always left with his hands full, but many did not get off the stage alive. The list of these latter is long. A few outstanding names only need be mentioned: Hidalgo, Morelos, Matamoros, Iturbide, Maximilian, two Carranzas, Villa, Zapata, Diéguez, Obregón, Serrano, Gómez, Maycott, Vigil, Alvarado. But, except for the five first mentioned, all the others had financial rewards before they were killed. The living are the wealthy men of Mexico today, with ranches, corporation stock, palaces, and money. No one knows how much of the latter is stored up outside against the day of the "getaway," though it is forbidden for just ordinary citizens to take or send out any money. One train of the Carranza retreat to death had boxed gold and silver enough to take care of all who went with him. It was fired upon and destroyed before it got out of the suburb of Guadalupe. Those who witnessed the destruction picked up the scattered coins from the place of the wreck. Easy Money! What an attraction for deeds of glory done in the name of liberty!

There is always the hatred. So much of it as to be utterly incomprehensible to normal human beings. But it is not entirely incomprehensible. It takes no scientific study to know that in the human race the pull is downward. Teaching is not a process of assisting wings to grow on a man, but the process of making and attaching them. Teaching is from without. Leave man lessonless and even what is of instinct in him will deteriorate. Then he retreats backward in the direction of savagery, pulling his environment back with him. Civilizing is not a job done once and for all. It is a progressive effort, not only to advance but to save itself from retrogression. It is like an artificial lake on an open plain. Nature filled it with rain when the dam was built, but evaporation constantly lowers its level unless there are springs to feed and freshen it all the time. Planting trees, growing gardens, and building cottages around the lake, will beautify but not save it. Only the rains and replenishing stream can do that. The expression, "he has fallen back to the level of the beast," is used often to illustrate the completeness of a man's fall. But the level of the beast is not the lowest possible level for man.

History is full of examples showing that he can fall, and has fallen, far lower. Science, especially medical science, upholds the finding of history. Quite recently an editor called attention to some remarks of Sigrid Undset about religious persecutions in her late book *Stages on the Way.* The distinguished Swedish novelist places much of the responsibility for them on "a disease which brings with it a pathological impulse to cruelty." It is, of course, sadism. Many individuals have it. When such individuals are brought together under leadership, and the combination achieves power over others, the result is always the same, excessive cruelty, hatred, lust, greed, even wholesale murder. This kind of human deterioration quite often attempts to avoid the open appearance of sordidness, of ignorance, of poverty. In group action it flies to platitudes, patriotism, resounding words. It apes the reformer, dabbles in philosophies it cannot understand, rolls idealogy off its tongue as if it knew the meaning of the word; is out to remake all things, to elevate the race or the nation, to destroy the "uncultured," to save the world in spite of itself. But under the surface the thing lives according to its degradation. Off parade it is worse than bestiality, for the beast kills only to eat. This thing kills in the refinement of hate. Its joys are all in orgies of vice and shedding of blood, like Dzerzhinsky of the OGPU whom the Russians called "the man with the eyes of a gazelle and the heart of a tiger."

I have found no other explanation for the men who rule Mexico today. No other seems possible. From the French Revolution to this hour there has been in Mexico a procession of abnormal human beings following one another through the sad record of its history, only a noisy few, always half-educated, always full of wild eloquence poured out in ill-understood words, always greedy, always bloodthirsty, always godless, always showy, always dissolute. They are part of the world's great unrecognized major problem, ridiculous enough to be passed by with a thought-less laugh, but persistent and smooth enough to take advantage of such careless and dangerous mirth. Mexico has had more than its share of them.

Of course religious persecution is so abhorrent to English-speaking peoples of this day and generation as to verge on the unthinkable. But these good people fail to understand the type of character represented by the criminal pervert. A century without so many of him has convinced them that he is only a bad dream. But if we dip into the history of the half century that followed the Reformation — of Münster for example — that bad dream will be shown to have had flesh and blood. If we go back farther and learn something of Mohammed's conquests the thought of the bad dream will forever be dissipated. Religious persecution is the child of hate, and hate is to such a pervert the only virtue. This is particularly true of those who, brought up in childhood as strong practicing Christians, lose their faith in youth or manhood. It is a sad truth that such people are the outstanding haters of the world. And, in producing them, those of the races once most deeply religious are the most fertile. Wherever the State has used the ecclesiastical establishment to further its own ends, the turn from love to hate has always been marked. But marked also is the fact that great saints grow up beside the sinners.

But there must be a deeper cause — a cause that reaches the very soul — to explain why seemingly civilized men, at least instructed men, will cut into the unprotected breasts of their fellow humans and fellow citizens to reach their hearts, tear them out, and offer them on the blood-drenched altars of hate, only because they failed to beat as commanded. That hidden reason does exist. The Apostle of the Gentiles wrote: "I live, not I, but Christ liveth in me." The words sound like nothing more than a simple line of preaching, so simple indeed that they have passed in and out of the ears of millions without being fully understood. But the sentence writes down the tragedy of the Christian and the tragedy of the Church. It does more: It exposes the secret of Christian civilization, which remade a world because it remade its spirit. It did that by putting sacrifice and self-denial into it, by teaching it the lesson of the fertility of suffering, by raising human values through pain to the plane of the Divine. It is "The Folly of the Cross."

The Church is the Mystical Body of Christ or nothing. She lives, not she, but Christ lives in her. Of no import are her garments. They may be silks or rags, as His was the seamless robe or the blood-stained linen band around His loins on the cross. She may be riding over a carpet of the strewn garments of love, with palms of devotion waving before her, or she may be hiding in caves. But she must reproduce every detail of the Life that lives in her. She must grow in pain. She is greatly loved or greatly hated. She must be ever ready for a crucifixion, a denial, or a Judas kiss. Read her story and the truth will be plain.

It is all compassed in a few simple words: "You shall be hated by all men for My name's sake" (Matt. x).

An American visiting the late Bishop of Querétaro, with whom he had been made acquainted during that prelate's exile in Chicago, expressed his wonder at the passivity of the Mexican bishops in the face of persecution.

"If I read the signs of affection for you and your clergy aright," he said, "the remedy for all these evils is in your own hands. The people are yours. They would gladly fight and die for you. Why don't you say the word and let them go? Or is it that I am mistaken in thinking that they would go?"

"You are not mistaken," replied the Bishop. "Apart from the people you have seen here in this city, there are those in the mountains, Indians attached to their religion and glad to die for it. Were I only to lift my finger I could have twenty-five thousand of them sweep into this city and, even with their bare hands, kill every persecutor in it. And I am but one of the bishops who not only could do that but who knows that he could do it. Our enemies are living by the unfailing toleration of Christ. They know as well as we that the finger will not be lifted, no matter how they make us suffer."

"But why?" asked his American friend, "Why is it not legitimate to defend justice even with the sword?"

The Bishop replied: "Christ said 'put up thy sword into its place for he who takes the sword shall perish by the sword.' But let that pass as something hard for the world to understand. We cannot be responsible before God and man for bloodshed. It is better that we should die and that out of the blood of martyrs should come a new growth — as it is sure to come."

No men or women calling themselves civilized ought to misunderstand or to underestimate the value of these pathetic words, but alas! many will. Perhaps I can bring the force of them home by an appeal to a terrible record that anyone can verify.

There are serious men and women in Europe who continue to utter warnings against a hidden and powerful sect bent on nothing less than the complete overthrow of Christian society. No one can read the history of Western Civilization without at least a fear that these warnings may be fully justified. But, strangely enough, the proofs of the existence of this organized secret fight are all, or nearly all, taken from events and utterances on the other side of the Atlantic. Russia is accepted as the greatest. There every threat since those of the Illuminati has been made good. Is Mexico too far from London and Paris to be taken into account? Since before 1810 it has been writing its part of the Red record and few have read it. Nowhere does the Red Sequence show its slimy track better than in Mexico. The Abbe Barruel's words were of far greater significance than the people of his day attached to them: "You thought the Revolution ended in France, and the Revolution in France was only the first attempt of the Jacobins. In the desires of a terrible and formidable sect, you have only reached the first stage of the plans it has formed for that general Revolution which is to overthrow all thrones, all altars, annihilate all property, efface all law, and end by dissolving all society."[2]

Four stages mark the development of these universal anti-civilization plottings. Each may be known by the character of the men who exploited them: Intellectuals, Bourgeoisie, Liberals, and Radicals. The fight passed from one group to the other, as the movement was used to further different political ends. Sometimes one snatched it from the other. If politics make strange bedfellows this super-political movement made stranger ones. In the semi-obscure professor of law, Weishaupt, the movement was of the Intellectuals, and to it was drawn the influence of such men as Rousseau, Voltaire, and Frederick the Great; the latter using it against France by favoring and working with Frenchmen to overthrow the Kingdom. From the Intellectuals it passed quickly into the care, but never the full control, of the merchant and professional middle class. Its lights then were such as Couthon, Robespierre, Sieyès, and other makers of the French Revolution. The idea was re-christened because of popular contempt for Jacobins, so that a more attractive name might be found both to make dupes forget the bloody past and look to what they intended would prove a more bloody future. The new name was Liberal. It was under this name that it gained to its cause Joseph II of Austria, Ferdinand VII of Spain, and Maximilian of Mexico; though it had dethroned the second and was to kill the third. It came to Mexico to find a freer field for its operations than could be found anywhere else in the world. Spain could not hold its fairest and richest territory. Mexico was abandoned, but abandoned before it was ready to walk alone. The Liberals seized it, and after long struggles won it with the swords of Juárez and Díaz.

Gradually the plan of destroying Mexico was worked out through the successive revolutions. After each came a tightening, not of the talons of the Eagle on the Snake, but of the coils of the Snake around the Eagle. The Liberals, having served their purpose, were cast aside in the end — many into graves — and the Radicals took full control under Calles, Morones, and the secret guidance of the Third International. The ride to power of the Red Sequence is apparently ended in Mexico, but not its work.

What was that work? Here is Weishaupt's philosophy: "Liberty and equality are the essential rights that man in his original and primitive perfection received from Nature. Property destroyed Equality; Governments and Religions destroyed Liberty; therefore to reinstate man in his original rights it was necessary to destroy all Religions, all Civil Societies, and all Property. . . . Princes and nations shall disappear from off the face of the Earth. Yes, a time shall come when man shall acknowledge no other Law than the great book of Nature."[3]

The Third International, if not more frank, is more diffuse. Its plan of action is well known: "Immediate universal dictatorship of the proletariat, involving the seizure of governmental power to replace it by the apparatus of proletarian power. This implies the setting up of working-class institutions as ruling power, and the principle of all rights to workers and no rights to any but workers, and is to be effected by the displacement of all bourgeois judges and establishment of all proletarian courts, the elimination of control by Government officials, and substitution of new organs of management of the proletariat. The disarming of the bourgeoisie and the general arming of the proletariat in order to make revolution secure. The dictatorship of the proletariat should be the lever of the immediate expropriation of capital and the suppression of the right of private property in the means of production which should be transformed into the property of the whole nation. The fundamental principle is to subordinate the interest of the movement in each country to the general interests of the international revolution as a whole."[4]

When Russia sent Madam Kollontai to Mexico as Minister the lady came to a nation which had practically no trade with her own and no great diplomatic questions to occupy her attention. Nevertheless she needed an office force of more than one hundred clerks. Why? Perhaps her sudden exit, suspected to have been managed by Washington, might explain. But the bond between Mexico and Russia was not severed. It still exists and still explains what is now going on. Dzerzhinsky is dead but his counterparts are in Mexico. While they have the hearts of tigers, however, they have not the eyes of gazelles.

What we are doing, the Government of Mexico says, is a necessity. It is either religion or us. One of us must go. But by *us* is meant the National Revolutionary Party, not the Republic. As that Party stands today the statement is quite true. It would likewise be true of Hell. God cannot be in Mexico if the country is to be made over according to that Party's plans. He does not figure in them. In the schools of Chihuahua there are inscriptions on the walls which read: "God does not exist . . . never has existed." The man who saw and read them saw "churches being torn down while the faithful were kneeling before the empty altars." Let it be well understood, Christ is now on His way out of Mexico, and behind Him on this new Via Dolorosa the whips are swung by the Communists who, when they have finished below the Rio Grande, will not wait long before crossing — if they can. Already the ground is being prepared. The record shows it.

What bulks largest in the Mexican problem, in spite of the twisted and intertwined ball of wires called national debts, oil, mining, and land interests is the religious persecution. Once it was possible to conceal that fact because the persecution was restricted to the Catholic Church. Though technically all religious bodies were involved before, in application the laws were made against one and one only. It is different today. The properties of Protestant denominations have been confiscated, their clergy forbidden to conduct religious services in the buildings they built with their own money — chiefly American — their schools either closed or conducted as socialist institutions in which doctrines alien to the creeds of their founders are taught, their charitable works suppressed. Where once these Protestant missions bought toleration at the price of blindness to injustice inflicted on others, or, in certain cases, at the price of active assistance, today there is no tolerance for religion at any price. The religious part of the Mexican problem has, then, widened out till its proportions throw all others into relative insignificance. There is no denying that fact. It is admitted.[5]

The present-day excuse for the persecution too has been widened. Once it rested on charges that the Church possessed too much wealth, had an avaricious clergy, or stood for conservatism as against democracy. Today no one pretends that there is any democracy in Mexico. The government sternly upholds the doctrine that the minority in power must be infallible in all things, political, economic, spiritual; and has a right to impose its views on the majority because it has the power to do so. The United States has always opposed the setting up of a monarchy on the American Continent, but it has been set up nevertheless in Mexico; if not in name, certainly in practice. The United States objected likewise to Old World political influences on the American Continent. Today Old World influence, which for years it would not even recognize, is planted on the American border. The excuse of an avaricious clergy, which never had any great value, is more worthless today, for everyone in Mexico and the world knows that the clergy, still there or in exile, are homeless and in want. As to the wealth of the Church herself, whatever its proportions were, it is now in the hands of the State or the friends of those in power. The excuse for persecution today is an open admission that the objective of the Mexican Government cannot be reached unless the Church and all religion, God Himself with His eternal principles of goodness and right, be crushed. In former Mexican persecutions of religion there was a sense of shame that forced the guilty to have recourse to falsehood and deny their existence at least in part. In this one even that sense of shame has disappeared though over the worst atrocities the veil of censorship is drawn. That there may be no room for misunderstanding or for lack of knowledge of the true aim of the Mexican

Government, the words of the promoter of it, the managed dictator of Mexico, were spoken out by Calles at Guadalajara: "The Revolution has not ended. The eternal enemies lie in ambush and are laying plans to nullify the triumphs of the Revolution. It is necessary that we enter a new period of the Revolution. I would call this new period the psychological period of the Revolution. We must now enter and take possession of the consciences of the children, of the consciences of the young, because they do belong and should belong to the Revolution. It is absolutely necessary that we dislodge the enemy from this trench where the clergy are now, where the conservatives are — I refer to education, I refer to the school. It would be a very grave stupidity, it would be a crime for the men of the Revolution to fail to rescue the young from the claws of the clericals, from the claws of the conservatives; and, unfortunately, in many States of the Republic and even in the capital of the Republic itself the school is under the direction of clerical and reactionary elements. We cannot entrust to the hands of our enemies the future of the country and the future of the Revolution. With every artfulness the reactionaries are saying and the clericals are saying that the children belong to the home and the youth to the family. This is a selfish doctrine, because the children and youth belong to the community; they belong to the collectivity, and it is the Revolution that has the inescapable duty to take possession of consciences, to drive out prejudices and to form the new soul of the nation. Therefore, I call upon all Governors throughout the Republic, on all public authorities and on all Revolutionary elements that we proceed at once to the

field of battle which we must take because children and
the young must belong to the Revolution."⁶

That these words expressed only the purposes of one
man is not the case. On October 20, 1934, the Secretary of
the National Revolutionary Party, Senator Padilla, said:
"Religion is something that is in the heart, in the convictions of men. It cannot be destroyed by brute force. It can
be destroyed, if at all, only by persuasion. For this reason
the Mexican Revolution has made a chief instrument of its
policy the diffusion of education which is eminently socialistic. Those who have studied history know too well that
openly to fight religion would have gotten us nowhere. In
the French Revolution priests were hanged and guillotined
in every province. Who would have thought after this that
clerical power would still live? Nevertheless, only a few
decades were required for Catholicism once more to raise
her powerful head in every part of France. Religion is to
be combated with the book, by teaching and by persuasion."⁷ These words followed an appeal by the majority
of the Mexican Chamber of Deputies addressed to the
President to exile all bishops. Nine days before, the Constitution was amended, illegally because not by the operation required by its own provisions, so as to take away
even from private schools the right to teach religion.

To accomplish the end in view, that is the elimination of
God from Mexican life, a spokesman for President Calles
said: "Liberty of conscience, of teaching, of association and
assembly, of the press and all the other liberties demanded
by the reactionaries and clericals, are, at bottom, nothing
but imaginary, words without substance. . . . Liberty of

conscience in a socialist society is a contradiction in terms."[8]

Before any of these utterances were made, however, the Governor of Vera Cruz had closed all churches and schools; and the Governor of Tabasco likewise. There is no clergyman living now in the State of Tabasco. And the man who put an end to all outward practice of religion in Tabasco has been promoted to the Mexican Cabinet. He is the leader of the "Red Shirts."

Enough has been quoted from Dictator, President, Congress, and Cabinet, to show that the religious persecution is a planned affair. That it will be carried out, legally or illegally, is certain, as the news dispatches show. The murder of people coming out of church at Coyoacan, a suburb of Mexico City, is only one incident on the illegal side. The fact that President Cardenas was in sympathy with these murderers and intends to have that fact known to all is proved by his action in forbidding public demonstrations except by those who were actually responsible for the murders, his own political party.

To Americans, then, the persecution is of alarming interest, not only because of its horror, but principally because of the purposes behind it. "Liberty of conscience, of teaching, of association, of the press," are privileges especially cherished by Americans, and recognized by the American Constitution as part of that heritage of natural rights referred to in the Declaration of Independence as "inalienable." Such rights are recognized as beyond the legitimate power of government to deny. When religious belief is referred to as "fanaticism," not alone the religious people of Mexico, comprising more than 90 per cent of the population, are insulted, but well over 95 per cent of the American people. When abomination for actual sin, especially that of lewd character, is called a "prejudice," the insult to both peoples is of a nature that almost passes belief. If the Mexican Government wished metaphorically to spit on the face of its Christian neighbor, it could have selected no more appropriate word for such a crowning affront. When such words were used in reference to Catholics there was at least a selection of only a fifth of our population thus mortally to injure. Since all religion has been included formally and by act under the prescriptive laws of the Revolution, there can be no question but that the insult is intended to be general. The one saving thought about it is that of recognizing the source from which it comes. There is not an educated man or woman in the whole world who would be willing to stake his or her reputation for culture and refinement on the pompous, superficial, and blasphemous platitudes, that pour out of Mexico. In the face of them, that charity which is "patient and kind" and "dealeth not perversely" can only, as a supreme manifestation of its presence, allow the thought that Mexico is governed today by madmen, for our only choice is between men mad or men possessed.

Mexico today, like Russia, is a challenge to all that is decent, honest, and just in the souls of men. Every cherished ideal of Christian civilization has there been defied by this refinement of barbarism; every human right, even the most fundamental, has been questioned and, as far as possible in action, denied; the stability of the family upon which rests the authority of the State, has been struck at, and not blindly; the painfully won cultural advance of twenty centuries has been stamped worthless; the moral guardianship that was a protection around all human relationships — last word of honesty in the dealings of trade and commerce — is denounced; the body is exalted over the soul. Slowly, it is true, but we thought surely, man had come up from slavery and woman from degradation. With joy did we hear the noise of what was thought to be the last of fetters falling. Steadily gains were made as the years passed, so steadily that we could look with confidence to the rise of each new century's sun as it broke from the future into the present and sent its first rays to salute a still standing Cross. Triumphantly the march of civilization entered new and untouched fields of human endeavor with conquering scythes. We were as jealous of our principles as the lover of his bride, ready to defend, even at the cost of life, what we had won with so much sacrifice. Who would believe that we could without resentment now hear them derided? The message that comes out of Mexico today is a defiance of truth, a challenge to universally accepted and tested ideals, a threat to twenty centuries of progress, a promulgation of war upon the dearest possession of the human soul.

EPILOGUE

IT WOULD BE no matter for wonder to see a lion play with a mouse and kill it for the very fun of his savage game; but it would be decided matter for astonishment to see the situation reversed and the mouse play the lion to death. This is the astonishing thing that the story of Mexico discloses to anyone who cares to shut his ears to platitudes and falsehoods, and look for himself below the surface of passing events. A small minority is playing death to a nation.

To all appearances Mexico is dying, but not because of those evils which the historian is accustomed commonly to recognize as unmistakable symptoms of incurable national disease. Mexico is not being killed by a foreign army; her physical resources are more than sufficient for all her needs; her people are for the greater part fundamentally good; and she has shown herself quite capable of producing both talent and devotion. What, then, is the disease?

Every race which for a long time lived in terror is for centuries after by its memories made fearful. Suspicion is constantly being reborn, and with it a certain jealousy, a marked characteristic of which, in those who have little to lose, is short-lived loyalty for any leader who panders to the vice and takes the risk of being hated in his turn. Out of such fear revolutions burst like explosions; revolutions to no purpose and for no cause save the passing glory of a meaningless name. This revolutionary class is always a minority. Because it does not reason, but acts without thinking, it is better known than the class which, thinking, is slow to act, and therefore misses a place in history.

The story of Mexico is fantastic. It begins in myths. No one knows much about Mexican racial origins, but these origins contribute mightily to the fantastic character of the story. In spite of the shame of them once so keenly felt by the Indians, the horror and degradation of them, the people were able to receive a foreign culture and come near to improving upon it. Sylvester Baxter was right: the result of the Conquest came as quickly as the rubbing of an Aladdin's lamp. What took centuries for others to do Mexico actually accomplished in decades; and for a very great part by herself. There is a touch of the marvelous as well as the admirable in such a people.

But as quickly as the rise came the fall. After three centuries its sign was the unorganized and brutal mob surging out of Dolores, the unthinking minority; the throwback to savagery, blood-lust, and the red altar. It was not a mob urged on by hunger. It was a *jealous* mob, an embodiment of blind hate, with no grievance beyond the thought that others had something it wanted. Mexico's permanent misery is the fact that this mob has never been broken up. It was and is there to meet each new leader; his friend first and his enemy after. It is the killing disease.

The result is more fantastic than were the acts and the actors: cheers and joy for peace seemingly attained, hope and comradeship in fancied relief, curses and maledictions on the still dissatisfied; then swift falling back into the abject misery of a fight that must be gone through all over again. For what? Ask the story and it will answer as only fact can answer — *for nothing*. Of gains there were none; of losses there were many. Every move of the mob brought the nation nearer the end.

The promises made by the military politicians of Mexico may be set down about as follows: Free Elections, Liberty of Conscience, Education, Democratic Government, Human Rights, Property Rights, and a Free Press. Let us take up each in turn.

1. FREE ELECTIONS: They were held but once, and even then their results were accepted only in part. I refer, of course, to the election of Madero and the setting aside of the popularly chosen Vice-President as well as many elected senators and deputies. But for a whole century the people have been asking for free elections, and have always been refused. They are still being refused today — by the leaders of the mob.

2. LIBERTY OF CONSCIENCE: I have shown that the Constitution itself of the Mexican Republic denies that right. It is useless for the Mexican Government to proclaim that such liberty exists. The long list of confiscated churches, and other buildings used for religious purposes, as well as thousands of martyrs, give its words the lie. There is no liberty of conscience in Mexico. The mob leaders do not want it.

3. EDUCATION: There were once free schools in every parish; colleges in all the large towns and cities. They are now no more. In spite of the few show schools in the Federal

District, there are still 3,000,000 children without educational opportunity in Mexico. These are in training for the mob.

4. DEMOCRATIC GOVERNMENT: The story of the elections tells what has happened to it. Worse still is the story of the courts. Justice and injustice are both for sale. Judges rule according to the commands issued by those who made them judges, and these latter rule the mob.

5. HUMAN RIGHTS: Of all such the first is that of conscience and the second that of the family. Neither exist in Mexico. The Dictator has proclaimed that the child belongs to the State, to the Revolution, to the Mob. Instruction for the child must be in socialism and corruption. The teacher has no freedom. Here literally translated is the pledge every teacher must sign in the State of Yucatan:

"I, before the Federal Board of Education, solemnly declare, without any reservation whatever, to accept the program of the Socialist School and to be its propagandist and defender; I declare myself an atheist, an irreconcilable enemy of the Roman, Apostolic, Catholic religion, and that I will exert my efforts to destroy it, releasing the conscience from every religious worship and to be ready to fight against the clergy in whatever field it may be necessary; I likewise declare myself ready to take a leading part in the campaigns of disfanaticizing and to attack the Roman, Apostolic, Catholic religion wherever it manifests itself; also I will not permit in my home any religious practices of any kind whatever, nor will I permit any images; lastly, I will not permit any of my household to take part in any religious act whatever" (From *La Prensa,* Feb. 23, 1935).

6. PROPERTY RIGHTS: Already the State has issued worthless agrarian bonds amounting to 800,000,000 pesos, which constitute an indisputable record of the private property taken from its owners within the last few years.

7. LIBERTY OF THE PRESS: I need only quote again one recent news dispatch about it:

"Mexico, D.F. (Feb. 12). A reform in the postal laws was decreed today to prevent the circulation in the Republic of all printed matter except that containing affairs of 'positive social interest.' According to belief, the said law is directed principally to prevent the circulation of those publications opposed to the government. According to the clauses of the law, publications from foreign countries and containing forbidden matter, in the judgment of the government, will be returned to their place of origin, and Mexican publications found in like condition will be confiscated by the Department of Communications" (From *La Prensa*, Feb. 13, 1935). No one may criticize the mob.

We have been told that all this is none of our business. *The Christian Century,* opposed as it is to the very thought of persecution for conscience' sake, warns us thus: "Is it conceivable that the Mexican Government would suffer the indignity which would be involved in submitting its acts and policy to review by a legislative committee of another nation?" This expression of editorial opinion opens up an interesting question: Have the citizens of this other nation — our own — the right to inquire into the acts of the Mexican Government as far at least as they affect themselves? If they have, then they have also the right to ask their elected representatives to make such inquiry in their name.

For a hundred years, as I have shown, all the successive governments of Mexico, by their acts, admitted dependence on American public opinion. It is an old and accepted saying in Mexico that no government set up there could last a year without the support and friendship of the United States. Mexican revolutionists asked our help. We went to the length of actual invasion to give it to them. That is history and there is no denying it. Even at the present time the Mexican Government is recognizing the right of American public opinion to inquire into and pass judgment on its acts. If not, why the propaganda? Why the White Book of its Attorney General circulated among American legislators, even State governors? That book is an appeal for a favorable judgment or its publication was a worthless gesture. The Mexican revolutionists themselves decided the question long ago.

Nine years ago the American Bishops called attention to the fact in this paragraph of a joint Pastoral Letter: "Through its diplomatic and consular agents in the United States that Government [the Mexican] appeals to the American people to justify its actions. In consequence we have before us the extraordinary spectacle of a foreign government not only filling our country with propaganda in favor of its own internal plans and policies, but even attempting to justify and defend, in our nation, laws and conduct at variance with fundamentals set down in imperishable documents by the Fathers of this Republic. Misinterpreting our good-natured tolerance for a neighbor still disturbed by consequences of many military upheavals, the Government of Mexico has thus presumed to appeal to our fellow citizens for approval. This actually amounts to the submission of its case for judgment to a court beyond its own boundaries; pleading, not before its own citizens who, according to its Constitution, form the only court competent to pass upon it, but before strangers who claim no jurisdiction over their neighbors' political affairs, and whose only interest in them is a desire for the well-being of the people of Mexico and their own peace in amicable mutual relations. The Government of Mexico cannot, therefore, object, under such circumstances, if the case it has thus presented for judgment be considered in the light of American principles, as embodied in our fundamental laws; and in the light of Christian principles, since it appeals for the sympathy of Christians."

Madam de Stael, looking back over the French Revolutionary Terror, wrote: "There is a whole life full of reflections that these two years have given, and I have to read my baptismal certificate to know that I am only twenty-four years old." Looking back over the twenty years I have known of this Mexican Terror, I find in me the same feeling of stupor, the same difficulty of realization. But it is not Mexico's blood-drenched altars that appall me most. It is the invasion of the home and the threatened destruction of the rights of the family, forerunning inevitable ruin to the State and nation, as well as a universal evil example.

The thought is being forced upon many that in matters of government the world is retrograding. We are changing the simple for the complex, thus multiplying our difficulties and inviting the disasters of revolutions, which have become what Jubert said of them: "Times when the poor man is not sure of his probity, the rich not sure of his fortune, nor the innocent sure of his life." The same philosopher said truthfully that "to govern one's home is to be truly a citizen." Surely that is reducing the essential to simplicity itself. But the trend is from the simple to the complex when it should be the opposite. As a matter of fact, our modern political notions and experiments have made the democratic and popular form the most complex of all governments. Some may be rich enough or tolerant enough to enjoy that without danger, but who can answer for those ambitious ones who take advantage of the opportunities thus offered to prey upon their fellows? If the father no longer finds himself the ruler of his own fireside, if he discovers that "political liberty" moves the State out of the Congress into his home, if he is told that what he has always considered personal rights no longer exist because he is just a cog in a machine, he will either rebel against the tyranny or go out from that home to take a part himself in tyrannizing over others. In either case the home and family suffer and a pillar of the State is shaken down. A danger to popular government lies in its complex overexpansion. As long as it remains the simple thing its makers planned, the simple thing that stems up from the true unit of society which is the home, it is a blessing. The moment it invades the sanctity and independence of the home it becomes first a potential and then an actual destroyer. It is all wrong to make the State the only center of a citizen's interest, its welfare his first responsibility. It is all wrong to say that the family is communal property. Men care for their own better than for that in which they only share. The home makes the State and not the State the home. Human nature wants to have one door that can be closed and locked, one responsibility that is its very own, one fortress into which no other power but God and love can enter. That fortress is the family. Transfer its rights to the State and not only does it fall, but the State crashes to the dust with it. The present Government of Mexico is the result of a process of evil evolution directed against the citadel of the home upon which the State depends. The war on religion is an attack on the protecting wall around the family and, since education was part of that wall, it, too, is to be destroyed. It only remains to be seen what grace or inherent power the home possesses to save itself. If it saves itself, it saves the nation. If it falls, the Mexican nation becomes only a memory and a warning.

In a preceding chapter of this book I stated that the strength of religious bigotry in these United States had been greatly exaggerated. I was there expressing a sincere conviction. But I would not dare to state that what there is left of it does not constitute a very real and pressing danger. The attitude of American Protestants on the subject of religious persecution in Mexico brings that danger into the light; for there are those who, having thrown aside the moral law common to all Christians, no longer feel bound by any of its commandments. There is too great a tendency in the American religious majority to accept the assurances of such people as the truth. This was well illustrated by the attitude of even Protestant religious bodies who for selfish reasons cast a doubt, not only on the facts of the persecution, but even on the destructive nature of its plans.

On our own accepted American principles there can be no choice for anyone who has not rejected them in favor of Marxian absolutism. That the Mexican persecution is directed chiefly against Catholics does not enter into the fundamental issues of the case. What does enter is simply the fact of the persecution itself and the avowed reasons therefor. What is to be considered is the threat of a return to the world of conditions universally admitted to have been antagonistic to Christian ideals of justice and morality. Protestants cannot play with that danger any more than Catholics. Even less than Catholics can they afford to do so, since Protestantism lacks a bond of unity which, when the precious pack of principles becomes loose, can be used to pull them together again and out of the danger of being dropped one by one along the way.

Conditions in Mexico are not, then, alone a challenge to the Catholic Church. They do not constitute an exclusively Catholic problem. They are first and foremost a challenge to justice and the moral law of nature. They are, secondly, a challenge to all Christian civilization. When Catholics fight them they are not fighting only their own battle; they are fighting what all men of good will know in their hearts to be a battle for principles. If out of Mexico's misery the world learns that lesson, for the nonce the devil will unwillingly have been turned into a schoolmaster.

PART TWO

CHRONOLOGY

NOTES AND DOCUMENTATION

CHRONOLOGY

A.D.

5th Century. Visigoths occupy Spain as Arian Christians.

586. King Reccared becomes a Catholic.

711. Arabs win battle of Algeciras. Begin possession of Spain.

1492. Spaniards conquer Granada.

Columbus discovers America.

1517. Córdoba expedition to Yucatan.

1518. Grijalva visits Yucatan, and Mexican coast to Pánuco.

1519. Cortés lands.

1521. Cortés takes Tenochtitlán and subdues the Aztecs.

1523. Friar Gante and two companions arrive.

Pedro de Alvarado to Guatemala.

1524. Famous twelve Franciscan missionaries arrive.

Cortés to Honduras.

1528. Juan de Zumárraga, first Bishop; then Archbishop.

1535. Antonio de Mendoza, first Viceroy.

1538. Francisco de Montejo to Yucatan.

1539. Fray Marcos de Niza to New Mexico.

1540. Francisco Vázquez Coronado to Northeastern Kansas.

1767. Jesuits expelled.

1803. Napoleon compels Spain to pay subsidy as price of neutrality.

1804. Dec. 26. Spanish decree seizure trust funds ($44,500,-000) in Mexico.

1808. Napoleon occupies Spain. Spanish Royal family prisoners in Bayonne; resign throne. Joseph Napoleon King of Spain. Spaniards rebel.

1809. England helps Spain.

1810–1811. Height of French power in Spain.

1810. Hidalgo revolt in Mexico.

1812. Radical constitution adopted in Spain.

1813. French abandon Spain.

1814. Ferdinand VII returns and rejects radical constitution.

1820. Jan. 1. Military revolt in Spain forces readoption of constitution of 1812.

Iturbide revolt in Mexico.

1821. Treaty of Córdova between Iturbide and O'Donojú, Mexico independent.

1822. May 18. Iturbide proclaimed Emperor.

1823. Iturbide abdicates, March 19.

1824. Oct. 4. Constitution, Federal.

Oct. 10. Victoria President to April 1, 1829.

1829. Guerrero President from April 1 to Dec. 17.

Bocanegra Acting President to Dec. 23.

Supreme Executive Council to Dec. 31.

1830. Bustamante (Anastacio) President, Jan. 1, 1830, to Aug. 14, 1832.

1832. Melchoir Múzquiz acting President to Dec. 24; Manuel Gómez Pedraza President to April 1, 1833.

1833. Santa Anna President to Jan. 28, 1835. Gómez Farías acting in the absence of Santa Anna.

1833. Laws attacking the Church. Confiscations.

1843. Another Constitution.

1846. United States forces defeat Mexicans, occupy capital. Force treaty ceding territory.

1848. Treaty signed Feb. 2.

1855. Until this year Santa Anna, Bustamante, Bravo, Pedraza, Corro, Echevarria, Gómez Farías, Canalizo, Herrera, Paredes, Barragán, Múzquiz, Bocanegra, and Salas, chase each other in and out of the National Palace. Then came Juan Alvarez, Comonfort, and Juárez.

1856. Beginning of great confiscations under Juárez and Lerdo (Miguel).

1857. Another Constitution, imposed by a minority faction.

1858. Juárez driven out but returns and sets up government in Vera Cruz. Zuloaga President; then Miramón.

1860. March 6. Near midnight the American warship *Saratoga* seizes the warships of the Mexican Government, and the U. S. later gives them to Juárez.

Dec. 25, Miramón leaves. General pillage begins.

1863. May 31. Juárez leaves capital.

1864. June 12. Maximilian arrives in Mexico City.

1866. United States gives Juárez arms.

1867. June 19. Maximilian shot.

1872. July 18. Juárez dies. Lerdo de Tejada (Sebastian) President to

1876, Nov. 21, when he is displaced by Porfirio Díaz to

1880, Nov. 30, when Manuel González becomes President to

1884, Nov. 30, when Porfirio Díaz resumes presidency until

1911, May 25, when De la Barra becomes provisional President until Nov. 1, when Madero steps in, and steps out when assassinated,

1913.   Feb. 19, on the evening of which day Pedro Lascurain is President for 28 minutes; then General Victoriano Huerta, who leaves

1914,   July 15, after United States army and navy take possession of Vera Cruz and blockade Mexico, April 21.

1914.   Nov. 23. Americans abandon Vera Cruz on approach of Carranza. Villa supports Gutiérrez for President. Obregón supports Carranza.

1915.   Feb. 4. Villa announces he is in charge of Presidency. Jan. 28, Villa abandons capital. Jan. 29, Carranza enters it. March 10, Carranza and Obregón flee capital before Zapata. Carranza back in April but unable to remain he retires to the castle of San Juan de Ulloa in front of Vera Cruz. July 10, back in Mexico City. Oct. 19, recognized by United States. — Orders American Red Cross to leave.

1916.   Jan. 10. 18 Americans massacred at Santa Isabel. Mar. 9, Columbus attacked and 17 Americans killed. Gen. Pershing pursues Villa unsuccessfully. His expedition out of Mexico by Feb. 5, 1917. Cost of same $130,000,000 Priestly, *The Mexican Nation*, p. 434).

1917.   Feb. 5. New Constitution promulgated.

1918.   Nov. and Dec., Carranza proposes amendments to Constitution permitting religious liberty.

1920.   May 18, Carranza assassinated. Dec. 1, Obregón President.

1923.   Dec. De la Huerta revolt. United States gives arms to Obregón who wins.

1924. Dec. 1. Calles President.

1926. June. Calles begins new persecution. August 1, Clergy forced to cease services in the churches. Revolt begins and spreads. Secretary of State Kellogg sends warning note to Calles.

1927. Nov. 13. Bomb attack on Obregón. Nov. 23. Miguel Pro, priest; Humberto Pro, his brother; Luis Segura, a civil engineer; Juan Tirado, laborer and innocent bystander, all arrested and confined incommunicado; then shot by order of Calles without trial.

1928. Holy Week. Conference between Calles and Rev. John J. Burke arranged by Morrow. In May another conference including Archbishop Ruiz y Flores. Archbishop goes to Rome. July, Obregón "elected" and assassinated, July 17.

1929. Escobar in revolt, May 3, is defeated. May 1. Provisional President Portes Gil makes advances. June 21, Agreement reached. Clergy permitted to return and churches opened.

1930. Persecution renewed and continued to date.

DOCUMENTATION

I

INTRODUCTION

[1]*Vide* pages 1274 and 1289 of the Senate Report of the United States Senate Investigating Mexican Affairs (Government Printing Office, 1920).

[2]At one time there were complaints in the Mexican papers from official circles inspired by poorly discharged obligations by foreign writers who had been handsomely entertained at public expense and paid liberal honoraria.

[3]Bruce, *Romance of American Expansion,* page 35.

[4]Humboldt, *Political Essay on New Spain* (Ed. 1811, V. I), p. 139: "The capital and several other cities have scientific establishments, which will bear a comparison with those of Europe."

Same, page 159. "No city of the new continent, without even excepting those of the United States, can display such great and solid scientific establishments as the capital of Mexico."

[5]The underlying motive for the Mexican policies of Polk, Buchanan, and others, before the war between the States, was the extension of slaveholding territory. As the desire for the acquisition of "free" territory was active in the North, we have there the opposition of the abolitionists to the acquisition of Mexican territory, and the opposition of the South to the advocates of "54-40 or fight." (Livermore, *War with Mexico Reviewed,* Chapter III, *passim.* Jay, *Review of the Mexican War,* Chapter I, *passim.* Livermore, *War with Mexico Reviewed,* pp. 17, 18.) Mr. Upshur, Secretary of State, wrote to W. S. Murphy, *charge d'affaires* of the United States in Texas, in a letter dated Washington, August 8, 1843, as follows: "The establishment in the very midst of our slaveholding States, of an independent Government, forbidding the existence of slavery . . . could not fail to produce the most unhappy effects upon both parties."

[6]Evidences in favor of Cortés are his ordinances; especially regard-

ing the treatment of the Indians. An interesting fragment is preserved in Alamán, *Disertaciones,* Vol. I, pp. 138–143.

[7]*Spanish Pioneers,* p. 24.

Riva Palacio — introduction to the second volume of *México Á Través de los Siglos,* p. x. — "The House of Austria closed the registry of its legislation with a jewel that with great injustice has passed unperceived by American writers . . . the *Recopilación de las leyes de Indias* (Compendium of laws of the Indies) code of honorable protection to the natives of the New World, and of justified energy with those who saw in them only beasts of burden and tireless tributaries."

The last Monarch of the House of Austria called sharp attention to a notation made by his father, Philip IV, on the margin of a decree for the protection of the Indians, presented to him for signature as follows: "I demand satisfaction of you to me and the world for the treatment of these my vassals, and if this be not done, that I may see by the reply to this letter that exemplary punishments have been imposed upon those who have offended in this matter, I shall take it as a personal affront; and if you do not remedy this I shall remedy it, and I charge you to have a great care for the slightest omissions in it, for they are against God and against me, and totally ruinous and destructive of these Kingdoms, whose natives I esteem and require that they be treated as deserve vassals that so greatly serve the Monarchy, and so greatly have enhanced and adorned it."

After copying the above, Riva Palacio refers to the *Consejo de Indias* (Indian Office) and the *Casa de contratación de Sevilla* (Seville Chamber of Commerce) saying: "The first framed the laws establishing the mode of government and administration in New Spain, always diligently promoting the order and progress of the colony." Hence the growing prosperity, the proverbial honesty of Mexican business, the less difficulty of making the colony progress in the reign of Charles III. The good fortune that Mexico attained at the close of the XVIII century was the resultant of a social evolution in New Spain and the civilization and culture of the centuries. Contributed powerfully, it is true, the wise direction of affairs rendered at home by the learned ministers of Charles III; but the difficulties encountered by this government and the attention given to the interior affairs of the colony, cannot be compared with those [difficulties] encountered and [the attention] given prodigally, by the Kings of the House of Austria and the Indian Office."

[8]According to the tables offered by Alamán (V. 5, app., docs. 1, 2, and 3), the native troops were three to one as numerous as the expeditionary forces. (Alamán, I, 455. — Bustamante, *Campañas de Calleja*, p. 12) — Calleja was obliged for lack of arms to refuse a large number of those who presented themselves. Those retained were mounted and armed with lances.

[9](Alamán, *Hist. de Mex.*, V, I, p. 379). Hidalgo inscribed this motto on his banner, which was a painted image of Our Lady of Guadalupe: *"Viva la Religión, Viva Nuestra Madre Santisima de Guadalupe; Viva Fernando VII; Viva la America y Muera el Mal Gobierno."*

(Alamán, I, p. 384). "Hidalgo made his entry into Celaya on the 21st with great solemnity; himself at the head of his people accompanied by Allende, Aldama and other chiefs, carrying the painting of the Virgin of Guadalupe taken from the sanctuary of Atotonilco; following him was the band of music of the Reina regiment with one hundred dragoons led by an officer who carried a standard with the portrait of the King Fernando VII."

[10](*Á Través*, II, xi). "Agriculture, commerce, and mining, were the foundation of fabulous wealth in New Spain; and it can be asserted that during many years the City of Mexico was one of the most opulent cities in the world for the accumulated riches of its inhabitants if not for the splendor and grandeur of its edifices."

(Humboldt, *Essay on New Spain*, Ed. 1811, V. I, pp. 139–140). The prosperity observed by Humboldt when he visited Mexico in 1803 is treated as follows: "In the intendencias of Oaxaca and Valladolid, in the valley of Toluca, and especially in the environs of the great city of la Puebla de los Angeles [the present States of Oaxaca, Michoacán, and parts of Mexico and Puebla] we find several Indians, who under an appearance of poverty conceal considerable wealth. When I visited the small city of Cholula, an old Indian woman was buried there, who left to her children plantations of *maguey* [*agave*] worth more than 360,000 francs [$72,000]. These plantations are the vineyards and sole wealth of the country [that is, they are the popular 'cash crop' of that particular region because of the demand in the capital for the pulque, or native wine, derived from them]." Humboldt then gives the names of a number of wealthy Indian families and remarks: "Each of these families possess a capital of 800,000 to 1,000,000 livres [$166,680 to $208,350]."

II

SPANISH BACKGROUND

After the first draft of this Chapter had been made, chiefly on the foundation of Bertrand's *Histoire de Espagne,* a translation of the work into English, greatly enlarged by the addition of a Second Part made with the collaboration of Sir Charles Petrie, M.A., F.R.Hist.S., came to hand. The original French Edition ended with the reign of Philip II. Petrie with Bertrand carry on from the reign of Philip III to our own time. It was not thought necessary, in view of the fact that nearly all of Chapter II is really a review of Bertrand, to do more of documentation than refer the reader to his book, now made additionally valuable by the collaboration of Petrie and its translation into English. It was all the more necessary to do this because of the lengthy notes required for the Mexican Background in Chapter III; too valuable for the student to be shortened. The Bertrand-Petrie History of Spain is published by the Appleton-Century Company, New York. Additional good material may be found in *Charles of Europe,* by D. Bevan Wyndham Lewis, published by Coward-McCann and Edwin V. Mitchell, New York and Hartford.

III

MEXICAN BACKGROUND

[1]*Letters of Cortés*, by Francis A. McNutt, I, p. 234.

[2]*Relación de Andrés de Tápia*, in *Colección de Documentos para la Historia de México*, Icazbalceta, Vol. II, p. 580.

[3]*Prehistoria de México*, Obra Postuma del Ilmo. Sr. Arzobispo de Linares, Dr. D. Francisco Plancarte y Navarrete, 1923.

[4]Motolínia, *Epistola Proemial, Col. de Docs.*, Icazbalceta, I, p. 12.

[5]*Peabody Museum Reports*, II, Bandelier, pp. 95–161; *Nueva Col. de Docs.*, Icazbalceta, III, *Relación*, Zurita, pp. 71–227; *Relaciones Antiguas*, pp. 228–308; Duran, *Historia de las Indias de Nueva España;* Motolínia, *Historia de los, Indios;* Motolínia, *Memoriales;* Mendieta, *Historia Eclesiástica Indiana;* Sahagún, *Historia General de las cosas de Nueva España.* Passim.

[6]Liberal mention of cannibalism is made by all the early writers. Cortés tells of roasted children being found in provisions abandoned by a routed Indian force (*Letters*, McNutt, II, p. 104); and he tells of his Indian allies killing and eating their prisoners (*Ibid.*, p. 111); Sahagún tells us that the Indians killed and devoured a great many children (I, p. 84); that they devoured their captives (*Ibid.*, p. 87); that a thigh was always sent to Montezuma (*Ibid.*, p. 89); Motolínia refers to it (*Col. de Docs.* Icaz., I, pp. 40–44); so does Duran (*op. cit.*, Cap. LXXXI); also Pomar (*Nueva Col. de Docs.*, Icaz., III, 17); and Las Casas (*Bartholomew de las Casas*, McNutt, p. 356); and the laws of the Indies take cognizance of it by prohibiting it (*Recopilación de Indias*, Lib. I, Tit. I, Ley VII).

[7]*Historia Antigua de México*, Orozco y Berra, IV, p. 679.

[8]*The Story of Mexico*, Susan Hale, pp. 8–9.

THE NATIVES. The native peoples encountered by the Spaniards in Mexico were composed of a multitude of tribes speaking many languages and innumerable dialects, living in autonomous villages (Plancarte, *Prehistoria de Mexico*, pp. 1–76) possessing varying degrees of barbarous culture, or wandering about naked, or partly clothed in skins and houseless, over certain areas, eating raw the food spontaneously provided by nature (Plancarte, pp. 1–214; Mendieta, *Historia Ecclesiastica Indiana*, p. 144; Motolinia, in Icazbalceta, *Coleccion de Documentos para la Historia de Mexico*, I, pp. 4, 173). The more cultured lived by fighting, making frequent raids, to subject the conquered to the condition of tribute payers (Plancarte, I, pp. 70, 77), and to obtain captives for the sacrifice. The bodies of these latter were devoured. Slaves were killed and eaten; and so were little children. The tribute was paid in products of the soil and loom, in gold and slaves. In the slave market in Atzcapotzalco, slaves were purchased to be fattened for a feast. Prices were thirty to forty pieces of cloth, depending on condition and appearance.

Of nation there was none. Bandelier (*Peabody Museum Reports,* Vol. II, 1876–79, pp. 699, 477, 698) says: "There was in aboriginal Mexico, neither state, nor nation, nor political society of any kind . . . the social organization and mode of government was a military democracy, originally based upon communism in living . . . the notion of the abstract ownership of the soil, either by nation or state, or by the head of the government, or by individuals, was unknown . . . the procuring of subsistence, by means of warfare, is the widest field of tribal action known to aboriginal Mexico."

THE TOLTECS. The tribes in the valley derived their culture and their aristocracies from a common source, a people called the Toltecs, or people of Tula. Not alone the modern Tula, in the State of Hidalgo, but a very ancient Tula, whose fame inspired a wealth of legends and the naming and renaming of other places in honor of its memory, like ancient Troy. Back still further, the Toltecs become the Olmecs, who in turn are, or are the descendants of, a people coming from the east in ships. (Sahagún, III, p. 114, shows Nahoas are those left by Quetzalcoatl; p. 121, Nahoas descend from Toltecs; 136, Olmecas are Toltecs, Motolinia, *Col. Docs.,* I, p. 12, reference to Aristotle, Orozco y Berra, *Hist de Mex.* II, pp. 468, 469, 470, cites another version of Aristotle, and an anonymous writer, and Diodorus, to the same effect. Plancarte, Tam. 73, Ulmecs in Tamoanchan. *Prehist.* I, p. 151, Ulmecs bring culture. Plancarte, *Prehist.,* I, p. 451, oldest traditions are to be found in the myths. *Col. Docs.* II, p. 580, Andrés de Tápia, *Relación. Letter of Cortés,* McNutt I, p. 234, Montezuma's statement to Cortés. The statement of Montezuma continues further, among other things saying: "Do not believe more than you see with your own eyes. . . . My enemies . . . have told you I have houses with walls of gold. . . . The houses you have seen are of lime and stone and earth" [earth, that is, mud bricks], p. 235.)

Having landed at Panuco, the ancient immigrants "built cities where they lived" (*Rambles,* etc., B. M. Norman, p. 145, Panuco. Plancarte, *Tamoanchan,* pp. 20, 46). The aborigines they encountered were apparently near relatives of the primitive Chichimecas. Plancarte separates them into two distinct linguistic stocks; the ancestors of the families related to the Otomi and the ancestors of the families related to the Aztecs. (Motolinia, Col. Docs. 4, manner of living; Plancarte, I, 503, strangers find savages; Motolinia, 253, Chichimecas nomads.) The name nearest at hand for the former is the Quinametin; for the latter, it is the Nahoa or Naua. The first appear to have entered the country from the northeast; the latter from the northwest. (Plancarte, I, 309, Nauas from Asia to Mexico, 157, Otomi from the northeast, 80, the most ancient inhabitants.) Between them they formed the basic racial stock, while the immigrants who came from the east in ships, form the cultural stock. The origin of the racial stock is lost in an antiquity whose remoteness is suggested by the finding of human artefacts beneath layers of dung deposited by the ground sloth; a contemporary of the saber-toothed tiger, Imperial Elephant, Mammoth, Mastodon, Giant Bison, American Horse and Camel, and other creatures long extinct. The artefacts are nothing more nor less than the darts like those used by the Indians, especially the Mayas, when the Spaniards came. (Recent discoveries in Gypsum Cave in Nevada near Boulder Dam.)

Up the course of the Panuco and its southern affluent, the Montezuma, the civilizing immigrants, spread their settlements. Eventually they entered the valleys about the great volcano, Popocatepetl, and the "white mountain." The valleys of the present Puebla, Mexico and Cuernavaca, the land of Tamoanchan (Plancarte, *Tam.* Cap. III, *Prehist.* I, p. 152). There they appear to have encountered their first serious opposition; the Quinametin, or giants, who subjected them to slavery for a time (Plancarte, *Prehist.* I, p. 99, Tello,

Cronica Miscel. 34, tells Indian story of giants 35 feet tall appearing fifty years before the Spaniards came). Freeing themselves from this slavery by a strategem, they proceeded to build cities whose vestiges remain concealed beneath later and inferior constructions (Plancarte, I, p. 100). Others of the descendants of the immigrants extended their settlements onward to Guatemala, where their descendants built the cities whose ruins astonish those who penetrate the humid jungles, or see them from the air (Sahagún, III, p. 139. Plancarte, *Tam.* p. 21).

The Olmecs built Tula and so were called Toltecs or people of Tula (Plancarte, *Tam.* p. 86, Ulmecs and Toltecs). For many centuries the people prospered under the rule of beneficent chiefs or astrologers, priests who perpetuated the name of Quetzalcoatl (Sahagún, I, pp. 243 *et seq.*). But at last evil days came for Tula and the Toltecs. Dreadful things happen; a mountain burns; there is a shower of stones, fetid gases. Myriads perish (Sahagún, I, pp. 245, 254. Duran, I, cap. XXX. Plancarte, I, pp. 347–48). There may have been two great calamities separated by a long interval, as may be deduced from the two widely separated strata of ruins reported beneath the City of Mexico. Tula suffered a four-year drouth in the time of Quetzalcoatl. Again we read of all being forced to leave, but with no mention of why. The survivors depart and wander away in groups, the Toltecs leading (Sahagún, III, p. 144. Plancarte, I, p. 443). We are left to guess if this may be the departure referred to in the picture record mentioned.

To these natural phenomena we have added the appearance of a malignant figure, a powerful and evil necromancer and sorcerer. He employs various fantastic enchantments to force Quetzalcoatl and his people to leave (Sahagún, I, pp. 245 *et seq.*). The machinations apparently are applicable to the most ancient Tula; but again they seem to belong to the Tula of a much later day. Quetzalcoatl and his people depart toward the east; that is, to Tabasco and Yucatan and Guatemala. In these districts we find traditions that confirm this.

THE QUICHES. The Quiches of Guatemala preserved a tradition of having come from the east, but not directly. They were first in Tulan-Zuiva, as written by Brasseur, or Tulanzu, according to Ximenez; and this is also called Vukub-Pek, the seven caves. This is to be recognized immediately as the Chicomostoc of the Aztecs, seven caves, so very frequently mentioned, and often given as the origin of the tribes. The Quiches were at that place a very long time and did many things. They were obliged to leave because of famine (Plancarte, I, p. 348). They claimed as brothers the Yaqui of Mexico (that is, in the restricted sense of the Valley, p. 349). (It is interesting to note that our Cherokees are said to have claimed relationship with the Yaqui. Yaqui is from the Aztec *yauh,* meaning to go some place. It was applied to traders. Settlements of Yaqui were found in Central America. And there are the Yaquis in Sonora.) Four chiefs lead the people. The Yucatan traditions agree with the Quiche (p. 350). The four chiefs are the four Tutulxiuh and Tulan-Zuiva becomes Zuina and Tulapan. The Quiches preserve traditions paralleling those of Tula. The fourth or fifth King of the Quiches, Gucumatz, is the same as Quetzalcoatl the fourth or fifth King of Tula (Plancarte, I, pp. 360, 361). He becomes Kukulcan in Yucatan, and Chuchulchan in Chiapas. After leaving Tula he went to Tlapallan (Nonoalco). Nonoal is Tabasco or perhaps a more extensive region. In Yucatan they said they came from Nonoal. In Chichen Itza is a temple pyramid credited to Kukulcan. After exploring its interior, Thompson appears to be justified in assuming it to be the tomb of that interesting personage (*The City of the Sacred Well,* T. A. Willard, The Century Co., 1926, p. 260). If this be true, the age of the ruin makes him a figure relatively modern as compared with the known antiquity of other remains and those evidently still older.

OTHER MYTHS AND LEGENDS. The god that has most engaged the interest and attention of students is that baffling figure, Quetzalcoatl, god of the Olmecs, a great necromancer and another Hercules, as Sahagún calls him (Sahagún, I, p. 243). "He was much esteemed and long worshiped in Tula where he had a very high Cu [temple pyramid], with many steps very narrow without room for a foot." In these misty legends and traditions of Quetzalcoatl and Tula, Plancarte tells us to seek the ancient history of Mexico (Plancarte, I, p. 451). The ruins of Teotihuacan may be the ancient Tula.

ORIGIN OF THE AZTEC TRIBE. That all the tribes of the valley derived from a common origin with common but varied traditions is evident from Sahagún who took pains to seek out these traditions from separate sources. The Aztecs differed from the others only in being later arrivals to the valley of Mexico. *But with the rest they also appear to have returned to a starting point* (Sahagún, III, 146–47, I, *Prologo*.) Olmos, whose works have disappeared, pursued the same plan as Sahagún, interviewing the chiefs of many towns (Mendieta, p. 75). A people called the Chichimecs had taken possession in their absence. Chichimec is a term used to designate a manner of living as well as a people. Wholly unrelated tribes are called Chichimecs, "because they lived like Chichimecs," that is, nomads. In claiming descent from the Chichimecs, the Aztecs and their relatives clothe them with some respectability by calling them Teochichimecas, or venerable Chichimecs (Mendieta, p. 147; Sahagún, III, p. 147; Plancarte, I, pp. 124, 127; *Nueva Col.* III, p. 271).

TULA. By tracing the traditions of the Aztecs *backward* from their settlement on the site of the present Mexico City in 1325, we can follow them through a number of well-known places in the valley; then out of it to Tula, in the present state of Hidalgo, a short distance from Mexico City. This Tula is not the ancient place of that name. It was known as Xicocotitlan until occupied by the Toltecs who renamed it Tula after the old Tula which they had been compelled to abandon. Here we find that the Aztecs have paused in their *return* from the west to take part in the destruction of Tula. *Into* that west the Aztecs or Mexicans had gone after passing Tula (Xicocotitlan), and before that we trace them *back* again in the valley to their point of departure.

The picture record at this point depicts an inhabited place surrounded by water from which a departure is shown. On the mainland or on the island, is the name Aztlan, and also Culhuacan or Teoculhuacan. Aztlan is a former name of the well-known Chapultepec, and Culhuacan still exists. Apparently the point of departure was the point of later return, the site of the present Mexico City (Plancarte, *Prehistoria*, I, pp. 201, 202; Plancarte, *Tamoanchan*, p. 47; Sahagún, III, pp. 138, 147; *Á Través de los Siglos*, Vol. I, passim; *Peregrinacion de los Aztecas, Tira del Museo*, in the National Museum, Mexico City; *Nueva Col.* III, pp. 248, 239).

The above assumption is supported by the remains which are reported discovered beneath the present city. There are reported two strata of ruins whose ground levels or pavements are said to be ten and one-half feet, and "over twenty" feet below the present level. That both of these levels cannot belong to the pavement of Montezuma is obvious. That the ten and one-half foot level cannot belong to him is also obvious because the large stone objects, Calendar Stone, Sacrificial Stone, etc., that were buried soon after the conquest by the Spaniards, were unearthed at a shallow depth below the present level. (Batres, Díaz, *Arch. Explorations in Escalerillas St. Mexico,* 1900–1902, as to depth of 10½ feet or 3.2 meters. *Science* for July 29, 1927, supplement, p. 14, as to the "over twenty feet" depth. Bandelier, *Arch. Tour Mexico,* p. 52, shows objects found and their depths: Calendar Stone, at 1 ft. 5 in.; Large Idol, top at 3 ft. 8 in., bottom at 2 ft. 8 in., Sacrificial Stone, at 1 ft. 8 in.)

Continuing backward beyond the departure shown in the picture, legends and traditions merge into fantastic myths, with only here and there a trace of something credible suggesting history. The traditions and their chronologies were edited to conform to sixteenth-century interpretations of ancient history, as we are warned by Plancarte, who suggests that we may find the truth in the myths (Plancarte, *Prehistoria,* I, pp. 95, 96, 133, 526).

WHITE GODS. The early history of Carthage is obscure because the Romans destroyed it so utterly. Very early, it was establishing colonies in distant places. It must have been still young for its Senate to be disturbed by any departures. The translator of Rollin provides a note (Rollin's, *Ancient History,* I, p. 47) referring to Howel as authority, that according to Appian, "the port, or Cothon, was built fifty years before the fall of Troy; Megara, or Karthada the new city, according to Eusebius, was built 194 years later; and Byrsa, the citadel, was built, according to Menander (cited by Josephus) 166 years after Megara, and probably by Dido." Herodotus, who derived his information from the Egyptian priests, places the fall of Troy during the rule of Proteus in Egypt, who was succeeded by Rhampsinitus, who was followed by Cheops, who built the Great Pyramid. Proctor the astronomer places the building of this structure, according to the period and position of the star by which it must have been oriented, Alpha Dragonis, at about 3400 B.C., or "within fifty years or so on either side of this date" (Proctor, *The Great Pyramid,* pp. 154–55). 3400 B.C. is the date he gives "when the descending and ascending passages thus commanded both these stars," Alpha Dragonis and Alpha Centauri. The "zero date" used by the Mayas in their astronomical calculations is equivalent to October 14, 3373 B.C. (Spinden, in *Scientific American* for March, 1928, p. 234).

According to ancient writers the Great Pyramid was originally a platform from which the priests made observations (Proctor, p. 177). In that form, Proctor declares it the most perfect instrument for the purpose until the perfection of the telescope (Proctor, p. 165). It must have marked an important period in the science of astronomy.

From the story told by Montezuma it is apparent that an attempt was made to repatriate the people; an attempt that we might expect after such a drastic stoppage of any migration. In the leader of that enterprise we may see as well the basis for that most baffling figure in Mexico's ancient history, Quetzalcoatl. He is a god, a deified hero, a high priest, a dynasty of high priests, a famous astrologer and magician, and a benign ruler responsible for a veritable golden age. Though usually clothed in the varying grotesqueries of Indian symbolisms, at times he appears in a garment covered with crosses and a pointed cap, quite like those we are accustomed to see worn by the astrologer of the middle ages, long before Columbus sailed (Plancarte, *Prehist.* I, p. 451, the oldest historical traditions are wrapped in the myths about Tula and Quetzalcoatl).

Quetzalcoatl was god of the night wind and his temples round (Plancarte, I, pp. 506, 505, 528). But this apparent nonsense becomes serious when we find that the round temple was an observatory, which also explains the association with the night wind.

The legend or prophecy regarding the return of Quetzalcoatl was taken very seriously by the people of Mexico. When Cortés landed, Montezuma sent him a rich collection of presents. They included the habiliments of the god Quetzalcoatl (Plancarte, I, p. 313).

THE AZTECS entered the valley of Mexico as a small, wandering group of miserable gypsies about the middle of the twelfth century (*Nueva Col. de Docs.* III. *Historia de los Mexicanos por sus Pinturas,* p. 242) to find every desirable site occupied by related tribes speaking the same language, with like customs and traditions, and heirs to the same culture (Sahagún, III, p. 145). Until A.D. 1325 they continued as despised vagabonds wandering about the valley, sometimes compelled to scatter to conceal their self-evident character of pilfering nuisances, as the indignation of their victims was aroused. At last, a particularly horrible atrocity almost brought about their extermination by their enraged neighbors who forced them to seek refuge in the marsh which became a lake in the rainy season (*Nueva Col.* III, p. 248. Duran, I, Cap. LV). By the digging of ditches they made raised places upon which to rear shelters, just as may be seen today in the present gardens or chinampas (called floating gardens by Americans) in the town of Xochimilco, a suburb of Mexico City. Of picture writings they could have preserved little under such unfavorable circumstances. More than a hundred years later they had become a powerful warrior tribe, thanks to their naturally defensive position that permitted them to raid their neighbors, as favorable opportunties presented themselves, and then find there a safe retreat. It was about that time (1427–1440) that occurred the reputed destruction of picture writings by order of Itzcoatl and the leading men (Sahagún, III, p. 140).

PICTURE WRITING. Regarding the destruction of picture writings, Icazbalceta in the Biography of Zumárraga has made an extended analysis of the matter (Zumárraga, *Estudio Biografico,* pp. 305 *et seq.*). Clavijero (*Hist. de Mex.,* Navarro, Ed. Mex. 1853, pp. 8, 9) deplores the loss of material, but in refuting Robertson who had said that *all* was destroyed, he shows us that what has survived is relatively abundant. Alfredo Chavero, in the first volume of *Á Través de los Siglos,* gives a list of important documents of that nature, and among them is one "picture writing" with an interpretation in Aztec that still remained untranslated into Spanish at the time he wrote. He says it is the most notable in that it covers a good part of the ancient history of Mexico (*Á Través,* Vol. I, p. 26). Orozco y Berra (*Hist. ant de Mex.* I, pp. 400, 1) also discusses the matter to arrive at much the same judgment. Plancarte (*Prehistoria,* I, p. 94) rejects the reasons given for the burning of the paintings, preferring to believe that it was to erase the record of a humble origin. We are prompted to suspect that it may have been an excuse to account for something that never existed. George Creel (*The People Next Door,* p. 1) mentions the date 1500 and then says that "some twenty years later," Juan de Zumárraga gathered a "mountain heap" and applied the torch while "swarming priests chanted. . . ." What must have remained for him to burn is indicated by Ixtlilxochitl (Zumárraga, *Biografía*, p. 351) who says that when the Tlaxcalan allies of Cortés entered Tezcoco in 1520, they burned the palace of Nezahualpilli and with it "all the archives of all New Spain." The siege and destruction of Tenochtitlán must have left little there. So that when Zumárraga arrived in December of 1528 he must have found practically nothing in those places (Zumárraga, *Biografía*, p. 21). In May of 1532 he returned to Spain. Instead of destroying material, he collected it, as did Bishop Fuenleal (Icazbalceta, *Nueva Col. de Docs. para la Hist. de Mex.* III, pp. xl, xli, xlii; Icazbalceta, Zumárraga, *Biografía*, Cap. XXII).

When the famous "Twelve Apostles" arrived together from Spain in 1524, they found six other Friars on the ground who had come the year before. On seeing the Indians still at their idolatry, the twelve inquired of them what they had been doing. One of them replied: "Learning theology entirely ignored by St. Augustine." That is, they had been learning the language (Cuevas, *Hist. de la Iglesia en Mexico,* I, pp. 162, 163, 170). Two left with Cortés on his march to Honduras where they died of hardships. The sixteen were divided among four places in groups of four. Four in Mexico and the remainder in Tezcoco, Tlaxcala, and Huejocingo, provinces with 60,000, 200,000, and 80,000 inhabitants respectively. It was not until New Year's Day of 1525 that the Friars in Tezcoco laid hands on anything. Then they went to the temple and destroyed the idols, while the native priests fled. In 1537 the Bishops, including Zumárraga, advised the King that ". . . the teocallis are not yet all destroyed and in them the Indians have their idols with their customary veneration" (Zumárraga, *Biografía*, p. 345). Zumárraga returned to Mexico in 1534. By then the Friars were collecting those native pictures and interpretations which form the basis of the numerous documents that have survived and of the histories which have been written.

WORSHIP. The settlements in and about the valley of Mexico became to all intents and purposes the beginning of things for the Mexicans. Here the great lord of all created the world and the gods who in turn created the sun and moon and man; and demand hearts to eat and blood to drink, for which they create men to be killed in sacrifice to them; and the gods themselves are sacrificed (Sahagún, I, pp. 232 *et seq.,* II, pp. 244 *et seq; Nueva Col. de Docs.* III; *Origen de los Mexicanos,* p. 287; Plancarte, I, p. 128; Mendieta, p. 79). In one account, the sun shoots an arrow to earth and from the hole made emerge a man and a woman, the first pair (Mendieta, Cap. IV). In another account, one of the many gods is deputed to obtain from the realm of the dead some bones, which placed in water, become two children (Mendieta, p. 78). Every community has its own account and, as Mendieta says, they differed as to the gods, even doubting and blaspheming them when not satisfied with favors received (Mendieta, pp. 77–83). But in the Fire we find they all dissolve; we hear the priest say to the Fire, as he casts the copal incense on the blaze: "Lord, thou art the father and the mother of the gods, and thou art the most ancient god" (Sahagún, I, 12).

According to Mendieta (p. 101) "they sacrificed all the white men and women they could find to placate the sun. In which it seemed to bring to memory the death of their gods for the sun" (p. 79). The gods, after the creation of the sun, found they could not prevail against it and submitted to be sacrificed. Each left his mantle to his particular devotees.

CIRCUMCISION — SOUL FOOD. Circumcision was practiced among the Totonacs. At the age of 28 or 29 days, the child was taken to the temple where the high priest and assistant performed the operation with a stone knife. Also with the Totonacs it was customary every three years to kill three children, to mix their blood with certain seeds and make a dough. This was partaken of every six months by men above the age of twenty-five and by women above sixteen. It was called "food of our soul" (Mendieta, pp. 108–9).

AZTEC ARISTOCRACY. The aristocracy, claiming descent from the legendary white immigrants, held the masses in contempt and exploited them to the limit of their endurance. The medicine men, sorcerers, necromancers, conjurers, wizards, not to mention women playing the part of witches, kept the people in terror with grisly superstitions, and bound to them through the necessity of consulting them on every occasion that these "masters of the count" might determine from their calendric tables the most propitious days for their purposes. The gods were veritable demons demanding myriads of human hearts and torrents of human blood for food and drink. Small wonder that the Spanish Friars believed themselves confronted with Satan and his hosts.

ANCIENT MONUMENTS. The more ancient cities in Central America contain dated monuments that were erected from time to time for some purpose. To the assumption that they commemorate events or honor personages or celebrate conquests, might be added the suggestion that they may have an important astrological significance. These places were abandoned to the jungle about A.D. 600 (Spinden, *Ancient Civilizations of Mexico*, pp. 69, 134).

The observatory in the "new" Chichen Itza (the round temple of Quetzalcoatl) bears a date equivalent to A.D. 1207. The presence of the Toltec (also Aztec) ball court in that and contemporary cities, evidences the presence of invaders from the Mexican highlands; and that they built new cities out of the ruins of the old suggests a not very prosperous condition of the original inhabitants who appear to have become serfs or slaves of the strangers. If we are to gather anything at all from the chronologies and the traditions accompanying them this was not the only invasion from a similar source. Constant warfare and destruction followed, or continued, until there was not much left for the Spaniard to damage or destroy. "All in all, there is little to be said in favor of the frequent plaint that the coming of the white man snuffed out a culture that promised great things. The golden days of the Mayan civilization had already passed, and, if we may judge by the history of other nations, would never have returned" (Spinden, *Ancient Civilizations of Mexico*, p. 137.)

In the highlands the culture was still more decadent; while all about were hostile tribes seeking to burn the temples of their neighbors (the picture of a burning temple being the sign of conquest), their homes, make them pay tribute, and devour them in cannibal feasting.

IV

THE CONQUEST

[1]Alamán, *Disertaciones*, I, App. pp. 105, 117, 119, 137.

[2]*Á Través de los Siglos*, II, p. 353. Riva Palacio says: "Not only does he become the protector of the conquered, but they themselves consider him, instead of their conqueror and enemy, to be their chief and prefer him to their natural chiefs and leaders, while he prefers them to the Spaniards."

The regard of the Indians for Cortés is best demonstrated by the joyful reception given him by them on his return from Honduras. *Historia Verdadera de la Conquista de la Nueva España*, Bernal Díaz del Castillo, cap. CXLIX (CXC).

[3]The Tributo Roll of Montezuma. Reproduced in *Monumento del Arto Mexicano Antiguo*. Plates 228 to 259 — the actual number there shown is 355 towns paying tribute to Montezuma.

[4]Bernal Díaz, Cap. XXIX. This was in 1511. But Columbus encountered near the isle of Pines a canoe from Yucatan loaded with merchandise for trade, in 1502.

[5]*Ibid.*, Cap. VIII.

[6]*Ibid.*, Caps. II to VII.

[7]*Narratives of de Soto*, Bandelier, *passim*.

[8]Bernal Díaz, Cap. LI.

[9]*Op. Cit.*, p. 245.

[10]Sunday, Oct. 7, 1571: *Don John of Austria*, by Margaret Yeo, pp. 224–232.

V

QUICK RESULTS

[1]Remesal, *Hist. Gen.* Madrid, 1620, p. 141.
[2]Icazbalceta, *Col. de. Docs,* II, 204.
[3]*Cavo. Tres Siglos,* Lib. IV, Par. 10.
[4]Alamán, *Disertaciones,* I, App. 2⁰, p. 137.

In explaining in a letter to the King, the reasons for not obeying the King's order not to establish *repartimientos* or *encomiendas,* Cortés relates how the people were oppressed by their native masters. He says they were compelled to surrender everything, retaining barely enough to keep life in them; and besides, from them were taken their children and relatives, and even themselves, to be sacrificed to the idols; that in the principal temple alone in the city, in a single feast of the many they celebrated for their idols, they killed eight thousand victims. Giving them in *encomienda* to the Spaniards is to release them from captivity and give them liberty, and relieve them from many insupportable burdens. Then Cortés says: "It has happened, and happens every day, that to scare some towns into serving well the Spaniards to whom they have been apportioned, they tell them that if they do not do well they will return them to their old masters (*señores antiguos*); and this they fear more than any other threat or punishment that might be made them" (*Col. de Docs.* Icazbalceta, Vol. I, p. 473, Letter of Cortés to the King, dated Oct. 15, 1524).

[5]Rogers, *Six Centuries of Work and Wages,* pp. 394–395. Law of Elizabeth, 1584. In the fifteenth century it was 8 hours — *op. cit.,* pp. 327, 542.

[6]*Recopilación de Indias,* Lib. VI, Tit. XX, Ley I; Tit. VIII, Ley I.
[7]*Ibid.,* Lib. VI, Tit. IX, Ley XXX.
[8]*Ibid.,* Leyes IX to XXVIII.
[9]*Ibid.,* Lib. VI.
[10]*Ibid.,* Tit. X, Ley VII. Clergy charged to report directly to King

"by every ship or fleet" on observance and enforcement of laws and condition of Indians.

[11]*Ibid.,* Lib. V, Tit. XV, Ley XXVIII.

[12]Mora, *Mexico y sus Revoluciones,* I, 194.

[13]Alamán, *Disertaciones,* I, p. 177.

[14]1696–1701.

[15]Velásquez had played the same trick on his own superior in occupying Cuba.

[16]Alamán, *Disertaciones,* I, 182.

[17]*Ibid.,* pp. 68, 69.

[18]*A New Survey of the West Indies,* Second Ed., London, 1655, pp. 104 *et seq.*

[19]Humboldt, *Political Essay on the Kingdom of New Spain,* Ed. 1811, I, pp. 139–40.

[20]The present States of Oaxaca, Michoacán, and parts of Mexico and Puebla.

[21]$166,680 to $208,350.

[22]Alcavala or Alcabala — *octroi* or municipal customs dues.

[23]Mora, *op. cit.,* I, p. 197. On page 198 he states that the law required that when a certain number of families had settled upon any spot and had built a chapel or church, that this should form a village, even though it be upon private property, the owner being obliged to give up the necessary land to provide properly for the needs of the people.

[24]*Ibid.,* p. 274.

[25]Humboldt, *op. cit.,* I, pp. 142, 147.

[26]*Á Través de los Siglos,* II, p. 226.

[27]*Recopilación de Indias,* Lib. IV, Tit. XIV.

VI

EDUCATION

[1]The Telpuchcalli and Calmecac have been taken for "schools" but were really for the selecting and training of fighters and a selected few as "medicine men." The entrance age was 15 (*Á Través*, I, p. 590).

[2]Genaro Garcia, *El Clero de Mexico Durante la Dominación Española,* p. 106.

[3]Conc. III Prov. Mex., Ed. Mariano Galvan Rivera, 1859, p. 18.

The Church law says that every curate must "procure with all diligence" the establishment of schools in their towns where the children may be taught to read and write Spanish.

[4]*Recop. de Indias,* Lib. VI, Tit. L, Ley XVIII.

The laws of the Indies required that "where possible schools must be established to teach them to read and write Spanish and at no cost to them."

[5]*Bibliografia Mexicana del Siglo,* XVI, p. 37.

[6]*Ibid.,* p. 38.

[7]Thomas C. Moffett, *The American Indian on the New Trail,* p. 157.

[8]Juan de Zumárraga, *Estudio Biográfico,* p. 3.

[9]*Á Través de Los Siglos,* Vol. II, p. 354.

[10]*Estudio Biográfico,* p. 225.

[11]*Ibid.,* p. 210.

[12]*Ibid.,* Appendix, p. 96.

Friar Gante taught the Indian boys art and crafts as well as reading, writing, and other studies (Torquemada, *Monarquia Indiana,* Lib. 2, Cap. 19).

In 1531 both Zumárraga and Martin de Valencia wrote letters in which reference is made to schools. The latter says that in "nearly twenty" establishments they in some cared for "a little less than five hundred boys and in others many more." Thus 10,000 or more would be accounted for (Torquemada, *op. cit.*, Lib. 20, Cap. 33, Cap. 16; Agustín de la Rosa, *La Instruccíon en Mexico,* p. 56).

[13]*Ibid.,* p. 215.

In reporting on their establishments (Nov. 8, 1569) in the diocese of Nueva Galicia, the Franciscans mention fourteen towns in their care where they have schools where the children are taught by an Indian "maestro" to read, write, cipher, music, and singing (*Nueva Col.* Vol. II, pp. 167–169).

Beaumont (*Cronica de la Provincia de franciscanos de Michoacan,* tomo 3, caps. 18, 19; Rosa, *op. cit.,* p. 58) says that many children were taught and sent to their homes to teach others.

A significant item appears in Torquemada (*op. cit.,* lib. 15, cap. 12; lib. 20, caps. 18, 19; Rosa, *op. cit.,* p. 55). The three first Friars, Juan de Tecto, Juan de Aora, and Pedro de Gante, came in 1523. They took up their residence in Texcuco where the Indian Chief, their host, requested that they not appear in public to avoid a disturbance by the Indians. For more than a year, while they were engaged in learning the language and teaching the children, the Indian priests continued to occupy and use their temples for their pagan worship, though they were not supposed to continue their human sacrifices and cannibalism.

In the province of Huainamota labored two Friars, Andres Ayala and Andres de Medina. They established 15 towns of 230 to 300 each. Two children from each were trained and returned to teach (Rosa, 60, citing frag. mss. *de la Cron. de franciscanos de Xalisco,* lib. 3, cap. 12). Even some of the native pagan priests were converted and educated and placed in charge of schools (Rosa, 59, citing Beaumont, *Cron. de la Prov. de franciscanos de Mich.,* tomo 3, p. 22). In the Province of Zacatecas the Franciscans established schools in the towns teaching reading, writing, and Spanish (Rosa, 61, citing Arlegui, *Cron. de Zacatecas,* Parte 2a, cap. 9).

[14]*Ibid.,* p. 351.

[15]McNutt, *Letters of Cortés,* II, pp. 213–214.

[16]Mendieta, *Hist. Ecc. Ind.* Lib. III. Cap. XI.

[17]*Ibid.,* Lib. IV, Cap. I.

[18]*Ibid.,* Lib. IV, Cap. II.

[19]In a report rendered in 1570 covering the regular clergy of the Archdiocese of Mexico (*Nuevo Collección de Documentos para la*

Historia de Mexico, Vol. II, Informe al Visitador . . .), it is shown that there were present 215 Friars to care for 222,680 "tributaries" representing a population of more than a million, served by 51 stations or "monasteries." Attached to each was a school where the children were taught to read and write. A similar report covering the secular clergy in the same territory reveals a school attached to each of their churches (*Descripción del Arzobispado de Mexico, hecha en 1570*).

[20]*Descripcion del Arbpdo. de Mex. hecha en 1570,* pp. 53 *et seq.*

[21]Sahagún, *Hist. Genl.* III, pp. 81 *et seq.*

[22]*Col. de Doc. para la Hist. de Mexico,* Vol. II, p. 148.

[23]*Documentos para la Historia de México,* 2a Serie, Mexico, 1855, Vol. IV.

[24]*Boletín de la Sociedad Mexicana de Geografía y Estadística,* 2a Época, Vol. III, p. 531 *et seq.,* Obispado de Michoacán, por el Dr. D. José Guadalupe Romero.

[25]*Boletín,* etc., Primera Época, Vol. I, p. 137.

[26]*Op. cit.,* p. 250.

[27]*Boletín,* etc., 3a Época, Vol. VI, pp. 62–65; Oaxaca, Manuel Martinez Gracida. Lummis, *Spanish Pioneers,* p. 24, says: "by 1575 — nearly a century before there was a printing press in English America — many books in *twelve* different Indian languages had been printed in the City of Mexico, whereas in our history John Eliot's Indian Bible stands alone; and three Spanish universities in America were nearly rounding out their century when Harvard was founded. A surprisingly large proportion of the pioneers of America were college men; and intelligence went hand in hand with heroism in the early settlement of the New World."

Encyclopedia Americana, Vol. XVIII, p. 572.

When the nineteenth century opened, there were only three medical schools in the United States, and only two of importance, the University of Penn. and that connected with Harvard; and only two general hospitals. There were at that time at least eight hospitals in the city of Mexico alone. Two of them, the San Andres and the Hospital Real for Indians, were large. The San Andres had 400 beds, all endowed, while the Indian Hospital cared for 350 to 400 patients. In a severe epidemic it cared for over 8,000. Humboldt gives the number of beds available as 1,100 in 1803 (Humboldt, *Political Essay on New Spain,* Vol. II, p. 55).

The San Andres Hospital was founded in 1779 by Archbishop Haro who supported it for a number of years, spent large sums upon it, and endowed it heavily (*La Beneficencia en Mexico,* by Juan de Dios Peza, August 20, 1861, in *Boletín,* etc., 3a Época, Vol. V, pp. 524 *et seq.*). From September 26, 1784, to February 10, 1790, the Bishop spent on it $459,586. In 1790 the funds amounted to $1,454,657 and the yearly income to $66,142. At one time it possessed 56 houses worth $576,525 (Duarte, *Diccionario de Curiosidades Historicas,* p. 83).

The Maternity Hospital was founded in 1760 by Rev. Ortiz Cortés, leader of the Cathedral Choir. The institution was found abandoned by Carlota who caused it to be refitted (*La Beneficencia en Mexico,* by Juan de Dios Peza, August 20, 1861, in *Boletín,* etc. 3a Época, Vol. 5, pp. 524, *et seq.*).

The Hospital del Divino Salvador was founded in the late 17th century by a carpenter named Jose Sayago, who, with his wife, gathered the demented women they found wandering the city's streets and cared for them in his home opposite the church of Jesus Maria. The Archbishop learned of this and aided Sayago by paying the expenses of caring for these unfortunates and paying the house rent, moving the establishment to a larger house opposite the College of San Gregorio, where it remained until 1698. The Congregation of El Divino Salvador took charge in 1700 and built a new building (*La Beneficencia en Mexico,* by Juan de Dios Peza, August 20, 1861, in *Boletín,* etc., 3a Época, Vol. V, p. 545). Closed and looted by Juárez.

The Augustinian College of San Pablo, founded in 1575, was one of the institutions forced to close by the revolutionary chaos following independence. It was used partly as a barrack, and during the war with the United States, in 1847, it was occupied as a hospital and so continued, being dubbed later the Hospital Juárez. In 1861 being under government management, it was discovered to be in an indescribable condition of decay and dirt, the patients neglected and in filthy beds (*Ibid.,* pp. 552–554).

In 1572, Dr. Pedro López founded two hospitals, the San Lázaro and Desamparados, the latter came under the management of the Friars of the Order of San Juan de Dios in 1604, who added to it a refuge for foundlings (Duarte, *Diccionario de Curiosidades Mex-*

icanas, p. 305). It later fell into the hands of the Sisters of Charity. In 1874 they were expelled and the government seized the funds. The name was changed to that of Hospital Morelos (*Boletín,* etc., 3a Época, Vol. V, p. 569).

The Board of Trade built the Hospital de San Hipólito, for the insane, which was opened in 1777 (Duarte, *Dic. de Curi. Mex.,* p. 301). Along with several other institutions of like nature it was under the direction of one of the Hospital Orders and when these were suppressed by the Spanish Government in 1820 they fell eventually into the hands of the republican government with results that might be expected. The San Hipólito funds and properties were disposed of by Santa Anna for an eighth of their value or given to his military officers in lieu of salaries. In 1853 it became a barrack (*Boletín,* etc., 3a Época, Vol. V, p. 574). In 1863, under Maximilian, it was again in use and in a fair state of preservation (*Documentos Historicos de Mexico,* Vol. V, "Informe Sobre los Establecimientos de Beneficencia," pp. 53, *et seq.*). In 1881 it was in a ruinous condition (*Boletín,* etc., *loc. cit.*).

The asylum for the poor, founded in 1763 by Rev. Ortiz Cortés. Archbishop Haro gave $200 monthly to it, and a total of $62,000. Captain Zuñiga founded the orphanage and a school in connection with this institution at a cost of $400,000, which was opened in 1806. He left a fund of $250,000 and one third of the output of his mines as a support for this orphanage and school (*Boletín,* etc., p. 582). The children were taught useful crafts, which they were permitted to choose for themselves (*Colección de Ordenanzas,* etc., Vol. I, N. 7). This establishment was very large, covering an area of nearly eleven and one-half acres. As the supporting funds and properties were sequestered or wasted by thieving politicians and revolutionary chaos, portions of the building were rented as shops to help support it. These portions were appropriated by the tenants under the law of Juárez. Other portions were seized and sold, and still other portions were destroyed to open new streets. Two thirds of the establishments were thus disposed of. Deprived of means of support, and neglected by the ignorant politicians, it was found by Andrade, in 1863, to be in a condition unfit to shelter the inmates who numbered some 300. The roof leaked badly and had fallen in places; the windows were without panes or shutters, and admitted the rain and wind, exposing the unfortunate inmates to all the inclemencies of the weather; the doors were rotting from their hinges, and many were gone entirely; and vegetation had taken root about the walls and roof (Andrade, *Informe,* pp. 6 *et seq.*).

Maximilian endeavored to resuscitate this, as well as other beneficent institutions, but after his death, and the return of Juárez, it was abandoned to utter ruin.

The Foundling Asylum, two insane asylums, the Maternity Hospital, other hospitals, and connected institutions, had similar beginnings and met a like fate (*Boletín,* etc., p. 582).

The Foundling Asylum (Casa de Ninos Expositos, or "La Cuna") was founded by Archbishop Lorenzana in 1767 from his revenues. He supported it while in Mexico, and continued to contribute after he had returned to Spain as Cardinal Archbishop of Toledo. Archbishop Haro, his successor, contributed $200 monthly, besides other sums at frequent intervals (Andrade, *Informe,* etc. Published by Garcia Pimentel, *Documentos Historicos de Mexico,* Vol. V, p. 33).

The San Lázaro Hospital, founded by Dr. Pedro López in 1572, was closed by Juárez in 1872 (*Boletin,* etc., 3a Epoca, Vol. V, p. 659). The buildings were sold to private parties. The church was turned into a warehouse by the Mexican Packing Company (*Practical Guide of the City and Valley of Mexico,* by Emil Riedel, Mexico, 1892, p. 312).

The Belemitas Hospital was founded in 1674 by two Friars, who also founded a primary school (800 boys) in connection therewith that became famous. The buildings were seized in 1862 and sold by Juárez, to be converted into dwellings and the church into a library (*Boletín,* etc., p. 659).

The Hospital Real, founded in 1553 for poor Indians, was seized by Juárez in 1862 and sold, to be converted into a tenement house, and the church into a Protestant mission (*Boletín,* etc., p. 661).

The Hospital de Terceros de San Francisco, founded in 1756, was closed in 1861 by Juárez who sold it to private parties who converted it into a hotel. It was later resold to the government for $75,000 to be used as a commercial school and for other purposes (*Boletín*, etc., p. 662). It was finally torn down to make way for the new post office.

The Hospital de la Santisima, founded in 1579, was closed by Juárez in 1861 (*Boletín*, etc., p. 663), and its buildings and properties sold to private parties.

The following hospitals were located in the city of Mexico:

San Hipólito for insane men. Founded 1777.

Maternity Hospital. Founded 1760. Rev. Ortiz Cortés.

Hospital del Divino Salvador for Insane Women. Late seventeenth century.

San Lázaro for contagious diseases. Founded 1572.

Desamparados. Founded 1572. Later merged with San Juan de Dios.

San Hipólito for insane men. Founded 1777.

Belemitas. Founded 1674.

Hospital Real for Indians. Founded 1553.

Hospital de Terceros. Founded 1756.

Hospital de la Santisima. Founded 1579.

Hospital de Jesus. Founded by Cortés.

Hospital de San Juan de Dios. Founded 1604.

Hospital del Amor de Dios. Founded by Zumárraga 1540.

Hospital del Espiritu Santo, 1600 (gave its name to a street).

Hospital San Antonio Abad, 1787, for lepers.

Hospital La Santisima Trinidad, 1681, for clergymen.

Four "provisional" hospitals in 1737.

The College for Girls, Colegio de Niñas, was founded by Friar Gante in 1548. It was closed by Juárez and sold — to become the Deutsches Haus, the German Club (Riedel, *Guide,* p. 334).

The College of San Miguel de Belen, for women, was founded in the latter part of the seventeenth century by Rev. Domingo Pérez de Barcia. It grew to be a very large establishment. The revolutionaries converted it into a city jail (Andrade, *Informe,* p. 65).

The Brothers of Charity had a college near by. It was turned into a barrack (Riedel, *Guide,* p. 349).

The Casa de Recogidas, founded in 1698 as a refuge for women, became a military hospital (Riedel, *Guide,* p. 322).

The famous Indian college of Santa Cruz, founded by Bishop Zumárraga in 1536, was converted successively into a barrack, a political prison, a military headquarters, and finally into a military prison. The church was occupied as a customs warehouse and dubbed the Almacen Juárez (Riedel, *Guide,* p. 364).

The College of San Pedro and San Pablo and the Indian College of San Gregorio, were transformed into a House of Correction (Riedel, *Guide,* p. 368). This is of interest as illustrating the consequences of "Reform." An Institution dedicated to the education of honest youth must be converted into an asylum for the criminals bred by revolutionary chaos.

To the colleges already mentioned may be added the College of San Luis in Puebla, founded in 1585; the College of Santa Cruz, in Zacatecas, founded by Father Antonio Margil de Jesus, who arrived there in 1683 (Duarte, *Dic.* etc., pp. 131–132).

The College of San Diego, for girls, in Guadalajara, was begun by a poor woman who took poor girls into her home and taught them to read and write, and to sew and perform other domestic duties. In 1707 the Bishop lent his aid. In 1712 a clergyman purchased the ground and put up a building suitable for the purpose (Duarte, *Dic.,* etc., pp. 131–132). This institution was closed by Juárez and converted into a military prison.

The Girls' School in Guadalajara, founded by Bishop Alcalde, was closed by Juárez and occupied as a military hospital.

The Hospital of San Juan de Dios, of Guadalajara, was closed by Juárez and sold to private parties. A part of it is now used as a public market.

The Boys' College of San Agustín, in Guadalajara, was closed and sold to private parties.

The Girls' College of Santa Maria de Gracia, in Guadalajara, was closed and a part sold to private parties, a part used as a barrack, and the remainder for various public purposes.

The University of Guadalajara was closed and the building devoted to a variety of uses. It is now the Court House.

The present Federal Building in Guadalajara was once a college.

The College of San Juan, in Guadalajara, continued to be used as a school because the donor stipulated that when the buildings ceased to be used for this purpose they must pass to the heirs of the estate.

Besides the colleges already mentioned as existing in Mexico City during colonial days there were the following:

Colegio del Coliseo, founded in 1548 for girls by Friar Pedro Muria (Duarte, *Curiosidades Historicas,* p. 131).

San Pablo, founded by the Augustinians in 1575. Turned into a barrack by the radicals (Riedel, *Guide,* p. 317).

San Ildefonso, founded 1588 by the Jesuits. Seized by the government in 1767.

Santa Maria de todos Santos. Founded 1573 (Cavo, *Tres Siglos,* lib. 5, par. 3). Closed 1843.

Colegio de Cristo. Founded 1612 (Duarte, 132). In 1774 it was absorbed by San Ildefonso college for girls.

San Ramon. Founded 1623 for boys. Mercedarios (Cavo, 6-22). Closed 1838.

Nuestra Señora de Guadalupe. Founded 1708 for girls (Duarte, 133).

Belem de los Padres. 1734 for boys by Brothers of Charity. (Hypólitos) made into barracks (Riedel, 349).

San Ignacio, for girls, founded in 1734 by some wealthy Spaniards (Riedel, 324), (Viscainas).

School of Mines founded in 1792 (Riedel, 225).

School of Fine Arts founded in 1791 (Riedel, 226), Academia de San Carlos.

Colegio de Hijas de Caridad (Duarte, 83).

San Gregorio.

San Bernardo, 1575–1576 by Jesuits (Rosa, 76).

La Santisima (Riedel, 311), or Infantes, 1725.

Other institutions mentioned by Rosa (76–77) San Juan de Letran, 1553.

San Andres, Jesuits. Porta Coeli. San Pedro Pascasio. San Buenaventura. De Abogados. De Jurisprudencia.

Colegio de la Santisima la Antigua, Nuestra Señora del Pilar, 1754.

Colegio de San Ignacio. Founded by the Archbishop Manuel Rubio y Salinas for Indian girls, 1754.

Colegio Anexo a la casa de niños expositos. 1766.

The government report (Congreso Nacional de Educaçión Primaria, 1911–12, Vol. 3, p. 616) shows the following:

> 9,692 Primary schools, Public.
> 2,726 Primary schools, Private.
> _____
> 12,418 Total.
>
> 698,117 pupils in public schools.
> 191,392 pupils in private schools.
> _____
> 889,509 Total.

Wallace Thompson (*The People of Mexico,* p. 201) says: "Theoretically, the Catholic schools are nonexistent, though large numbers of them functioned in every diocese in the time of Díaz, 'over 30,000 parish schools' with an attendance of 300,000 being mentioned unofficially."

According to the government report above mentioned (Vol. II, p. 269) in the State of Jalisco the private schools provided for nearly one half of all those attending all schools. The exact percentage is 40 per cent of the enrollment, but 45 per cent of the average attendance.

In the city of Querétaro the industrial high school, operated by the Salesians, is now (1926) a barrack, and the Franciscan college is now a tenement crumbling to ruin. The college of the Propaganda Fide (La Cruz) is also a barrack. In Zapotlan the girls' high school, that cared for some thousand pupils, is now a barrack. In Querétaro, parish schools were scattered all over in small units in private houses to avoid attention (1926).

Tannenbaum, *op. cit.,* pp. 296–7 — end of 1929, total number schools in Republic 13,412 — all schools — Federal, state, county, private; kindergartens, rural schools, primary schools, normal schools, preparatory schools, professional schools, schools of technology and fine art. Of these, 6,106 were Federal rural schools, 4,574 rural maintained by the state, 1,799 private rural — really maintained by large estates, industrial or mining companies.

12,479 rural schools.

July, 1933 — 6,850 Federal rural schools.

3,459 Federal rural schools served by 4,527 teachers.

4,162 no normal training.

2,439 in single room.

Registration in rural schools, 467,137.

Average attendance, 273,253.

Also, 95,449 adults.

Total enrollment all rural schools, 1929 (end of) 1,662,371 — in Federal, state, and private, 1,560,786.

Federal and State appropriations, 7,000,000 pesos.

VII

THE CHURCH

[1]*Thomas More,* by Christopher Hollis, pp. 245–246.

[2]Italian News Dispatches of December 26, 1934.

[3]Mendieta, Lib. III, Cap. LIX.

[4]From table by Navarro y Noriega in *Boletín de la Sociedad de Geografía y Estadístca, Segunda Época,* Vol. I, pp. 290–291. The mixed bloods numbered 2,053. Though he says this is for 1810, it would appear that he derived his figures from the census of 1793. Brantz Mayer, *Mexico,* etc., II, p. 369, shows total population of California missions as 23,025 in 1831.

[5]Englehardt, *Missions and Missionaries of California,* Vol. II, Chapter XVI. The comparison of the accomplishments of the Friars with almost no resources with the costly failures of the United States Government in all its tragic magnitude is well depicted in the pages of Englehardt (*The Missions and Missionaries of California,* Vol. II, Chap. XVI). The United States Government finally discovered what the Friars had demonstrated successfully nearly four hundred years before.

"The product of the field was garnered in graneries, and the goods produced in the shops were stored in the mission warehouses for the benefit of the community. All, Indians and missionaries, shared alike from the common property. The missionary himself received no more. When there was an opportunity, the missionary would sell to foreign merchants what could be spared, and in turn he purchased groceries, dry goods, and especially iron and ironware. Most wearing apparel was manufactured by the Indians." Hides, tallow, grain, wine, and olive oil were sold to ships from abroad, and trinkets purchased and distributed. "On such occasions the missionary was only too happy to be able to make his wards happy; he shared everything with them just like the thoughtful father of a family." An enemy (Forbes) is quoted by Englehardt as admitting reluctantly that "Their labor is light, and they have much leizure time to waste in their beloved inaction, or in the rude pastimes of their aboriginal state." In the matter of education the Friars made equally contrasting discoveries. Giving the Indian "book" education only unfitted him. Englehardt quotes Charles F. Lummis, well experienced with Indians, as follows: "What is an education? Is it the ability to repeat what you have heard? A phonograph can do that, and a phonograph is about the measure of modern education. To older fashioned folks an education is what fits a man, or woman, to live happily, decently, usefully. And whatever parrotry of text-books fall short of this isn't an education" (*Land of Sunshine,* June, 1900, p. 50).

In Chapter XIV Englehardt shows the incredible bestiality of the California native. And after reading the descriptions of the ancient Mexican Chichimecas it is not difficult to recognize the intimate relationship.

[6]A sensitive Mexican Liberal might be tempted to call attention to the wholesale dispossession and exile from their homes of the so-called civilized tribes in the southeastern United States by American land-grabbing politicians.

CHURCH FEES. Few writers neglect to charge the clergy with exhorbitant fees for their services. Callcott (*Church and Mexico,* 211), says: ". . . the fact remains that for laborers to be forced to pay twenty pesos for a marriage fee, when they earned only fifty pesos a year, was a direct invitation to most of them to ignore the ceremony entirely." The Church law (Concilio III, Mexicano, p. 274) specifically forbids the exaction of any fee for services, all offerings to be voluntary. But a schedule of fees was published covering the non-essentials demanded to lend grandeur to the occasion. Marriages in the Parish church occasioned no fees; if celebrated elsewhere, four pesos. This was for Spaniards. The Indians paid half (*Arancel Para Todos los Curas del Arzobispado de Mexico.* Issued in 1767, republished in 1827). As every Catholic knows, missions are held as often as possible, when all are given an opportunity to receive the sacraments, no one of which was ever denied for lack of a fee.

VIII

RETURN TO SPAIN

[1]"More than two centuries passed without more permanent troops in New Spain than an escort of halberdiers for the Viceroy" (Alamán, I, 77). ". . . in 1568 . . . Enriquez of New Spain could have only twenty soldiers for a guard" (*Viceregal Ad. in Sp. Amer. Col.,* Fisher, p. 277). When the English took Habana in 1762 there was much excitement in Mexico from fears for an attack on Vera Cruz. In Mexico City there were 346 under arms including 23 halberdiers for a ceremonial guard; in Vera Cruz 960; in small detachments from Pensacola, Florida, to California, 1,140 — a total of 2,746 (*Á Través,* II, 819). For the purpose of organizing a local force there was sent over in 1765 a number of officers and two thousand Walloons and Swiss (*Ibid.,* 820).

[2]*Catholic Encyclopedia,* Art. "Mexico."

[3]Sylvester Baxter, *History of Spanish Architecture in Mexico,* quoted by Bertrand, *op. cit.,* p. 300.

[4]Alamán, *Disertaciones,* III, p. 352. The Conde de Aranda, in a personal communication to Charles III of Spain, warned him of the possible consequences of the creation of the new Republic of the United States as affecting the Spanish colonies in America. First would come the seizure of Florida, and later of Mexico; if worse did not befall. To avoid this, he recommended erecting three Kingdoms, of which Mexico would be one, and the others in South America; to place princes of the Spanish royal house on their thrones, with the King of Spain the Emperor of the whole.

[5]The expulsion of the Jesuits from the Spanish dominion in 1767 demonstrates the authority of the Spanish monarch over the clergy, as well as the regard for the clergy by the people. Every precaution was taken to keep the intention of expulsion secret until the last minute.

The Jesuit establishments were descended upon everywhere at a prearranged moment by the armed authorities, and the Jesuits put under arrest and hurried away to be embarked at Vera Cruz for exile. Besides missions in Lower California and other places the Jesuits were noted for the excellence of their numerous institutions of higher learning. In addition to five colleges in the City of Mexico, and three in Puebla, they possessed others in 17 cities throughout Mexico. These institutions and the missions were supported by the income from endowment funds invested in loans and productive city and country properties (*Á Través,* II, p. 843; Cuevas, IV, pp. 414 *et seq.,* p. 452). The need for secrecy in the fear of popular protest, and possible uprising, is revealed in a letter from the Viceroy of Mexico to his brother, in which he said (*Á Través,* II, pp. 836-7): "As all the inhabitants, from the highest to the lowest and the richest to the poorest, are worthy pupils and zealous partizans of the Company, you will readily comprehend that I carefully avoided trusting any of them to execute the King's orders." Nevertheless, serious riots occurred in several places, which were suppressed with thoroughness and punished with severity. A large number of political appointments at good salaries at once became available to take over, administer, and sell the confiscated Jesuit properties. Purchasers were granted unusually favorable terms (*Á Través,* II, pp. 842-843; Bustamante, *Sup. a Los Tres Siglos,* Cavo, Año 1767, par. 3). In one report were listed 124 properties, of which 41 were in the Archdiocese of Mexico, 53 in Puebla, 2 in Oaxaca, 13 in Michoacán, 3 in Guadalajara, 12 in Durango. The income from the haciendas, etc., totaled $6,850, from invested funds, $132,000, from rented city properties, $4,200. The total over five years $863,746, 1 real, a yearly average of $172,749. All this to support 30 colleges with *free* tuition, in addition to the many missions (Cuevas, IV, pp. 451-452).

THE FIRST REVOLT

[1]Mora, *Mex. y sus Rev's.* IV, p. 10. In a note Mora gives a copy of the instructions sent to revolutionary agents.

[2]Bustamante, *Campañas de Calleja,* p. 4.

[3]Mora, *op. cit.,* IV, pp. 1 *et seq.*

[4]Ignacio Rayon, Hidalgo's Secretary, in a letter said: "From practical experience we know that not only the people and persons are indifferent, but many that are fighting under our American banners, lacking these essential understandings, find themselves embarrassed to explain the system adopted and the reasons why they should uphold it" (Alamán, *Hist. de Mex.* II, app. Doc. 16, p. 37).

[5]Mora, *loc. cit.,* p. 8.

[6]Alamán, I, pp. 350, 351, 353.

[7]Mora, *Mexico,* etc., IV, p. 8.

[8]Dávalos, *Col. de Docs.* I, p. 79.

[9]*Ibid.,* p. 123.

[10]Mora, *op. cit.,* IV, p. 7.

[11]HIDALGO'S MOTIVES. According to Hidalgo in his testimony at his trial, Allende was the instigator. The impending change of Viceroys with its consequences might account for the apathy with which reports of impending revolt were received in the capital. The affair of Allende and Hidalgo finally brought an inquiry and the discovery sent a hurried warning to Allende who was not at his home in San Miguel but with Hidalgo. It was received by Aldama who hurried to warn them. On that same day, September 15, the new Viceroy, Venegas, arrived at Mexico City and took command. Aldama reached Dolores at two in the morning of the 16th and aroused Hidalgo who proceeded to dress. As he was pulling on his stockings he paused to say "Gentlemen, we are lost; there is nothing left for us but to nab Gachupines." With 10 armed men from his household he went to the jail, where with a pistol he compelled the jailer to permit the release

of the 80 prisoners therein; thence to the local militia armory where the mob was armed with swords and was joined by some soldiers. They then proceeded to "nab Gachupines" to the number of 20 and sack their establishments (Alamán, I, pp. 375–376), (Dávalos, *Col. de Docs.* p. 65, Aldama's reply to 3rd question. P. 193, *Fragmento de las declaraciones del Sr. Hidalgo,* replies to questions 12, 21, and 29). Bancroft (*Hist. of Mex.,* IV, p. 117), without citing his authority, puts these words into the mouth of Hidalgo as the latter stood in his pulpit that Sunday morning: "Will you become Napoleon's slaves? Or will you as patriots defend your religion and your rights?" Apparently no Mass was celebrated that morning — Hidalgo jailed his assistant — nor did Hidalgo engage in the theatricals suggested by Bancroft. Instead, after pillaging and terrorizing the place, he commanded the presence of the surviving respectability and informed them that his movement had no other purpose than to shake off the rule "of the Europeans who have surrendered to the French and want us to do the same." Later, he admitted this to be false, and that it and the device on his banner had been invented to entice and excite the people (Dávalos, *op. cit.,* I, p. 193, replies to questions 12 and 30. Also *Manifesto,* p. 119). At every town he released prisoners without regard to the enormity of their crimes (reply to question 29). He permitted pillage in order to attract the rabble (reply to q. 21). In general the leaders gave as reasons the fear that the Spaniards intended delivering the country to the French whom they believed to be atheists and would endanger their religion (*Ibid.,* I, 65, Aldama reply to question 3. Alamán, I, p. 379).

[12]Mora, *op. cit.,* IV, p. 8, note pp. 10–17. Revolts in America cut off help to Spain to fight the French.

[13]Hidalgo said his forces were composed of "Indians and rabble" (Dávalos, *loc. cit.,* reply to question 17; Alamán, I, pp. 380 *et seq.*).

[14]Alamán, II, pp. 167–226.

HIDALGO'S MARCH. The mob entered San Miguel the evening of the 16th and pillaged it as they had Dolores, making the Europeans prisoners. More militiamen joined him here. A band and a hundred dragoons with their banner picturing Fernando VII serving as an escort for the entrance into Celaya on the 21st, where more Spaniards were seized and their establishments pillaged. More militia joined him here (Alamán, I, pp. 375-386). On September 26 the Viceroy sent two battalions — of presumably 500 men each — to Querétaro. For the defense of the capital volunteers were called for who could afford their own uniforms and had independent means. Three battalions of 500 men each, a squadron of cavalry and a company of artillery, were thus organized. Alamán (I, p. 400) calls particular attention to the fact that the troops on both sides were natives of the country, and that even much later the troops from Spain did not exceed 11,000 or 12,000 men while the natives exceeded 30,000 plus many from haciendas and towns. The newly arrived Viceroy applied to the rebels the same term "insurrectos" that was applied to those in Spain refusing to submit to the French (Alamán, I, p. 401). The military commander in Guanajuato received word on the 18th of the uprising. To his call the people responded with alacrity and preparation for defense was made. For reasons not clear he then decided to dismantle these defenses and shut himself up in the Alhondiga — the grain-market warehouse already referred to — where with some 500 or 600 men, soldiers and civilians, he hoped to hold out till help came. What with more than $600,000 of public funds and the money and valuables of the Europeans, he had to defend a treasure of some three millions. The Alhondiga — still there — is a large substantial building of stone with two entrances. For some unaccountable reason the commander closed only one entrance and disposed his forces *outside* the building. On the 28th the mob attacked and the commander was killed. The defenders retired within the edifice, the doors were burned, and the mob swarmed in to massacre and pillage. Alamán (I, p. 432) says it was the work of the rabble of Guanajuato. To them had been added the 300 or 400 malefactors from the local jail released by Hidalgo. Some of the defenders escaped by divesting themselves of their uniforms and mixing with the mob. Alamán (I, p. 434) says some 200 soldiers and 105 Spaniards perished. The survivors, stripped naked and covered with wounds, were driven through the streets to the jail. It was not until October 28 that Calleja joined Flon at Dolores to begin an active campaign against the insurrection. On October 8 Hidalgo set out for Valladolid — now Morelia — which he entered on the 17th without resistance. A large body of militia joined him there. He had offered Iturbide a commission to do so but the latter refused, and with 70 loyal soldiers left for the capital. Later in his manifesto from his exile in Leghorn, Iturbide said that the offer (Lieut. General) was attractive but he was "persuaded that the plans of the priest were ill conceived, could produce only disorder, bloodshed, and destruction, and never attain the object sought." Though Hidalgo had agreed to respect property and persons, his undisciplined mob proceeded to pillage. Only after a number were killed was the disorder quelled. Hidalgo increased his supply of cash, and Alamán (I, p. 466) remarks that with no more money Calleja had raised an army, but Hidalgo only wasted it in confusion. On October 19 he set out for the capital stopping at Acambaro to hold a review and find that he had 80,000 men. The Viceroy sent a small force to oppose him. Mora (IV, p. 74) says 2,500. Alamán (I, p. 475) says scant 1,000 infantry, 400 calvary, and 2 pieces of artillery. Bancroft (IV, p. 175) says 50 volunteers went with these. On October 30 the opposing forces met at the mountain pass of Las Cruces between Toluca and the capital. After fighting from 11:00 in the morning till 5:30 in the afternoon and losing both cannon and a third of his men, Trujillo, the royalist commander, retreated to the capital. Hidalgo retired in the opposite direction — to encounter Calleja on November 6 at Aculco where on the 7th the insurgents were completely routed and all their arms, ammunition, baggage, and cattle were captured. With the remnants of his forces Hidalgo hastened to Valladolid. On the 17th he left for Guadalajara, having learned that Torres had occupied it.

In the meantime Calleja moved on Guanajuato, but not without resistance nor in time to prevent another massacre of Spanish prisoners who to the number of 247 were in the Alhondiga. A few were able to barricade themselves in a room and hold out until a cry that Calleja was coming scattered their assailants permitting them to escape. More than 200 perished that November 24th. On the 25th Calleja took possession, and from the survivors learned the facts. Some 505 victims in all were butchered in the Alhondiga, the second attack being a savage slaughter of prisoners. Calleja rounded up a lot of the rabble and decimated them summarily, executing 23. Further inquiry found 18 more. Then 8 who had served with Hidalgo and then 5, made a total of 54 (Alamán, II, pp. 57–60). Having established order in Guanajuato, Calleja departed in pursuit of Hidalgo who had arrived in

Guadalajara, November 26. There the latter had recruited a new army including 95 cannon (Alamán, II, p. 119). Mora (*op. cit.,* IV, p. 126), says that more than 700 Spaniards from Guadalajara alone had their throats cut by order of Hidalgo. Many of his victims carried his safe conduct in their pockets (Dávalos, replies to questions 16, 17, and 20).

On the 17th of January, 1811, at the bridge of Calderon over the river of the same name some miles east of the city of Guadalajara, the forces of Hidalgo, with his 67 heavy cannon and 100,000 men, of whom 20,000 were cavalry, met Calleja with 5,000 to 6,000 men and ten guns (Alamán, II, pp. 126, 131). The rout was complete. The leaders and some 1,500 headed north cutting the throats of any help-less Europeans they encountered (Alamán, II, pp. 131–132). On the 21st of March, 1811, near the town of Monclova at a water hole called Acatita de Bajan they were captured as they approached, by a force that awaited them. After trials those condemned to death were executed, some on the 10th of May, Allende on June 26th, Hidalgo, July 30th. Some not until July the following year.

[15]Alamán, II, pp. 178–181.

[16]Mora, *op. cit.,* V, p. 3.

[17](*Á Través de los Siglos,* III, app. Doc. 11). Julio Zarate gives a list, prepared by Dr. D. Ramón Mejía Gonzáles of Morelia, of 155 priests and religious — 46 of the latter — concerned in the revolution.

[18]Dávalos, I, *Hidalgo Declaración,* Manifesto.

[19]Alamán, IV, pp. 316–334.

Morelos. Morelos was born in Valladolid — later renamed More-lia in his honor — September 30, 1765. His father was a poor carpenter and his mother the daughter of a schoolmaster in the same city. Through both parents he derived a mixture of Indian and Negro blood. He claimed to be Spanish. After following the calling of cow-boy until the age of 32, he studied for the priesthood, taking only those subjects indispensable to ordination, working day and night. He was given the parish of Caracuaro (Alamán, II, pp. 315–16). His original force consisted of 25 armed men with which he recruited more and took arms where he could find them. Unlike Hidalgo, he proceeded first to drill and discipline his force. But like him he recog-nized the loyalty of the masses to the King though he deplored the deceit of proclaiming that loyalty to attract recruits. The ayuntamiento of Oaxaca, set up by Morelos, and *compelled* by *him* to serve, December 5, 1812, swore to "recognize, respect, and obey, His Majesty the supreme governing junta of America in representation of our august sovereign Fernando VII" (Alamán, III, p. 329, note 28). The Junta referred to was that set up by Rayon in Zitacuaro. This "Junta" was named in a meeting, called August 19, 1811, by some fifteen, mostly military leaders and others, associated with Rayon and Liceaga. It was to consist of three to five members. Having organized themselves as such they proceeded to demand of the local authorities of the Indian villages within reach that they give oath of allegiance to this "Junta" that "governed in the name of Fernando VII and during his absence" (Alamán, II, p. 379). Invited to become a fourth member of the "Junta" Morelos criticized the hypocrisy of pretending to serve Fernando VII, whereupon the others wrote him that they had found this subterfuge very profitable and even necessary (Alamán, II, p. 382). It was an effort to provide some central authority and semblance of government for the innumerable armed bands operating independently. The dissentions continuing, Morelos convoked the "Congress" of Chilpancingo consisting of 8 men — later increased to 16 — appointed by himself. A "Declaration of Independence" was prepared, and signed by seven of them on November 6, 1813. It declared for the Catholic Religion to the exclusion of all others. A proposal by Bustamante in favor of Fernando VII was crossed out by Morelos (Alamán, III, pp. 570, 560). The mask was no longer needed. The ideas of Morelos are clearly set forth in his "Medidas Politicas" — political measures — that must be taken by the military chiefs: All those who have anything must be dispossessed, one half to the military chest, the other half to the poor to gain their favor; the same with all valuables in the churches; all public archives, except parish records, to be burned; all large haciendas to be destroyed, aqueducts, and buildings; all tobacco to be destroyed (evidently Morelos did not use it); all mines to be destroyed to leave no trace; and the same with all sugar mills. "This plan is the result of profound meditations and experiences. If executed to the letter our victory is attained." Alamán (III, p. 559), says Morelos, was strongly inclined to socialism and communism. Like Matamoros he shot prisoners. The anarchy he had hoped to restrain continued. Juntas and congresses only served to turn suspicions and jealousies into hatreds and quarrels. The "Congress" moved to Tehuacan, expecting help from the United States (Alamán, IV, p. 304). Morelos was captured. Some of the insurgent forces at Tehuacan mutinied; the Congress was dissolved and dispersed (Bustamante, *Cuadro Historico,* III, p. 330).

[20]Alamán, V, pp. 1–48.

Calleja had no difficulty in securing enlistments to fight the insurrectos under Hidalgo and his successors. But for a time the royalist forces made less headway as the disorders became more widespread. The sentiment for independence grew, perhaps because of this. At any rate, Calleja could write, August 18, 1814, in a manner indicating a universal desire, and co-operation, for independence. Yet two years later the revolt is a failure. The royalist forces, in great majority well-trained natives, are veterans. There is money in the treasury, business and traffic resumed, the mail service uninterrupted (Alamán, IV, p. 746). The few honest men fighting for independence were greatly outnumbered by the dishonest. The Secretary of Rayon said the leaders in Michoacán were naught but outlaws and robbers; Liceaga painted a horrifying picture of the leaders in Michoacán and Guanajuato; equally unfavorable the characters of Osorno, Gómez, Sanchez and others in the Plains of Apam as shown by Morelos in his letters to Rayon and Bustamante: Bustamante has the same to say of Bocardo, Arroyo, Anaya and others; likewise appear Aguilar, Olarte and others in Vera Cruz according to the testimony of Rayon, Rosains, and Teran; Rayon paints a melancholy picture of Oaxaca in the power of the insurgents, and his secretary an equally disagreeable one of the work of the Villagran family and their followers from Huichapan to Jalpan. The total European population in the census of 1793 appeared as 7,904, and Navarro y Noriega (Boletin, etc. 2a. Ep. Vol. I [1869], p. 281), estimated that in 1810 the number did not exceed 15,000. These were scattered over a territory half the size of the present United States, with numbers in the cities, especially the capital. There was nothing to fear from them as was proved. The rabble made less and less distinction as time passed between friend and foe. The capture and execution of Mina and his men left the country almost at peace. Guerrero with a few followers remained at large on the Pacific coast, while Victoria was a lone fugitive in the mountains of Vera Cruz.

[21]Alamán, V, pp. 49–348.

(Alamán, V, p. 40). After a year or more of quiet the proclamation (1820) of the Constitution of 1812 was a bombshell in Mexico. The attacks upon educational and charitable institutions and upon the clergy made way for wilder attacks in the press given its freedom. The election of delegates to the Cortés (Congress) in Spain sent a group from Mexico, among them Alamán who says (V, p. 47) that when they waited on the Viceroy for his farewell Alamán and another expressed the hope of finding him in good health on their return. "Find me here when you return!" said the Viceroy. "Do you know what is going to happen in your country in your absence?"

X

AMERICO TRIUNFO

[1]Alamán, V, *loc. cit.*

The mental confusion and political aberration consequent upon the royal "patronage" is apparent in the pastoral of the Archbishop Fonte declaring obedience to the constitution of 1812 *an obligation* (Cuevas, *Historia de la Iglesia en Mexico,* V, p. 99). The Viceroy Apodaca reported that the publication of the decrees had excited uncertainty, disquiet, and suspicion, with open discussion of independence, some for a republic, some for a prince of the reigning house (Cuevas, V, p. 100). The real project for action was the work of the "junta de la Profesa," a gathering of priests in the church of that name in the capital. They selected Iturbide as military commander (Cuevas, V, pp. 99, 100, 101, citing official documents in Spanish archives). In 1816 Iturbide had been removed from his command on charges preferred by a number of persons many of whom failed to appear when their object, his removal, was attained. The charges of atrocities could not greatly affect the Viceroy, and those on trafficking still less so, because those of the regular forces, from the Viceroy on down, were equally involved, though expressly forbidden by law, while Iturbide and others like him were exempt because belonging to the provincial troops. On the 3rd of September the charges were declared unmerited. But he was not restored to his command (Alamán, IV, pp. 446–451). Iturbide's sentiments on independence are revealed by a conversation he had with Filisola who repeated it to Alamán (Alamán, V, pp. 56–57). On the 4th of March, 1815, when besieging Cóporo, after a costly and unsuccessful assault, Iturbide lamented the useless bloodshed, and remarked the ease with which independence might be attained, co-operating with the insurgents were it not for the atrocious system they proposed; that it was necessary first to dispose of them before attempting anything. Filisola assented, and Iturbide remarked that some day he might remind him of their conversation, to which Filisola agreed. In similar vein Iturbide discussed the subject with his intimate friends. In his manifesto he revealed confusion of ideas. Independence was desired but the numerous parties could agree neither how to attain it nor what government to have after it (Alamán, V, p. 60). Alamán (V, p. 62, app. Doc. 5) presents, for what it is worth, a copy of a letter from Fernando VII to Apodaca, and found among the papers of the latter, in which the King expressed his disapproval of the Constitution, his recommendation that Mexico become independent, and his hopes of going there. The letter is dated December 24, 1820. A paraphrase was published in France, by the man said to have carried it, and was promptly denied by Fernando.

The activities of the surviving insurgent forces in the south, and the lack of a suitable commander to send against them, prompted the Viceroy to recall Iturbide on November 9, 1820; verbal instructions being given to endeavor to persuade Guerrero to accept amnesty (Alamán, V, p. 67). By various artifices Iturbide hastened to assemble resources and troops, some of whom, not knowing the idea of Iturbide, planned to desert and declare for independence, fearing he had discovered their previous intent to do so. Advised of this, Iturbide suddenly appeared before the officers at supper and, after assuring them that his opinions were not different from theirs, secured a promise to await events. Thus was the revolt begun (Alamán, V, pp. 72–73). But before making this openly, certain military movements against Guerrero and his lieutenant Ascensio were required. In one of these a detachment of Iturbide's men consisting of 108 were cut off by Ascensio with 800 and all but some four exterminated, the prisoners being shot, among them the commander González mortally wounded — which fact did not deter Ascensio from having him immediately shot. This was a blow to Iturbide who had persuaded González to forego his permit to retire, just received; revealing his plans to influence his decision to remain (Alamán, V, p. 82). Another similar disaster convinced Iturbide that his plan, first to dispose of Guerrero and then launch his campaign for independence, was impractical, so he decided to treat with Guerrero. In the meantime he communicated with numerous friends, seeking their support. Then came a convoy with $525,000 bound for Acapulco and Manila. He seized it, and published his "Plan" on the 24th of February, 1821 (Alamán, V, pp. 96, 99).

[2](Alamán, V, app. Doc. 6). After the customary oratorical flourishes, he outlines his project in 23 propositions, among them being the Catholic religion without tolerance of any other; absolute independence; a monarchical form of government; Fernando VII or some member of his house to be Emperor; a Regency to govern until this is determined. A congress to be assembled to form a constitution; this to be established at once; all inhabitants are citizens without distinction; all persons and their properties to be respected and protected by the government; all clergy to retain their rights and places; all public employees to remain but those not favoring the plan; army to be organized; to observe strict discipline; employment to be by merit; laws of Spain to prevail until Congress acts; elections to be held as soon as possible for the Congress.

[3]With the first burst of enthusiasm subsiding, desertions began. Officers led small bodies of troops to rejoin those loyal to the King. Alamán (V, p. 141) says one of them, named Almela, made a colonel by Iturbide, left with three companies. He was a Mason and, as these were in favor of the Constitution of 1812, they had declared against independence, and had ordered Almela, under pain of death, to return to his allegiance. He and his men were Europeans.

After two months' negotiation Iturbide was visited by the cautious Guerrero. He was left to look after the region he had always controlled while Iturbide returned to a more healthy altitude. Presently royalist commanders began declaring for him and old insurgents appearing in the field so as not to be left out. The Viceroy issued proclamations and sought to hold commanders to him by offers of promotion. Cities were occupied without resistance or surrendered after investment without a fight. Iturbide prepared to invest the capital, first marching by way of Cuernavaca from Querétaro, only arriving at Puebla after the surrender (Alamán, V, p. 256). This released troops to invest the capital where Apodaca had been forced by his remaining officers to resign naming one of them in his place. On the same day that Iturbide entered Puebla a new Viceroy arrived at Vera Cruz and was amazed at what he found. The place was threatened by Santa Anna who had deserted to Iturbide. The new Viceroy O'Donojú issued a proclamation asserting his lone helplessness and assuring the people that if he were not satisfactory they might elect someone else (Alamán, V, p. 267). In most friendly terms he wrote to Iturbide at Puebla begging a safe conduct to the capital where he might confer with him. Iturbide selected Córdova as the place of conference where both arrived on August 23rd and on the 24th signed the Treaty of Córdova.

⁴Alamán, V, p. 274.

The opposition to Iturbide arose early. His "plan" had provided that Spanish public employees who wish to remain and recognize the new government keep their jobs. An exodus at once began. Iturbide endeavored to prevail on one of them, holding an important position, named Bataller, to remain, who replying professed entire lack of confidence in the promised security. Iturbide responded by declaring he would stake his head on it. "Your head?" said Bataller, "Sad security, it will be the first to fall in this country" (Alamán, V, p. 367).

The Army of The Three Guarantees entered the capital on the 27th of September. The next morning 36 prominent citizens, including O'Donojú, assembled and formed a governing committee, and at once named a Regency composed of five, though the treaty had only called for three. Here arose a dispute (Alamán, V, p. 338).

The deliberations of the Junta (Alamán, V, Chap. 2) reveal first a split over the return of the hospital orders that had been expelled by the Spanish Constitution. Then their utter lack of any knowledge of how to conduct an election either as to time necessary or machinery involved to secure even a semblance of response to popular will. A complicated system for choosing 162 members of the Congress was invented which time, distance, and utter unfamiliarity made impossible of successful operation.

Alamán says (V, p. 411) that to those who supported the Plan de Iguala and liberalism were joined the Spaniards who wanted to remain in the country and saw their only hope in it; the republicans who did not believe it would go into effect, and the old insurgents who detested it. Opposed to them Iturbide counted on the army, the clergy, and the people.

The Congress was elected and assembled, and was duly organized the 24th of February as ordered. The majority professed the liberal ideas popular at the time (Alamán, V, p. 480). About this time the Spanish Cortes annulled the Treaty of Córdova (Alamán, V, p. 573). The enemies of Iturbide then became the republicans, joined with the monarchists who would have none but a prince from Europe, all liberals; the supporters of Iturbide being the monarchists who wanted that form of government, his personal following, and the clergy who dreaded the liberals, and who were in closest contact with the people (Alamán, V, p. 590).

[5] Alamán, V, p. 220.

[6] Alamán, V, pp. 322, 323.

[7] Alamán, V, pp. 602–642.

While the Regency still ruled, on April 3rd Iturbide presented a letter he had received from the Spanish commander, who still held the fortress of San Juan de Ulloa in front of Vera Cruz, declaring there were traitors in the Congress and the Regency. A tumult arose and when the letter was read the deputies could find nothing in it substantiating the charge. They called for more facts. He returned only to name some eleven he suspected. The Congress absolved its members (Alamán, V, pp. 535, 536, 537). The strife continued for weeks becoming more bitter as numerous questions and disputes added fuel. The liberals, republicans, and Bourbonists — as the monarchists were called — were Masons. Zavala, who was one of them, reveals in his book (Alamán, V, p. 589) that in a meeting he attended a certain colonel in the heat of the discussion declared that if there was lacking a Brutus to take the life of the Tyrant he offered his arm for the country. And in another presided over by a Colonel Valero, who had come with O'Donojú, it was resolved to assassinate Iturbide. But the latter, warned by his spies, voided the attempt and the affair became noised about. As Valero about this time was made a Brigadier, he was charged with having sold a secret of the society and his punishment decided upon; whereupon he returned to Spain (Alamán, V, p. 590).

[8] Alamán, V, pp. 622–740.

It was while Iturbide was in trouble with his Congress that Poinsett first visited Mexico (*Notes on Mexico* — made in the fall of 1812 — Joel R. Poinsett, London, 1825). He established contacts with the troublemakers some of whom were in jail.

[9] Alamán, V, pp. 740–804.

The papers of Iturbide were brought to Mexico by a Mexican bishop who discovered from them that Iturbide had been obliged to leave Italy and was denied asylum elsewhere.

[10]Alamán, V, pp. 358–685.

The rabble, as then and since, thought only of pillage. The thoughtful were concerned with the protection of life and property, the maintenance of law and order, and the preservation of their religious institutions. Independence was attractive to those who sought to gain some personal advantage from it, but not with anarchy. The hatred for the Spaniard was largely due to the "high-hatting" of a few officials and the jesting insolence of a number of young "smart alecks" of the "counter jumper" class, with a superiority complex.

[11]Alamán, V, pp. 358–546.

Iturbide, while still occupied with his enterprise, had decreed, while in Querétaro, the abolition of a number of special war taxes, such as 10 per cent on house rents (234). The Alcabala was reduced from 16 per cent to 6 per cent, but the Indians who had enjoyed the exemption of this impost were now subjected to it on the theory that it was incompatible with equality to be exempted therefrom (234). Many other changes were made as equally costly and reasonable (413–423). Needing many millions a voluntary loan was called for. It realized $277,067. Independence was nice to have, but nobody wanted to pay the cost of it (424–430).

[12]*Concilio Tercero Mexicano*, p. 569. *A Través*, IV, p. 47, 58, 201.

[13]Alamán, V, p. 384.

[14](Bocanegra, *Memorias*, I, p. 38). To this may be added from the same "The Scottish Rite lodges, which according to all authorities existed in Mexico, were actively at work at the time, and, according to information later acquired, arranged in their meetings that which was to be proposed in the congress and that which was to be agreed upon by the majority."

Rocafuerte, one of the bitterest enemies of Iturbide, said that (*Bosquejo Lijerisimo*, p. 164), "The Congress smothered every measure that might prove favorable to the Generalisimo; it took its time with the constitution to give opportunity for the propaganda to take effect; it elicited a remembrance of the first and true patriots of independence; and meanwhile continued a covert war of opinions within itself."

[15]Alamán, V, pp. 492–493.

XI

THE HIDDEN HAND

[1]Alamán, *Hist.*, V, 5-6.
[2]Bancroft, *History of Mexico*, IV, 698.
[3]Alamán, V, 409.
[4]Bocanegra, *Memorias*, I, 38.
[5]Poinsett, *Notes on Mexico* (London, 1825).
[6]Alamán, III, 479-480, app. Doc. 12.
[7]Poinsett, *Notes on Mexico*.
[8]Also see *La Missión de Poinsett á México, por* Wm. R. Manning.
POINSETT. He arrived in Mexico as Minister from the United States in May, 1825. A religious fiesta was in progress in San Augustín, a suburb of the capital, which he attended, and in describing it in his report reveals his hostility and contempt. His instructions from Clay included the revealing a discreet disposition to explain the functioning of the United States Constitution to the Mexican Government. He at once plunged into Mexican politics embracing and favoring the faction promising the creation of an "American party." To aid in this, he favored the York Rite to oppose the Scottish Rite which was the instrument of the factions already referred to. He reported in January, 1826, that Masonry was in its apogee; to it belonging the cabinet and principal men and some of the highest clergy; the President excepted. He expected Guerrero, who was without education, to be President, but under the influence of Zavala, one of the head men of the Yorkinos, the party favorable to the United States. On July 8, 1827, he wrote to Clay that the Yorkinos were already there before his arrival but unrecognized; that certain of them, viz., Guerrero, Esteva, Alpuche, Arispe, and Zavala, had requested a charter from the Grand Lodge of New York which he had not hesitated to obtain. It had not occurred to him that such men would disorganize the government, and he had ceased to attend the meetings as soon as the Yorkinos were publicly accused of being perverted to political ends. The Scottish Rite had long been established and the Yorkinos had done no more than follow their bad example of political activity. The progress of the York Rite had been so rapid that the people had attributed it to some secret cause and the success of the republican cause and

liberal principles were due to Poinsett's influence. Zavala says Alpuche was responsible for the York idea; that Esteva, Arispe, Victoria, and others joined them in organizing five lodges; that they requested charters from the Grand Lodge of New York; this and the installation of a Grand Lodge in Mexico, was all that Poinsett had to do with it. But Poinsett was the center of a highly disturbing influence in Mexico during his incumbency. Constant protests and demands for his recall were uttered against him by the people of Mexico. He received his recall December 9, 1829. The Mexican President *ad interim* assured the President of the United States that it was a testimony of sincere friendship of the United States for Mexico. The facts in this note are taken from *La Misión de Poinsett á México, por* William R. Manning.

Mariano Cuevas, S.J., in his *Historia de la Iglesia en México,* devotes a chapter (Capitulo V, Vol. V) to what he calls "El Pacto Secreto de Nueva Orleans" (The Secret Pact of New Orleans). Well documented, it reveals the machinations of Gómez Farías and his group in co-operation with American sympathizers in New Orleans, whose interest in the extension of slave territory may be taken for granted. The plan agreed upon in the so-called Amphictionic Council of New Orleans (Sept. 4, 1835) is the goal to which the radicals have always aspired, and to which the present regime believes it has arrived.

[9]Cuevas, *Hist. de la Iglesia en México,* V, p. 150.

Á Través, IV, 165—January 7, 1828—Legislature of Vera Cruz pronounces against all secret societies and Masons in particular.

DÁVILA AND ITURBIDE (Alamán, V, 530). The Spanish Commander, Dávila, in Vera Cruz had retired to the fortress of San Juan de Ulloa built on a rock a few hundred yards off shore in front of the city. There he remained to the chagrin of the impotent Mexicans. Iturbide wrote him a letter mixing persuasion with empty threats in an effort to secure his surrender but Dávila refused. Evidently kept well informed of what was passing in the capital, and shrewdly calculating his opportunity, Dávila wrote a letter to Iturbide expressing his personal regard and his admiration for his achievements from which he had hoped so much for his country, but far from realizing this he saw the country taking gigantic strides toward ruin and anarchy; that the deputies in Congress were not the ones to save the ship of State which would sink with all on board because of their selfishness and lack of sense; that the hostility in the Congress against him was daily increasing and would end in his ruin because of the way of those determined to destroy him. He reminded him that to retrace was no dishonor, and proposed co-operation to that end. It was this letter that Iturbide offered to the Congress as evidence of there being traitors in its ranks and which only served to make more determined the rancor of his enemies. But this did not deter Gómez Farías and 46 other deputies from offering a resolution signed by them for the election of Iturbide as Emperor (Bocanegra, *Memorias,* I, 58), and his election in May, by 67 votes for to 15 against. Of the six names of those protesting (*Á Través,* IV, 77) most loudly, only one, Lombardo, appears among the 19 ordered jailed August 26 by Iturbide to checkmate a conspiracy for a revolt (Alamán, V, 645-650). It was these and their friends with whom Poinsett conferred, and doubtless arrived at some arrangement (Poinsett, *Notes*).

[10]Alamán, V, 824. "Zavala, . . . who belonged to the York Rite, said that the Grand Lodge was attended by Congressmen, Generals, Senators, Ecclesiastics, Governors, Merchants, and every class of persons of influence; and there they discussed and arranged elections, drafts of laws, cabinet decisions, placing of employees, and everything of interest or importance" *Á Través,* IV, 208; Cuevas, *Hist. de la Iglesia en Mexico,* V, pp. 131–153.

[11]The conspiracy referred to was uncovered in January, 1827. A Friar named Joaquin Arenas, who had been sent to Mexico from Durango in irons by his Bishop, had attempted with a few friends to enlist partisans among government employees to restore Spanish rule. At the time, Arenas was conducting a counterfeiting plant under cover of a soap factory. When he approached the Comandante General Mora the latter laid a trap and caught the lot (Alamán, V, 825-831).

Alamán, V, 836 *et. seq;* Bancroft IV, 39.

[12]Alamán, V, 845; Bancroft, IV, 401.

[13]Alamán, 846 *et. seq.* Alamán is the accepted authority on this period. Both Bancroft and *Á Través* follow him closely. Bancroft lists a multitude of authorities in his bibliography but does not question Alamán except in a partisan way. George Creel, *The People Next Door,* app. p. 886, reveals the real authors of the Bancroft volumes on Mexico.

[14]The report referred to appeared in *The Builder* for October, 1920, published by the National Masonic Research Society of Cedar Rapids, Iowa.

MASONRY. A Mason of thirty years' standing contributes the following two notes of explanation:

1. There is a Masonic lodge in Edinburgh, Scotland, called Mary's Chapel. Its records long antedate the Reformation, being continuous for many centuries. Tradition has it that it was brought to Scotland with the men who built Holy Rood Cathedral by order of King David. From fragments of ancient "charges" (instructions to candidates) preserved in some lodge archives in England, it would appear that members were expected to be Catholics in good standing. In the beginning of the eighteenth century some of the existing lodges began accepting nonprofessional members, while other lodges for some time refused them. There was certainly no attempt at secrecy beyond the exclusion of nonmembers from meetings, a practice common to fraternal organizations, because parades were held, and members wore insignia advertising their membership. With the growth of the Order, in the acceptance of nonprofessionals, variations in procedure began to appear, and it soon became apparent that some authority was necessary to assure uniformity. Doubtless to obtain Royal patronage, the lodge at York became the "Grand Lodge." Hence the designation of the "York Rite." While the social phase was emphasized, there was also the phase of mutual benefit. But so far as any religious phase is concerned there never has been any more than would be expected in any organization of men belonging to any Church, such as opening and closing proceedings with prayer, and the inevitable references to Diety and religious precepts in the induction of candidates. It was not originally intended or used as a substitute for the Church. The change came about, at least in my opinion, when political refugees in England from the Continent made friends with their hosts, and those who seemed eligible were accepted as members. On returning to their homes later, these continentals preserved only the name of the organization. Otherwise they preserved secrecy as to membership, as to meetings, and as to purposes. They invented altogether new and fantastic ceremonies for the initiation of candidates, and in every way made an entirely new organization; though they did preserve some of the means of recognition, such as signs and passwords.

Instead of being a charitable organization with a religious background, it became a conspiracy against religion and a means to revolution. Also see *The Builders*, by Joseph Fort Newton, 1916, the Torch Press, Cedar Rapids, Iowa.

2. Like the continental he really was, Poinsett was most unethical in the perversion and misuse of his Masonic membership, and misled both Americans and Mexicans. He used any means to gain his ends. The results of his efforts in Mexico paralleled those of his revolutionary predecessors in France. American sympathizers with Mexican revolutions, with or without honorariums therefor, have attempted to use their membership in American lodges to procure for the Mexican lodges recognition by the American bodies. These activities were sufficiently vigorous during the "constitutionalist" revolution to inspire an inquiry by the Grand Lodge of Alabama (there is no national grand lodge). The report on this inquiry was published in *The Builder,* a Masonic publication, for October, 1920. It concludes by saying: "Owing to the unsettled conditions in Mexico, both from the Masonic and the political point of view, not to speak of any other reason, we do not recommend recognition of any of the Mexican bodies claiming to be Masonic." The "Mexican bodies claiming to be Masonic" were not Masonic at all, they were atheistic and opposed to every principle for which American Masonry claims to stand. If American Masons are Protestant it is not because they are Masons but because they were born Protestants, and if as individuals they are hostile to the Catholic Church it is for a like reason. While the Southern Jurisdiction of the Scottish Rite is composed of men who are Masons, it is a separate and distinct organization which has permitted those in charge of its publication, a monthly magazine, to make use of it as a weapon against the Church in aid of the Mexican revolutionaries. This need not be surprising when there is considered the Southern mind and the Southern background. Because of these the Southerner has preserved prejudices that in the North are mere shadows by comparison. But he is not an atheist; being, in fact, more warmly religious than his northern neighbor. There is a sincerity in his anti-Catholicism that would make him a neutral, if not a convert, if only someone would take the trouble to inform him.

XII

THE GREAT STEAL

[1]Callcott, *Church and State in Mexico*, pp. 51-52; *Á Través*, IV, 97. In addition to all this the forced sale was ordered of the properties belonging to the Jesuits and the hospitallers.

[2]*Á Través*, V, 31; Laws of Oct. 19, 24, and 27, Nov. 6, Dec. 17, 1833, and April 22, 1834.

The ecclesiastical authorities could consult the public records to ascertain the facts regarding legacies involving bequests for purposes subject to ecclesiastical oversight. This inspection was called *"visita de testamentos."*

[3]*Á Través*, V, 331.

MISSION FUNDS. Having prepared the destruction of the California missions with the decree of August 17, 1833, on the 31st was decreed the seizure of the funds and properties of the Philippine missions; (*Á Través*, IV, 331) it being declared that such should belong to the nation and not be used by a Spanish colony. Evidently charity was not only to begin at home but stay there for the exclusive benefit of the politicians. On October 19 the University and a number of other institutions were ordered seized, among them being the Hospital de Jesus, founded by Cortés with all its supporting properties, the old and the new Belen hospital, the asylum of Santo Tomas, the convent and temple of San Camilo, and the printing establishment in the great asylum for the poor (*Á Través*, IV, 332). The Camilos served in the hospitals. Their establishment was converted into a tenement.

(Helen Phipps, *Some Aspects of the Agrarian Question in Mexico*, p. 100). "The national government sold a mission in Lower California with its furniture, chapel, garden, orchard and six or eight square leagues (26,340 to 35,120 acres) of irrigated agricultural land to an American for thirty dollars. About four hundred square leagues (1,756,000 acres), also in Lower California, were sold to a Mexican for two hundred dollars. (Vicente Manero, *Documentos*, etc., Mexico, 1878, p. 51.)" Helen Phipps does not give the date of these transactions, but presumably they took place, when the California missions were taken, in the early thirties.

THE WORK OF GÓMEZ FARÍAS. The decree of December 17, 1833, asserted the right of the President, for the Federal District and territories, and the Governors in their states, to appoint the parish priests (in permanent benefices); it suppressed the *sacristias mayores* (administrators of temporalities) in all parishes; and provided for banishment of bishops who fail to comply with the law. On April 22, 1834, it was decreed that within thirty days the bishops and clergy must formally agree to obey the law under penalty of exile and confiscation. Having prayed for fortitude and guidance, the Cathedral Chapter presented themselves before Santa Anna to voice their written protest: "There stands the Church with her treasures we have viewed as sacred and have preserved and guarded religiously, not the smallest stone is lacking in the custodias, not a piece of silver devoted to the service of the Lord. We are four old men that, bowed with the weight of our years and our sorrows, are on the way to die in the perpetual exile to which we are condemned. But we take with us our piety, our obedience to the law and a clear conscience. We are to suffer because we have preferred to obey God instead of men" (*Á Través,* IV, 340).

During the month of May the bishops and clergy were driven into hiding or exile.

Bancroft (V, 128) says that Santa Anna absented himself ". . . intentionally, as believed by many, to permit the initiation by Gómez Farías of the reforms demanded by the radical wing of the progressive party without incurring himself any responsibility in the event of these innovations not finding general support."

Gómez Farías made Ramos Arizpe Minister of Justice and Ecclesiastical Affairs. Both men were close associates of Poinsett.

The law of April 22, 1834, was the last straw. Or as Callcott say (p. 100): "By the last date the sentiment of the country had become crystallized, and further delay had become unnecessary." Santa Anna returned to the capital, but appears to have been moved to extreme caution because of the *Thing* that controlled the little band of desperate men forming the extremists of the most extreme radicals.

In referring to the attempts of Gómez Farías and the "progressives"—as he calls them—Callcott (p. 99) says: "The real liberals who could be relied upon for support in time of trouble were a small minority of the Mexican people, who were ready to break with the past." A number of Liberal writers are quoted by Planchet (*La Cuestión Religiosa,* pp. 119-121) who support this. One of them, Bulnes, says: "In the Mexico of 1858, the nine millions of population, with the exception of not to exceed a thousand persons, all were devout, superstitious, and attached to their religion like bark to a tree. It seems impossible at first sight that in ten years four or five·free thinkers could form a small school of less than a hundred educated and daring young reds and upon a great country impose laws that would destroy the absolute sovereignty that the clergy had enjoyed for three centuries; laws that the nine millions of inhabitants detested with all the strength of their souls. This proves that our people are made to be tyrannized with impunity. Just as some people are formed for liberty, the Mexicans are formed for tyranny. The laws of Reform were received by the majority of the people with rage, horror, disgust, and desperation, and only arms imposed them, only arms have sustained them effectively, and only by arms have they gained any favor little by little in the national conscience. The Mexican people have never felt any need for the laws of Reform. Even in 1905 the majority of Mexicans did not know what thing the reform is. Francisco Bulnes, *Juárez y las Revoluciones de Ayutla y de Reforma,* pp. 363-384.

FORCED LOANS. American advocates of the Mexican liberals follow the lead of Bancroft in calling attention to the war cry of the conservatives *"Religion y fueros"* without explaining its origin which was the attempt to destroy schools, colleges, hospitals, and asylums. Santa Anna heeded temporarily the popular anger, and by permitting the bishops to return calmed the storm. The chronic lack of funds drove him again to the Church. As usual, when only questions of cash were concerned, the clergy reluctantly surrendered what force demanded. We have no record of the conversations that led up to what we quote but their tenor should not be difficult to guess. *Á Través* (IV, 342) does not give the date, but presumably it was in June that in the Official Bulletin appeared a notice of which

Á Través gives a fragment, as follows: "His Excellency, the President, accepting the desires manifested by some ecclesiastical corporations and pious (charitable) establishments, to aid the government in its present straights with a voluntary loan that may be collected from among those existing in the Federal District furnishing it each month for six months a sum of forty thousand or more pesos with interest at 6% per year. . . . His Excellency has deemed it well to accept the offer. . . ." Ferrari calls this "thirty pieces of silver," and "the salvation of the Church" which "was never in greater danger of perishing" (*Á Través*, IV, 342).

George Creel (*The People Next Door*, p. 66), treats it as follows: "One of Santa Anna's first acts was to accept a salary of forty thousand dollars a month from the Church."

Santa Anna arrived on August 16. Juan Álvarez is in correspondence with Gómez Farías. The Americans apparently are following the plan suggested to Mr. Polk by Santa Anna (Callcott, 152-153). Santa Anna's proposal to raise $25,000,000 on Church property (the November notes failed) is in a letter to Gómez Farías dated January 2, 1847, given by Callcott, pp. 182-183, from Gómez Farías' papers. Gómez Farías issued a decree January 11, 1847, pledging Church property, or selling it at auction to raise $15,000,000 (Bancroft, V, 305; *Á Través*, IV, 603; V, 42, 43; Planchet, *Cuestión Religioso*, 19; Callcott, 184).

Alamán, V, 863-864; Callcott, *op. cit.* 91; *Á Través*, V, pp. 32, 33, 34; Callcott, 103.

Besides forced loans, bonds to raise $500,000 were sold April 10, 1835, for 45 per cent of their face value. On April 27, a loan of $200,000 for 4 to 6 months called for 4 per cent per month. On November 4, one for $1,000,000 for 5 months went at 4 per cent per month (Callcott, 113).

[4]Bancroft, V, 129-136. Callcott, 123, 162, 163, 171. Zamacoiz, XII, 297-299.

[5]*Á Través*, IV, 598-603; V, 41-43; Callcott, 182, 185, 194; Bancroft, V, 305; Planchet, *Questión Religiosa*, 19.

William Jay, *Review of the Mexican War*, p. 116; Callcott, *op. cit.*, 154, 155, 157; *Á Través*, V, 41. In May of 1846, Parades called upon the several Church dioceses to pay the government $2,400,000 in installments of $200,000 per month, the share of the Archbishop of Mexico being set at $98,000. The Archbishop, however, was able to show that this was more than the gross income of his diocese and secured a reduction to $25,000, the first payment being made in July. The barrack revolt of August, 1846, instigated by Santa Anna and sponsored by Gómez Farías, placing Salas in charge, raised this sum to $60,000 monthly should the war go beyond the seventh month.

On November 19, 1846, the government (Salas) issued $2,000,000 of notes which the Church authorities were ordered to endorse and distribute as best they might among those who had money; the funds thus obtained to be secured by Church property; $1,000,000 on Mexico, $400,000 on Puebla, $250,000 on Guadalajara, $160,000 on Michoacán, $100,000 on Oaxaca, and $80,000 on Durango (*Á Través,* IV, 597–598).

[6]Callcott, 200; Planchet, *op. cit.,* 21.

The law of January 11, 1847, caused a multitude of protests and threats of revolution. Bancroft says (V, 305): "Several state governments protested against the measure, and erelong revolutionary movements broke out in various places. At the capital on the 15th of January occurred a serious one, proclaiming 'religion y fueros.' In Querétaro the effect of the publication of that law, which had been made the 17th of January, was still more dangerous. The government was kept in constant alarm by the hostile popular demonstrations, but persisted in the purpose of enforcing the law." A decree of January 16 forbade criticism of it. At the end of March, returning from his defeat at Angostura (Buena Vista) Santa Anna ousted Gómez Farías and—March 29—revoked the law of January 11. Vigil, author of Vol. V, of *Á Través de los Siglos,* panegyrist of Gómez Farías, says that the latter was stripped completely, with but a handful of men of the people left him (V, 633).

TEXAS. Rippy (*The United States and Mexico,* pp. 15–19), gives an interesting and well-documented account of the question of acquiring territory, annexation, and Trist's mission. George Creel (*The People Next Door,* p. 121), discussing the separation of Texas from Mexico, its annexation to the United States, and the latter's war with Mexico, says: "The unhappy conflict between the United States and Mexico affords another impressive illustration of the manner in which history can embalm a lie." This lie is the belief that the war was "deliberately forced for the purpose of seizing territory from which additional slave states might be carved." How far this is from being a lie is abundantly testified by the record. Speaking of the value of slaves, Mr. Upshur in the Virginia Convention in 1829 said: "If it should be our lot, as I trust it will, to acquire Texas, their price will rise" (Livermore, *War with Mexico Reviewed,* p. 15). In 1832, Mr. Gholson, in the Virginia Legislature, speaking of slaves, said that he believed "the acquisition of Texas would raise their price fifty percent at least." And Mr. Calhoun, in the United States Senate, May 23, 1836, said there were "powerful reasons why Texas should be a part of this Union. The Southern States owning a slave population were deeply interested in preventing that country from having the power to annoy them; and the navigating and manufacturing interests of the North were equally interested in making it a part of the Union" (p. 16). In 1843 Mr. Upshur wrote to Mr. Murphy, *charge d'affairs* of the United States in Texas; "Few calamities could befall this country more to be deplored than the establishment of a predominant British influence, and the abolition of domestic slavery in Texas" (p. 17). As a smoke screen to obscure the truth Mr. Murphy wrote to Mr. Upshur, Sept. 23, 1844, as follows: "Saying nothing therefore which can offend even our fanatical brethren of the North; let the United States espouse at once the cause of civil, political and religious liberty [?] in this hemisphere; this will be found the safest issue to go before the world with" (p. 18). (Debates of Virginia Convention, 1829; *Journal of Virginia Legislature,* 1832; 28th Congress, 2d Session, *Congressional Globe,* p. 495; 28th Congress, 1st Session, 341, pp. 21, 22, 46, 25.) Southern politicians in legislatures and in Congress, Southern editors in a multitude of papers, refute Mr. Creel. (See also Ladd, *The War with Mexico;* or Wm. Jay, *Review of the Mexican War;* H. Rippy, *The United States and Mexico.*)

The Mexican politicians were now confronted with the annexation of Texas by the United States. No government of Mexico had dared to recognize the independence of Texas that Santa Anna in defeat was compelled to grant. Much less would they agree to its annexation by the United States, so they made it inevitable by declaring that such an act would be accepted as a declaration of war. On the passage of the joint resolution for the annexation in March, 1845, by the American Congress, Mexico severed diplomatic relations and prepared for hostilities (Rippy, *United States and Mexico*, 10; *Á Través*, IV, 543).

In October of 1845 offers from President Polk to negotiate and "adjust all questions in dispute between the two governments" received an evasive and truculent assent, but when Mr. Slidell, sent in response thereto by Mr. Polk, approached the Mexican capital, early in December, he was met at Puebla by a request to defer his arrival because he was not expected until January. The real reason was a lively fear of the politicians that the opposing factions eagerly would embrace the opportunity to charge the administration with being too friendly with Washington (Wm. Jay, *Review of the Mexican War*, 111–113), a fear only too well founded, and that was justified by the revolution which placed Paredes in power on the 4th of January, 1846.

Attempts were made, in November, 1845, to raise funds by issuing sight drafts against the clergy (Callcott, 182). Mr. Slidell was even less successful with Paredes who "evinced marked hostility towards the United States and dismissed the American envoy in short order" (Rippy, 11–18).

Trist reported (Dec. 26, 1847) that he feared the annexation party in Mexico would be too strong and might delay negotiations in order to bring about annexation. The Mexican President justified his hasty action in signing the treaty by the assertion that, had he delayed, the whole country spontaneously would have annexed itself to the United States because of the peace and order and security that prevailed where the American forces were stationed, and that these paid cash for their supplies to the amazed incomprehension and delight of the people. A delegation of prominent Mexican citizens waited on General Scott and begged him to remain in the country with his army. At a banquet attended by American and Mexican officers to celebrate peace, annexation was toasted and cheered. One of those present being no less than Miguel Lerdo de Tejada (Miguel Roja O'Brien, *Quienes son los Traidores de Mexico*, p. 22; Regis Planchet, *La Cuestión Religiosa en Mexico*, p. 21).

[7]Callcott, 200–229; Planchet, 20–21; *Á Través*, V, 51; Rabasa, *La Constitución y la Dictadura*, 39–40.

MAKING REVOLUTIONS. Brantz Mayer (*Mexico*, II, 109), shows that the interest charges alone on the debt were nearly nine millions while the income of 1849 was $5,540,112 with expenses of $13,765,435, not counting that interest. The total deficit being $17,213,754. Callcott (208) mentions two more attempts to mortgage Church property without result. Callcott (229) quoting Garber (*The Gadsden Treaty*, 153), says Gadsden "actively sympathized with the rebels and urged Pierce to break off all relations with Santa Anna and send an army to aid the Liberals." The latter were principally Álvarez, Juárez, Comonfort, Ocampo, Lerdo de Tejada and others of a confessed minority. How such a minority operates is explained by Munguia (Planchet, 114). ". . . every revolt begins by collecting a considerable number of fugitives from justice, of those that live by avoiding the vigilance of the authorities, engaged in robbery and assassination, or, like those released by Hidalgo to begin his revolution in 1810, in jail waiting sentence or purging their crimes. They fall upon defenseless communities seizing by force the peaceful inhabitants to serve as soldiers and conclude by over running the country with these heterogeneous armies held together in part by the bait of pillage, and in part by the oppression of violence." Rabasa (*Evolución Historica de Mexico*, 43) says that "In 1810 war, murder, undisciplined rebellion against law and order was unknown to the people of New Spain; in 1820 disorder was a means of livlihood." It continued to become more and more so. Vigil (*Á Travės*, V, 202) says that the leaders "live off the country"; . . . "disposing at their pleasure of the lives and properties of peaceful citizens." A multitude of such admissions could be cited. Such lawless marauders are the pawns in the revolutionary game. Vigil admits (*Á Travės*, V, 108) that the ecclesiastical authorities endeavored to impress upon the people that they should obey the authorities and keep the peace; that the Archbishop of Mexico never ceased to inculcate in the clergy the obligation of submitting to the temporal authorities (*Á Travės*, V, 188); and he gives in full (*Á Travės*, V, 104) the letter of the Bishop of Puebla admonishing the people to keep the peace and obey the authorities, and another letter reprimanding the parish priest of Zacapoaxtla for his action in forwarding a revolt. This has been a constant and consistent policy of the Mexican Bishops and the consequence has been the withdrawal from strife of the vast majority of the people *especially those best fitted for leadership,* leaving in the field of battle those restless or contemptuous of authority to lead the lawless and the vagabond.

[8]*Á Través,* V, 66; Planchet, 29–33, 146–158; Rippy, *U. S. and Mexico,* 216–219.

PLAN OF AYUTLA. The Plan de Ayutla, the ostensible revolutionary pronouncement against Santa Anna by the liberals, was announced by a Colonel Florencio Villareal on March 1, 1858 (Callcott, 228). As the Colonel did not long lead this effort those familiar with the revolutionary procedure will recognize the customary "muscling in," this time by Álvarez and his intellectual guides. The latter seldom are military leaders and the military leaders seldom are intellectual.

This Plan de Ayutla called for the removal of Santa Anna, to which everyone agreed, and for other demands to which no one could object except perhaps the limited period set for the calling of a constitutional congress—two weeks (Rabasa, *La Constitución y la Dictadura,* 39, 40; Callcott, 229). Innumerable independent bands took part in this revolt and continued in the field after his departure (*Á Través,* V, 84). Many joined the conservatives later (Rabasa, *op. cit.,* 39).

ALVAREZ. Planchet (29) cites Santa Anna (*Memorias*) as authority for the statement that Álvarez was a mulatto and (30–31) other publications for a few of his more atrocious crimes. Also other details referred to.

Vigil (*Á Través,* V, 66) makes a brave attempt to explain the revolutionary kaleidoscope with leaders fighting for different sides, changing sides, and against each other on the same side, acknowledging few superiors. From the utter confusion he derives at least four parties or military factions. He then identifies four principal factions jockeying for position. Álvarez won. Mr. Gadsden, the American Minister, rushed to Cuernavaca and recognized Álvarez before his government was established (Rippy, 221) and congratulated him with an impassioned eulogy that included the revolution; and refused co-operation with the diplomatic corps because he did not wish to embarrass his government (*Á Través,* V, 77–78). The

leaders in possession of the government quarreled among themselves
(84). Álvarez entered the capital with his Pintos on November 15,
1855. These Pintos are not as Callcott (228) says called so "because
of the dark spots on their skins," or because "they were of mixed
Indian and negro blood," but because of a peculiar tropical disease
prevalent in the Mexican "hot country." The victims become covered with red, white, and blue blotches in irregular sizes and shapes
in spots or all over the body. The decree issued by Álvarez, November 23, interfering in Church affairs, threw the fat in the fire, and
on December 9, Álvarez resigned naming Comonfort to succeed
him. The latter declined but offered to protect Álvarez, which offers
a hint as to the reason why neither wanted the responsibility.
Álvarez insisted, so Comonfort took charge December 11
(*A Través,* V, 88).

LIBERALS AT WORK. The liberals distrusted Comonfort because they
suspected him to be lukewarm; the conservatives because they saw
no promise of protection for those interests the liberals were sworn
to destroy (91). Revolts multiply against the liberals; every day
brings word of more revolts (95–99). Troops desert the government,
revolts everywhere (102). Bishop of Puebla admonishes people to
keep the peace (101). The government could not trust its own
(103). Troops desert radicals to conservatives (104). Again the
bishops endeavor to "inculcate the obligation in conscience to obey
the constituted authorities" while "revolutionary outbreaks occur
daily" (108). But the liberals are determined to prevail (110), in
spite of the fact that there is widespread opposition to them (119–
120). The liberals concentrated upon a group of conservatives in
Puebla and laid siege to the city. The Bishop, in co-operation with
the foreign consuls, prevailed upon the latter to capitulate (117).
The revolt was charged to the clergy and a large amount of property
was confiscated as a reprisal (123). Criticism of this decree was
made punishable with two to six years imprisonment (Planchet,
35). By protesting against this the clergy "close the way to any
conciliation and provoke in consequence revolutionary reprisals"
(*A Través,* V, 125). To justify confiscation Vigil (125–126) cites confiscations by Carlos III. It is necessary at all costs to disarm clergy
by confiscating all wealth (132–133). Any hint of opposition is
called "subversive" and intended to excite "fanaticism" and drive

the people to "revolt." The Bishop of Puebla was charged in a radical paper published in Mexico City on May 11 with uttering from his pulpit the following incendiary words: "With great regret I see that the Christian people view with indifference attacks upon ecclesiastical properties." So on May 12 he was arrested and sent into exile (136). That the Bishop denied uttering the words charged to him made no difference (137). Vigil agrees with the Bishop that the real reason for his exile was his opposition to the con- fiscations. So Vigil says: "The priests and other clergy had to follow the example of their superiors; their sermons could be nothing more at bottom than seditious proclamations however soft the terms with which they were invested, and these burning words falling on multitudes already ill disposed were readily interpreted as revolu- tionary excitements that were converted into revolts and mutinies without much delay" (138). The "Ley Lerdo" was decreed June 25, 1856. This law called for the compulsory sale to the tenants of all properties owned by all civil and religious corporations. As the law expressly included all such corporations as colleges, hospitals, asylums, houses of correction and beneficence. In other words, all educational and charitable institutions which, as has been previ- ously explained, were chartered by the State as *civil* corporations. The *religious* corporations were such incorporated bodies or asso- ciations as were devoted to pious and charitable purposes.

Bancroft (V, 693–694) says that "three-fourths of the landed property in the country had been vested in mortmain." Of course, this statement is a most gross exaggeration; but even if it were true, would it not be most remarkable and most praiseworthy for any people to devote so much wealth to purposes of education and charity?

Bancroft (V, 694) says in a note that the value of the property transferred by the end of December, 1856, totaled $23,019,281. Callcott (p. 250), citing a report by Lerdo de Tejada, gives the estimated total value of urban and rural real property at $1,355,000,000. Of this amount $250,000,000 to $300,000,000 "was owned by the clergy."

Bancroft (V, 692) speaks of the Archbishop of Mexico, Lazaro de la Garza y Ballesteros, as one "who had done so much for public instruction"; and in a note volunteers the information (691) that

"His gifts for charitable and other useful purposes are said to have exceeded $200,000."

The Constitutional convention called by the radicals was chosen according to the laws for the gathering of 1843 which were designed expressly to give Santa Anna the greatest possible power. The citizens in primary assemblies designated primary electors who gathered in the county seats to name secondary electors who in turn went to the capital of the state to name the representatives for that state in the Congress. Of the 155 electors or representatives chosen for the Congress only 80 were present at the opening. The greatest number ever present was on the day when the voting occurred on the article on religious "liberty"; 110 were there. That any moderates whatever appeared was due to the carelessness of the liberals who had just gained a military triumph (Rabasa, *La Constitución y la Dictadura*, 39, 40, 41). The Congress that drafted the Constitution also adopted it and signed it and then called in the President to take the oath to support it. He promulgated it— and said: ". . . its observance was impossible, its unpopularity a palpable fact; the government whose fate was linked to it was a government lost" (*Á Través*, V, 219–222). The articles disapproved by the clergy were 3, 5, 6, 7, 9, 12, 13, 27, 36, 39, 72, and 123, or (3) removal of education from clerical control; (5) outlawing of religious orders; (6) free speech; (7) free press; (9) free association; (12) outlaws titles of nobility; (13) fueros suppressed; (27) all corporations forbidden to own land; (36) obligation to inscription in poll lists and enlistment in National Guard, and to vote in elections; (39) sovereignty resides in the people who have the right to change or modify their form of government; (72) fixes faculties of Congress; (123) gives federal government exclusive power to interfere in religious worship and discipline as designated by the laws. The suspected hostile interpretation intended was more to be feared even than the clauses themselves, some of which were harmless appearing, while others were frankly restrictive and destructive. Perhaps the former were included in the protest so as to have something to trade against the latter. But the radicals were uncompromising. Justo Sierra (*Mexico y su Evolución Social*, I, 250) says: "The Congress that resulted from the revolution of Ayutla was not in reality representative of the people. The country people did not vote, the city and industrial population obeyed the orders of its leaders, or also abstained from voting; neither did the conservative party take any part in the elections. The new assembly represented in reality a minority of the citizens capable of taking part in political affairs."

CONSERVATIVE INACTION. Romero (*Mexico and the United States,* 354, 355) calls the conservatives "Church Party," because his material was prepared for American consumption. He says: "The Church party, being so wealthy and powerful, and having so much influence in the country, could very easily have brought about a civil war of so serious a character as would have made it difficult for the liberal side to defeat them." It will be observed that he says they "could" have done so, not that they "did" it. Vigil gives us the answer (*Á Través,* 325): "Here we must pause before a fact unfortunately overly frequent in the history of civil disturbances. The belligerent parties having in sight only the triumph of their respective political causes, by the destruction of their enemies, have been little scrupulous in the choice of means, gathering beneath their banners fugitives from justice, without law or control to restrain their depraved instincts. A destructive scourge rather than political adversaries, the services they might render, to the party they pretended to defend, were dearly purchased with the fortunes, the honor, and the lives of a multitude of victims sacrificed to their savage passions. Perhaps it will be said that an unescapable necessity compelled the parties to seize such means in time of armed struggle, in as much as all have operated in this manner; so be it, but it is no less certain that this has been a fertile source of immorality whose pernicious influence has made itself felt when some one of the factions has succeeded in making itself the government."

The destruction of numerous educational and beneficent institutions aroused the clergy to protest, but this was precisely what the liberals were seeking to effect. Vigil says: (*Á Través,* V, 330) ". . . the ecclesiastical properties which assuredly constituted the most positive and material part in the struggle, were those that in a direct manner suffered the blows delivered from both sides, as though there had been set up a sort of contest as to which might be the first to put an end to that considerable mass of wealth accumulated through a long series of years."

Bancroft says (V, 707) that Comonfort was charged by the conservatives with having sought an alliance with the United States, basing their charges on American press notices. "The liberal press with indignation rejected the reports, which, though purely sensational, served to give weight to the slanderous charges of the reaction. It is true that a treaty was concluded with the American Minister for pecuniary assistance, to be repaid, which treaty was not ratified by the Senate of the United States, and therefore was void."

Evidently the conservatives were justified. But this raises a very interesting question. Obviously the reference is to the McLane-Ocampo treaty, and quite obviously, therefore, it was being sought by the liberals at a much earlier date than generally considered.

Rippy says (*op. cit.,* 213) that by February 10, 1857, Forsyth had negotiated five treaties, one granting a loan to Mexico. And he quotes Forsyth as saying: "I regarded a loan to Mexico as a species of floating mortgage upon the territory of a poor neighbor, useless to her, of great value to us, which in the end would be paid by a peaceful foreclosure with her consent. In short, finding it impossible to acquire territory immediately, I did the next best thing, which was to pave the way to acquisition hereafter."

On December 17, 1857, a revolt was organized in Tacubaya to set aside the Constitution and charging Comonfort to call another constituent congress. On the same day the existing congress declared Comonfort deposed and all his acts void. Thereupon Zuloaga and his brigade entered the city and arrested Juárez and a number of his intimates. Comonfort vacillated between one side and the other and finally decided for the liberals and released Juárez who promptly deserted the capital. Comonfort's army deserted to the conservatives, so on January 21, 1858, he left the capital and on February 7 sailed on the American steamer *Tennessee.* Juárez claimed the presidency and set up his government in Guanajuato. In all previous contests it had been an accepted rule that the abandonment of the capital meant the end of any government sustained by any such faction or leader so doing. Fleeing from Guanajuato, Juárez sought refuge in Guadalajara where some of the liberal troops mutinied and made him prisoner. But the temporary strengthening of the liberal forces—and $6,000—secured the release of Juárez, who at once left the country, April 14, by way of Manzanillo, going· by way of the Isthmus of Panama to Habana to New Orleans to Vera Cruz where he arrived the 4th of May, 1858 (Planchet, 61).

Zuloaga was at once recognized by Forsyth who demanded a cession of territory. Being denied this, he withdrew recognition (Rippy, 216, 217). The pretext was the expulsion of an American citizen; but as the rights of its citizens have always been secondary to the peculiar Mexican policies of its politicians the refusal of the cession remains paramount. Forsyth was recalled and in December, 1858, Churchwell was sent to negotiate with Juárez. Rippy (p. 219) says: "While writing Churchwell's instructions Cass took occasion to remark: 'From the President's message to Congress at the opening of this session, you will have gathered the views of the administration upon the subject of Mexican affairs. The liberal party of Mexico has our hearty sympathy, and we are disposed to give it any moral support which may result from our recognition of its supremacy, whenever such recognition can take place in conformity with our usual policy on such occasions.' "

What that "conformity" was has been indicated by the demands upon Zuloaga by Forsyth.

On March 7, 1859, McLane was given instructions saying that "the sympathies of the United States have been strongly enlisted in favor of the party of Juárez." One month later he was given the coveted recognition.

Then followed attempts to secure from Juárez what Forsyth had failed to get from Zuloaga but Juárez hesitated. By November, however, the position of Juárez had become so precarious that he accepted the terms offered and the famous (or infamous) McLane-Ocampo treaty resulted. The objections of the Mexicans to intervention were overcome by the assurance that the United States would intervene sooner or later whether they signed or not (Rippy, 223). Juárez was to receive $2,000,000. The significant fact is in the revelation of the situation of Juárez which Rippy (p. 223) says: ". . . was now almost in desperation." Juárez was penned up in Vera Cruz and was threatened with intervention by England, France, Spain, and Prussia, which gave occasion for Cass to declare that "any attempt to establish European ascendency in Mexico would be met by the armed opposition of the United States" (Rippy, 227).

JUÁREZ AND THE UNITED STATES. The action of Juárez in accepting United States demands aroused severe criticism in his own camp. So much so that he felt compelled to write an apology. This is what he says: "I regret with you that the great liberal family could not alone, without help from the foreigner, pulverize the reaction and raise upon its remains the altars of liberty. My friend, if the Tacubayists had not exploited the fanaticism of our masses, do you think that Benito Juárez would have asked for help from the United States to triumph over his enemies? No, never! My love of liberty compelled me to take the great step, and God knows the great sacrifice it cost me. Some tepid liberals reprove my conduct, believing that without the winds from the north I might arrive at the capital of the republic to chain beneath my soles the reactionary hydra. Those who think thus deceive themselves. Miramón had arranged perfectly his plan of campaign against this port, bulwark of liberty, so that if the North-American steamers had not captured the ships of Marín and made him prisoner, the place would have surrendered, and the reaction certainly would have triumphed. You ask me in your favor that I reply if you may now announce officially our alliance with the sons of Washington, and I must say to you that it is not yet convenient to make such a declaration. The people are very susceptible, are impressed by everything, and I wish to keep them in doubt. Some accuse me of treason, others do me justice knowing that there is no treason on my part, but an imperious necessity obliging me not to halt at any means to attain the end" (Planchet, 158). This letter was addressed to Epitacio Huerta, and dated April 25, 1860.

This astonishing confession by Juárez is matched by another letter excusing the "excesses" committed by the bandit forces upon which he relied. These "excesses" were unspeakable atrocities comparable only to those nameless horrors committed by the most degraded savages—though quite typical of American Indian warfare. In this letter he says:

"I lament with you the excesses committed by some of the guerrillas aiding us. But it is necessary to tolerate their hatred for the reactionaries, for otherwise they would leave us. I believe that you would, as I have, stipulated, on casting accounts, not to molest nor pursue those who have so effectively aided us. Although our allies look askance at Rojas, Carbajal, Gonzalez Ortega, and Pueblita I have given them to understand that they have acted according to my orders to deprive the enemy of all resources" (Planchet 146). Letter addressed to Epitacio Huerta, dated March 2, 1860.

CHURCH PROPERTY. The confiscation by Juárez became a scramble to grab. The bishops and higher clergy who might organize or inspire resistance were driven into hiding or exile and the remainder terrorized along with those that might be inclined to protest. The "Colossus" had given such practical demonstration of its military might and its sympathy, that it were folly to defy.

In the capital an attempt was made to maintain some order and records, but in the provinces this was difficult. For many years one might hear tales of how carts were loaded with books and taken to no one knew where. A certain foreigner for many years conducted a business of handling old books and papers that were gradually disposed of to foriegn libraries and collectors. A vast amount of valuable material went to the makers of fireworks.

The real estate called Church property may be divided into four classes: First; Church edifices and attached buildings used as priests' residences, schools, etc. Second; establishments used and occupied by the religious orders for various purposes. Third; establishments used and occupied under charter as educational or beneficent purposes. Schools, colleges, hospitals, asylums, correctional establishments, etc. Fourth; the rented properties, urban and rural, whose rents went to support the activities of the three classes above named, including numerous lay associations.

In addition to the real estate the Church, the religious orders, and the institutions and societies, possessed funds which, placed out at interest, contributed to their support or were devoted to some charity.

The bishops and some of their clergy were trustees for certain funds called "chaplain" and "pious" whose objects were different charities including scholarships. These particular funds in 1804 (Dávalos, *Col. de Docs* Vol. 2, p. 866) amounted in round numbers to $44,500,000. The King of Spain attempted to seize this fund but after taking $10,507,957.47 he had to stop because of the distress and protests. (*Boletín,* etc., Ép. I, Vol. II, p. 44). Humboldt says

(*Political Essay on the Kingdom of New Spain*, English Edition, Vol. I, pp. 174, 175) that "The lands of the Mexican clergy (*bienes raices*) do not exceed the value of 12 to 15 millions of francs ($2,500,000 to $3,125,000); but the clergy possess immense capitals hypothecated on the property of individuals. The whole of the capitals (*capitales de Capellanias y obras pias, fondos totales* [*dotales* is what it should be, not *totales*] *de Comunidades religiosas*—capitals—or funds—of Chaplaincies and pious works, endowment funds of religious communities) of which we will give a detail in the sequel, amounts to the sum of 44 millions and a half of double piastres, or 233,625,000 francs." Humboldt and his translator were misled by the term "double piastres." In the document from which Humboldt derived his information the figure is clearly shown as pesos (*Representación*, etc. *Colección* Dávalos, II, 866). The use to which this money was put is best described by some of the liberals who laid hands on it.

José Guadalupe Romero says (*Boletin*, etc., 2a Epoca, Vol. 3, p. 556), in 1860, regarding the Church, the clergy, and the funds handled by them: "They formed a perennial loan bank for agriculture and commerce. There had not been, in the Republic, a farmer or worried capitalist who had not remedied his needs or increased his business with the capitals of the Church loaned at so moderate a charge that while these funds existed the loan sharks were unable to effect a rise in the rate of interest."

Matías Romero, a partizan of Juárez, and long Mexican Minister in the United States, tells us that, "The wealth of the Church was loaned out at a moderate rate of interest . . . and to its credit be it said was not at all usurious, exacting only a fair rate of interest and being hardly ever oppressive in dealing with delinquent debtors" (*Mexico and the United States*, p. 93).

And this is what Juan A. Mateos had to say: "In the days of the old regime, when the clergy possessed a great number of city and country properties, year after year went by without the shameful evictions to which so many poor families are the victims today. The sordid avarice of the landlords of today has no compassion in contrast to the clergy who, animated by a spirit truly Christian, overlooked and excused. The Church loaned its capital at a low rate of interest; 4%, 5%, or at 6% which was called the legal rate, a rate unknown today. Very rarely was a foreclosure notice published against a property pledged for a loan from these funds. For this reason I proposed, at the time of their confiscation, that a bank for the poor be established from the millions of the clergy, but my voice was drowned in the midst of the tumult of passions of the revolution. Because of this, the selfish interests and exactions of to-day have left homeless the many families who formerly enjoyed the tolerance and charity of the clergy" (From a speech by Juan A. Mateos in the Mexican chamber of deputies on the 20th of October, 1893). *Boletín,* etc., Primera Época, Vol. I, p. 137.

By "the lands of the Mexican clergy" Humboldt must have meant the Church establishment itself, because the total in the lands of the educational and beneficent institutions was much more than that. Even to prepare a list of those in existing records would require considerable space. If the total really amounted to that given by some writers, who seek to condemn the clergy with it, it reveals the astonishing fact that the Mexican people devoted a very large share of their wealth to education and charity, a share unequaled by any other people, anywhere, at any time in the world's history. The liberals gave this system an ugly name—the dead hand—and then killed it, meanwhile profiting in its demise by the seizure of the properties that had been the support of it.

How the booty was disposed of and how little the government profited by it is revealed by a lawsuit inspired by a quarrel over the spoil. The details are set forth at some length in a pamphlet containing the brief of the complaint of the loser. It is entitled:

"Monjardin, Ocurso que Presentó en 28 de abril de 1862 al Juez cuarto de lo Civil reclamando el despojo que se le infirió en 24 de mayo de 1861 de una casa de su propiedad de la que dió posesión a Don José Ives Limantour; Mexico; Murguia Imprenta, 1862."

The José Ives Limantour above mentioned was the father of the famous finance Minister of Díaz. He was given judicial possession, on March 11, 1861, of some fifty houses in the City of Mexico, valued at $525,528. They previously had been assessed in 1856 at $587,419. (*Noticia de las fincas pertenecientes a corporaciones civiles y eclesiasticas del Distrito de Mexico; 1856; publicada por el Min-*

istro de Hacienda, D. Miguel Lerdo de Tejada.) The law in the matter called for two-fifths to be paid in cash, and three-fifths in government due-bills in payment for confiscated property of this character. (Law of July 13, 1859, Art. 11). Limantour, however, secured the property for $1832.40 in cash, and the remainder in government due-bills that had cost him $40,077.90 (*Monjardin,* etc).

[9]*À Través,* V., 354–470; Planchet, *op. cit., passim.*

[10]*Boletín,* etc., 3a Época, V, 659–663; Reidel, *Practical Guide to Mexico City and Valley,* 312–368; *Documentos Historicos de Mexico,* Icazbalceta, V, Andrade, *Informe.*

[11]Poinsett, *Notes on Mexico.*

XIII

SEMICOLON

[1]Carleton Beals, Foreword, *passim*, in *Maximilian, Emperor of Mexico*, by José Luis Blasio. Translated by R. H. Murray, Yale University Press.

THE UNITED STATES AND MAXIMILIAN. The attitude of the United States Government toward Maximilian is a matter of history and public record. How the United States Government worked covertly to aid Juárez is revealed by General Sheridan in his memoirs as follows: General Sheridan tells that he used two United States Army corps to "impress the Imperialists, as much as possible, with the idea that we intended hostilities"; that he demanded from them war material given them by the confederates; how "As the summer wore away Maximilian gained in strength until all the accessible portions of Mexico were in his possession, and the republic under President Juárez almost succumbed"; how he made another demonstration as though preparing for invasion, interviewed Juárez in an ostentatious manner, and let it be known that he waited only the arrival of troops "to cross the Rio Grande in behalf of the Liberal cause." This movement caused the Imperialists to withdraw from northern Mexico and so encouraged the Liberals that they were able to collect an army of their followers. Then he tells us that "Thus countenanced and stimulated, and largely supplied with arms and ammunition, which we left at convenient places on our side of the river to fall into their hands, the Liberals, under General Escobedo—a man of much force of character—were enabled in northern Mexico to place the affairs of the Republic on a substantial basis." Then he says: "During the winter and spring of 1866 we continued covertly supplying arms and ammunition to the Liberals—sending as many as 30,000 muskets from Baton Rouge Arsenal alone—and by mid-summer, Juárez, having organized a pretty good sized army was in possession of the whole line of the Rio Grande" (*Personal Memoirs of P. H. Sheridan*, V. 2, pp. 213 *et seq.*).

How the United States Government took sides against the decency and respectability of Mexico is revealed by the following: "The Mexicans who, in 1863, invited Maximilian to the throne, before applying for help in Europe, having failed in securing the intervention of the United States Government in their behalf, 'raised a large sum,' says Mr. Sylvester Mowry, 'and proposed to certain influential and intelligent gentlemen in the United States to unite with them in establishing in Mexico a strong government. Several officers of the old regular army were enlisted in the cause, some of them now distinguished and dear to the American people. The arrangements were being perfected; a government with probably Iturbide at its head was to have been established—with the administration of affairs in American hands. Money to an adequate amount to secure success was obtained—eight millions alone from Mexico. A memoir prepared by one of the leading men of New York today, assisted by McClellan, Charles P. Stone, the writer, and the most intelligent, wealthy, and influential Mexicans, which, I am informed, has been perused with great pleasure and profit by the Emperor Napoleon, embodied the statistics and plan of the enterprise. When success was certain if let alone, the United States Government, whose neutrality was implored by all worth recognizing in Mexico, put out the hand of authority, and the enterprise was reluctantly abandoned. Failing in getting either private or public assistance here, the Mexicans, who had property and life at stake, appealed to Europe, and the throne of Maximilian is the result.'

"Subsequently one of these Mexican gentlemen said to Mr. Mowry:

" 'We tried, as you know, for years to get the United States to help Mexico. She would neither do it as a government nor permit an association of private individuals to do it. As a last hope, we came to Europe and got the help we needed. If the United States will recognize Maximilian, or say that they will remain neutral, and keep so, we can get all the money in Europe needed for our government until the home revenues are sufficient to sustain it and pay the interest on our national debt. If the United States makes war on Maximilian she makes war on Mexico. Europe will furnish us money and men, and we, the gentlemen of Mexico, will gain in the army at least the glory of dying for our country, in defence of the only government worthy the name it has had or can hope to have.'

"This was the simple, truthful sentiment of the intelligent, wealthy, decent, responsible people of Mexico" (*Mexico Under Maximilian,* Flint, pp. 35, 36).

MEXICO AND MAXIMILIAN. The attitude of the Mexican people toward Maximilian when he was set up as Emperor in Mexico is best evidenced by his bitterest enemies. Said Ireneo Paz (Panchet, 177): "The national defense was beaten; more than that, it was expiring. The sense of patriotism had been going dull, and all desired now that there govern an emperor or any demon whatever. As the intervention began to establish its dominion over the country, after gaining the easiest triumphs, few there were who retained any atoms of faith whatever inside them, and from this augmented so prodigiously the number of men who betrayed their country."

Another famous liberal, Genaro García, says: "Almonte was absolutely right when he told Napoleon that Mexican society was monarchical in habits, sentiments, traditions, ideas, laws, religion, interests, education. . . . Republican ideas were professed only by the middle class represented by a few. . . . Whence resulted that an immense number of Mexicans declared themselves enemies of the country." And Bulnes says: "The majority of the acts of submission to the Empire were voluntary. The majority did not then believe that Intervention compromised Independence, and the remainder, excepting the energetic liberal group, were willing even to lose independence to secure respect for property rights, for human life, for personal liberty, the inviolability of labor, sleep without nightmares, authority without brutalities, law without license, courts free from influence and without venality." Also he says: "The leaders and officers of the republican army deserted their ranks to present themselves in squads, and battalions, and by brigades to receive the hot bread of Intervention. The arrival of the Archduke gave the death-blow to the republican cause. . . . The extreme liberals went on presenting themselves in great number, many of them convinced of the advantages of an opulent and truly liberal monarchy in place of the old republic deformed, false, tyrannical, miserable, Jacobin, anarchic."

Porfirio Díaz himself said: "The work of the renegade liberals so demoralized the troops under my command that entire guards deserted."

The discouraged Colonel Escamilla wrote to Juárez: "I can no longer arouse with blows men consumed with fever and hunger only to kill them instead of making them march. They throw themselves on the ground and say 'kill me, my chief, for I can go no farther,' and in a tumult their women cry 'we can do no more; we want our sick and mistreated men to come home to die in their huts; we care only for our husbands, brothers and sons; we want no country.' "

Zamacona, a minister of Juárez, had the courage to tell him in substance that the Intervention won even the very liberals; that upon the fingers of one hand might be counted the circle of the government of Juárez; that the towns praised Heaven when the liberals departed, and that the policy of Juárez inspired repulsion (Planchet, 181). How betrayal stood at the elbow of Maximilian is illustrated by the following:

"The French troops were being concentrated on the line from Mexico City to Vera Cruz, getting ready to take ship for Europe. Napoleon III was naturally much concerned to provide against the risk that the evacuation should be disgraced by some untoward incident. Bazaine was no less desirous to come off with good grace. The atmosphere was favorable to intrigue, and a letter which Díaz wrote at the time to Don Matías Romero records that he was asked to take part in one of truly extraordinary character. Romero was Mexican Minister at Washington. The Republican officers in the south were cut off from Juárez, who was in the northern provinces, and were compelled to communicate with him through the United States. So it was to the Minister, and not to the President, that Díaz made his surprising statement: "General Bazaine, through a third party, offered to surrender to me the cities which they (i.e., the French) occupied, also to deliver Maximilian, Márquez, Miramón, etc., into my hands, provided I would accede to a proposal which he made me, and which I rejected, as I deemed it not very honorable. Another proposition was also made me by authority of Bazaine, for the purchase of six thousand muskets and four million percussion caps, and if I had desired it, he would have sold me both guns and powder."

The witness for the fact that Bazaine made these proposals is manifestly the third party who reported them to Díaz. Twenty years after the letter to Romero was written (1886), it came to the knowledge of Bazaine, who was then living in great misery at Madrid. It provoked him to write an angry expostulation to Don Porfirio, who at that later date had been well established for some time as President of Mexico. The unhappy exile recriminated by a counter-charge that Díaz had written a compromising letter to him in 1865, and asked very reasonably for the name of the alleged agent. Don Porfirio's answer is explicit: "With regard to the second point, although some years have now passed, I do not think you will have forgotten Senor Carlos Thiele. I must tell you, since you ask me, that he was the person whom I sent to you to arrange the exchange of Mexican prisoners who were in your power for those taken by me in the actions of Nochistlan, Miahuatlan, La Carbonera, Tehuantepec and Oaxaca, an exchange which was made with great advantage to the French army, because I sent as a favor all the chiefs, officers and soldiers that were left with me when you had no officers of ours of equal rank to exchange for them. This Senor Thiele it was who, in your name, made me the proposals which I reported in the letter which has aroused your resentment, and who, a few months after the circumstances to which I refer, settled in Guatemala, where he can still be found. I should be very pleased if you could some day persuade me that the whole affair was an imposture on the part of this gentleman, and I would make it known to the public who read my letter; but for this I need Senor Thiele's own declaration, as the knowledge that I have of him does not justify me in doubting his honor' " (*Díaz*, by David Hannay, pp. 104–106).

[2]His father, José de la Cruz Díaz, is said to have been a pure-blooded Spaniard, his mother half Mixteca and half Spanish (*Diaz*, Hannay, pp. 1, 2).

"Old Indian" is what some Americans called him. To the Mexicans he was "Don Porfirio."

[3]Díaz was neither illiterate nor uneducated—he had four years seminary training and studied law under Juárez, apparently for another four, at least he took his examinations for civil and canon law in 1853 (*Diaz*, Hannay, p. 5).

[4]Edward I. Bell, *The Political Shame of Mexico*, p. 53.

[5]*Ibid.*, p. 11.

[6]Carey, *The Catholic Church from Without*, pp. 4–5; Lecky, *History of Rationalism*, Vol. II, p. 37; Canon Farrar, *Hulsean Lectures*, 1870, "The Victories of Christianity," p. 115.

XIV

DON PANCHO

[1] Rabasa, *Evolución Historica de Mexico,* pp. 201, 202, 203, 204.

[2] The Creelman interview was published in *Pearson's Magazine* for March, 1908 (Rabasa, *op. cit.,* p. 193).

[3] Rabasa, *op. cit.,* p. 206.

[4] THE CATHOLIC PARTY. When the Madero revolution broke out in 1910, the Bishops of Linares and Sonora warned the people against the disturbers of order, and counseled them to respect and obey the constituted authorities. This was not done to favor either Díaz or his government, but in obedience to the Church policy to oppose violence and to urge respect to constituted authority. Indeed, the Bishop of Linares was a warm personal friend of the Madero family, as is evidenced by the correspondence which passed between them.

The revolution which destroyed the dictatorship of Porfirio Díaz, offered the people full freedom in the choice of their public officials, and in the establishment of a real democracy. Trusting in this promise, many citizens, early in the year 1911, formed political groups, one of which was composed of Catholics who gave to it the name of the National Catholic Party.

The platform adopted by the organizers of this party made no secret of its principles, and the adoption of the name itself was a frank announcement to the country at large of the principles themselves.

Very naturally the Bishops looked with favor upon the organization of the Catholic Party. It is not surprising that they should welcome the formation of a party founded upon principles instead of personal leadership, and expressing in its principles a respect for the rights of others as well as voicing a desire to attain the fundamental human rights of religious liberty, enjoyed by the citizens of all civilized governments, in the pursuit of which it proposed to use only the peaceful instrument of the ballot.

The Bishops confined themselves to reminding Catholics of their duty to vote conscientiously in order that the public offices might be filled with worthy men. And they urged them repeatedly to respect the constituted authorities, even though there might be irregularities in the elections, and particularly when they might not be in accord with their rulers.

This counsel of the Bishops attracted the attention, and even the approbation, of the Madero government. When the Bishop of Monterrey was promoted to the diocese of Michoacán, he so informed President Madero, who replied, December 18, 1912, "Gratefully acknowledging the proofs of loyalty and respect for the Chief Magistrate of the Republic," and added: "Be assured that this attitude is the reflection of that of the Mexican Clergy in general, and will make much easier for me the policy which I desire to follow of concord among all Mexicans, blotting out all the ancient divisions which no longer have any reason for existence."

Soon after this, the Minister of Finance, uncle of the President, wrote to the Archbishop of Michoacán as follows: "I have just been informed that on the twentieth of the coming month you will preach a sermon in which you will speak of the present situation and will touch on certain points of general politics. I am well aware of your patriotism and general intelligence, as well as of your tact, and on this account I hope, that in treating a question that is now so delicate, you will direct attention to that which our country needs so much, namely, that you will make your faithful Catholics see the necessity which exists and the obligations they are under to contribute to the pacification of our beloved country. . . . You may rest assured that I will feel gratified if your intelligence and eloquence shall succeed in leading the faithful of your archdiocese on the right road." It should be needless to add that the Archbishop already had arranged his sermon along the lines indicated.

The Catholic Party adopted its name not to make religious capital of it, but to indicate clearly the principles advocated by it. The Clergy had no part in its management and confined themselves to the expression of such generalities as their sacerdotal character called for and such active participation as their rights as Mexican citizens permitted.

The Catholic Party supported no reactionary principles whatever. It did not seek to promote interference by the Church in the affairs of the State. On the contrary, it sought to bring about a real separation of the Church from the State in which it might be guaranteed the same rights enjoyed by religious bodies in all civilized countries.

The Catholic Party accepted the existing form of government and rejected any resort to violence for the purpose of changing the existing order. It sought to convince its enemies of the injustice of certain laws by peaceful argument, and to change those laws by means of the ballot.

The Catholic Party named Madero as its candidate for the Presidency and voted for him, in spite of the fact that he declared his hostility to their platform before the convention of the Liberal Party held eight days after that of the Catholic Party.

In the elections held for deputies to the national congress, the Catholic Party won one hundred seats, but was arbitrarily deprived of seventy-seven. In the State of Aguascalientes, the Catholic Party cast three-fourths of the vote. Similar results were obtained in other States. In many of the States, the winning candidates of the Catholic Party for the State offices were arbitrarily ousted. In spite of this injustice, the Catholic Party, in several announcements, declared its intentions to abide by the results regardless of the injustice; an action wholly unique in Mexican politics.

The elections in Mexico, in 1911–12–13, were very nearly real elections. The conservative elements did not refrain from voting to so large an extent as formerly. Enough of them attempted the experiment of the franchise to augment to a notable extent the number of votes cast. In the presidential elections, the State of Jalisco cast over 81% of its vote for de la Barra for Vice-President. Pino Suárez received less than 13% of the vote for that office, and Vasquez Gómez a trifle over 6% (*El Partido Católico,* October 22, 1911). In the State elections on the 21st of January, 1912, the vote reported, from 82 districts out of 115, totaled 92,388. Of this number the Catholic Party polled 59,507, or 64.4% (*El Partido Católico,* January 28, 1912). It is important to note that its enemies counted the votes. No data are available indicating the vote cast in the 33 towns not reported. If the proportion held, the total vote cast would appear to have been 129,570 (the total vote recorded in Jalisco at the "election" of Carranza was 34,215, of which Carranza received 34,135. Ackerman, *Mexico's Dilemma*, p. 280), a truly remarkable showing for Mexico, and one that will compare favorably with many elections in the United States. Those refraining from voting were, as usual, conservatives, whose appearance at the polls would have made the conservative majority all the more impressive. Today, it is safe to say that a real election would result almost unanimously conservative. Especially would this be true if Mexico had a secret ballot.

Members of the Catholic Party were approached with a view to enlisting them in the revolution headed by Feliz Díaz, but they refused. Notice of this reached the Bishops, and they immediately condemned the revolution, and cautioned Catholics not to take any part in it.

When Huerta made himself dictator, the members of the Catholic Party, and the Bishops, held aloof. They asked no favors from him; they did not recommend him to their followers, nor did they take any part in any of his political acts. When, later, the situation became acute, two Archbishops, those of Mexico and Oaxaca, had the courage to go to him, in person, where they, as Mexican citizens, urged him to resign.

The Congress, elected during the administration of Madero, called for the election of a President and Vice-President, and the Catholic Party representatives met in convention in August, 1913, and decided not to take part in any such election because they were convinced that the situation would not permit the proper exercise of political rights.

When Mr. John Lind, the personal representative of Mr. Wilson, demanded the resignation of General Huerta, the Minister of Foreign Relations, Señor Gamboa, replied that an election had been called and that General Huerta was by law ineligible as a candidate. The Catholic Party thereupon decided to take part in the coming elections and therefore called a new convention and nominated Gamboa for President and General Rascon for Vice-President, both gentlemen being well-known members of the Liberal Party.

The purpose of the Catholic Party in thus deciding to take part in the elections was to afford Huerta a chance to save his face; to avoid foreign complications; and to protect the sovereignty of the country; for a great many Mexicans were fearful that the demands upon Huerta were but the entering wedge for occupation.

After the *coup d'état* of October 10, the Catholic Party saw that it would be useless to enter any candidates for the election, but they agreed that they would keep on their course in view of the attitude of the American President.

Huerta sought to secure the aid of the Catholic Party, but this was refused, and to show him that they disapproved of his program, the Party put up its candidates, especially after it had received authentic copies of the instructions sent by the Federal authorities to the governors of the States to the effect that they should frustrate the elections. (Consul Davis in Guadalajara reported to Charge d'Affaires O'Shaugnessy that [in the "election" for Huerta]: "There were reported to have been cast, in this city of 200,000 population, about three hundred votes. At about 6 o'clock P.M., the Jefe Politico had all the voting booths visited, the boxes containing the votes gathered in, and — that was the last heard of the matter. I understand that the same procedure was followed throughout this Consular District." *Experiences,* etc., Davis, pp. 8–9.)

To punish the Catholic Party for this action, Huerta suppressed the Party organ, arrested its editor, and drove the party leader (not the candidate Gamboa) from the country. All of which is good evidence that the Party did not render any aid to Huerta.

The Mexican Clergy were not a party to the revolt in 1913; they gave it neither moral nor material support, either directly or indirectly. They gave no support of any kind whatever to Huerta.

On July 16, 1913, the Bishops, who were assembled in Zamora, issued a pastoral letter from which the following is taken:

"In virtue of the freedom which the Church grants to its people to adopt the form of government which suits them best, provided only that the principles of justice and morality be preserved; and in virtue of the historical circumstances of Mexico, we believe that the National Catholic Party ought always and everywhere to be, and declare itself heartily, in favor of our present form of government substantially as it exists. This will not prevent them from seeking and endeavoring, with due prudence, to bring about those minor changes which will make this form of government at the same time democratic, representative, and Federal, and better suited to our condition and manner of life. We believe, further, that the National Catholic Party ought, for the present, to limit its action to the defense of the rights which the constitution grants to the Church, to the Clergy and to Catholics, without striving for remedies, which however just, might arouse the feeling of their opponents."

The foregoing is the viewpoint of the Catholic authorities as outlined at that time, and in it they claim that there is no excuse whatever for persecuting Catholics, their Clergy, or their Religion. It may be said that it epitomizes the political viewpoint expressed in all the pastoral letters of all the Mexican Bishops during the past hundred years.

The Clergy realized full well that with the downfall of Madero would go the promise of liberty that his administration had offered, and that with the downfall of Huerta would come the deluge. They knew that in mob violence no permanent nor just democracy could be established, and so they constantly urged peace. Bulnes, *The Whole Truth about Mexico* (p. 168), says: "Of the one hundred seats in the House of Representatives fairly won by the Catholics, the censoring board, having recourse to the most barefaced frauds, nullified more than forty of the electoral college votes. The Catholics then held sixty places when they appeared before the electoral college of the Lower House, and here, in the most shameful, dirty, illegal and despotic manner, the majority of their votes were discredited and thrown out, leaving them only twenty-three. The same tactics were followed with the Independents, with the ultimate result that the Catholic and Independent representation, combined, was reduced to forty-two out of a total of two hundred and thirty-three." Again: "When the Mexican Constituent Congress discussed the Federal electoral law in 1856, Señor Ignacio Ramirez, an implacable reformer and a talented, high-minded politician, impugned the indirect electoral system, basing his objection upon the fact that there is no real vote of the people except when the election is direct, and that all really free countries had recognized this fact in their electoral laws. The commission which sustained the opposite opinion frankly replied that the indirect election was necessary, because if the direct vote were granted to the people, it would be the parish priests, the chapters, the bishops, and the guardians and priors of convents who would name the representatives, senators, magistrates, aldermen and the president of the Republic, and that the granting of the direct vote to the illiterate, fanatically Catholic people, would be signing the death warrant of the glorious democratic revolution proclaimed at Ayutla. Señor Ramirez replied that democracies cannot be farces; that all governments based upon the opposition's plan were either corrupt or tyrannical, or both; that if the Mexican people were not fitted for democracy, a Constitution adapted to their capabilities should be drafted; and that if a direct vote were not granted to the people nothing but a fraud would result from the indirect vote, leaving the people condemned to the rule of political charlatans, because any one guilty of such a fraud could not be anything but a knave.

"The delegates decided in favor of the indirect vote, excusing themselves by saying that it was better to educate the people in democratic principles from the start, and that in no wise would this be better accomplished than by the indirect electoral vote.

"Señor Ramirez's prophecy was verified. When the Madero revolution triumphed, all honest persons who believed in good faith that the Mexican people were now ready for democracy, resolved that the direct vote should triumph. The demagogic corporation, knowing that the masses, cut loose from the influence of the clergy, can be molded to their views—as happens everywhere when the voter is unworthy of the vote—energetically supported the reform of the electoral law, aiming at having the elections of 1912 carried out in conformity with the strict rules of the direct popular vote. The result was a surprise to honest liberals and to the demagogic herd. They believed that after forty-nine years of an anti-Catholic policy, an atheistic press, and obligatory lay schools, the popular masses had been totally emancipated from the tutelage of the clergy. The elections of 1912 proved that the clergy possessed the power to organize a real disciplined political party, and to carry the Federal and local elections in almost all the states. If the Catholics did not have a complete triumph in the elections of 1912, it was owing to pressure brought to bear by the Maderista government, and the frauds practised by the *porra* against the Catholics. The situation was clear to all.

"In order to make democracy with the free vote possible in

Mexico, it is necessary for the Catholics to be a permanent political factor because they are in the majority and are strong enough to organize legislative bodies, and to prevent any other powerful, well-disciplined political body from obtaining a complete triumph in the parliamentary field. What the Mexican Catholics lack is the power to rise up in arms and assert their rights when the liberal minority nullifies their honestly won triumphs by means of frauds and violence. This lack of assertive power is due to the fact that the Indians and mestizos of the rural districts, who vote with the Catholic party, do not go to the polls pistol in hand as their opponents are ready to do. Owing to that stony passivity, of which I have already spoken, they will vote for or against Catholicism, just as they will fight for or against it, if superior authority brings pressure to bear upon them.

"The politicians know that they cannot be the controlling power in a real, or even in a corrupt, democracy, so long as a majority of the Mexicans are Catholics, and this explains their anxiety to destroy the Catholicity among the popular classes by any and every possible means. As the lay schools did not accomplish this, the revolutionists have had recourse to another species of anti-Catholic education of the masses carried on by desecrating churches, breaking images, outraging nuns, expelling and assassinating priests, closing churches, and even by prohibiting private worship. From this also springs the cry for more lay schools. To the reformer 'regeneration of the people by the school' means getting control of the conscience of the popular class by driving Catholicity out. Bulnes, *op. cit.,* pp. 274–276.

"This accounts for the hatred of the political revolutionists for Catholicism, and their care to encourage the bandits of the north to commit all kinds of outrages against the clergy and the Catholics in that section."

[5]H. L. Mencken, *Notes on Democracy,* p. 3.
[6]For election figures see Note 4.
[7]Bell, *op. cit.,* p. 151.
[8]*Ibid.,* pp. 153–154.
[9]*Ibid.,* p. 155.

XV

FIRST CHIEF

[1]*Senate Investigation of Mexican Affairs,* p. 769; Rabasa, *op. cit.,* p. 219, says "more than \$70,000,000." Bell, *op. cit.,* p. 188, says \$63,000,000, but that only \$45,000,000 was available and had been reduced since the advent of de la Barra during ten months to less than \$20,000,000 because of extraordinary expenses on account of the Madero revolution and subsequent revolts of other groups. Bulnes, *The Whole Truth about Mexico,* p. 108, says 72,000,000 pesos.

[2]*Senate Investigation,* p. 769.

[3]The telegraphic correspondence between Carranza and Huerta was captured from Carranza and taken to the United States where it was published in the *Revista Mexicana* of San Antonio, Texas, June 24 and July 21, 1917. Also see *Senate Investigation.*

[4]*Senate Investigation,* pp. 2820–2822; Tannenbaum, *Peace by Revolution,* p. 233.

Contract with Casa del Obrero Mundial (I.W.W.), signed by: General Alvaro Obregón; Engineer M. Rolland; Gen. Salvador Alvarado; Gustavo Espinoza Mireles; Gen. Maclovio Herrera; Rafael Nieto; Engineer Alberto Pani; Gen. Gabriel Gavira; Jesus Urueta; Dr. Atl (who appears to have been the real evil genius); Luis Cabrera; Gen. Manuel M. Diéguez; Rafael Quintero (signed for Venustiano Carranza) (p. 2822).

[5]Innumerable details of incredible atrocities are recorded in the pages of the *Senate Investigation of Mexican Affairs.*

[6]Carranza by decree limited the vote to his supporters. The vote cast represented less than 2 per cent of the population. Gibbon, *Mexico under Carranza,* p. 56; p. 14.

[7]July 23, 1914.

XVI

WILD GOOSE ASTRAY

[1]Important and interesting revelations on the situation in Guadalajara at that time may be found in *Experiences and Observations of an American Consular Officer in the Recent Mexican Revolutions,* by Will B. Davis, M.D. Mr. Davis' letters cover the period from the autumn of 1913 to the summer of 1916.

[2]Obregón confiscated a number of endowed charity properties, schools, and hospitals, etc., amounting to some millions in value. The trustees carried the matter to the supreme court which decided for Obregón on the remarkable grounds that the clergy had been responsible for the three years' war (1858–1861).

XVII

THE IRON MAN

[1]Gibbon, *Mexico under Carranza,* p. 56, says: ". . . in his call for the election (for the constituent congress that made the constitution of 1917) First Chief Carranza expressly provided that the elective franchise should be exercised only by those citizens who were known to have been the supporters of his revolutionary party."

[2]*Church and State in Mexico,* Nov., 1926.

[3]NUMBERS OF CLERGY. The tabulations of Navarro y Noriega were published in the *Boletín de la Sociedad Mexicana de Geografía y Estadística,* 2a Época, Vol. I, pp. 290–291. The figures for different periods with those giving them may be tabulated as follows:

1810—Mexican population, 6,122,354.
Navarro y Noriega (*loc. cit.*).
4229 Secular Clergy.
3112 Regular Clergy.

———

7341 Total Clergy.
2098 Sisters.

———

9439 Total Religious Persons.

1826—Mexican population, 6,204,000.
Brantz Mayer, *Mexico,* Vol. 2, p. 132.
4150 Secular Clergy.
1918 Regular Clergy.

———

6068 Total Clergy.

1931 Sisters.

———

7999 Total Religious Persons.

1831—Mexican population, 6,382,284.

Mora, *Obras Sueltas,* Vol. 1, p. CLX (From a report by the Minister of Justice and Ecclesiastical Affairs).

3282 Secular Clergy.

1688 Regular Clergy.

———

4970 Total Clergy.

1911 Sisters.

———

6881 Total Religious Persons.

Mora, *México y sus Revoluciones,* Vol. 1, pp. 496–498 (From a report by the Minister of Justice and Ecclesiastical Affairs).

In 1833.

Number of Secular Clergy not given.

1363 Regular Clergy.

1797 Sisters. (Mora gives 1847, but made a mistake in repeating the numbers in two establishments).

R. A. Wilson, *Mexico and its Religion* (Harpers, 1855), p. 321 (From *Cuadro Synóptico de la Republica Mejicana en* 1850, by Miguel Lerdo de Tejada).

1850—Mexican population, 7,661,919.

2084 Secular Clergy.

1139 Regular Clergy.

———

3223 Total Clergy.

1541 Sisters.

———

4764 Total Religious Persons.

[4]NOTES ON THE CHURCH-STATE NEGOTIATIONS OF 1928–9. In 1927 Archbishop Ruiz read a letter from Mr. Morgan to Gen. Calles, the president of Mexico, in which he spoke of the debts owed by Mexico to the bankers, and concluded with the indication that the financial affairs of Mexico required religious peace for the prosperity of Mexico.

In November of that same year, Mr. Morrow was appointed Ambassador to Mexico. Mr. Morrow began by inviting Gen. Calles to make an arrangement with the Church. In Holy Week of 1928, Mr. Morrow arranged a conference between Calles and Father John J. Burke which took place in San Juan de Ulloa, Vera Cruz, without result.

In May of 1928 there was another conference, Calles consenting that Father Burke be accompanied by Archbishop Ruiz. Calles there offered to write a letter that in general terms would say that the Government would permit religious services if the Clergy would submit to the laws.

At once Archbishop Ruiz went to Rome to present the case to the Pope who decided that this was not enough.

The Pope and the Government were in communication through Mr. Morrow when the assassination of Obregón caused everything to be suspended.

In May of 1929, at the conclusion of the revolt of Escobar, the new President, Portes Gil, declared in the press that the Catholics had not aided Escobar, and that with a little good will by both sides the conflict between Church and State might be ended.

Archbishop Ruiz answered through the press that this good will existed.

The President, through the press, invited Archbishop Ruiz to a conference, and the latter replied in a personal letter thanking him for the invitation but saying that he could not accept it because he was without authority from Rome to do so.

The Pope asked for a report on the matter and then appointed Archbishop Ruiz his delegate *ad referendum*. Archbishop Ruiz reported this to the President through the Mexican Ambassador in Washington, Sr. Tellez. The President set a date for the conference. Through the Ambassador, Archbishop Ruiz proposed that it be held in Washington with the Ambassador. The President replied that he would think it over; then decided against it. So Archbishop Ruiz left for Mexico accompanied by Bishop Díaz as secretary. On the same day, in another train, Mr. Morrow departed for the same destination, arriving there twelve hours behind them. It was agreed that the statements appear simultaneously in the newspapers, and the arrangements were concluded on the 21st of June, 1929.

It is to be noted, that in authorizing Archbishop Ruiz to sign, the Pope imposed two conditions: (1) that amnesty be granted to all those in arms who surrendered; (2) that there be returned all temples with connections, priests' houses, episcopal residences, and seminaries. The President immediately accepted both conditions, but unfortunately none was fulfilled, neither was the agreement published in the Official Daily, as promised.

XVIII

THE AMERICAN FRONT

[1] *The Cause of the World Unrest* (Putnam's, 1920), pp. 1, 2, 3.
[2] "Whoopee."
[3] Gruening, *Mexico and its Heritage,* p. 390.
[4] Two other important leaders on the "American Front" were Lincoln Steffens and George Creel.

Autobiography of Lincoln Steffens (p. 716), "As I said to President Wilson once . . ." (p. 718) "I remember that in conversation with President Wilson once . . ." (p. 733) "I was seeing President Wilson, who made me sure we would not go fighting in Europe and that he had no intention of intervening in Mexico, but he might. (p. 736) But once when I was in New York he was on the verge of a war with Mexico. I hurried to Washington. . . . In despair I went to the law office of Charles A. Douglas, the American attorney for Carranza in Washington. We often held hands in mutual sympathy. He tossed me a deciphered private wire from Carranza. . . . I read these communications . . . and went over to the White House. Since I could not see the President, I dictated to his stenographer a message. . . . 'A war due to irresistable causes is bad enough, but a war made by misinformation is unforgivable, and I, for one, will never forgive it.' "

Then he tells (pp. 738–40) of his conversation later with Wilson and how he convinced him of the sterling honesty and super-high-mindedness of Carranza, and how Wilson assured him that there would be no war.

Lincoln Steffens flavors his interesting narrative with a little humor in telling how worried property owners chased Carranza about the country—as he moved his peripatetic "government" from place to place in the only available train—in frantic endeavors to secure some protection from pillage and extortion (p. 732); how they resorted to Washington with equal lack of success; how they eventually contacted Luis Cabrera who reminded them that he had been their advocate in similar circumstances during the rule of Díaz, but that now he was on the other side and proposed to take full advantage of his position and knowledge to fleece them completely (p. 733).

From what Consul Davis has to say about the meeting of the business men with Sr. Cabrera, it would appear that Mr. Steffens' account of it is wholly imaginary, and much more to the credit of Sr. Cabrera, though not very complimentary to his abilities as an economist or financier (*Experiences,* etc., Davis, pp. 217–220).

Steffens paints Carranza as a man of the humanities and great honesty (p. 734). How honest he really was we may judge by his decree obliging merchants, under savage penalties, to accept the paper money that Carranza himself had declared to be counterfeit. His humanitarian instincts are revealed in the horrible and unprintable atrocities he permitted his followers to commit constantly and universally. One need only read the published correspondence of Will B. Davis, M.D., American Vice-Consul in Guadalajara (*Experiences and Observations of an American Consular Officer During the Recent Mexican Revolutions,* by Will B. Davis, M.D., printed privately, Chula Vista, California) to realize that the American State Department must have been deluged with reports from its representatives in Mexico on the Carranza atrocities and his incompetence and rascalities. To recognize Carranza's so-called government without knowledge of the information in these reports would be nothing short of criminal negligence—to recognize him after reading them requires, to adequately qualify it, condemnatory terms not available in the English language. Recognition merely decided which of two major groups of gangsters should murder and pillage with United States sanction. Carranza's "humanitarianism" is noted by Gibbon (*Mexico Under Carranza,* p. 10) in relating how, when the American Red Cross was feeding 26,000 families daily in Mexico City, Carranza was exporting 37,000 tons of foodstuffs through the port of Vera Cruz alone. When the reports of the Red Cross became public with facts that showed Carranza and his savages in their true light, Carranza expelled the Red Cross. The true character of Luis Cabrera, for whose "honesty" Lincoln Steffens so earnestly vouches, is shown in his own statements made in reply to charges of mishandling funds. His defense is that ". . . great quantities of private property have been seized in the beginning for the nation, but the confiscators have used them for personal profit or sold them for money," that "This goes from the mere 'loan' of a horse or saddle, from the requisition of grain and fodder which are not used for the troops, to the occupation of houses, property, and ranches . . ." (Gibbon, p. 167).

George Creel (*The People Next Door*, p. 357, note 1), says: "The author of this volume served as President Wilson's representative in the negotiations, interviewing Generals Obregon and Calles and President de la Huerta in the City of Mexico and accompanying Mr. Pesqueira to Washington." The note just quoted refers to the following: "From his bed of pain, President Wilson has been closely watching the progress of Mexican affairs, eager for an opportunity to aid. When the free and peaceful election gave final proof of the restoration of law and democratic processes, he let it be known, unofficially, that he would be glad to discuss and remove every question that Carranza had raised to divide the two republics."

The events referred to were the assassination of Carranza and the assumption of power by Obregón and Calles. Creel gives the details of a conversation between Calles and Carranza alleged to have been dictated by Calles himself to Creel. "Betraying the revolution," is the charge thrust into Carranza's beard, and Calles threatens to rebel with others against him.

Gruening (p. 329), speaking of the "incubus" of "military rapacity," says: "Obregon tolerated it, and his government would have been swept under but for the fortuitous aid of the United States."

[5](From *Mexico and the United States*, by Matias Romero, p. 95.) Regarding the introduction of Protestant missionaries into Mexico, Romero says: "I am in a measure responsible for that step."

One of these Protestant clergymen, a Mr. Riley, proposed, says Romero, ". . . to buy one of the finest churches, the main church of the Franciscan convent, which had been built by the Spaniards, located in the best section of the City of Mexico, and which could not now (Romero's book is dated 1898) be duplicated for a very large amount of money; and with the hearty support of President Juárez, who shared my views and who was perhaps a great deal more radical than I was myself on such subjects, I sold the building which had become national property after the confiscation of the Church property, for a mere trifle, if I remember rightly about $4,000, most of that amount being paid in Government bonds which were then at a nominal price." On page 363 Romero gives this price as "about five per cent." He says further: "The magnificent building bought by Dr. Riley's community was bought recently by the Catholic Church to restore it as a Catholic temple, for the sum of $100,000, as I understand." It was said that some $50,000 were expended in repairs.

Romero says further: "I do not think that the American Protestant missionaries in Mexico have made much progress, and I doubt very much whether Mexico is a good field for them; but they are satisfied with their work, and they think that under the circumstances, they have made very good progress.

"The number of Catholic churches and chapels in the country was, in 1889, 10,112, while the number of Protestant places of worship was 119. On August 12, 1890, there were in the municipality of Mexico 320,143 Catholics and 2,623 Protestants."

About the time Sr. Romero was writing his book the writer of this note heard a Protestant missionary admit that after nearly twenty years of labor in a large city he could not truthfully say that he had obtained one genuine conversion to Protestantism. When visited by interested parties he prepared a congregation for them by the simple process of distributing pennies at the door after the services were concluded and the guests gone. The latter, being ignorant of the circumstances and the language, departed convinced of something that did not exist. Another missionary said that in nine years he had obtained eleven converts, but as one of them, on his deathbed, had called the priest, he was doubtful of the sincerity of the remaining ten.

In 1934 there appeared, apparently from official sources, in the press the following figures covering the Federal District (presumably for 1930):

Catholics	1,182,431	or	96.175%
Protestants	16,895	or	1.373%
No Religion	14,438	or	1.172%
Other Religions	9,242	or	.750%
Jews	5,980	or	.483%
Buddhists	590	or	.047%
Total	1,229,576	or	100. %

It is safe to assume that by far the greater part of the Protestants are foreigners. Likewise, must be foreigners many of those listed as of no religion or other religions, whatever the latter may be. Among those of no religion safely may be grouped the few choosing, for the moment at least, to consider themselves atheists. Here we have the little group that is ruling Mexico.

[6]Gompers, *Autobiography,* II, p. 312.

XIX

INTERNATIONAL ASPECT

[1]News Dispatches, 1934.

[2]Montavon, *The Church in Mexico Protests,* p. 12.

[3]*Religious Prohibition under the Mexican Constitution before the League of Nations and the permanent Court of International Justice,* by Martin T. Manton (Judge of the Circuit Court of Appeals, New York), p. 6.

[4]Manton, p. 18.

[5]Manton, p. 18.

[6]"No one can give what he himself does not possess."

[7]Introduction.

[8]Manton, p. 30.

[9]Manton, p. 31.

[10]Portes Gil, *The Conflict between the Civil Power and the Clergy.*

[11]*Idem.,* pp. 118–132.

[12]Tannenbaum, *Peace by Revolution,* p. 127.

[13]Gruening, *Mexico and its Heritage,* p. 664: "In executing Generals Serrano and Gomez, the Calles government could pursue no other course." See also, p. 662.

[14]Quoted in *The Cause of the World's Unrest.* Gwynne.

XX

SOLUTIONS

[1]Husslein, S.J., *The Christian Social Manifesto,* p. 150.

[2]Bandelier, *Reports of the Peabody Museum of American Archaeology and Ethnology,* Vol. II, p. 447. "The notion of abstract ownership of the soil, either by a nation or state, or by the head of its government, or by individuals, was unknown to the ancient Mexicans."

[3]Enoch (London, T. Fisher Unwyn). "National lands have been set aside in vast areas; and any inhabitant of the republic may 'denounce' or acquire a piece of such land, and retain it by paying an annual tax payment, the prices varying from 2 pesos, in the remote regions, to 20 or 30 pesos per hectare, equal to two and a half acres, in the more settled states" (p. 157). The vast majority of the Indians prefer the old Indian system of land tenure. The Spaniard introduced a new system and a new use. The new system was cultivation for profit on land privately owned; and the new use was the pasturage of herds of animals.

[4]Gruening, *Mexico and its Heritage,* pp. 162–163.

[5]*Foreign Affairs,* Vol. V, No. 1, 1926.

[6]Half the diocesan revenue of a certain Diocese ten years ago came from one man. I knew this because I lived in the Bishop's house as his guest. And I knew the man. The average annual offering to the Church by the mass of the people would not amount to one-half peso each family. — E.C.B.

[7]LANDS. The "land question" is always resorted to as a last defense when the various falsehoods, offered in justification of the persecution of the clergy, have been destroyed.

There are several phases of the "land question" all of which are slightly contributing factors all more or less exaggerated except one. That one contains the real grievance. This is the share-crop or share-tenant system. In all of its evil features it is precisely identical with the same system prevailing in the cotton-growing regions of the United States. These causes of dissatisfaction are not "land hunger" but the evils consequent upon greed, incompetence, and brutality—

the brutality of overseers, the greed of proprietors, and the incompetence of both tenants and owners. Where the landowner is competent and operates his property on Christian principles—there *are* owners who do this—we find satisfied tenants who are much more prosperous and contented than many of those who own their own small farms.

In a great many cases the hacienda, or plantation, gives employment to its tenants and to neighboring small landowners. By destroying the hacienda system just that many people are deprived of employment. This appears also from Mr. Tannenbaum who shows (*Peace by Revolution,* 194): In 1910 there were 56,825 resident plantation communities with an average population of 97 each, or a total of 5,512,025. In 1921 (p. 206) there are 46,381 such places with an average of 84, or a total of 3,796,004—a loss of 1,716,021. They are not in the villages because there were 12,724 with an average of 541 in 1910, or a total of 6,883,684. In 1921 the villages were 13,388 with an average of 495, or a total of 6,627,060; a net loss of 256,624, though the villages have increased by 664, possibly at the expense of the plantations.

From the above figures it appears that the agricultural population has lost nearly two millions, due to the attacks upon the haciendas which have lost over 30 per cent of those employed. The hacienda system is not by any means extinct; if it were it might add some six million more people to the list of unemployed. Perhaps this accounts for the problem that confronts the cities with their increases of population, largely unemployed and compelled to beg.

George Creel (*Wilson and the Issues,* p. 13) says: "In a country of fifteen millions, ten thousand owned every inch of the land." President Wilson, in a campaign article in the *Ladies Home Journal* for October, 1916, published too late to be refuted, expressed much the same thing without committing himself to exact figures. They are supported, however, by would-be authorities, such as Phipps (*Some Aspects of the Agrarian Question in Mexico*) and McBride (*Land Systems of Mexico*).

In 1809, in preparation for a census to be made the following year, there was made a list of "inhabited places." Navarro y Noriega (*Boletín,* etc. 2a Ep. Vol. I, pp. 290–291) evidently made use of this in making up his table which shows 3,749 *haciendas,* and 6,684 *ranchos.* The haciendas would be inhabited places because of the villages of tenants on them. *Rancho* has several meanings in Spanish: a soldier's victuals; a farm; and—in the sense intended above—an agricultural village without a resident authority. For reasons unknown subsequent writers have fallen into the error of assuming that Navarro y Noriega meant a farm. Hence the repeated references to that meaning where all appeared to have depended upon guesswork for their figures. In these there are at times included the 2,082 (1910) undivided Indian communes (Rabasa, *Ev. Hist. de Mex.*, p. 300), (Bulnes, *The Whole Truth about Mexico*, p. 85).

Mr. Wilson, at least, might have determined the facts by calling on his consular agents in Mexico to ask the local taxing authorities for their assessment lists. Most certainly these lists would not show a number in excess, and few properties would be permitted to escape.

These lists customarily are kept in the local offices of the taxing districts, but one State, that of Jalisco, has made a collection and tabulation of all its districts. That State shows that in 1910–11 there were 162,851 (Rabasa, *Ev. Hist.*, 302) separate rural holdings. In 1911–12 the total is 164,815, divided as follows (from the published list itself):

		Taxed	*Exempt*
Less than $	100 in value	59,744	41,018
$ 100 to	1,000 in value	54,507	77
1,000 to	5,000 in value	7,073	20
5,000 to	10,000 in value	1,108	6
10,000 to	20,000 in value	569	10
20,000 to	30,000 in value	192	3
30,000 to	40,000 in value	122	1
40,000 to	50,000 in value	64	3
50,000 to	100,000 in value	160	1
100,000 to	200,000 in value	79	2
Over	200,000 in value	55	1
		123,673	41,142
		41,142	
		164,815	

$ = pesos.

El Universal for January 1, 1926, gave the taxed total as 144,590.

The State of Jalisco is located in the western part of the Central Highlands of Mexico with a density of population nearly double that of the average for the whole country. Its admitted Indian population is small. The area is 33,486 square miles, and the population for 1910 was given as 1,202,802.

The laws of reform of Juárez and Lerdo, confiscating all corporation property and forbidding all corporations to own land, fell also upon the Indian communities, which were corporations, and therefore required by these laws to distribute their lands in severalty to the individuals forming the community. This partition was begun in 1877, and by 1895 there had been issued 12,422 titles covering 1,202,727 acres (Romero, *Mex. and the U. S.*, p. 227).

Rabasa says (*op. cit.,* p. 288), that the distribution was carried into effect in some villages, was partially realized in others, and became a mere pretense in those where it was feared disturbances might result. In many places the local governments made no regulations for a distribution. In general it may be said that little change was made in the system of communal lands throughout the Republic. The villages continued to be represented by their *ayuntamientos* in their corporate capacity before the courts and administrative authorities, thanks to legal subtleties and fictions which the government accepted and authorized in its decisions.

Where the distributions were actually carried out the Indians often sold their lots as soon as they found themselves in possession of a property right they had never known. This has been called "robbery," and the purchasers of such lots "exploiters." This half truth has been offered as proof that all the Indians in the country have been the victims of a violent and iniquitous outrage.

In the State of Oaxaca is an example of what has happened in many States: The government early dictated the regulations for the division of the lands according to the laws. All the cultivable lands were distributed, legally or otherwise, to the satisfaction of the Indians. But not so with the common woods and pastures because the villages were opposed, and continue to administer them for the common use (p. 289).

Nor does the Indian limit his pretended right to the surface.

With only less zeal he lays claim to the subsoil, declaring the mines to be his and the labors of the mining operators to be usurpations. In many districts the Indians resolutely oppose the locating of claims, uphold their traditional property rights, and are so persuaded of it that not rarely, when addressing the government, they declare them as "Our Mines" (p. 292).

The assessment lists for Oaxaca are not kept in the offices of the capital but in the Districts, or County Seats. Partial figures from five of these Districts were available when Rabasa wrote. They gave a total of 6,534 subject to tax because above $100 assessed value, and 13,579 exempt because less than that; total 20,113. Applying this proportion to the remaining Districts would give a grand total of more than 100,000 individual holdings (p. 303) El Universal, January 1, 1926, gave the State 19,174 taxed.

In 1890 there were in the State of Vera Cruz 16,138 rural properties subject to tax, and 9,650 exempt by reason of being less than $100 in value; a total of 25,788 (Memo presented to the Legislature by the Treasurer). But this is not the number of proprietors in the State. There are many collective properties, besides those belonging to the Indians, due to several generations of undivided inheritances, a condition common to other States (p. 301) El Universal, January 1, 1926, gave 6,876 taxed properties.

Guanajuato had in 1909 a total of 6,935 above $1,000 value. Applying the proportion in this category found in Jalisco, the total should have been 17,680. El Universal, January 1, 1926, showed the number of taxed properties to be 17,096.

In the State of Chiapas the lists carried no information on properties assessed at less than $100, because exempt. They should have numbered many thousands. In 1893 the taxed properties numbered 5,015; in 1910 they were 10,684 (p. 302) El Universal, January 1, 1926, gave the taxed total as 15,718. Besides these properties every community has an *ejido* of several thousand acres amply sufficient for its needs. Besides all that, there were available, in 1910, several million acres of public lands at a few cents an acre: incredibly fertile land with abundant and well-distributed rainfall where it is possible to plant or harvest any day in the year.

In 1908 the Governor of the State of Puebla, in a message to the

Legislature, stated that in the State there were 277,680 rural properties (note on p. 303). *El Universal,* January 1, 1926, gave 4,123 as taxed. Rabasa explains the large number by the successful breaking up of the Indian commons and the large collective estates. Puebla has an area of 12,204 square miles and a population of 1,092,456 (1910).

Rabasa calls repeated attention to the 2,082 Indian communes. He estimates the families involved as averaging not less than 200 each. This would give a total of more than 400,000 proprietors to add to the grand total for the whole country.

The State of Yucatan is given a population of 337,020 in the census of 1910. This is equivalent to 67,404 families. Of farm owners there were 26,961. This is a proportion of persons to one farm of 12.5. The importance of the hemp industry is evidenced by the employment of 49,244 laborers on the plantations. Most of them were engaged directly in cutting the leaves from which the fiber is extracted. These laborers were paid 50 centavos for the first thousand leaves cut, and 75 centavos for each succeeding thousand. On the average a laborer cut 2500 leaves by two or three P.M.; some did 3000. He could thus earn two pesos per day if he chose. Many, however, preferred to cease work when they had cut the second thousand, for one peso was considered a fair wage. That these laborers could make more money cutting leaves than they could raising corn on their own land has been well demonstrated by one of the revolutionary pamphleteers who shows: that they could earn but a fraction of their customary wages if they tried to raise corn; that to attempt to raise hemp they would fail for lack of capital to sustain themselves during the seven years they would have to wait for the plants to mature; that they would fail for lack of the necessary capital to purchase the machinery to prepare the fiber; that this machinery requires a large investment and in turn requires a large acreage to warrant that investment. Furthermore, the soil of Yucatan, in the hemp district, is suited only to the cultivation of this particular plant. Agriculture is not encouraged in a land of doubtful rainfall, where but a few inches of poor soil overlie a limestone plain where there are no surface streams. As a matter of fact, the people of Yucatan have found it much cheaper to import their foodstuffs from other parts of Mexico, or even from the United States, than to attempt to raise any themselves.

The urban population of Yucatan formed 63 per cent of the total and was engaged in various lines of endeavor necessary to the commerce and industry of the country. It thus may be seen that the entire population of the State was occupied in one way and another and that there was no class demanding land. As a matter of fact, there was an ample area of public land available at a very cheap price. What was needed was capital to develop it.

Before the development of the hemp industry, Yucatan was considered fit only for cattle raising. The natives found it difficult to raise sufficient corn for their sustenance. Indeed, the land was a synonym for poverty. With the growth of the hemp industry, Yucatan became relatively the richest State in Mexico, and the prosperity of its people was evident on every hand. And now the invention of the combine and the planting of the henequen plant elsewhere has left Yucatan a problem to solve.

The henequen plant (*Agave rigida*) requires seven years to mature and leaves can be cut during some eighteen years. About one fourth of the planting is thus in a condition of constant renewal. Failure to make these renewals must result inevitably in a scarcity of the fiber when the present planting has given out.

When Porfirio Díaz took charge of Mexico the large areas of public lands were unsurveyed, and to make them available for settlement it was necessary to have them surveyed. There was no money to pay for this and the best the government could do was to contract for the surveys on the basis of giving the surveyors one third of the land surveyed for doing the work. At the time this arrangement was made it was considered a good bargain for the government. The government placed a price on its own share of the lands that made the ultimate returns to the surveyors appear to be of very doubtful value. Of course the only way the surveyors could cash in on their work was to sell their lands in competition with the government.

By the year 1896 there had been surveyed, according to these contracts, a total of 149,030,444 acres. In addition to the surveyors' share of one third, there were sold 26,734,853 acres, leaving the government with 72,618,776 acres of surveyed lands ready for sale and settlement (Romero, *Mexico and the United States,* p. 125). One of the revolutionary pamphleteers (Brinsmade, *Mexican Problems,* p. 9) shows that the public land, presumably in 1910, amounted to 108,-844,000 acres.

In 1896 the prices for government lands (Romero, *op. cit.,* p. 126) averaged less than 87c Mexican money per acre. This sum was payable one half cash with the balance in bonds of the interior debt that were worth about 15c. The best lands in the Republic are in the State of Chiapas, and there the price was less than 81 cents an acre. The American plantations in that region paid 50 cents to $1 a day with house and rations, and would have employed many more men than they did if the men had been available. It was, therefore, possible for any enterprising Mexican to earn, in two months, enough money to buy a 100-acre farm. If the Mexican preferred he could settle on the village "Ejido" at no cost at all. Chiapas is a terrestrial paradise, and if it were American territory its lands would exceed those of California in value.

The large landed properties in northern Mexico are mostly cattle ranches and much of the area embraced in them is useless for agriculture for lack of water with which to irrigate. The large plantations in the central and southern Mexico are similar to, and have the same reasons for existence as, the large plantations in the United States, especially those south of the Mason and Dixon Line.

As a rule corn is raised from the summer rains which vary considerably, sometimes ceasing almost altogether. Wheat is raised in the winter with irrigation. In general, the large properties in the *mesa central* are equipped with some sort of irrigation system, some primitive, some quite modern and extensive, representing heavy investments of capital. Efforts to introduce modern agricultural machinery have discovered a diminishing enthusiasm therefor, because it deprives the tenants of employment.

All of the large properties have laborers resident upon them. These laborers crop on shares, as is done in the southern United States, the owner furnishing seed, plow, and oxen. Between times the laborer finds employment on the plantation. By confiscating and dividing up such a property the laborer is deprived of his chance of such employment, and there is no one to provide him with seed, plow, and oxen. Moreover, he is confined to a certain piece of ground, and loses much more than he gains. If he really wants land there is an ample area and variety from which he is free to select at a very cheap price. But, of course, he must leave his home to find it, just as our American pioneers did to settle the great west. This he refuses to do.

Only a few Americans secured lands direct from the Mexican Government, and such lands were purchased at the government price. Many thousands of Americans bought land from private parties. Many of these properties were subdivided and sold to American farmers who improved the land, built substantial homes and buildings, purchased modern farm machinery, and imported blooded stock from the United States. That the Mexicans benefited therefrom is a fact sustained by abundant testimony. That land was "taken" from anyone by Americans is a fabrication invented by the socialist propagandists.

The oil companies in Mexico purchased their lands from private parties or made leases just as is done in the United States. Only one concern, that of Lord Cowdray, ever made any deal to get oil on public lands, and that arrangement was to pay a royalty to the Mexican Government for the oil obtained. But no oil was ever developed from these lands (*Investigation of Mexican Affairs,* p. 2386; Gibbon, *Mexico under Carranza,* p. 103).

There has been no lack of public land in Mexico nor any impediments to its acquisition by any Mexican. There are still many millions of acres of vacant lands, especially in the most fertile regions of Mexico. Carranza granted some two million acres of land to several colonizing enterprises (*Chicago Tribune,* Nov. 14, 1919, citing the "official publication of the Mexican department of industry, commerce and colonization, under date of March 15, last, and bearing the official seal").

[8]PEONAGE. Common laborers in Mexico are frequently referred to as "peons," which is the proper application of the term. The word "peonage" in the English language, however, has come to mean a condition of labor such as exists in the southern United States among negroes; that is, laborers who are indebted to their employers for various sums and who are expected, or are obliged, to labor for them until the sums owing have been paid. Americans, and other foreigners, hearing the word "peon" used, in its proper sense, have jumped to the conclusion that the laborers referred to were subjected to the conditions implied by the word "peonage" as understood in the United States.

Peonage was unknown throughout the greater part of Mexico. It existed only among the tropical plantations in parts of Vera Cruz, Tabasco, and Chiapas. Whatever may have been the cause of its beginning, its persistence was due, in part, to the scarcity of labor. On the large plantations there were employed two classes of labor. Gangs of laborers were recruited from among the towns and villages and paid by the day. In general they camped on the work where they might remain for a week or a month, as the fancy seized them. A few might remain as long as three months, rarely longer. This system provided a labor supply that varied in a manner compelling some other arrangement whereby a permanent force of men might be had for the necessary work that was carried on continuously from day to day. To do this advances of wages were made to men who would bring their families and live on the plantation. Or the amount owing by some man would be paid and he would remove to the plantation. The latter might be any amount, but the former would be at least $50. The laborer, depending on the demand for his services, would try to secure from the employer as large a sum as possible. It thus will be seen that the system was forced upon the planters by the laborers. Many planters endeavored to talk their laborers into abandoning the system, but with indifferent results. The system was, in a sense, self-regulating. The planter hesitated to make too great advances to the shiftless, and the thrifty hesitated to ask for them. Many laborers looked upon the debt as a measure of their financial standing which increased in the ratio of the amount they were permitted to owe. The writer has heard the matter discussed by the laborers in that sense. The long-established custom of the system decreed that when a man became dissatisfied with his employer, he might call for his account and go forth to seek someone to pay it for him. This was a matter of easy arrangement, because the demand for labor was so great that the first planter called on would eagerly grasp the opportunity to secure a steady hand. Indeed, some of the most prolific sources of discord among the planters were the efforts that some of them made from time to time to entice laborers of this character from their neighbors.

No one disliked the system more than the planter who was compelled by it to tie up a considerable sum of money in a manner contrary to law and liable to total loss at any moment should the laborer die. Losses by absconders were so few as not to be considered. It must be said that the laborers of this class were generally trustworthy and discharged their debts conscientiously. The planter had to be on the alert to prevent the appeals for continued advances increasing the debt unduly, few of them being for any real necessity. The debts might run from $50 to $300, in very exceptional cases to as much as $600 where the laborer received a wage in proportion. These laborers earned from 75 cents to $1 and more a day.

In addition to their wages these laborers received a house in which to live and rations for the family; they usually had at least a flock of chickens about the place and frequently pigs. The women drove a lively trade in eggs and fowls in the village, and often at the plantation headquarters; in addition they were privileged to plant as large an area as they cared to cultivate, keeping all the produce for themselves.

The style of house furnished was that common to the country with whose construction everyone was familiar and whose materials were procurable, usually on the ground. They were built at the expense of the planter. Some American plantations imported materials to build comfortable frame cottages with tile roofs.

There were a few plantations in Mexico employing convict labor. Mr. John Lind visited a plantation of this character in Vera Cruz, and returned to the United States to relate what he saw in a manner calculated to cause Americans to believe that such conditions were general throughout Mexico, and especially typical of American plantations in that country.

Peonage existed in Mexico to a very limited extent and in the manner shown. It never at its worst reached the condition indicated by the following advertisement printed in the *Atlanta Journal*.

$25 REWARD

For the return of Walter Banks, yellow negro, about twenty-five to twenty-eight years old, about five feet ten inches tall, weight 240 or 250 pounds, raised at East Point, thick lips, and has big eyes. Will pay $25 for this negro delivered to Estes Bros., Gay, Georgia.

(From the *Atlanta Journal* of May 8, 1914. Referred to by *Colliers,*

June 27, 1914, p. 17, in an editorial headed "Wilson and Mexico."

The writer worked on a plantation in the *tierra caliente* or "hot country" of Mexico, in the State of Chiapas, on the borders of Tabasco, where the peonage system prevailed. The greater part of the labor on the place, however, came from distant Indian villages to remain a week or more and then return home. The peons were residents on the place, but before agreeing to come always demanded an advance of at least $50 when not already owing someone else. An attempt was made to compel these peons gradually to liquidate their accounts by a restriction of credit, only to incur their displeasure and distrust. These particular peons were paid a minimum of 45 cents a day with house and rations for family, or quarters and meals with the same wage if without family. The "ration" was a monthly allowance of 125 lb. of shelled corn (or 400 ears, a "tzontli"), 25 lb. beans, 4 lb. salt, and lime to cook with the corn. The Indian laborers were paid 50 cents a day with food and shelter. The "store" carried only the minimum of articles demanded by the people for their convenience, and these were sold practically at cost.

In that particular region the labor problem was being solved by a growing custom of contracting small areas with local people who, in partnerships and by the employment of small groups of laborers, usually their own neighbors, cleared, planted, and cultivated the land during definite periods, or for definite purposes. Practically all those engaged possessed their own farms from which they derived an abundant subsistence as well as some cash crops. Gangs of Indians, all of whom possessed their lands, came down to labor for short terms for day wages. Several million dollars were thus invested by Americans in plantation of tropical products, especially rubber.

Regarding the matter of the company or plantation or hacienda store, Matias Romero (*Mexico and the United States,* p. 511) reminds critical Americans of their dirty hands as follows: "It seems that something similar to this is done in the United States, as is shown by the following extract from Gen. Rush C. Hawkin's article, entitled 'Brutality and Avarice Triumphant,' published in the June, 1896, number of the *North American Review,* page 660:

" 'One of the most facile means in the hands of avarice for cheating the poor and helpless is the corporation and contractor's store. It is usually owned by corporations whose employees are the only patrons, and the rule is to sell the poorest possible quality of supplies at the highest price obtainable. In many instances employees are given to understand that they are expected to trade at the company and contract stores, or, failing to do so, will be discharged. This oppressive method of cheating is not confined to any particular part of the country, but prevails, with varying degrees of malignancy, wherever under one management, whether corporate, partnership, or individual, any considerable number of employees are assembled together. Since the close of the Civil War many thousands of ignorant blacks have been made the victims of this common and heartless swindle which has absorbed their scant earnings. At the end of each month, year in and year out, it has proved to their untrained minds an astonishing fact that the longer and harder they worked the more they got in debt to their employers.' "

(The two concerns in Mexico, operating "company" stores, for which the writer worked in his youth, did not require employees to trade in them, yet they did so. The only complaints came from the storekeepers in the neighboring towns. E. C. B.)

In view of the agitation in the United States for a five-day week and a six-hour day, it is interesting to read what Señor Romero has to say regarding the holidays formerly customary in Mexico (*Mexico and the United States,* p. 542): "The Catholic clergy in Mexico encouraged the custom of having a great many feast days, which were, besides, very profitable to the church. Over one-third of the year, not counting the Sabbath, was given up to religious festivals, during which all work was stopped. So objectionable were the results of this system that when, in 1858, the laws of reform were enacted separating the church from the state, the feast days were reduced by law to a very limited number — about six only in the year."

CONCESSIONS. The matter of "concessions" and "concessionaries" has been greatly confused and misunderstood. The Mexicans imitated the Americans in encouraging new industrial enterprises. The Mexicans, however, were more canny in driving a bargain, and more exacting in assuring themselves of the fulfillment of it. The promoters of new enterprises were required to put up a bond to guarantee the fulfillment of their promises. They were required to employ a given number of people (at least 20) and to invest a given sum (at least $100,000) in the enterprise. The only favors they received were a permit to import the machinery for the plant in one shipment free of duty and exempt from Federal taxation during five, and sometimes ten, years. No monopolies were granted. Anybody was free to take advantage of the same arrangement.

Mining "concessions" are mining patents or claims differing little from the same thing in the United States. Railroad "concessions" are railroad franchises, nothing more nor less. In the United States the transcontinental roads were built by government aid; the government guaranteeing the bond issues and giving enormous extensions of public land to the railroad companies. No control was exercised over the roads nor were any favors exacted in return for the government assistance.

In Mexico the plan was adopted of paying a subsidy that averaged $8,935 Mexican money per kilometer ("The subsidies paid for railroads up to December, 1892, averaged $8,935 per kilometer of road built and in operation at that date. This average is much less than that of the subsidies paid by other Latin-American countries, the Republic of Chili having averaged $17,635 per kilometer, and the Argentine Republic $31,396, $14,379, $28,380, $50,525 per mile, respectively." Romero, *op. cit.* p. 119. Exchange not considered. Also see treatment of this subject by Gibbon, *Mexico Under Carranza*.), a very small sum when compared to the bonds guaranteed and the land given away by the United States Government for its transcontinental lines. This sum was paid in installments as certain sections of the lines were completed. The builders were compelled to put up heavy bonds to guarantee the fulfillment of their part of the contract. The roads were agreed to revert to the government in 99 years and were obliged to carry the mails free. The government reserved the right to fix the freight and passenger rates. Not a foot of land was given. About $100,000,000 were thus expended and nearly every dollar was paid out by the contractors in the territory through which the lines were built for materials and labor.

Some revolutionary propagandists have asserted that the railways of Mexico were built with subsidies so great that *"they were built solely for the sake of the subsidy"* (*The Mexican People,* De Lara and Pinchon, p. 336). Mr. Edward N. Brown, until October, 1914, for 27 years connected with the Mexican railroads, retiring as President of the merged systems, stated before the Senate Committee

(*Investigation of Mexican Affairs,* pp. 1787-1809) that the subsidies represented 15 to 18 per cent of the costs of construction. The propagandists claimed that Americans were employed to the exclusion of Mexicans; but Mr. Brown tells of the railroad schools for the training of Mexicans to replace Americans. (The various testimonies relating to this and similar subjects, regarding labor and wages and other relations of workmen with Americans, also as to the so-called concessions, should be read and pondered. See *Investigation of Mexican Affairs,* also Gibbon, *Mexico under Carranza.*)

XXI

THE ARK AND THE FLOOD

[1]Francis McCullagh, *Red Mexico*, p. 405.

[2]*The Cause of the World's Unrest*, p. 4.

We have availed ourselves only of matter quoted in this book; not accepting as authentic the "Protocols" upon which it chiefly relies to make its case.

[3]*Idem.*, p. 15.

[4]*Idem.*, pp. 199–200.

[5]From Gruening, *Mexico and its Heritage*, p. 284, note 2.

"Miss Hewitt, head of the Methodist Girls' School (Hijas de Allende) in Pachuca, told me in March, 1927: 'The new regulations of Article 130 of the constitution mean that we no longer teach religion in the school. Formerly we had Bible classes and a branch of the Epworth League. We have abolished both, because we are entirely willing and determined to obey the laws of the country. The children, however, may go voluntarily to church on Sundays and to Sunday-school. Our boys' school (Julian Villagran) which is situated next to our church and is in charge of a Mexican teacher, had a door connecting church and school. The authorities requested us to plaster it up and we did so. Our relations with the authorities are entirely friendly.' "

The members of the Villagran family acquired reputations for savagery, treachery, and assassination, during the revolution for independence.

[6]News Dispatches.

[7]Montavon, *The Church in Mexico Protests*, p. 19.

[8]News Dispatches.

INDEX

ARIZONA

NEW MEXICO

✝ TUCSON

EL PASO
JUARES

T

LOWER

SONORA

CANANEA

SIERRA MADRE

CHIHUAHUA

✝ CHIHUAHUA

Rio Grande

Gulf of CALIFORNIA

✝ HERMOSILLO

BELEM

SIERRA TARAHUMARE

COAH

CALIFORNIA

PACIFIC

S I N A L O A

DURANGO

✝ CULIACAN

SIERRA MADRE

✝ DURANGO

ZACATECA

ZACATECAS

CAPE
SAN LUCAS

SIERRA DE NAYARIT

TERR

CAN

✝ TEPIC
TEPIC

OCEAN

ISLAS
TRES
MARIAS

GUADALAJARA

SAN JACIN

CAPE
CORRIENTES

CHAPALA

JALIS

S

MANZANILLO

✝ COLIMA

M

MEXICO

● VICARIATE APOSTOLIC ‒ ✝ ARCHBISHOPRIC ‒ ✝ BISHOPRIC ‒ ✝ BISHOPRIC VACATED OR TRANSFERRED

HUNT
BROS